Designing and Developing

Web-Based Instruction

Designing and Developing

Web-Based Instruction

Haomin Wang
Dakota State University

Deborah L. Gearhart
Dakota State University

PEARSON

Merrill
Prentice Hall

Upper Saddle River, New Jersey
Columbus, Ohio

Library of Congress Cataloging-in-Publication Data

Wang, Haomin.
Designing and developing web-based instruction / Haomin Wang, Deborah L. Gearhart.
    p. cm.
Includes bibliographical references and index.
ISBN 0-13-098780-8 (pbk.)
1. Web-based instruction—Design. 2. Education—Computer network resources. 3. Internet in education. I. Gearhart, Deborah L. II. Title.
LB1044.87.W37 2006
371.33'44678—dc22
                              2005011587

Vice President and Executive Publisher: Jeffery W. Johnston
Executive Editor: Debra A. Stollenwerk
Assistant Development Editor: Elisa Rogers
Editorial Assistant: Mary Morrill
Production Editor: Alexandrina Benedicto Wolf
Production Coordination and Text Design: Thistle Hill Publishing Services, LLC
Design Coordinator: Diane C. Lorenzo
Cover Designer: Terry Rohrbach
Cover Image: Getty One
Production Manager: Susan W. Hannahs
Senior Marketing Manager: Darcy Betts Prybella
Marketing Coordinator: Bryan Mounts

This book was set in Garamond by Carlisle Communications, Ltd. It was printed and bound by Courier Stoughton, Inc. The cover was printed by Courier Stoughton, Inc.

Pearson Prentice Hall™ is a trademark of Pearson Education, Inc.
Pearson® is a registered trademark of Pearson plc
Prentice Hall® is a registered trademark of Pearson Education, Inc.
Merrill® is a registered trademark of Pearson Education, Inc.

Pearson Education Ltd.
Pearson Education Singapore Pte. Ltd.
Pearson Education Canada, Ltd.
Pearson Education—Japan

Pearson Education Australia Pty. Limited
Pearson Education North Asia Ltd.
Pearson Educación de Mexico, S.A. de C.V.
Pearson Education Malaysia Pte. Ltd.

10 9 8 7 6 5 4 3 2 1
ISBN 0-13-098780-8

PREFACE

Designing and Developing Web-Based Instruction is about designing, developing, and delivering courses for Web-based instruction (WBI). The overarching goal of the book is to provide comprehensive coverage of important aspects of WBI from theoretical, pedagogical, technological, and managerial perspectives, with theoretical discussions integrated with practical considerations.

This book has three sections: foundation, application and implementation, and management. The first section includes an introduction to distance education and Web-based instruction, instructional design, and assessment. The second section covers interaction, interactivity, multimedia, and instructional hypermedia. The last section includes copyright and intellectual property, course management systems, utilization of Web resources, and policies and management.

This book is intended primarily for those who will be designing and developing online courses—whether they are novice Web course designers or are well versed in Web development and instructional design—as a course textbook or as a reference.

Web-based instruction is a vast field that a single text can hardly cover adequately. We are therefore selective in the content we cover. Throughout the book, we focus on course design and development for Web-based instruction and talk briefly about content pertaining to general instruction, but not specific to Web-based instruction. We use a case study with scenarios to illustrate some of the points discussed and to help readers relate concepts and ideas to possible practice.

The case study is partly based on our actual experience in Web-based instruction. It is set in the context of a small public university in the Midwest, which we have named Mid-State University (MSU). The university has been a pioneer in utilizing educational technology and integrating it into the curricula as part of its institutional mission. With the growth of the Internet and the World Wide Web, the administration decided to extend these educational opportunities to a broader student population by offering some of its key programs online over the Internet. This text is based significantly on what we have learned in designing and developing Web-based courses.

PEDAGOGICAL FEATURES

Each chapter of the book has the following pedagogical features to help the reader make better use of the chapter content:

▶ **Chapter introduction.**

▶ **Chapter objectives:** Advance organizers help the reader focus on the important topics for discussion and reflection.

▶ **Case study:** Scenarios provide a context for relating the issues discussed to possible practical situations.

▶ **In Practice:** Boxed feature stories introduce what is happening in instructional technology and Web-based instruction in industry and academia. These feature stories serve as mini-cases and provide a broad range of examples of the issues discussed in each chapter.

▶ **Chapter summary:** The summary synthesizes key issues and important topics.

▶ **Review questions:** Questions help readers recall the chapter objectives and check comprehension.

▶ **Tips:** Practical guidelines and tips are given throughout the chapter.

▶ **Exercises:** Suggested learning activities relate the chapter's content to learners' personal experiences and application needs.

▶ **Resources:** Internet resources related to the topics discussed facilitate additional learning activities.

▶ **References.**

COMPANION WEBSITE

This book's Companion Website (http://www.prenhall.com/wang) provides supplementary materials and resources that cannot be appropriately and effectively included in the text. The Companion Website provides:

▶ Additional dynamic, interactive content that is best presented in hypermedia and/or through server support.

▶ Annotated links to the In Practice examples in the book.

▶ Updated links to the Web resources at the end of each chapter.

▶ Additional Web resources that become available after the publication of the text.

▶ Updated content, such as URLs, that has changed since the publication of the text.

ACKNOWLEDGMENTS

First of all, we would like to thank our executive editor, Debbie Stollenwerk. This book would not be possible without her consistent support and insightful guidance throughout the process.

We are also grateful to the following reviewers for their valuable comments and feedback: J. Michael Blocher, Northern Arizona University; Janet L. Bohren,

University of Cincinnati; Scott Fredrickson, University of Nebraska, Kearney; Clarence R. Geier, James Madison University; Robert M. Hill II, Tulane University; Andrew L. Hunt, University of Arkansas, Little Rock; Matthew J. Koehler, Michigan State University; Linda Lohr, University of Northern Colorado; S. Kim MacGregor, Louisiana State University; Sara McNeil, University of Houston; Kay Persichitte, University of Northern Colorado; V. Richard Persico, Georgia Southern University; Jennifer Summerville, Emporia State University; and David VanEsselstyn, Long Island University.

In addition, we would like to thank the staff at Merrill/Prentice Hall, particularly Editorial Assistant Mary Morrill, Assistant Development Editor Elisa Rogers, Senior Production Editor Alex Wolf, and Project Editor Amanda Hosey at Thistle Hill Publishing Services.

Finally, we want to thank all the faculty, staff, and students who have been involved in Web-based instruction at Dakota State University and have contributed to the growth and formation of this book in many different ways.

Haomin Wang
Deb Gearhart

BRIEF CONTENTS

Part I Foundation   1

Chapter 1 — Introduction 2

Chapter 2 — Instructional Design for Web-Based Instruction 13

Chapter 3 — Assessment in Web-Based Instruction 31

Part II Application and Implementation   59

Chapter 4 — Interacting with Learners 60

Chapter 5 — Making Content Interactive 96

Chapter 6 — Instructional Hypermedia Design 121

Chapter 7 — Multimedia for Web-Based Instruction 156

Part III Management   190

Chapter 8 — Copyright and Intellectual Property 191

Chapter 9 — Course Management Systems 207

Chapter 10 — Utilizing Web Resources 243

Chapter 11 — Policy and Management for Web-Based Instruction 273

Glossary 286

Index 291

CONTENTS

Part I Foundation

1

Chapter 1 — Introduction 2

Brief History of Distance Education and E-Learning   3

The Growing Popularity of Web-Based Instruction   4
    Contributing Factors   5
    Impacts of Web-Based Instruction   6

Challenges and Constraints of Web-Based Instruction   7
    Digital Divide   7
    Challenges for Designers and Instructors   7
    Challenges for Learners   9
    Costs and Returns   10

Chapter Summary   11

Review Questions   11

Resources on the Web   12

References   12

Chapter 2 — Instructional Design for Web-Based Instruction 13

Instructional Design for WBI   14

Needs Analysis   15
    Institutional Readiness   16
    Faculty Readiness   17
    Learner Readiness   18
    Instructional Materials Readiness   20

Designing for Constructive Learning   21

Designing for Online Communication and Collaborative Learning   22

Designing Interactive Multimedia Content   24

Designing for Utilization of Internet Resources   25

Designing for Alternative Assessment   25

Review Questions   27

Summary of Tips   28

Exercises 29

Resources on the Web 29

References 30

Chapter 3 — **Assessment in Web-Based Instruction** **31**

Fundamentals of Assessment 32
　　Assessment as Part of Instructional Design 33
　　Learner Authenticity and Prevention of Cheating 33
　　Formative versus Summative Assessment 35
　　Criterion-Referenced versus Norm-Referenced Assessment 37

Technology and Web-Based Assessment 39
　　Objective Tests in Web-Based Instruction 40
　　An Online Quizzing System 41
　　Adaptive Testing 43
　　Multimedia Tools 44

Alternative Assessments 45
　　Performance Assessment 46
　　Authentic Assessment 48
　　Portfolio Assessment 49
　　Assessing Collaborative Learning 52

Chapter Summary 53

Review Questions 54

Summary of Tips 54

Exercises 55

Resources on the Web 56

References 57

Part II Application and Implementation **59**

Chapter 4 — **Interacting with Learners** **60**

Importance of Interaction in Learning 61
　　Cognitive Effects 62
　　Affective Effects 63
　　Social Effects 63

Collaborative Learning 63

Factors That Affect Interaction in Learning   65
    Beliefs and Perceptions   65
    Teacher Direction   66
    Learner Motivation   66
    Learning Styles   67
    Nature of Task   67
    Media   67
    Technical Support   68
    Immediacy of Feedback   68

Asynchronous and Synchronous Communication   69
    From a Pedagogical Perspective   69
    From a Psychological Perspective   71
    From a Technological Perspective   71

Using The Right Tools   72
    E-Mail   72
    Discussion Boards   73
    Mailing Lists   74
    Usenet (Newsgroups)   75
    Internet Chat   76
    Internet Conferencing   77

Designing and Managing Interaction in WBI   79
    Time Flexibility   80
    Group Composition   81
    Learning Tasks   84
    Instructor's Role   84
    Learner Engagement   86
    External Resources   86
    Quality Feedback and Formative Assessment   86
    Time Management   87

Conclusion   89

Chapter Summary   89

Review Questions   90

Exercises   90

Resources on the Web   91

References   92

Chapter 5 — **Making Content Interactive** **96**

Interaction and Interactivity   97

Factors That Affect Interactivity   98

Levels of Interactivity   99
    Attention   99
    Content Relevance   100
    Cognitive Engagement   100
    Supportive Context   101
    Learner Control   102

Adaptive Instructional Content   103
    Adaptive Hypermedia   104
    Navigation Branching and Learning Paths   105

Learner Response Opportunities and Instructional Feedback   107
    Selection of Learning Paths   108
    Selection of Web Form Items   108
    Data Entry Into Web Forms   109
    Mouse and Stylus Action   110
    Voice Input   110
    Programmed Instructional Feedback   110

Server-Supported Interactivity   112
    Client-Side Programs   112
    Server-Side Programs   113

Conclusion   116

Chapter Summary   117

Review Questions   117

Summary of Tips   117

Exercises   118

Resources on the Web   119

References   119

Chapter 6 — **Instructional Hypermedia Design**..................................... **121**

Hypermedia Defined   122

Hypermedia and Knowledge Construction   123

Navigation Schemes and Content Structure   125
    Linear Structure   125
    Hierarchical Structure   126
    Grid and Mesh Structures   128
    Balance Between Breadth and Depth   131
    Content Modularity   131

Navigational Guidance   132
    User Orientation   132
    Navigational Cues   133

Interface Consistency and Variation   **135**

Web Content Accessibility   **136**
 Speed   **136**
 Section 508   **137**
 Assistive Technology and Tools   **138**
 Browser Compatibility   **139**

Content Legibility and Salience   **140**
 Foreground and Background Contrast   **140**
 Color Associations   **141**

Text Layout and Legibility   **142**
 Text Line Length   **142**
 Table to Delimit Text Area   **143**
 Space Between Lines   **144**
 Font Type   **145**
 Downloadable Font   **145**
 Graphic Text   **146**
 Font Size   **146**

Page Layout and Navigation   **147**
 Frameset and Frames   **147**
 Grouping and Listing   **150**
 Page Length   **150**

Chapter Summary   **151**

Review Questions   **151**

Summary of Tips   **151**

Exercises   **152**

Resources on the Web   **153**

References   **154**

Chapter 7 — **Multimedia for Web-Based Instruction** **156**

Do Media Matter?   **157**
 Media Attributes and Effects on Learning   **159**
 Multimedia versus Single Medium   **159**
 Media and Context   **160**

Functions of Visuals   **160**
 Decoration and Perceptual Enhancement   **161**
 Realistic Representation   **162**
 Analogous and Metaphoric Representation   **164**
 Organizational (Spatial) Representation   **166**

Audio for Web-Based Instruction   169
    The Appeals and Constraints of Audio   169
    Digital Audio Protection   170

Instructional Use of Video   172
    Action and Motion   172
    Affective Impact   173
    Accessing the Inaccessible   173
    Manipulating Time and Space   173
    Capturing Screen Action   174

Digital Video Production   175
    Advantages of Digital Video   175
    Digital Video Formats   177
    What to Consider When Using Video   177

Streaming Media   179

Animation and Interactivity   179

Virtual Reality   181

Print Textbooks   183

E-Books   183

Chapter Summary   185

Review Questions   186

Summary of Tips   186

Exercises   187

Resources on the Web   188

References   188

Part III   Management   **190**

Chapter 8   Copyright and Intellectual Property **191**

What Is Copyright?   192

Traditional Regulations and Practice   192

New Copyright Issues in the E-Learning Environment   193

Current Practices—Establishing Guidelines for Fair
Use in Distance Learning   199
    Making Sure You Meet the Fair Use Guidelines   199
    Finding the Rightful Author   200
    What to Do If the Author Does Not Respond   201

Intellectual Property Rights and Ownership of Online Course Materials **201**
  Changing Your Institution's Intellectual Property Policy
    and Procedures **202**
    Scenario: Multimedia Production—Faculty **202**
    Scenario: E-Mail Copyright and Privacy **203**
    Scenario: Entrepreneurial Faculty **204**

Chapter Summary **204**

Review Questions **204**

Summary of Tips **205**

Exercises **205**

Resources on the Web **205**

References **206**

Chapter 9 **Course Management Systems** **207**

Key Components of a Course Management System **208**
  Browser-Based Interface **210**
  User Management **211**
  File Management **212**
  Content Organization and Presentation Structure **215**
  Assessment Tools **216**
  Communication Tools **220**

What to Consider in Adopting a Course Management System **222**
  Cost and Portability **222**
  Standardization **224**
  Customization **228**
  Online Quizzing **229**
  Support for Collaborative Learning **236**
  Open-Source Endeavors **236**

Chapter Summary **238**

Review Questions **238**

Summary of Tips **239**

Exercises **239**

Resources on the Web **240**

References **241**

Chapter 10 **Utilizing Web Resources** **243**

The Growth of the Web   244
　　Learn to Manage Web Resources   245
　　Check Offline Resources First   246

Finding Resources on the Web   246
　　Search Engines   247
　　Search Agents   249
　　Search Directories   250
　　Specialized Databases   251
　　Virtual Libraries   251
　　Online Journals and Periodicals   252
　　Online Reference Resources   252
　　E-Books   253
　　Primary Data Providers   254

Evaluating Web Resources   254
　　Authorship   255
　　Site Goals   256
　　Nature and Scope of Content   257
　　Accuracy and Credibility of Information   257
　　Currency and Stability of Content   258
　　Accessibility of Site and Ease of Navigation   258
　　Privacy and Security   258

Build Your Own Web Resource Repository   259
　　Recording and Archiving   259
　　Bookmarking   260
　　Creating a Database   260
　　Consulting Experts and Colleagues   263

Assessing Students' Information Skills   263
　　Information Search and Evaluation Skills   264
　　Information Presentation and Exchange Skills   264

Chapter Summary   265

Review Questions   265

Summary of Tips   266

Exercises   267

Resources on the Web   267

References   271

Chapter 11 — **Policy and Management for Web-Based Instruction 273**

Distance Learning Institutions   274

Planning Your E-Learning Program   275

Developing Policy for Your E-Learning Program   277

Marketing Your E-Learning Program   280

Providing Services to Distance Students   282

Evaluating Your E-Learning Program   283

Chapter Summary   283

Review Questions   284

Summary of Tips   284

Exercises   284

References   285

Glossary   286

Index   291

Note: Every effort has been made to provide accurate and current Internet information in this book. However, the Internet and information posted on it are constantly changing, so it is inevitable that some of the Internet addresses listed in this textbook will change.

PART I

FOUNDATION

Chapter 1   Introduction

Chapter 2   Instructional Design for Web-Based Instruction

Chapter 3   Assessment in Web-Based Instruction

Chapter 1

Introduction

CHAPTER INTRODUCTION

This chapter begins with a brief history of distance education and the evolution of e-learning. It then examines various factors that contribute to the growth and popularity of the Web as a learning medium. The chapter also discusses the impact that Web-based learning can have on how teaching and learning are carried out, assessed, and evaluated. Finally, the chapter discusses the challenges and constraints that Web-based instruction presents to institutions, designers, instructors, and learners.

LEARNING OBJECTIVES

After studying this chapter, the reader will be able to:

1. Give a brief description of the history of distance education and the evolution of e-learning.

2. Describe various factors that have fostered the growth of the World Wide Web as an e-learning environment.

3. Describe and discuss challenges, constraints, and costs of Web-based instruction.

BRIEF HISTORY OF DISTANCE EDUCATION AND E-LEARNING

Before we embark on Web-based instruction, some background knowledge of distance education will be helpful. **Distance education** has been generally defined as any form of instructional activities in which instructor and learner are separated from each other by physical distance. When it started, distance education relied on the postal services and often was called **correspondence study,** now referred to as independent study. In Europe, correspondence courses were offered in Germany, Great Britain, and Sweden as early as the 1830s (Holmberg, 1986). In the United States, William Rainey Harper helped establish one of the earliest correspondence degree programs at Chautauqua College of Liberal Arts in New York in 1883. When Harper became president of the University of Chicago, he established the University Extension Division in 1892. Other universities that also started offering correspondence programs included the University of Wisconsin (1885) and The Pennsylvania State University (1892). The majority of participants in these programs were adult learners who wanted to upgrade their occupational and professional skills. This characteristic of distance learners remains true today.

As radio became widely available in the 1920s, some universities such as the State University of Iowa, Ohio State University, and the University of Wisconsin converted the content of their correspondence courses and programs so they could be delivered over the radio. Radio-delivered instruction remained popular for a few decades as an affordable and convenient means of distance education, but in the 1950s it was gradually replaced by television as a more powerful tool for distance education. Public Broadcasting Service (PBS) has been one of the primary providers of distance education via television. Because of the relatively high cost of cable TV network and satellite technology, early television distance education programs were mostly state-supported and affiliated with major universities. Today, cable TV–based distance education programs are still more prosperous and successful in metropolitan areas.

Compared with other countries, distance education in the United States is less extensive. Nevertheless, the U.S. Department of Education (1999) estimates that there were approximately 1.6 million enrollments (counting students enrolled in more than one course) in distance education programs offered by college and universities in the academic year 1997–1998. Furthermore, 1,230 of the programs also delivered degrees and 340 of them delivered certificates.

Many terms have been used over the past several decades to refer to education delivered over distance, including *distance education, distance learning, distributed education, distributed learning,* to name a few. In recent years, the term *e-learning* has emerged to refer to learning through electronic media, with or without the involvement of the World Wide Web. This text focuses on **Web-based instruction (WBI),** although the term **e-learning** can cover more than that.

Two other terms, **blended learning** and **hybrid learning,** are also sometimes used in the discussion of Web-based instruction. Both blended learning and hybrid learning use a combination of electronic media and traditional face-to-face approaches to enable teaching and learning. Circumstances that may justify the adoption of blended learning or hybrid learning include a mix of any of the following:

▶ The technology infrastructure is not available or not ready to deliver completely Web-based instruction.

▶ The same course or program is offered to both distance and on-campus students.

▶ Some courses or curriculum components require students to come to campus for face-to-face, hands-on learning activities.

▶ All students are on the campus and electronic media are used to enhance teaching and learning effectiveness.

Since the practice of blended learning and hybrid learning can vary significantly in accordance with institutional contexts and needs, a comprehensive discussion of blended learning and hybrid learning is beyond the scope of this text. Instead, we will address blended learning and hybrid learning only where it can deepen the discussion of Web-based instruction.

THE GROWING POPULARITY OF WEB-BASED INSTRUCTION

Online learning is growing at an exponential rate. Since the advent of the Internet and the World Wide Web, more and more educational institutions have started offering courses and programs online. Institutions that a few years ago had never contemplated WBI are now anxious to have trained designers take a major role in renovating their instructional or training systems.

The National Center for Education Statistics of the U.S. Department of Education conducted an extensive survey in 1999 that included 5,000 two-year and four-year postsecondary education institutions that offered distance education opportunities. The study found that about 58% of the institutions surveyed used the Internet as a primary mode of instructional delivery for their distance courses and programs in 1997–1998 (U.S. Department of Education, 1999). Five years later, the Sloan Consortium conducted a survey of more than 1,100 colleges and universities with a report titled "Entering the Mainstream: The Quality and Extent of Online Education in the United States, 2003 and 2004." The survey results indicate that 1.9 million students were enrolled in online courses in the fall of 2003, and the schools expected the number of online students to be over 2.6 million by the fall of 2004 (Allen & Seaman, 2004). The U.S. Army has created one of the most innovative programs of higher education in the world: eArmyU, which is a collaboration of the Army and 29 educational institutions. eArmyU offers approximately 146 programs and participating soldiers can earn certificates or degrees by taking Web-based courses at any time, anywhere around the globe (eArmyU, 2004).

Some well-established educational institutions that have been successful providers of distance education are going online. The British Open University, Jones University, and the University of Phoenix are enrolling more students in Web-based courses and programs than in face-to-face settings. Public and private educational institutions have formed consortia to deliver learning opportunities across regional boundaries. These consortia include the Western Governors University (WGU), the California Virtual Campus (CVC), the Southern Regional Electronic Campus, and the Electronic University Consortium (EUC) in South Dakota. Many educational institutions that had a dubious attitude toward online learning have now become anxious to enter the realm of Web-based instruction to gain their share of the market.

The emergence of course management systems has further pushed the movement toward Web-enhanced and Web-based instruction. According to Casey Green (2003), a third of all college courses now use course management tools, up from 26.5% in 2002, 20.6% in 2001, and almost double the level in 2000. We discuss course management systems in chapter 9.

Contributing Factors

The growing popularity of Web-based instruction can be attributed to several factors. A predominant attraction of Web-based instruction to most distance learners is certainly its geographic independence and time flexibility; learners do not need to travel to attend classes on campus. As the Web-based Education Commission (2000) describes, the Internet is bringing learning to students instead of bringing students to learning. For rural communities, Web-based learning can provide a great means of overcoming geographic barriers between teachers and learners, and among peer learners. As Internet connection reaches farther and wider, Web-based courses will be accessible to a broader range of learners. With the growth of wireless mobile computing, the Web is also becoming an attractive instructional medium for on-campus classes. Time flexibility is another important advantage of Web-based courses for those adult learners who have full-time employment and cannot attend classes during the day. Asynchronous Web-based learning allows them to find time slots in their busy schedules to access course materials, do homework, communicate with peer learners, and conduct research projects.

WBI also accommodates the growing need for continuous, lifelong learning. As technology advances at an ever-increasing pace, continuous knowledge and skill updating have become necessary. Today's knowledge-based economy requires higher levels of skills. According to the Web-based Education Commission (2000), 85% of current jobs in the U.S. economy require education beyond high school, up from 65% in 1991. In most industry sectors, the need for just-in-time training has become constant. Lifelong learning is perceived by a growing number of people as essential in this information age.

At the same time, the cost of attending traditional higher education institutions has been rising. College expenses have soared at both public and private institutions. In the last decade, average tuition and fees at public colleges have increased by 44%, and the average cost at private colleges shows a 40% increase after adjusting for inflation (Green, 2000). With online courses, students can stay at home and save on travel and living expenses.

Another contributing factor in the growing popularity of WBI is that learning outcomes from e-learning have been found comparable to those from traditional classroom instruction (Hanson et al., 1997). A widely cited report by Tom Russell (1999) found that learning outcomes from technology-supported alternative forms of education are similar to, and sometimes better than, the learning outcomes of traditional on-campus learning. Online institutions and programs have been accredited as meeting established academic quality standards. For example, the Commission on Institutions of Higher Education of the North Central Association (NCA) has evaluated and accredited the University of Phoenix, Capella University, and other private online higher educational institutions.

Impacts of Web-Based Instruction

Web-based education brings more than freedom across space and time; it is changing the ways students learn, instructors teach, and educational outcomes are evaluated. First of all, the Web provides worldwide access to authentic data and primary resources. This makes it easy for instructional designers and instructors to incorporate authentic materials and multiple perspectives in course content to encourage situated learning.

The networked learning environment also encourages collaborative learning. In a virtual learning community, students have more opportunities to communicate and interact with each other through a variety of means, including e-mail, chat, discussion board, net conferencing, and application sharing.

In a hypermedia learning environment, students must actively navigate through the course; they cannot just sit back and passively listen to a lecture (Horton, 2000). With asynchronous communication mode and time flexibility, learners have more control over their learning pace, too. Using appropriate time management skills, students can arrange their learning activities to fit their schedules. Thus, Web-based instruction has made a long-cherished dream become reality: holding learner achievements constant by allowing learners to vary in the amount of time needed to accomplish their learning tasks.

In addition, the nonlinearity of hypermedia allows instructional designers and developers greater flexibility in content organization and presentation to accommodate different styles of learning: deductive or inductive, field-dependent or field-independent, associative or sequential learning. Furthermore, with database support and artificial intelligence, learning paths in hypermedia can be dynamically and interactively adjusted and customized to meet individual learners' needs and progress.

CHALLENGES AND CONSTRAINTS OF WEB-BASED INSTRUCTION

Although Web-based education can offer unprecedented learning opportunities to a larger population of students than ever before, it may not be the educational solution for everyone, given the current practical constraints. For those who find Web-based instruction a promising solution, there are usually some barriers to overcome.

Digital Divide

Although some countries such as Finland and Iceland have been able to develop an extensive network infrastructure that can give broad Internet access to the majority of the population, many developing countries are still trying to provide basic telephone and television services. Even in developed countries, millions of people do not have access to the Internet yet, particularly in remote and less developed areas, among low-income households, and minority families. In places where people do have access, many of them do not know how to use the Internet effectively to tap its rich resources. They do not know how to use the various interfaces of computer applications, where to find needed information, how to sort through the thousands of links returned by search engines, how to evaluate the resources that are very uneven in information quality, how to integrate new information into their existing knowledge, and how to use the communication tools to interact with others to build a virtual learning community.

Challenges for Designers and Instructors

Web-based instruction also presents new challenges to many instructional designers and instructors who have only recently become acquainted with the virtual learning environment. A Web-based instructional program cannot be built simply by converting existing courses from traditional format into electronic form and posting them on the Web. It requires very different information presentation and processing techniques, and thus a different instructional design and development process from the traditional models. Bork (2001) suggests that Web-based education should not be an effort to replicate traditional classroom teaching online. Keegan (1993) points out that new technologies have created new learning conditions and virtual environments that have made many existing theories of learning less applicable. Keegan (1996) also suggests that virtual learning might be treated as a new field of study itself rather than a subset of traditional distance learning.

In order to use hypermedia to help students achieve optimal learning outcomes, instructional designers and instructors need to have an understanding of the information attributes of hypermedia and their impacts on instructional content organization and presentation, such as associative versus sequential learning and information focus versus information richness. Without appropriate guidance and organization, the flexibility of information organization in hypermedia can easily cause cognitive overload and navigational disorientation for less experienced learners. Although the World Wide Web provides abundant resources to be incorporated into online courses, these resources tend to be very uneven in quality. Consequently, instructional designers and course developers need to select top-quality resources and make sure that learners really benefit from them.

Online instructional designers and instructors also need to be prepared for a paradigm shift in pedagogy from teacher-directed to student-centered learning, from a highly structured, directive approach to a flexible, constructive approach. Generally, an instructor in a Web-based learning environment needs to address the following apparently antithetical issues:

▶ Associative versus procedurally structured learning

▶ Collaborative versus independent learning

▶ Exploratory versus instructed learning

▶ Situated (context-specific, field-dependent) versus abstract (context-free, field-independent) learning

▶ Asynchronous versus synchronous communication

▶ Formative versus summative assessment

To organize and present course content in a scheme that utilizes the various link possibilities of hypermedia, instructional designers and instructors need to examine the nature of the course content, identify the knowledge structure, and decide how different types of content organization structures can be combined to provide flexible learning paths. The World Wide Web seems to be particularly appropriate for teaching certain subject matters. The survey previously cited by the National Center for Education Statistics of the U.S. Department of Education (1999) found that in the U.S., the most popular fields of study in which distance courses were offered by colleges and universities were in English, humanities, social and behavioral sciences (70% of all institutions surveyed), and business and management (55% of the institutions).

A virtual learning environment also requires significantly more interaction between instructor and learners and among peer learners. Instructional designers and instructors must be able to create varied channels to promote online communication and interaction. The instructor needs to develop skills in coordinating online interactions through e-mail, chat, discussion board, net conferencing, application sharing, and other communication channels. The instructor also needs to be prepared to spend more time responding to students' e-mails and other electronic messages.

Finally, depending on the extent of technical support available, the online instructor may also need some knowledge of digital media and skill in converting, compressing, and distributing digital documents and files. Special software may also be required for authoring and presenting course content in

IN PRACTICE **Web-Based Math Courses**

Using special software, Scientific Notebook, Texas A&M University offered college algebra and calculus courses completely online. The software comes with a built-in computer algebra engine, MuPAD. Scientific Notebook provides an interface that allows users to create, edit, evaluate, solve, or plot mathematical expressions in a graphic user interface. The files produced in Scientific Notebook can be delivered over the Web and learners can view the files with a special browser they can download for free.

Source: http://www.math.tamu.edu/~webcalc/ and http://www.mackichan.com/

some subject areas such as chemistry, physics, and mathematics. Additional cost and faculty training are usually required to support the development and delivery of courses in these subject areas.

Challenges for Learners

Students who seek online educational opportunities are typically different from traditional students in motivations and lifestyles. Time is the most valuable asset to many of them (Boettcher, 2002), and the time flexibility offered by distance learning is a major attraction to them. However, time flexibility comes with a major challenge: time management. Often, a learner drops out or withdraws not because he or she does not have the academic potential to accomplish the course work, but because he or she lacks time management skills and soon lags too far behind to catch up.

Although Web-based instruction technically should work for any learners who have Internet access, the features of the virtual environment seem to make it work better for learners who have these particular characteristics:

1. The learners are highly motivated by the need to acquire new knowledge and skills, but cannot attend classes on campus because of geographic barriers or time constraints.

2. They are self-disciplined and have good time management skills.

3. They can learn independently as well as interactively and can work with people without actually seeing them.

4. They can express themselves clearly in writing, because the primary mode of communication on the Web is still written text.

5. They are tolerant of occasional technical glitches and are not easily frustrated and upset by small technical problems. (Web-based Education Commission, 2000)

Costs and Returns

For an institution that offers Web-based instruction, a primary challenge is generally the upfront cost. Web-based instruction typically requires a significant amount of initial investment in computer network infrastructure, services support, and faculty training. Web-based degree programs need to have a completely online system of registration, access management, and support services that include academic advising, course material ordering, multimedia and Web development, technical troubleshooting, and library resources. For individual Web-based courses, a single faculty member may be able to perform all the tasks of content collection, material development, media preparation, interface design, script writing, Web page authoring, course instruction, and class communication and interaction. For a completely Web-based program, much greater efforts are needed in planning, designing, developing, and implementing. The varied tasks are usually distributed among a team of specialists.

An accurate calculation of the total costs and returns from Web-based instruction is difficult, because many of the costs are long-term investments that are hard to quantify, and the benefits for the learners can be invaluable. Nevertheless, efforts have been made to assess the development costs for Web-based instruction in general. In partnership with the Western Cooperative for Educational Telecommunications (WCET), Dennis Jones (2004) from the National Center for Higher Education Management Systems (NCHEMS) has authored a comprehensive handbook discussing technology costing. (The 100-plus-page handbook is free to download from http://www.wcet.info/projects/tcm/.) The costs of Web-based instruction are generally calculated on a cost-per-student-hour-of-learning basis (Bork, 2001). Judith Boettcher (2004) has proposed some guidelines for predicting the costs involved in online course development and delivery. The available examples in the literature indicate that about $15,000 to $20,000 per credit hour is generally required for online course development (Boettcher, 2004).

Although Web-based instruction can cost a lot more initially to develop than face-to-face instruction, the long-term total return is generally expected to more than compensate for the initial development cost. That is probably a primary reason why more and more institutions are taking on the mission of online instruction and training. Nevertheless, there have been quite a number of unsuccessful cases of online program attempts from both for-profit ventures and nonprofit institutions.

Considering the significant costs that can be involved in developing and offering an online program, Boettcher (2002) suggests a micromarket segment approach for traditional nonprofit institutions. With this approach, an educational institution should adhere to its institutional mission and take advantage of its current expertise and strengths in developing and offering online courses and programs. The institution should also be selective and experimental with its first few online courses, test its capabilities for offering online courses, and build on initial success to expand its market share.

IN PRACTICE **Four Operating Principles for Building an Online Program**

The University of Massachusetts–Lowell has a successful online program that offers six full degrees and enrolls more than 6,000 students a year. Dr. Jacqueline Moloney, dean of Continuing, Corporate and Distance Education (CCDE), and Dr. Steven Tello, associate director of distance learning of CCDE, suggest four operating principles for building a successful online program:

1. Adhere to your school mission.

2. Use existing traditional resources to accelerate the development of an online program.

3. Start small, build incrementally, and think scalability.

4. Build learning communities that push the limits of new technology.

Source: Moloney, J., & Tello, S. (2003). Principles for building success in online education. *Syllabus, 16* (7), 14–17.

Chapter Summary

In this chapter, we defined this book as being both a text and a reference resource for anyone who is interested or involved in designing and developing Web-based instruction. We briefly reviewed the history of distance education and the emergence of the World Wide Web as a paramount medium for learning in a virtual environment. We examined key factors that contributed to the growth of the Web, the challenges of designing and developing Web-based instruction, the costs that can be involved, and the cautious approach an institution might want to take in starting its online program endeavor.

Review Questions

1. What advantages can you perceive in WBI as compared with cable TV–based instruction?

2. Do you think WBI eventually will be preferred by college students in general over on-campus classroom teaching? Why?

3. What new skills would an instructional designer or instructor have to learn in order to deliver WBI if she or he has never been involved in WBI before?

4. What kinds of learners are more likely to succeed in a Web-based learning environment?

5. What should be taken into account if an institution wants to start a Web-based instructional program?

Resources on the Web

We have listed some Web resources here for your convenience, but we ask that you please visit the Companion Website for the most current links to resources.

- Office of Educational Technology (http://www.ed.gov/Technology/)
- webcommission (http://www.webcommission.org)
- EDUCAUSE (http://www.educause.edu/)
- e-Learning Centre (http://www.e-learningcentre.co.uk/)

References

Allen, I. E., & Seaman, J. (2004). Entering the mainstream: The quality and extent of online education in the United States, 2003 and 2004. The Sloan Consortium. Retrieved January 5, 2005, from http://www.sloan-c.org

Boettcher, J. V. (2002). The changing landscape of distance education: What micro-market segment is right for you? *Syllabus, 15* (12), 22–27.

Boettcher, J. V. (2004). Online course development: What does it cost? *Syllabus, 17* (12), 27–30.

Bork, A. (2001). What is needed for effective learning on the Internet? *Educational Technology & Society 4* (3). Retrieved December 16, 2001, from http://ifets.ieee.org/periodical/vol_3_2001/bork.html

eArmyU (2004). About eArmyU. Retrieved December 24, 2004, from http://www.earmyu.com/public/public_about-auao.asp

Green, K. C. (2000). Campus Computing 2000. http://www.campuscomputing.net

Green, K. C. (2003). Tracking the digital puck into 2004. Retrieved December 1, 2004, from http://www.campus-technology.com/article.asp?id=8574

Hanson, D., Maushak, N., Schlosser, C., Anderson, M., Sorensen, C., & Sionson, M. (1997). *Distance education: Review of the literature* (2nd ed.). Washington, DC and Ames, IA: Association for Educational Communications and Technology and Research Institute for Studies in Education.

Holmberg, B. (1986). *The growth and structure of distance education*. London: Croom Helm.

Horton, W. (2000). *Designing Web-based training*. New York: Wiley.

Jones, D. (2004). Technology costing methodology handbook. The Western Cooperative for Educational Telecommunications. Retrieved December 1, 2004, from http://www.wcet.info/projects/tcm/

Keegan, D. (1993). *Theoretical principles of distance education*. London: Routledge.

Keegan, D. (1996). *Foundations of distance education* (3rd ed.). London: Routledge.

Russell, T. L. (1999). *The no significant different difference phenomenon*. Chapel Hill, NC: Office of Instructional Telecommunications, North Carolina State University.

U.S. Department of Education, National Center for Education Statistics. (1999). *Distance education at postsecondary education institutions: 1997–98* (NCES 2000-013). Washington, DC.

Web-based Education Commission (2000). *The Power of the Internet for learning: Moving from promise to practice: Report to the President and the Congress of the United States*. Washington, DC.

Chapter 2

Instructional Design for Web-Based Instruction

CHAPTER INTRODUCTION

Instructional design, the foundation of instructional content development, runs throughout the instructional process. Without well-grounded instructional design, the success of instructional practice will be largely contingent upon spontaneous performance, and this is true of Web-based instruction as well. Various instructional models have been proposed by theorists and researchers, and there are many good texts describing and discussing these models. Popular models include Gagné's nine-event approach (1985, 1987), Dick and Carey's instructional systems design (Dick & Carey, 1996; Dick, Carey, & Carey, 2001), Jonassen's constructive learning environment (1991, 1999), and Hannafin, Land, and Oliver's open learning environment (1999). This chapter will not elaborate on any of these instructional design theories and models, nor will it prescribe systematic procedures or steps to follow in instructional design. Rather, this chapter aims to highlight the attributes of the Web as a learning environment and then discuss its implications for instructional design and course development. Most of the areas highlighted in this chapter will be elaborated in following chapters.

LEARNING OBJECTIVES

After studying this chapter, the reader will be able to:

1. Explain the interrelations between the basic components of an instructional design process, namely, needs analysis, objective specification, development, implementation, and evaluation.

2. Summarize the basic characteristics of the Web-based learning environment and how they can influence instructional design.

3. Outline the basic preparations an institution must make to start Web-based instructional programs.

4. Describe the preparations necessary to involve faculty and students in Web-based instruction.

5. Discuss how constructive and collaborative learning can be facilitated in the Web-based learning environment, including the effective use of hypermedia, asynchronous and synchronous online communication, interactive multimedia, and utilization of Internet resources.

6. Explain how assessment differs in the Web-based environment from that in the traditional classroom setting and discuss alternative assessment methods.

ⒸASE STUDY

• Mid-State University (MSU) has a graduate program in information systems (IS). The program started out with all the courses being taught in face-to-face classroom settings on campus. Three years ago, the state procured enough funds to set up a statewide interactive TV (ITV) system with satellite sites distributed across the state and linking all higher educational institutions and K–12 school districts. The statewide ITV network soon became a popular tool for live interaction among educational institutions, and the university started using ITV to teach some of the courses in the IS program. The capability of distance delivery allowed many nontraditional students to enroll in the program. These nontraditional students generally have family and job commitments that prevented them from attending classes on campus.

As the program grew, it started attracting more and more students, many from out-of-state. Since the ITV system is statewide only and cannot reach out-of-state, the university is considering moving the courses online to make the program Web accessible, so that out-of-state students can enroll in the program. The program administrators and faculty all support the move, but they would like to take a gradual approach and start with a few courses that they feel would be better candidates for online delivery. They would also like to retain as much of the multimedia interactivity offered by ITV as possible when the program becomes Web based.

The university is currently using a commercial course management system (CMS) for its online course delivery. The instructional technology support team offers regular training workshops on using the course management system and other related instructional technologies. If you are an instructional designer and you are assigned to help redesign the courses of the IS program to make them Web deliverable, what approach are you going to take? What issues do you think you need to address before and during the redesigning and development process? Please keep these questions in mind as you read this chapter.

INSTRUCTIONAL DESIGN FOR WBI

Although instructional models vary in their emphasis on different aspects of instructional design, they converge on some underlying principles and inclusion of some key components. In general, the most fundamental components are needs analysis, objective (learning outcome) specification, development, implementation, and evaluation. The list may appear to be linear, but these components are not necessarily carried out sequentially. They can influence one another and need to be integrated, and the process of integration often requires revision of each component. For example, needs analysis may need to be further pursued later on in a program when new problems emerge and require inquiry and solutions.

According to Reigeluth (1999), one of the important principles of instructional design is that the methods offered by instructional models should be situational rather than universal; methods should be flexible and adaptable to context variables. For the Web-based learning environment, important attributes include: (a) hypermedia as the primary form of content delivery, (b) dynamic and interactive Web content, (c) worldwide resource sharing and communication, (d) asynchronous communication as the primary mode of class interaction, and (e) virtual collaborative learning.

The use of hypermedia as a primary form of instructional content delivery in Web-based instruction leads to some subsequent requirements, such as ease of navigation of course site structure, associative learning through hyperlinks, interactive and adaptive content, student-centered constructive learning, multimedia integration, and utilization of Internet resources. Because learners generally do not meet face-to-face in a fixed time schedule under the supervision of an instructor, WBI tends to be mostly asynchronous and more student-centered, and learners have more control over their learning activities. The asynchronous nature of communication has a significant impact on what types of teaching and learning activities are more appropriate and pursuable in the Web-based learning environment. Because instructor and students do not meet in a classroom setting, many of the traditional assessment methods are no longer as applicable in the virtual environment. Alternative assessment methods are playing an increasingly important role.

Web-based instruction is still in its infancy, and Web-based instructional design is far from a systematic discipline of science. This text is not intended to propose any model of instructional design or prescriptive framework for WBI. Rather, we attempt to highlight important areas that may deserve particular attention in designing and developing Web-based instruction. These areas are: (a) needs analysis, (b) hypermedia and constructive learning, (c) online communication and collaborative learning, (d) multimedia and interactive content, (e) worldwide resources and lifelong learning, and (f) assessment in a Web-based learning environment.

NEEDS ANALYSIS

Web-based instruction has some important technical and pedagogical characteristics that make it significantly different from traditional face-to-face classroom teaching. When designing and developing Web-based instruction, we need to be aware of these characteristics and be informed of the readiness

FIGURE ❷·❶   **Needs Analysis**

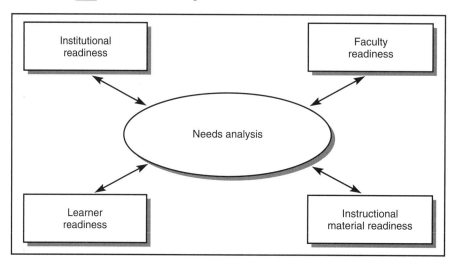

that the institution, instructors, and learners may need to have in these areas (see Figure 2.1).

Institutional Readiness

As a technology-dependent and resource-intensive medium of teaching and learning, Web-based instruction relies on strong technical infrastructure and adequate support services for smooth operation. Institutional readiness and support are crucial to the success of Web-based programs. Those who design and teach Web-based courses need to ensure that Web-based instruction is congruent with the institutional mission, know the amount of the institution's investment in Web-based course delivery, and know the amount of support resources the institution is prepared to provide. These resources fall largely into two areas: technical infrastructure and staffing. Specific infrastructure issues include servers and network connections, course management systems, Web development tools, online communication channels, and multimedia support facilities.

Web-based course development is a resource-intensive endeavor. Before starting to design an online course, we may want to check whether the institution has offered similar Web-based courses before. If so, we may want to reuse, with some adaptation and modification, those components that are still applicable. We should also find out if the course to be offered is part of a degree program or a stand-alone course. If the course is part of a degree program, it must contribute to the accomplishment of the program objectives. A common set of support resources can then be shared to support all the courses. When all the courses are designed and developed by the same team, coordination among courses is usually less of a problem. But if different individuals or groups are involved in designing and developing different courses, intercourse coordination can become a prominent issue. For the information systems (IS) program of our case study, we may need to assign an administrator or one of the faculty members to take care of coordinating the program curriculum and resources so that efforts can be consolidated to accomplish program objectives.

If an institution uses a course management system (CMS) such as Blackboard or WebCT, course development and faculty training can be very different from a situation that does not involve a CMS. Among other things, standardized courseware generally has a user management system that can support online registration, access control, usage tracking, online quizzing, and grade reports. Furthermore, a CMS usually has its own ways of structuring a course site and organizing course content. If a course requires an organization structure or functionality that is not adequately supported by the course management system, alternatives may have to be provided to compensate for the deficiency.

Another important aspect of support that may involve institutional coordination is the online access to library resources. Can the students access the library catalog and other resources via the Internet? Can the students check out books and request copies of journal articles online and through regular mail service? If online access to the library resources is available, such access may need to be integrated into the design of Web-based courses.

Faculty Readiness

A Web-based course can be very unproductive if the instructor is not ready to teach it online. Faculty readiness includes time availability and motivation to teach in the online environment. Teaching online courses generally requires far

C A S E   S T U D Y   MSU's Readiness for WBI

- Over the past few years, MSU has been using an in-house package instead of a CMS for its online courses. One of the advantages of an in-house solution is that it can combine the best application tools built for dedicated uses. For example, stand-alone discussion board systems and Internet conferencing tools are usually more versatile than those built into course management systems. As the institution migrates to an integrated course management system, adjustment and preparations need to be made in several areas, such as support resources and faculty training. One of the prominent issues will be to help instructors transfer their existing course materials into the new course management system with minimal cost of revamping. In addition, some instructors of the IS program have created quite a number of server-side programs to enhance the interactivity of their course content. Support staff and instructors need to find ways that can let the instructors continue using the interactive programs they have already invested a great amount of resources to develop.

more time involvement for instructors than classroom teaching. Faculty workload is a management issue and will be discussed in chapter 11.

Large institutions may have special support teams dedicated to designing and developing online course materials for instructors, who are only responsible for teaching the courses. A major issue in such situations is the coordination and cooperation required between designer and instructor. Instructional hypermedia is so flexible in content organization, so rich in multimedia possibilities, and so extensible in external resource inclusion that it is hard to imagine a functional separation between the designer and the instructor of the course. Ideally, course designer and course instructor should be the same person. When designers and instructors are different people, coordination and cooperation are crucial for the final success of the course.

Specifically, instructional designers and developers should be aware of instructors' prior experience in delivering online courses. If instructors have taught Web-based courses before, we need to find out what kind of experience they have had and if they have any cultivated preferences in developing and delivering Web-based courses.

Learner Readiness

Like a face-to-face course in a traditional classroom setting, a Web-based course can be designed and taught in various ways, depending on instructor and learner characteristics. Course designers need to have some knowledge about

©ASE STUDY   Training for the Instructors

- Mid-State University develops a series of training sessions to help instructors become comfortable and competent in instructional hypermedia and online communication tools. Following up on the initial course design and planning, designers and developers have also scheduled regular meetings with instructors to discuss technological needs and pedagogical issues that have not been fully addressed during the course planning phase.

  Surveys are conducted to discover instructors' needs for training. The training team has tried to be specific with the survey questions. For example, rather than asking whether instructors need training in using Web development tools, questions are asked on more specific topics such as managing course Web sites, designing navigation schemes, designing page layouts, developing Web graphics, administering online quizzes, and using online communication tools. Another challenge for the training team is to find time slots when most faculty members can come and participate in the training sessions. After trying different slots, they have concluded that lunch hour and the hour after 5:00 P.M. are the time slots when most people can come.

the incoming students, including their academic background, experiences with Web-based instruction, learning style preferences, and technical profiles, such as the types of Internet connection they have and the computer platforms they use. Students' technical capabilities are fundamental in helping us decide what type of Web content we can deliver. For instance, if the majority of the students are still using dial-up modem connections to access the Internet, it would not be a good idea to have them download large volumes of data or streaming media, which would be an extremely time-consuming, frustrating, and futile experience.

To learn about student readiness and needs, a survey before or when the course starts can help us determine what type of learning tasks might be more practical and what type of accommodations might be needed. Surveys on student needs should help us find out whether students are technically ready to undertake the learning tasks designed for the course. For courses that require students to post materials in hypermedia, we need to find out whether the students are able to create basic Web pages without much additional training.

One of the common problems many distance learners have is time management. Students without much experience in taking Web-based courses may not be aware of the challenge of time management required when taking courses online and eventually may find themselves lagging far behind the course schedule and unable to accomplish the course work in time. While allowing some time flexibility for students to complete assignments, it is usually necessary to have some explicit time requirement in course scheduling so that students have enough reminders to keep up with the course, particularly for nontraditional students who have family and job commitments, like many of those in the IS program of Mid-State University.

CASE STUDY Student Orientation to WBI

- Of the skills needed for successful learning experience in the Web environment, the ability to communicate with instructor and peers is crucial. Students have to be able to use various online communication tools from the very beginning of the course. If any students cannot use these tools, guidance and initial training should be provided before the course starts. The support team of the e-education services at Mid-State University has prepared some online orientation modules to help students assess their readiness for taking Web-based courses, and train novice students in using the required computer applications and communication tools needed. The online orientation package includes some tests that students are required to take with a passing grade. If a student fails the tests, additional help and training are provided to assist the student in acquiring the needed skills until he or she can pass the tests.

Instructional Materials Readiness

One of the popular misconceptions about Web-based education is that Web-based courses can be prepared simply by converting print-based course materials into electronic format and posting them on the Web. Such a misconception reflects a general lack of understanding of the attributes of hypermedia and the online learning environment. Although domain knowledge covered in a course should be very much the same regardless of the mode in which the course is delivered, content organization and presentation of instructional hypermedia and of print-based material are very different. In moving to the Web-based mode of instruction, many of MSU's IS courses may need to be redesigned in content organization and presentation to fit the hypermedia learning environment.

Another issue course designers and administrators need to be aware of is that Web-based instructional materials generally take a lot more time to prepare than traditional print-based course materials, primarily because of the modular approach and complex structuring required of hypermedia development. We need to find out how much of the existing course content is already in Web-deliverable form, how much needs to be converted into hypermedia, and how much needs to be prepared from scratch. Web-based course materials can take even more time to prepare if multimedia are to be incorporated, since multimedia content usually takes far more resources to prepare. So we may need to ask whether the multimedia content is instructionally justified before we decide to include it. Multimedia applications are further discussed in chapter 7.

IN PRACTICE   Worldwide Instructional Design System (WIDS)

WIDS was originally part of the Wisconsin Technical College System Foundation (WTCSF), a nonprofit organization dedicated to the advancement of education. In 1993, Wisconsin's 16 technical colleges partnered with WTCSF to create and implement a performance-based instructional design system, and the result is the Worldwide Instructional Design System (WIDS).

WIDS provides a framework for developing complete Web-based hybrid or traditional courses, programs, and training. The design information and input is stored in a database and can be exported to HTML or Microsoft Word format. WIDS consists of a set of software that serves as a large filing cabinet. The designer can put in learning outcomes, set performance expectations, create assessment measures, plan learning activities, and develop course outlines and lesson plans.

WIDS also provides consultation and training services to its clients. At the time of this writing, WIDS has clients in 33 states and six foreign countries.

Source: http://www.wids.org/

By the same token, time issues deserves attention and careful planning when courses are to be moved from one course management system to another. It is not a simple matter of data transfer without much need for redesigning or structure modification. Nothing can be farther from the truth. If the two course management systems involved have very different system structures, the process can be more time consuming and confusing than building a course on a blank template.

DESIGNING FOR CONSTRUCTIVE LEARNING

In today's mobile computing and networked learning environment, the control of knowledge construction is more in the hands of the learner than of the instructor (Lippman, 2002). This is particularly true in Web-based instruction. The primary advantage of hypermedia is flexible linkage across content units that may not be physically located adjacent to one another. Such flexible linkage allows us to arrange materials in ways that encourage learners to find possible interconnections among concepts and ideas, and to help learners navigate through learning paths that are most relevant to their personal experiences. Through active exploration and cognitive navigation, learners are encouraged to build connections between their past experience and new knowledge. This exploration is also known as **constructive learning.**

Linkage in hypermedia can support not only context-based and learner-built associations among concepts and ideas, but also multimodalities in presenting the same concept or idea. When information can be received concurrently in two or more modalities rather than one modality only, there is better accommodation of varied learning styles and a better chance for comprehension and understanding. According to the cognitive flexibility theory (Spiro, Feltovich, Jacobson, & Coulson, 1991), learners can often gain a better understanding of instructional content when the content is presented and "re-presented" (a pun) in multiple perspectives and modalities. Similarly, the elaboration theory (Reigeluth, 1983, 1999) supports associative learning and states that the learner needs to develop a meaningful context into which subsequent ideas and skills can be assimilated. Such customizable learning context with optional multiple perspectives can be effectively provided through hypermedia (Hoffman, 1997).

For designers of instructional hypermedia, important tasks are to identify associations that learners are most likely to make, select media for better presentations of the content, and appropriately place hyperlinks to encourage associative learning. The placement of hyperlinks in instructional content requires careful cognitive and pedagogical considerations. The decision on the type of resources to incorporate in each stage of learning and the choice of information modalities can have a significant impact on learners' successful processing of the instructional content. Inappropriate insertion of external resources can cause cognitive overload or learner digression. The design of instructional hypermedia will be further discussed in chapter 6.

⊙ A S E   S T U D Y   Constructive Learning for the IS Students ·······

- Many of the students in the IS program of MSU are nontraditional students with full-time or part-time employment. With their varied personal backgrounds and professional experiences, individual learners may not all attain the same learning outcomes. We may need to design course assignments and assessment measures that students could relate to their personal experiences and that accommodate their professional needs. This constructive approach calls for designing for collaborative learning and alternative assessment.

DESIGNING FOR ONLINE COMMUNICATION AND COLLABORATIVE LEARNING

With little chance to meet face-to-face with the instructor or with classmates, learners in the Web learning environment often feel alienated. Active and effective online communication can help learners overcome the sense of alienation. Class communication in Web-based learning environment can be synchronous or asynchronous, or a combination of both. The two modes differ primarily in the presence or absence of immediate feedback. In **synchronous communication,** participants are online simultaneously and interact with one another in real time with immediate feedback, whereas in **asynchronous communication** participants do not have to be online at the same time and feedback delay is expected. Synchronous communication over the Internet can be through text chat, multimedia conferencing, or application sharing. The latter two usually require a **broadband** Internet connection to maintain smooth and steady data transfer. For users without a broadband connection and for nontraditional learners who need time flexibility, asynchronous communication remains a primary mode of class communication. With its time flexibility, asynchronous communication can promote analytical and reflective thinking because learners have more time to carefully consider and construct their responses (Harasim, 1990).

The different strengths and constraints of the two modes of online communication can have important implications for course designers and instructors. For instance, synchronous communication provides instant feedback and usually works better for socializing and building interpersonal relationships. However, synchronous online sessions are often difficult to schedule for nontraditional learners with family- and job-related commitments and very tight timetables.

Participation in small groups is easier to manage with synchronous communication. In a text chat session that involves many active participants, messages can keep popping up about divergent topics, making it difficult to link the messages into a coherent thread. In a net conference, several people may try to speak simultaneously because they cannot tell whether and when other people are about to speak. Furthermore, in a large group, dominant speakers are more likely to talk and less vocal participants have fewer chances to contribute. Group composition and group size therefore need to be carefully controlled in designing online synchronous communication.

When immediate feedback is not needed, asynchronous communication is often more effective for learning tasks that require focused discussion, reflective thinking, and negotiation for team solutions. Among the asynchronous communication tools, the discussion board is probably the most popular. Messages posted in a discussion board are relatively permanent and typically organized in a way that allows the reader to see the path of the discussion. Participants can always review and follow up on previous postings, supplying additional messages for clarification and elaborating or modifying previous statements. With more evenly distributed opportunities for participants to post and respond, dominant speakers are less likely to monopolize the discussion.

Collaborative learning is valuable in a Web-based learning environment. Not only does it help learners to overcome any sense of alienation and to learn from one another, but it also trains students in effective teamwork, which is becoming increasingly important in today's workplace.

The concept of collaborative learning is based in the work of Vygotsky on social construction of knowledge and Bandura on peer modeling, which we discuss in chapter 4. The competence learners develop through collaborative learning will be transferred to their individual work. Compared with lecture-style teaching, a collaborative learning environment provides a relatively realistic, cognitively motivating, and socially enriched learning context. While collaborating with peers, learners often encounter fresh ideas, experience diverse interpretations, and see varied learning strategies that may not be congruent with their prior knowledge and experiences. The reciprocal give-and-take benefits all students, because people usually obtain a more solid grasp of what they know by tutoring others. We will further discuss online communication and collaborative learning in chapter 4.

CASE STUDY Synchronous Communication for IS Students

- For the adult learners in MSU's IS program, occasional synchronous sessions may be scheduled to provide opportunities for socializing and communication needs that require instant feedback, such as introduction sessions at the beginning of the semester or a group meeting for a project wrapup. If all students are in-state, the statewide ITV system may be used to host such net conferencing. If there are students from out-of-state, other conferencing tools such as NetMeeting or Messenger can be used for virtual meetings. Although it may be difficult to organize synchronous meetings for large groups, learners may find it convenient to set up sessions for small groups.

IN PRACTICE   **An Interactive Tool to Help Course Design**

The Module Organizer And Teaching System (MOATS) offers instructors and course designers multiple pathways into designing activities for course development, unit groupings, and specific lesson goals and objectives. Access the tool by selecting whatever area interests you. Corresponding choices will be offered along the way. You will also have the opportunity to save, download, and print your choices, permitting you to access them again in the future for alteration and reference as well as to build a library of useful reusable objects.

Source: http://moats.arizona.edu/moats/

DESIGNING INTERACTIVE MULTIMEDIA CONTENT

Historically, education has always been closely related to available media and technologies. As early as the 1960s, researchers pointed out that information attributes of different media differ (McLuhan, 1965). Media attribute advocates believe that a particular medium carries with it a means of interaction peculiar to it that colors its content, and comprehension of the message can be enhanced if the communicational symbol system has a closer match with the cognitive activities required by the information processing of the message (Salomon, 1974). The choice of medium is a frequent decision to make in Web-based instruction because a great variety of media is available in the Web-based learning environment.

Along with the rich variety of digital media, the ever-growing power of the computer has brought us interactivity potential not previously available. Database-supported libraries let the user search for needed information in a way far more effective and efficient than searching through the traditional index card system in a library. With programmed instruction supported by artificial intelligence and virtual reality, a computer-enhanced learning environment allows the learner to explore realistic scenarios or imaginary possibilities, test "wild" hypotheses, and simulate real-life situations.

Web-based instructional content can be designed to interact with learners at different levels. Logistically, interactivity usually occurs first at the perceptual level by getting the learner's attention. Based on content relevance and learning objective, the learner may either be led to study more about the topic or move to more interesting and relevant content. Once the learner is engaged with the instructional content, cognitive scaffolding sustains the interactivity between the learner and the content. To engage learners in a continuous dialogue with the instructional content, there must be opportunities for them to make active responses to the instructional content and produce their own output. Subsequently, instructional content should be adaptive and responsive to learner actions and variations in the learning process.

Designing instructional content with rich interactivity potential can involve varied degrees of pedagogical and technical expertise. The level of content organization and presentation generally does not require much programming expertise. Designers with sufficient experience and some skills in Web authoring should be able to design Web content that can interact with learners through a perceptually and cognitively engaging interface and navigation scheme. Instructional designers and developers are usually not required to develop anything that involves artificial intelligence or expert system support, which is usually developed by professional programmers and available as commercial software products. Nevertheless, instructional designers do need to keep well informed about the kind of interactivity potential current technology can support, whether the technology is available, and how the technology might be applicable in Web-based instruction. For example, computer simulations of network traffic flow and management could be effective learning aids for the IS students of our MSU case study. We will further discuss interactive Web content in chapters 5–7.

DESIGNING FOR UTILIZATION OF INTERNET RESOURCES

A major advantage of the Web as a learning environment is access to world-wide resources. Incorporating Internet resources in Web-based instruction can not only enhance course content with authentic materials from around the world, but also teach students how Internet resources can be leveraged for life-long learning. Appropriate utilization of Internet resources in WBI requires designers and instructors to be competent in both information search and information evaluation. Designers may even want to develop repertoires of Internet resources that fit the instructional needs of their local curricula.

Concentrated instruction on information search and evaluation usually is unnecessary for most courses. Instead, context-based guidance and just-in-time tips are often more helpful than general principles. A key point is to make informed decisions as to where to include such guidance and what resources to include. Inadequate resources may not satisfy learners' needs; too many resources can easily cause information overload and user disorientation. Making a good decision in placing appropriate resources in appropriate places is based on a good understanding of the learning tasks and anticipation of learner needs for supplementary resources. We will further discuss these issues in chapter 10.

DESIGNING FOR ALTERNATIVE ASSESSMENT

Assessment is an essential component in ensuring the effectiveness of any instruction. A major constraint for assessment in WBI is that the learner cannot be directly supervised in real time by the instructor in a face-to-face setting.

Without direct observation and supervision, a subsequent concern is learner authenticity. How can we be sure that the test-taker at a remote site is really the person who should be taking the test? In recent years, some new technology has emerged to help ensure learner authenticity, such as webcam monitoring of remote sites, digital signatures, and digital fingerprint scan. These measures are generally rather expensive or inconvenient to implement, however, and currently are unavailable in most areas.

There are proactive ways to promote authentic assessment. The essence of proactive authenticity is to have assessment aligned with instructional objectives and make the assessment an integral part of the learning experience, something perceived to be meaningful and valuable by the learners. For many nontraditional students, projects that integrate course objectives with their professional development are often most motivating and rewarding.

Although the adoption of **alternative assessments** may present a major challenge if standardized testing is required for accountability and credibility, alternative assessment can be a valuable means of assessing learner performances and improving the teaching and learning process. Among various forms of alternative assessment, authentic assessment, performance assessment, and portfolio assessment are three prominent approaches.

Authentic assessment and performance assessment share many essential characteristics. They both involve direct observation of student performance on authentic tasks or tasks that resemble those considered necessary in real life. Authentic and performance assessment value the process of constructive learning and problem solving more than the final result or product. Problem solving has been the focus of attention in some recent works on instructional design and practice (Jonassen, 2003). After reviewing instructional design theories for several years to identify prescriptive principles shared by various theories, Merrill (2002) has come up with five principles of problem solving. According to Merrill, the most critical characteristic of problem-centered instructional design is that learning activities should be based on authentic learning tasks that the learner has encountered or is expected to encounter in the real world.

Authentic and performance assessments in Web-based instruction can take various forms, such as journal writing, oral presentation, interview report, case study, demonstration of student project, audio and video recording of performances, role play, simulation, and portfolios.

Authentic and performance assessments may be easier to develop than objective tests, but more costly to administer and grade. For one thing, authentic and performance assessments are often time-consuming to conduct since they are usually process-oriented, extending as long as the student's tasks continue. Another constraint is that the knowledge and skills measured via authentic and performance assessment are not easily comparable across contexts and individual learners. We will further discuss alternative assessment in chapter 3.

C A S E   S T U D Y   Web-Based Portfolio for IS Students

In recent years, portfolio assessment has been gaining popularity as a form of alternative assessment, especially with the increasing applications of hypermedia. Since every student at Mid-State University is provided with a Web space, developing a hypermedia portfolio would be a very viable means of alternative assessment. The program coordinators believe that a portfolio should be a progressive collection of a student's work over the course of the IS program and should demonstrate the student's continuous progress of learning. As a process-oriented assessment method, the building of a portfolio should start at the very beginning of the program, rather than being an ad hoc collection put together near the end of the program. Designers and instructors should therefore include guidance and instruction on portfolio development from the outset and continue the guidance throughout the course of the program.

IN PRACTICE   **An Online Institutional Course Design System**

The Student Learning Objectives (SLO) system is a suite of four Web applications developed at the University of Washington. The university has 15 institution-wide standard learning objectives. All courses are encoded by the instructors in terms of the learning objectives that they offer. Every course has a total of 100 learning objective points, and each faculty member decides how to divide those points among the 15 university objectives and any custom learning objectives.

When compiled for a department, program, or major for a group of students, these data can be used as objective achievement indicators. Students can also have direct access to their own personal learning objective profiles and will be able to use learning objectives as an additional basis for choosing courses. The tool is designed to support continuous self-reflection on where the student has been and where she or he is going.

Source: http://www.washington.edu/slo/

Review Questions

1. What should we do to ensure that students who have limited experiences in WBI will have a comfortable head start in WBI, like many of the students in our case study of the IS program?

2. Do you think constructive learning and collaborative learning are more applicable or less applicable in WBI than in traditional classroom teaching? Why?

3. If you are going to promote constructive and collaborative learning in the IS courses of Mid-State University, what approaches are you going to take?

4. What kind of communication channels would you recommend for the IS classes of our case study? Why?

5. WBI lacks face-to-face contact and generally does not have much real-time synchronous communication. Does assessment become difficult because of this lack of face-to-face content?

6. What assessment methods do you think are more applicable for the IS program of our case study? How can different assessment methods complement one another?

7. How do we design Web-based instruction to integrate constructive learning, student collaboration, multimedia support, Web resource utilization, and alternative assessment?

Summary of Tips

1. Before building a new Web-based course, find out if there are any previous course materials that can be reused.

2. Encourage coordination between courses within the same program to avoid unnecessary redundancy in content development.

3. Conduct some needs analysis to find out faculty readiness for the Web-based courses they are going to teach.

4. Base faculty training on a good understanding of specific needs.

5. Schedule faculty workshops before 8:00 in the morning, during lunch hour, or after 5:00 p.m. to avoid conflicts with teaching duties.

6. Provide online orientation modules to help prepare students to take Web-based courses.

7. Find out students' technical capabilities to determine the accessibility of the online course materials.

8. Design synchronous learning activities for building interpersonal relationships and for information exchange that requires immediate feedback.

9. Design asynchronous learning activities to promote analytic and reflective thinking.

10. Design assignments in ways that can help students manage time well and keep up with the course schedule, especially nontraditional students with family and job commitments.

11. Design hypermedia in multiple perspectives and multiple modalities to accommodate varied learning styles and learner preferences.

12. Carefully plan the inclusion and placement of external Web resource links to keep learners concentrated on the learning tasks and not overwhelm them with excessive amounts of additional information.

13. Make assessment an integral part of the learning experience, and make it meaningful and valuable to the learners. For many nontraditional students, projects such as case studies and field reports that integrate course objectives with their professional development are often the most motivating and rewarding.

Exercises

1. Summarize the basic characteristics of the Web-based learning environment and how they can influence the instructional design.

2. Outline the basic preparations an institution needs to have to start Web-based instructional programs.

3. Select a school or college and study its readiness to offer Web-based instruction, including institutional readiness, faculty readiness, and student readiness.

4. Design a survey to learn faculty needs for training in Web-based course development and delivery.

5. Design a survey to determine student readiness for taking Web-based courses, including their experience in Web browsing, online communication, resource utilization, and time management.

6. What kinds of issues deserve attention when a print-based course is moved to the Web-based environment? Form a small group to share views on these issues and discuss possible solutions.

7. Five students are assigned to a team to work on a group project. The students live in different parts of the state. Their project is to research the state's water shortage situation and write a report on their findings to be presented to the class. The report should use hypermedia and multimedia to enhance the information presentation. What communication methods and tools would you suggest the students should use to interact and coordinate in working on the project?

8. Explain how assessment in the Web-based environment differs from assessment in the traditional classroom setting. Discuss alternative assessment methods.

Resources on the Web

We have included some related Web resources at the end of each chapter. However, because Web resources are generally updated very frequently, we ask you to check the Companion Website for updated and accurate resource links.

- Instructional Design Models (http://carbon.cudenver.edu/~mryder/itc/idmodels.html)
- David Merrill on Instructional Design (http://www.id2.usu.edu/Papers/Contents.html)

- Using Instructional Design Principles to Amplify Learning on the World Wide Web (http://edweb.sdsu.edu/clrit/learningtree/DCD/WWWInstrdesign/WWWInstrDesign.html)

- Distance Education Clearinghouse (http://www.uwex.edu/disted/)

- Evaluating Web-Based Instruction Design (http://www.chartula.com)

References

Dick, W., & Carey, L. (1996). *The systematic design of instruction* (4th ed.). New York: HarperCollins.

Dick, W., Carey, L., & Cary, J. O. (2001). *The systematic design of instruction.* New York: Longman.

Gagné, R. (1985). *Conditions of learning* (4th ed.). New York: Holt, Rinehart & Winston.

Gagné, R. (1987). *Instructional technology foundations.* Hillsdale, NJ: Lawrence Erlbaum.

Hannafin, M., Land, S., & Oliver, K. (1999). Open learning environments: Foundations, methods, and models. In C. M. Reigeluth (Ed.), *Instructional-design theories and models: A new paradigm of instructional theory* (Vol. II, pp. 115–142). Mahwah, NJ: Lawrence Erlbaum.

Harasim, L. M. (1990). Online education: An environment for collaboration and intellectual amplification. In L. M. Harasim (Ed.), *Online education: Perspectives on a new environment.* New York: Praeger.

Hoffman, S. (1997). Elaboration theory and hypermedia: Is there a link? *Educational Technology, 37*(1), 57–64.

Jonassen, D. H. (1991). Objectivist vs. constructivist: Do we need a new philosophical paradigm? *Educational Technology: Research and Development, 39,* 5–14.

Jonassen, D. H. (1999). Designing constructivist learning environments. In C. M. Reigeluth (Ed.), *Instructional-design theories and models: A new paradigm of instructional theory* (Vol. II, pp. 215–239). Mahwah, NJ: Lawrence Erlbaum.

Jonassen, D. H. (2003). *Learning to solve problems: An instructional design guide.* San Francisco: Pfeiffer.

Lippman, A. (2002). Lippman on learning: Fundamental changes. *Syllabus, 15*(7), 12–13.

McLuhan, M. (1965). *Understanding media: The extension of man.* New York: McGraw-Hill.

Merrill, D. (2002). First principles of instruction. *Educational Technology Research and Development, 50*(3), 43–59.

Reigeluth, C. M. (1983). Instructional design: What is it and why is it? In C. M. Reigeluth (Ed.), *Instructional-design theories and models: An overview of their current status* (pp. 3–36). Mahwah, NJ: Lawrence Erlbaum.

Reigeluth, C. M. (1999). What is instructional design theory and how is it changing? In C. M. Reigeluth (Ed.), *Instructional-design theories and models: A new paradigm of instructional theory* (Vol. II, pp. 5–30). Mahwah, NJ: Lawrence Erlbaum.

Salomon, G. (1974). What is learned and how it is taught: The interaction between media, message, task, and learner. In D. R. Olson (Ed.), *Media and symbols: The forms of expression, communication, and education* (pp. 383–406). Chicago: University of Chicago Press.

Spiro, R. J., Feltovich, P. L., Jacobson, K. J., & Coulson, R. L. (1991). Cognitive flexibility, constructivism, and hypertext: Random access instruction for advanced knowledge acquisition in ill-structured domains. *Educational Technology, 31,* 24–33.

Chapter 3

Assessment in Web-Based Instruction

CHAPTER INTRODUCTION

Perhaps no other topic in education has been as controversial as assessment, a complex issue that involves not only most sectors of education, but also many sectors of society as well. As Robert Linn (2001) notes, throughout the 20th century, Americans have had a love-hate relationship with educational testing. Lee Cronbach (1975) documented "five decades of public controversy over testing" (p. 1). This chapter will:

1. Briefly summarize some of the essential concepts of assessment and key issues for assessment in WBI.

2. Elaborate on various approaches to alternative assessment applicable to Web-based instruction.

3. Highlight some technological and pragmatic issues in Web-based assessment.

LEARNING OBJECTIVES

After studying this chapter, the reader will be able to:

1. Explain why assessment should be (or should not be) part of the instructional design process.

2. Summarize the various issues of learner performance authenticity in the Web-based learning environment and suggest ways to deal with the issues.

3. Explain the interaction between formative assessment and instructional objectives.

4. Explain the relationship between dynamic assessment, scaffolding, and the instructor's role in helping the student.

5. Create a criteria-referenced assessment rubric for a selected instructional topic or learning task.

6. Summarize the constraints and common problems in administering Web-based quizzes.

7. Suggest ways to minimize guessing and random picking on objective tests.

8. Summarize the benefits of having a large item bank for online quizzes.

9. Summarize the characteristics of adaptive testing and discuss its potential usefulness for dynamic assessment.

10. Compare and differentiate the characteristics of performance assessment, authentic assessment, and portfolio assessment.

11. Suggest various ways to carry out alternative assessments.

ⒸA S E   S T U D Y

- One of the courses taught in the IS program in our MSU case study is Introduction to Data Management Systems. The course is intended to help students acquire basic knowledge about relational databases and develop skills in actual database development and management. The textbook has extensive coverage of the course topics and will serve as the source for systematic readings by the students. Some additional Web-based resources have been gathered as complementary and supplementary materials for the course. By the end of the course, each student will be expected to be able to design a relational database to meet some personal or professional data management needs. If you are to assess the teaching and learning effectiveness of this course, what methods are you going to use? Will you focus more on the process of learning or the final products of students' course work? Are you going to use any alternative assessments? What about traditional objective tests? How should different types of assessment methods be combined to get a better idea of how the students are learning?

FUNDAMENTALS OF ASSESSMENT

Assessment is finding out how well learners perform in reference to a set of instructional criteria or in comparison with other peer learners or comparable groups of learners. The primary function of assessment should be to improve teaching and learning. In real life, however, assessment has taken on some extended functions, such as monitoring systemwide educational outcomes and informing decisions about selection, placement, and credentialing of students. Although these extended functions are inevitably involved in any discussion on assessment, this chapter will focus on the primary function of assessment: to improve teaching and learning.

The term *assessment* is sometimes used interchangeably with *evaluation* and *measurement*. Some researchers prefer to draw distinctions between the concepts. Patton (2000) calls attention to the importance of accurate use of language in assessment, evaluation, and measurement. Keeves and Masters (1999) observe that the evaluation implies a general weighing of the value or worth of something. Evaluation commonly involves comparing learners' performance with other groups of learners or against a set of standards or criteria externally imposed, though evaluation can be based on subjective perceptions without reference to any external standard. In contrast, assessment is generally based on a synthesis of a wide variety of evidence, including direct observation, interaction with learners, responses from surveys and interviews, learning outcomes, and test results. Measurement suggests assigning a quantitative value to what is assessed or tested. Thus, measurement is usually a component of both assessment and evaluation. Although direct measurement of some learning activities is possible, such as duration and length of writing, many characteristics of learner performances have to be measured indirectly, such as cognitive ability or psychological traits. In this chapter, we will use the term *assessment* to refer to any instructional activities that are designed to determine how well learners have learned and are learning.

Assessment as Part of Instructional Design

As pointed out in the nine principles of good practice for assessing student learning (AAHE Assessment Forum, 1992), assessment should be an integral part of instructional design, part of the continual cycle that includes design, development, feedback, and revision. When identifying and specifying instructional objectives, we should also be thinking of how we are going to assess the fulfillment of the objectives, because different types of instructional objectives require different approaches to assessment. For example, if the learning objective is to remember factual data, rote learning is generally effective and assessment that requires learners to recognize and recall facts would be appropriate. If the learning objective is to understand a particular concept, we can assess the learning outcome by asking the learner to paraphrase a statement, explain a causal relationship, or relate a phenomenon to personal experience, depending on the nature of the concept.

Without preidentified objectives, assessment would be ad hoc and we would not be able to tell whether the teaching and learning had been effective and successful in fulfilling the objectives. A valid assessment means that what is assessed is consistent with what is specified as instructional objectives. In order for teaching and learning to be deliberate and purposeful, instructional objectives and learning outcomes should be clearly stated and perceived by students as useful and desirable, and assignments should then be closely aligned to the course objectives (Hudspeth, 1997).

Learner Authenticity and Prevention of Cheating

As mentioned in chapter 2, a major constraint on assessment in WBI is that the student cannot be directly supervised by the examiner face to face, and without direct supervision, examinee authenticity is of concern. New technologies have emerged to help ensure learner authenticity, but these measures are generally costly or inconvenient to implement and not widely available. Other less costly methods of ensuring learner authenticity include the once-a-semester on-campus exam, open-book exam, or proctor supervision. When students are asked to come to campus to take a comprehensive exam during the semester, however, scheduling problems often result. In addition, on-campus exams are contradictory to the location-independence benefits of Web-based instruction (Cooper, 2000).

Open-book exams can be effective in assessing analytic thinking, but not factual knowledge, because quiz takers may easily find answers to factual questions by searching through textbooks and other resources. Well-designed questions in an open-book exam should require the students to apply what they have learned from the course to address an issue or solve a problem in an analytic, critical, and integrative manner. Answers should not be readily available in the textbooks or other resources.

Cheating is another problem with Web-based instruction. In recent years, some software tools have become available that are designed to make it harder for quiz takers to cheat. For example, one of the concerns many instructors have is that students may look up resources on the Internet while answering quiz questions. One solution is to require quiz takers to download a user interface to access the quizzes. When the user interface is launched, it locks up the desktop, preventing the quiz taker from accessing any other applications until he or she has completed or quit the quiz. This method may work well in a proctored environment. However, without proper monitoring, there are obvious ways to get around the desktop lockup, such as by calling someone, having someone stand by to help, or having two computers side by side, one for accessing the quiz and the other for accessing online resources. We need to find more proactive ways to encourage authentic learner performance and discourage cheating.

IN PRACTICE   **Secure Browser to Prevent Cheating in a Proctored Setting**

QuestionMark's Perception Secure Browser is a special browser that prevents cheating in a proctored testing environment. The secure browser can be downloaded for free and installed on any Windows system. It can be used only for taking online quizzes from a QuestionMark Perception Server. It is not for general Web browsing needs.

When a student uses the secure browser to take a quiz, the browser can stop the student from accessing any online resources, switching to other applications, using e-mail or a chat tool, or printing the quiz content. As noted by QuestionMark, while it is possible to lock down the PC or a laptop, there are still other ways to cheat in an unproctored situation, such as running two computers side by side, having a subject-matter expert on the phone, or having a coach sit next to the quiz taker.

Source: http://www.questionmark.com

The essence of proactive authentication is to have assessment aligned with instructional objectives and make the learning experience meaningful and valuable to the learners. When learners find the learning experiences beneficial and realize cheating would be harmful to themselves, they are much less likely to cheat.

Formative versus Summative Assessment

Ideally, assessment should both help improve teaching and learning and provide measures for academic credibility and fiscal accountability. Assessment that is well aligned with instructional objectives and integrated into the teaching and learning process is generally more formative than summative in nature. However, such an ideal integration is hard to come by in reality. For example, program assessment is often more focused on academic credibility and fiscal accountability, and is less concerned about the actual learning experience and process (Baker, 2001; Glaser, 2001). Program assessment is therefore mostly **summative,** administered at some key points during the course of a program in the form of standardized tests to stratify trainees for selection purposes, or surveys on student perceptions and satisfaction as a basis for teacher evaluation and program improvement, or statistic analysis of recruitment, retention and completion rate for academic credibility and fiscal accountability.

Many educators do not find standardized summative assessment helpful to teaching and learning because most summative tests can only reflect what skills may have been mastered by the students near the end of a course, but cannot adequately explain why learning has or has not occurred during the course and suggest ways to improve teaching and learning. Instead of having assessment focus on learning outcomes, teachers and students need **formative assessment** that is conducted on a more frequent basis and is focused on the actual learning experiences that lead or do not lead to the learning outcomes. Formative assessment can be administered through a combination of student performance tests, instructor interaction with students, observation of learning activities, and surveys of student perception and satisfaction. Findings from formative assessment can provide a just-in-time ground for adjusting teaching and learning processes in order to accomplish the instructional objectives. In formative assessment, learners are encouraged to look at the learning process with introspection and reflection. In doing so, learners become aware of how learning has taken place and how learning may be achieved more effectively and efficiently (Cyr, 1996).

Formative assessment is generally closely linked to course content and provides detailed information about specific skills. Effective formative assessment is based on clear specification of instructional objectives so that learners can relate the instructional objectives to their personal experiences and learning needs, particularly adult, nontraditional learners who are generally goal oriented. Before having students enroll in a course, we should post a course syllabus that specifies the course objectives so that students can know what to expect from the course. The statement of the objectives can serve as a kind of contract between instructor and student. Both can assess teaching and learning

◉ A S E   S T U D Y   **Macro and Micro Objectives** ····

Macro instructional objectives are specified at the course level and are usually included in the course syllabus. Micro objectives are specified at the course unit level and are usually aligned with particular learning tasks or assignments. The sample course in the MSU case study can include macro objectives such as "be able to describe principles of relational database design" and "be able to design a relational database to meet one's personal or professional needs," and micro objectives at the unit level such as "be able to identify levels of data normalization" or "be able to write subquery statements that involve multiple tables." The fulfillment of macro objectives is usually measured by the cumulative assessment of micro objective achievements, by the instructor's observance of student performance, and by the instructor's interaction with students, including office-hour talks and surveys.

effectiveness with reference to the specified objectives. Of course, the preset objectives should not be taken as fixed rules. As the teaching and learning process moves along, new needs often emerge and preset objectives may turn out to be unachievable or undesirable. Instructional objectives therefore should be adjustable and updatable.

When formative assessment is carried out on a frequent or constant basis, practically integrated into the teaching and learning process, it is **dynamic assessment.** The popular instructional approach of "scaffolding" is in essence dynamic assessment. The theoretic ground for dynamic assessment includes constructive learning, social learning (Bandura, 1986, 1971) and Vygotsky's (1978) zone of proximal development (ZPD). The primary goal of dynamic assessment is to keep students learning and growing. The instructor closely observes how the students are learning and what kind of help they need to accomplish the learning task successfully (Newman, Griffin, & Cole, 1989). However, dynamic assessment is not supposed to provide constant assistance to students as they learn. Rather, dynamic assessment is designed to control the amount of help to be provided to a learner in performing a task. The purpose of the control is to help the learner move from needing more help to needing less help, and eventually to become able to perform the task independently. In this apprenticeship approach, the instruction starts with an amount of help that has been found generally appropriate for the majority of learners. Based on the initial assessment of learner performance, the instruction adjusts the level of help until the learner appears to falter, and then increases help until the learner can perform the task again with expected competence. Once the learner's performance becomes stabilized, the instruction reduces the help again to see if the learner can accomplish the task with less help. The cycle continues to keep the learner moving forward (Newman et al., 1989, p. 87).

In dynamic assessment, the tutor has to be careful not to give more help than is needed. If too much help is given, it would be impossible to tell at what point the learner could have done the task with less help. With this type of withholding help, dynamic assessment may be pragmatically difficult or damaging to carry out in teaching practice, where the teacher can afford to err in the direction of giving too much help, but wants to avoid the detrimental consequences of giving too little help. If you want to try dynamic assessment, make sure that the instructor is there (virtually) to quickly pick up the learner when he or she does slip. In the Web environment, this means that the communication channels between instructor and students should be constantly open and students should be free to contact the instructor whenever they need help. This also requires the instructor to stay informed of students' progress and provide help in a timely manner only when help is needed.

Criterion-Referenced versus Norm-Referenced Assessment

Whether we use formative or summative assessment, a certain frame of reference is needed as the basis for assessment and judgment. The frame of reference can be a set of given criteria or the statistic of normal distribution of scores. **Criterion-referenced assessment** uses a set of performance criteria against which learner performances are measured. In using criterion-referenced assessment, learning outcomes need to be specified in observable and measurable terms so that we can tell whether students have met the instructional objectives. Using an evaluation rubric is a common method of stratifying performance

C A S E   S T U D Y   Minitests for Formative Assessment

A couple of instructors at MSU are using mini pretests to check students' preparation for each unit of the course content and posttests to check their comprehension of the unit content. Each minitest typically consists of 2 to 5 questions. The pretest is usually administered shortly before the start of each unit, and the questions are generally designed to find out whether students have read the assigned materials and what kind of comprehension difficulty they have in digesting the materials. The posttest is usually administered shortly before the end of each unit, and the questions are designed to find out whether a general grasp of the unit content has been achieved and if any remedial work is needed before the learners move on to the next unit.

The minitests are administered in a computer-assisted online quiz system with automated scoring, so that the instructor can see a report of the students' performances in a timely manner. If the instructor identifies any issues that need to be shared with the class, he or she can post the issues to the class in the course discussion board, add comments, and ask the class to share their views. Students' performances are used by the instructor as formative indicators to assess the learning progress. The instructor may optionally grade students' performances and let the scores count toward the course grade.

FIGURE 3.1   A Simple Grading Rubric

Grade	Indicators
A	Work demonstrates analytic thinking and flexible application of the concepts learned from the course. Work meets the assignment requirements in all aspects and is error free.
B	Work demonstrates limited application of concepts learned from the course, but lacks flexibility. Work meets the assignment requirements in most aspects. Work may have some minor runtime errors, but no compiling errors, and is basically functional.
C	Work demonstrates very limited application of concepts learned from the course. Work meets the assignment requirements in some aspects. Work has some major problems and has major runtime errors and/or some compiling errors.
F	Work lack functional understanding of the concepts covered in the course. Work has major compiling or runtime errors or does not run at all.

levels by differentiating criteria in tabular form for easy comparison (see Figure 3.1). In such a rubric, criteria for all levels usually focus on the same points of interests, but differ in degree of achievement satisfaction. The criteria can be termed "performance descriptors" or "indicators." Figure 3.1 is a simple evaluation rubric for a programming course. The rubric can be used for both course-level assessment and unit-level, task-specific assessment.

Bloom's taxonomy is a classic framework to use in developing a more comprehensive and systematic assessment rubric. Until recently, most attempts to incorporate cognitive skills into assessment were modeled on Bloom's taxonomy of cognitive behaviors. Assessments based on this taxonomy are organized according to a content-by-behavior matrix. A major advantage of the matrix approach to assessment design is that it provides an overview of the entire structure and relative emphasis on different components in one summative view. More recently, researchers (Anderson & Krathwohl, 2001) have revised Bloom's taxonomy into two dimensions of knowledge and cognitive process. Figure 3.2 shows an attempt to put in some observable actions into the grids of the revised taxonomy.

In contrast to criterion-referenced assessment, **norm-referenced assessment** evaluates learner performance in relation to other peer learners. In other words, norm-referenced assessment addresses the question: How well did each learner perform in comparison with the others? Norm-referenced assessment generally is used for candidate selection and placement purposes. It does have some side effects. One of these side effects is that since norm-referenced

FIGURE 3.2 **Actions Put into the Revised Bloom's Taxonomy**

Knowledge Dimension	Cognitive Process Dimension					
	Remember	**Understand**	**Apply**	**Analyze**	**Evaluate**	**Create**
Factual knowledge	List, recognize, preserve	Categorize, describe	Compile, express	Break down, outline	Appraise, compare, defend	Integrate, substitute
Conceptual knowledge	Label, recognize, reconstruct	Abstract, distinguish, paraphrase	Exemplify, formulate, illustrate, model	Diagram, infer	Critique, validate	Adapt, generate, revise
Procedural knowledge	Describe, reproduce, reconstruct	Explain, interpret, prioritize	Direct, instruct, operate	Diagram, infer	Assess, judge	Design, initiate, revise
Metacognitive knowledge	Reflect, reinforce	Elaborate, relate, summarize	Teach, tutor	Articulate, elaborate	Report, revise	Reframe, synthesize

Source: Lorin W. Anderson & David R. Krathwohl, *A Taxonomy for Learning, Teaching, and Assessing* © 2001. Published by Allyn and Bacon, Boston, MA. Copyright © by Pearson Education. Reprinted by permission of the publisher.

assessment is based on the presumption of a normal distribution curve, a subsequent expectation is that only about half of the students will perform above and half will fall below the mean. This expectation can foster students' self-fulfilling prophecy (Bloom, 1968). Another commonly reported side effect of standardized (norm-referenced) tests when used for comparative evaluation is that they encourage the practice of "teaching to the test."

TECHNOLOGY AND WEB-BASED ASSESSMENT

The interpretative and interactive power of the computer makes it a powerful tool for administering tests in ways that are more effective and efficient than tests conducted in a traditional paper-and-pencil manner. Advantages of computerized tests include the capability to administer a test to a large number of test takers simultaneously, with automated scoring and learner record keeping. Computerized tests also allow the instructor to see student performance distribution patterns through the built-in statistic analysis functions. Computerized tests in the Web environment can be conducted in varied formats. Test takers can enter input through the keyboard, mouse, tablets, touch screens, light pens, and voice. These alternative modes of input can be particularly valuable to learners with certain disabilities. We will discuss Web-based test assessment in three areas: (a) objective tests, (b) online quizzes, and (c) adaptive tests.

Objective Tests in Web-Based Instruction

Although objective tests have been criticized by many for lack of direct connection to school curricula and lack of direct guidance for improving teaching and learning, **objective tests** are still a predominant form of assessment used by instructors (Gearhart, 1999). Multiple-choice formats have been a popular form of standardized objective tests over the past few decades because they are easy to administer, broad in content coverage, generally high in validity and reliability, and can be machine-scored. Carefully designed multiple-choice tests can be used to assess some very high levels of analytic and logical thinking skills. For example, the ACT Science Reasoning Test uses multiple-choice items to assess interpretation, analysis, evaluation, reasoning, and problem-solving skills. The National Assessment of Educational Progress (NAEP) has also put considerable efforts into developing multiple-choice tests to assess analytic thinking and problem-solving skills. Other well-known tests that use multiple-choice items are the Graduate Record Examination (GRE) and the Graduate Management Admission Test (GMAT). Figure 3.3 shows a sample multiple-choice question designed to assess students' holistic understanding of scripting languages, which might be part of the Mid-State University IS curriculum.

One of the constraints of objective testing is that the answers are preset; test takers can only select what is given and generally are not allowed to enter their own answers. To overcome the limitation of preset answers, newer testing programs have been designed to incorporate more flexible and open-ended questions. A group of researchers at the Educational Testing Service (ETS) has developed a framework for categorizing such items along an "openness" continuum: selection, identification, reordering, rearrangement, substitution, correction, completion, and construction. The primary advantages of having students construct responses rather than select from given answers include the opportunities for students to reveal performance variations and errors unanticipated by test designers, the instructor's ability to

FIGURE ❸❸   **A Multiple-Choice Question**

Which of the following is NOT true of scripting languages?

A. Programs written in script are usually slower than compiled programs.

B. Programs written in script run on the client side only.

C. Scripting languages are usually easier to write than compiled languages.

D. Many scripting languages can be easily mixed with HTML code.

allow partial credit, and the elimination of students' guessing and getting cues from incorrect choices.

When conducted in a networked environment, objective tests can be administered simultaneously to a large number of test takers at different locations and can be scored with very high accuracy and efficiency. These attributes of objective tests can be a great help if a course has a large enrollment. Proctors can be arranged to supervise test taking if desired.

An Online Quizzing System

Administering objective tests in the Web-based environment requires a robust online quizzing system. Being able to conduct online quizzing is probably one of the major reasons why many institutions purchase a course management system (CMS). In this section, we will describe what we find are useful features of an online quizzing system.

A Web-based quiz system uses the browser as its only user interface for both instructor and students. Instructors create and manage quizzes and evaluate students' performances through the browser. Students take the quizzes and view their grades through the browser. Minimally, an online quiz management system supports multiple-choice, true/false, and short-answer questions. It is relatively easy to develop computerized scoring for the first two types of questions. For short-answer questions, computerized scoring is quite feasible if the correct answers are limited to a few key words. However, if answers are allowed to vary in content and length, computerized scoring can be extremely difficult to develop. Additionally, an online quiz system can include matching questions, arranging items, and fill-in-the-blank questions.

Item Bank and Item Reusability. Designing objective test items can be a time-consuming task. To save time, we can make test items reusable by building an item bank that is independent of individual tests. An item bank is generally very large, consisting of thousands of questions or more. Items are typically organized into categories and subcategories. Categorization can help the instructor select test items and analyze students' performances.

When an instructor needs to build a test, she or he can select test items from the item bank and have the options of arranging the items in default, customized, or random order. Alternatively, the instructor can choose to let the system generate a given number of test items randomly from the item bank. Random generation of test items requires the establishment of a large pool of test items. Once the pool is ready, random generation of test items can be very handy and valuable.

A major advantage of random generation of test items is to prevent test takers from sharing question and answer information, which can be very easy with the availability of telecommunication devices today. Distance students often have to take the same quiz at different times because of their schedule constraints or network accessibility. Giving students different questions can reduce the possibility of cheating through sharing question information. However, having students answer different questions can make it difficult to compare their performances.

With an item bank, quiz management is very easy for the instructor. Before releasing the quiz to students, the instructor can edit the quiz as desired, such as changing the selection and order of test items and resetting the points or weights of the items. However, once a test becomes current, only limited editing should be allowed because some students may have already taken or are taking the test. Computerized tests can be easily set to become accessible and inaccessible using the system clock. When the quiz is no longer needed, the instructor can delete the quiz, and the deletion will not affect any items in the item bank, because quizzes are separate from the item bank.

It can be time consuming for the instructor to answer student questions and explain the correct answers after a quiz. One solution is to let the instructor add an explanation of the correct answer for each test item and have the option to release the correct answers when students come to view their grades. The trade-off in releasing correct answers is that these test items may become less reusable since the questions and answers may be disseminated by the test takers.

Error Analysis. Error analysis is another valuable tool for the instructor to use in assessing student performance. Particularly helpful is a visual display of error distribution patterns like that shown in Figure 3.4. If almost every student

FIGURE 3.4 A Sample Error Distribution Chart

You can click on question # to review the question   wrong answers ■ correct answers ■

Multiple Choice Questions   Student Count: 6

cate	#	error frequency	A	B	C	D	E	✓
1	1	▬4 ▬2	4	2				B
1	2	▬4 ▬2	1	2	3			B
1	3	▬2 ▬4	2	4				B
1	4	▬2 ▬4	1		4	1		C
3	5	▬4 ▬2			1	3	2	E
3	6	▬4 ▬2	1	1		2	2	E
3	7	▬3 ▬3			1	3	2	D
3	8	▬2 ▬4			1	1	4	E
3	9	▬2 ▬4		1		1	4	E
2	10	▬4 ▬2	2			1	3	A
2	11	▬5 ▬1	1	1		1	3	A
2	12	▬4 ▬2			1	3	2	E
2	13	▬6			1	2	3	A
2	14	▬3 ▬3		1	1	1	3	E
1	15	▬3 ▬3	3		1	2		A

Error rates by 3 question categories: (category #, category name: # of wrong answers / total)
1. geography: 15/30 = 50.00 %
2. SAT Math Regular: 22/30 = 73.33 %
3. SAT Verbal Analogy: 15/30 = 50.00 %

had the correct answer on a particular question, it might indicate the question is a little too easy. But if few students got the correct answer, that question might be beyond the level of most students. If many students chose a particular wrong choice rather than the correct one, it might indicate some general misconceptions about the topic. Figure 3.4 is an example of error analysis that shows error rates by item categories. Each test item is also hyperlinked so that the instructor can click to open an item to see what it is.

One great potential benefit of administering Web-based quizzes is the inclusion of Web resources to supplement quiz content. Hyperlinks can be included in test items to point to external resources and let test takers view the external resources before answering the questions. The utilization of Web resources can add to the content authenticity of test items since the test items can now be drawn from the real world. This capability can be particularly useful for the IS students of Mid-State University. However, instructors must make sure that the linked Web resources are live and accessible when the test is given.

Adaptive Testing

An **adaptive test** is one in which questions are selected from an item bank and presented to the test taker based on the test taker's responses to the preceding items. With its responsiveness to individual performance, adaptive testing is also called response-contingent, customized, individualized, or branched testing. Variable branching requires the integration of item response theory, latent trait test theory, and item characteristic curve theory. Item response theory is based on the understanding that individual student performances can be assessed more precisely and efficiently if test items are selected and sequenced in reference to individual student competence levels. A test that uses item response theory generally starts by giving an individual test taker a question of medium difficulty based on the norm of the preidentified population. If the first question turns out to be too difficult for the test taker, the next question will be easier; and if the first question proves to be too easy, the next will be harder. The adjustment in item difficulty from one question to another usually starts with relatively large jumps and becomes smaller as the test fine-tunes its assessment of the learner's competence level. Adaptive testing can obtain more precise measurement of learner competence within the same length of time than conventional testing.

Adaptive testing is primarily designed to improve the efficiency of test administration because fewer items and less time is needed to measure each examinee's proficiency. However, initial development of the item bank and processing procedures can be costly, because analyzing erroneous answers and diagnosing error patterns are far more difficult to program than recognizing correct responses. Most item writing for computerized testing involves cooperation between content experts (teachers in the content areas), psychometric experts who can identify item-writing flaws, and programmers. A certain level of artificial intelligence is required for adaptive testing. When run as a server-side program, online quizzing can be programmed to be adaptive.

Adaptive testing can have a significant impact on traditional ways of test taking. For example, the test sequence in adaptive testing is more under the control of the test program, and it is harder for students to skip or review questions. In terms of reliability, results from adaptive testing may be less comparable across students because each test taker may receive different sets of items, which may have different context effects. For the same reason, adaptive testing may not be appropriate for norm-referenced assessment.

Multimedia Tools

Multimedia can provide a flexible means of assessing student learning in ways that can better fit instructional content and learning tasks. Multimedia also gives the instructor more options to provide feedback that is easier for learners to read than the standard paper-and-pencil text.

Digital Ink and Tablet Technology. Most instructors are probably more used to marking on a paper than typing on a screen. On a paper document, we can easily highlight certain parts of text or graphics with lines and shapes, cross out words, draw arrows to point to important points, and write remarks in the margin or between lines or paragraphs. With the keyboard and mouse as the data-entry devices, drawing is rather limited. Some applications such as Microsoft Word provide the "track changes" feature so that the instructor can add comments and mark changes on a student's paper in a different font and color, but this is still not as flexible and versatile as a pen on paper.

Now, all these actions can be done on a digital document by using a TabletPC and **digital ink.** On the screen of a TabletPC, the instructor can use a stylus (digital pen) to cross out words, handwrite comments, and draw lines and shapes to highlight or illustrate points on the student's work. The instructor can then save the file and send it over the Internet to the student. The student does not need to have a TabletPC to view the instructor's feedback. The only thing the student needs is a journal viewer to open and read journal documents generated from TabletPC. The journal viewer can be downloaded for free from Microsoft's Web site.

Video Presentation. Video applications for teaching and learning needs are becoming increasingly popular as digital hardware and software become more and more affordable. Video can be a powerful teaching and learning tool, and also an assessment tool. Making a theme-based, task-oriented video requires learners to be active, constructive, intentional, and collaborative (Jonassen, 2003). Learners can use videos to record their group discussion, field trip, project presentation, or storytelling. The recorded videos can be digitized and uploaded to a digital dropbox or student presentation area available in most course management systems, where they can be viewed by the instructor and the rest of the class.

C A S E   S T U D Y   **Presentation on Digital Video**

> The IS students at Mid-State University are required to complete a graduate project. The project is research based and practically oriented. The student must design, plan, and implement a real-world information systems project by applying and integrating the skills and knowledge learned throughout the program. Upon completion of the project, the student must give a presentation before the program committee, advising and supervising faculty members, fellow students in the IS program, and other interested audiences on campus. Telepresentation through net conferencing is also allowed for presenters who cannot come to campus.
>
> The presentation is the culmination of the program project. A good presentation can serve as a model for new IS students in planning their own projects. To make exemplary presentations available to those who cannot attend the live sessions, the graduate program office has asked the multimedia support services to record each presentation on digital video. Exemplary sessions are prepared and made available as on-demand streaming video to all IS students as part of the program orientation materials.

ALTERNATIVE ASSESSMENTS

Although standardized objective tests will probably remain a popular form to use for student selection and placement, primarily for their administrative efficiency and relatively high validity and reliability, they are often out of tune with local curricula because many standardized tests are designed to assess general knowledge and skills. For instance, most standardized tests in K–12 education are norm-referenced for comparing students with one another, not for helping teachers and students understand and improve the learning process. Robert Glaser (2001) identifies two types of estrangement that are preventing us from using assessment to improve learning. One is the breach between the study of cognition and the use of technology for measurement. The other is the disconnection between the assessment of learning outcomes and constructive feedback from learning activities. Researchers and educators have called for changes that would make tests more aligned with instructional objectives and learning activities and allow test results to be more informative for instructional improvement (Glaser, 1986; Linn, 1983). McClellan's (2001) study involving 130 undergraduate students indicates that students often view assessment as mainly a teacher-oriented activity and one that is not very helpful to them in learning.

The dissatisfaction with standardized objective tests, along with new understandings in the cognitive sciences, has driven many educators to start using varied alternative assessment approaches to complement traditional assessment methods. Central to the new understanding is the recognition that learning in the

FIGURE **3.5**   **Alternative Assessment**

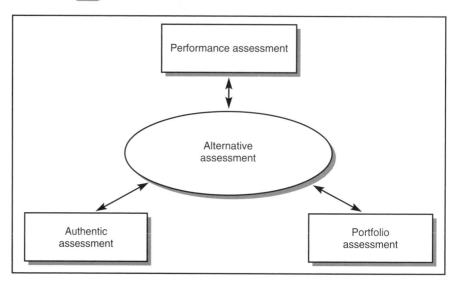

real world is a constructive process that involves interaction with other people and a multitude of knowledge-extending artifacts such as information-carrying media and intelligence-embedded tools (Pea, 1993; Salomon, 1993). For learning to be more constructive and productive at school, learning first of all must be meaningful to the students, and must be like what students encounter in real life. Assessment should be an integral part of the learning process. Meaningful learning has some characteristics: (a) active, (b) constructive, (c) intentional, (d) authentic, and (e) cooperative (Jonassen, 2003; Jonassen, Peck, and Wilson, 1999).

Alternative assessment is a general term covering a variety of assessment approaches that have grown largely out of dissatisfaction with the traditional objective test of student performance. Among the varied alternative assessments advocated, performance assessment and authentic assessment are two of the most prominent. Theoretically, both performance and authentic assessment are grounded in John Dewey's philosophy of education: Learning comes out of actual experience of the learning task in real life or lifelike contexts (Dewey, 1938/1968). Combining the essence of performance and authentic assessment, portfolio assessment is another form of alternative assessment that has been growing in popularity for its potential capability of assessing students' integration of learning and metacognitive development through reflective synthesis of the learning process and learning outcomes (see Figure 3.5).

Performance Assessment

Performance assessment involves direct observation of student performance on tasks that resemble those considered necessary in real life, though student performance may not be as authentic as in real life. The tasks can be group work as well as individual activities. Performance assessment values the process of problem solving more than the final result or product. Although performance assessment may be conducted at one time or at a few points during the course of study, it is more typical to distribute the assessment over an extended period of time to identify patterns of student work and consistency of performance (Office of Technology Assessment, 1992). While observing learners at task, the instructor can diagnose erroneous performances and identify possible causes of errors to help learners move along. Performance assessment is therefore formative rather than summative in nature.

Performance assessment can take many forms. Students may be asked to describe how they found a solution or explain how they reached a certain conclusion; to write a logical argument, draw a graph to interpret a quantitative relationship, design a scientific experiment, or write an essay on a given topic; to gather a portfolio of related materials over the course of study to demonstrate the learning experiences of an individual or a group of learners; or to document the process of reaching a solution to a given problem and holding a reflective discussion on the process. Performance assessment can usually help students develop metacognitive skills, becoming aware of their learning activities and thinking processes.

Experienced teachers have been using performance assessment in various forms, such as journal writing, oral presentation, interview report, case study, demonstration of student project, recording of student performances, role play, simulation, and portfolios. For example, the instructor can ask students to address a problem encountered in the course of study and then defend their decisions in an oral presentation or short essay. All these activities can be carried out through a discussion forum, e-mail exchange, and Internet conferencing in the Web-based learning environment.

Performance assessments may be easier to develop than objective tests, but more costly to administer and score. Although validity is mostly good in performance assessment, reliability can be a major concern. Many students have had the experience of taking an essay test and feeling "lucky" because the questions just happened to hit the topics they knew well. Reliability can be improved by increasing the number and variety of tasks. When there are only a few tasks, there is a higher chance for a learner's performance to be associated with a particular task and not indicative of her or his general competence level in the whole area of study.

Reliability can also be improved by using a criteria rubric. A rubric lays out a set of clearly defined criteria or guidelines that will be used to assess students' work. A good rubric should organize and clarify the quality criteria well enough so that two teachers who apply the rubric to a student's work will generally arrive at the same or similar score. The degree of agreement between the scores assigned by two independent scorers is a measure of the reliability of an assessment (Chicago Board of Education, 2000).

A rubric can also be a powerful communications tool. It is an effective way for the instructor to clarify a vision of excellence and convey that vision to the students. When it is shared among teachers, students, and parents, the rubric

IN PRACTICE **Chicago Public Schools Using Rubrics**

Chicago public schools are using performance assessment scoring rubrics to assess student performances in six fundamental learning areas: language arts, mathematics, science, social science, fine arts, and health and physical development. A rubric bank has been developed to provide many sample rubrics that have been used by schools, districts, and state departments of education throughout the country. Further information about the assessment efforts of the Chicago public schools can be found at http://intranet.cps.k12.il.us/Assessments/ and http://intranet.cps.k12.il.us/Assessments/Ideas_and_Rubrics/Rubric_Bank/rubric_bank.html.

communicates in concrete and observable terms what the school values most. It can also provide a rationale for assigning grades to subjectively scored assessments (Chicago Board of Education, 2000).

Authentic Assessment

Authentic assessment is a variation of performance assessment, with an emphasis on authenticity of learning tasks. Authentic assessment should be a genuine integral part of the learning process and part of real life too (Baker & O'Neil, 1994). The learning tasks in authentic assessment may be part of what the student is currently doing in real life or what the student is expected to do in real life in the near future. The fact that learners find this type of assessment both a meaningful learning experience and a valuable life experience is a defining characteristic of authentic assessment.

Like performance assessment, authentic assessment is grounded in constructive learning theory and Dewey's theory of learning through experience. In the constructivist view of knowledge, a primary instructional goal is to improve learners' ability to use the content in authentic tasks (Brown, Collins, & Duguid, 1989). Authentic assessment can provide a variety of opportunities to observe student learning and examine students' thinking processes. Grant Wiggins (1993, 1998), one of the key proponents of authentic assessment, describes the characteristics of authentic assessment as being:

1. Realistic and part of life experience

2. Application oriented and conducted through students' application of their knowledge and skills

3. Situated and embedded in a live context, either real or simulated

4. Integrated, requiring students to integrate many skills to accomplish a task

5. More for improvement than for measurement

CASE STUDY **Authentic Assessment**

- With nontraditional, adult learners like those in the IS program of Mid-State University, we often have to make some compromise or take some trade-off between task authenticity and assessment validity and reliability. To make the learning task meaningful and authentic to the learners, we often let learners choose a task that is related to their personal and professional experience. Some of the students in the IS program have extensive working experience in the IT field. For these students, choosing a task that can both meet the course assignment requirements and be closely tied to their personal and professional experience is relatively easy. The performances of these students cannot be compared to the performances of those students who do not have much working experience in the IT field.

  To make the tasks authentic, we usually give students options and allow students to choose their preferred ways of carrying out a task. In the IS program, we can ask the students to design a database management system that meets their personal or professional needs. The database can be a personal music CD repertoire or an extensive collection of Web resources on information technology or a quiz bank for a school district. We can also have the students conduct online interviews with field experts and report results to the class, holding a theme discussion on an issue of common concerns to the students, or ask the students to conduct a case study by gathering relevant online resources and presenting an analytic report in hypermedia.

Authentic assessment is not new; it has been traditionally used in the fields of arts, music, and many vocational education classes for many years. In the Web-based learning environment, authentic assessment can be carried out in many ways.

Although appealing to many instructors and students, authentic assessment may not be applicable in some instructional settings today. One constraint is that authentic assessment is often time consuming since it is usually process oriented, extending as long as the student's task continues. Another constraint is that the knowledge and skills measured via this approach are not easy to compare across contexts and individual learners. In other words, it is difficult to make the findings from these assessments generalizable across contexts. Assessment reliability is therefore often poor.

Portfolio Assessment

As a combination of performance assessment and authentic assessment, **portfolio assessment** is based on a cumulative collection of a student's work built over a period of time and usually involves multiple indicators and evidences to demonstrate a student's progress in learning. A portfolio is a process as well as a product. In this chapter, we will focus on process-oriented portfolio assessment, with ongoing data gathering for the purpose of reflection and growth (Janesick, 2001). As a process-oriented assessment method, portfolio building should start at the very beginning of the course, rather than being an ad hoc collection of evidences put together near the end of the semester. From the outset of the course, therefore, the instructor needs to guide the learners to plan and develop the portfolio.

Because process-oriented portfolio assessment is formative and criterion referenced, the instructor should make the instructional objectives and evaluation criteria clear to the students before the process starts, provide timely guidance and feedback as the students move on, and modify the objectives and requirements if necessary. The evaluation criteria can be specified as a list of requirements or in the form of a rubric (see Figure 3.6).

FIGURE 3.6   A Sample Rubric for Portfolio Assessment

	Media	Content	Organization	Integration
Excellent	Innovative use of multimedia, media complementing each other	Sufficient coverage, ample evidences, quality external resources	Innovative navigation, very smooth flow across parts	Outstanding theme(s), threading the complete portfolio
Good	Appropriate use of multimedia	Decent coverage, sufficient evidences, some good resources	Easy to navigate, logical connections between parts	Clear theme(s), reflected in many parts
Acceptable	Some use of interesting multimedia	Fair coverage, some evidences, some external resources	Functional navigation, some connections between parts	Theme(s) identifiable, reflected in some parts
Not acceptable	Improper or no use of multimedia	Insufficient coverage, minimal evidences, few or no external resources	Hard to navigate, little or no connection between parts	Theme(s) hardly discernible or no theme at all

Note: Student work should demonstrate originality and integrity.

Since reflective thinking is encouraged in portfolio development, students are usually allowed to revise previous work. But the instructor should emphasize that what is important in portfolio development is constructive reflection on learning, not perfect performance at every stage of the process. Rough workmanship is a natural feature of the developmental parts of a process-oriented portfolio.

Depending on the instructional objectives, some portfolios may emphasize comprehensiveness in record collection and evidence gathering; some may focus on the interconnections between parts and transitions between learning stages; and others may emphasize reflective synthesis of the learning process in a holistic manner. If comprehensive collection of data is not a goal of the portfolio, students should be encouraged to be selective in the material they include. Only those evidences and records that are significant indicators of the student's learning progress and representative of students' accomplishments need to be included. In any case, students should be encouraged to reflect upon the learning paths at different stages and wind up the portfolio development by creating a report or synthesis as a capstone of the whole process.

Process-oriented portfolio assessment has another major practical advantage: It can save the instructor from reviewing tons of materials near the end of the semester. In addition, we have found that collaborative learning and peer evaluation can be very helpful in portfolio development and assessment. Instead of having the instructor review all the portfolios near the end of the semester, we encourage students to assist and assess each other while working through their portfolios. Ongoing peer review and assistance make the portfolio assessment more formative than summative. In fact, peer reviews and responses can be made part of the portfolio development.

Web-based portfolio development has some additional advantages. First of all, hypermedia provides a very flexible and versatile means of data organization and content presentation. Content structure and navigation scheme can be linear, hierarchical, or a combination of both. Content can be presented in a great variety of media. Second, the anytime and anywhere accessibility of the Internet makes it very convenient for students to peer review others' portfolios or to work in teams and share a common virtual work space. Web-based digital portfolios are also more portable and easy to back up. Students can easily take their portfolios with them on a portable device when they graduate and republish the portfolios to new Web spaces. Finally, Web-based portfolios can include hyperlinks to students' additional projects on the Web and can incorporate various Internet resources to complement and supplement the portfolio content.

Please visit chapter 3 on the Companion Website (**http://www .prenhall.com/wang**) for an updated list of electronic portfolio samples.

The most effective way to help students build their own electronic portfolios from scratch is probably to check out some samples online. Another way to build their portfolios is for students to use a tool that guides them step by step through the process, like the Portfolio Builder used at the University of Washington, described in the accompanying In Practice box.

IN PRACTICE   An Online Portfolio Builder

The University of Washington has a Web-based Portfolio Project Builder that enables the instructor to guide learners through the process of creating online portfolios. With the Project Builder, the instructor can provide the learners with a set of Web pages that step them through the process of collecting and reflecting on their work. Each project page is interactive, not only providing questions or instructions to guide learners but also allowing them to work directly on the page. Learners can provide written responses, attach examples of their work or other artifacts, and submit their work to the instructor for review and comments. Learners are expected to collect their work and products in digital form throughout a course or their university career and then reflect on their work, skills, and accomplishments. Learners can also publish a portfolio to the Web with the click of a button.

Source: http://catalyst.washington.edu/how-to/portfolio/index.html

Assessing Collaborative Learning

Collaborative learning is an essential component of Web-based instruction not only because it is required in building a virtual learning community, but also because it trains the students in effective teamwork, which is becoming increasingly important in today's workplace. Assessment of collaborative learning can be formative, process oriented or summative, product based, or more often a combination. Usually, multiple assessment instruments, similar to triangulation in research methodology, are needed to assess student performances in collaborative learning. Summative assessment can be administered through student surveys, peer reviews or self-reviews, or by examining and evaluating the final products of student group work or team project. However, relying on the final group products alone to evaluate student performances can be problematic. It is not uncommon to find a final group product to be disjointed and uneven in quality, though each student has worked hard throughout the project process and has learned a lot. Often, it may not be fair to attribute the unsatisfactory result of a particular part of the project to the work of the student assigned to it. Instructors often need to be more participatory in student collaborative activities to observe student performances. If synchronous group meetings are part of the collaborative learning, the instructor can "sit" in students' chat rooms or conference sessions to observe students' performance. If students use e-mail for group communication and interaction, the instructor can ask the students to send the instructor carbon copies of their messages when they discuss their project and report their progress.

Assessment of student participation in online discussions should be based more on quality than on quantity of participation. Responses that basically agree with previous messages are not unacceptable, but they do not contribute much to a productive discussion. The instructor may want to demonstrate what

FIGURE **3.7** **A Criteria Rubric for Collaborative Learning**

Performance Level	Contribution	Leadership
Unacceptable	Is unaware of one's responsibilities and unable to contribute to group work	Is unable to lead any group work
Acceptable	Understands one's designated responsibility as a group member; fulfills one's assigned duties; shows respect for others; reports to the group	Recognizes the importance of teamwork; leads a group discussion; designates member responsibilities for group project
Good	Is aware of one's responsibilities and their impact on the group; contributes to group work regularly and constructively; does not dominate group discussion or work	Coordinates member efforts and responsibilities in group work; understands and accommodates the needs of group members; displays skills in time management
Excellent	Ties personal fulfillment to the success of the group as a whole; is observant of group needs and contributes when needed to promote cohesive and productive group work; achieves a balance between personal interests and group needs	Empowers and motivates group members to contribute; creates opportunities to utilize respective strengths of group members; leads the group in coordinating efforts to achieve the principal goal of group work while encouraging alternative thinking, creativity, and individuality

Please visit chapter 3 on the Companion Website (**http://www .prenhall.com/wang**) for further guidelines and support materials.

a productive discussion would look like by setting up a model conference with sample questions and responses as a simulated discussion. This is often more effective than verbal guidelines.

Specific criteria are usually needed for assessing student performances in collaborative learning. The criteria can be presented in the form of a rubric and posted on the course site for instructor and students to refer to in assessing performances. Figure 3.7 is an example.

Developing rubrics is a complex task. Criteria and parameters can vary significantly with differences in subject areas, topics, learning tasks, learner level, and so forth. It is beyond the scope of this chapter to elaborate on variations in rubric development.

Chapter Summary

This chapter begins by explaining why assessment should be part of instructional design and describing a major concern in administering online student assessment: learner authentication. The chapter then reviews the fundamentals of assessment, covering key issues such as formative versus summative assessment, criterion-referenced versus norm-referenced assessment, and standardized tests. The chapter highlights some prominent technical features of Web-based assessment including objective tests, online quizzing systems, adaptive tests, and assessment of information skills. In response to criticism of traditional objective tests for lack of connection to actual teaching and learning improvement, major alternative assessment approaches are introduced. The chapter discusses the epistemological and cognitive basis of the major alternative assessments and their pedagogical implications, focusing on performance assessment, authentic assessment, and portfolio assessment.

Review Questions

1. Do you feel standardized tests can provide a fair assessment of learners' knowledge and skills? How can we overcome the deficiencies of standardized objective tests?

2. Identifying and specifying learning objectives is the first step in integrating assessment into instructional design. Do you think the revised Bloom's taxonomy is applicable to defining instructional objectives across disciplines? Can you think of subject matter areas where the taxonomy may not be completely applicable?

3. Are performance assessment and authentic assessment synonymous? How do they differ?

4. Can the nature of instructional content affect the extent to which authentic assessment can be applied? If you think so, give some examples in which content nature constrains or promotes authentic assessment. If you think not, think of some subject matter areas in which authentic assessment is applicable.

5. How can performance and authentic assessment be used in our case scenario? What types of learning activities and assessment measures would be appropriate and effective?

6. Do you feel there are some types of learning contexts in which portfolio assessment is particularly appropriate? Learning contexts can include the nature of content, types of learning tasks, learner characteristics, and learning environment.

Summary of Tips

1. Make assessment an integral part of instructional design from the very beginning.

2. Design questions to assess analytic thinking, not factual knowledge, in online open-book exams. Answers to the questions should not be readily available from textbooks.

3. Use formative assessment to monitor students' learning and be ready to adjust the present instructional objectives.

4. Use dynamic assessment to control the amount of help needed for the learner. Help should not be more than is needed.

5. Design quiz questions that require students to enter answers rather than select given answers so that guessing or getting cues from answer options can be minimized.

6. Use random generation of quiz questions or random ordering of quiz questions to prevent students' sharing correct answers to multiple-choice questions.

7. Withhold instant grading in an online quiz until everyone has taken the quiz to help prevent sharing of correct answers.

8. Use an item bank (question database) to keep questions independent of quizzes to promote question reusability and facilitate question portability.

9. Use performance assessment to reveal students' erroneous performances and identify possible causes of error.

10. Use peer evaluation to promote collaborative learning in portfolio assessment, which can be very effectively carried out in hypermedia.

11. Make portfolio assessment more process-oriented than product-based to promote constructive learning and students' self evaluation.

Exercises

1. Summarize the various issues of learner performance authenticity in the Web-based learning environment and suggest ways to deal with the issues.

2. Summarize the constraints and common problems in administering Web-based quizzes.

3. Explain the relationship among dynamic assessment, scaffolding, and the instructor's role in helping the student.

4. Choose a topic that you feel you can teach well and design a series of instructional steps in which you can dynamically assess the process of learning. Keep in mind that it is a key point in dynamic assessment to control the amount of help given to learners.

5. Select a learning task in your field of teaching and write a rubric of assessment criteria to assess the accomplishments of the learning objectives.

6. Compare and differentiate the characteristics of performance assessment, authentic assessment, and portfolio assessment.

7. Develop a criteria-referenced rubric of your own for portfolio assessment in your field of teaching.

Resources on the Web

Electronic Portfolios

- Using Technology to Support Alternative Assessment and Electronic Portfolios is a collection of articles and resources gathered by Dr. Helen C. Barrett on theoretical and practical issues involved in using electronic portfolios for alternative assessment (http://electronicportfolios.org/portfolios.html).

- AAHE's Electronic Portfolios resources site has a constellation of useful resources on developing and using electronic portfolios (http://webcenter1.aahe.org/electronicportfolios/index.html).

- Electronic Teaching Portfolio by Professor Joseph A. Braun, Jr., Illinois State University (http://www.coe.ilstu.edu/jabraun/braun/professional.html).

- Mrs. Silverman's Webfolio—Susan Silverman is currently an adjunct professor at New York Institute of Technology and an instructional technology integration consultant (http://kids-learn.org/).

- Electronic Teaching Portfolio by Ima Sample, University of Iowa (http://www.uiowa.edu/%7Eedplace/portfolio/index.html).

- Electronic Portfolio Samples from the Center for Technology and Teacher Education, University of Virginia (http://curry.edschool.virginia.edu/class/edlf/589-05/sample.html).

- Music Teaching Portfolios from the University of Florida School of Music (http://portfolios.music.ufl.edu/studentport.html).

- Kathleen Fisher's Portfolio demonstrates some of the author's abilities and experiences arranged according to the Commission on Teacher Credentialing Standards (http://durak.org/kathy/portfolio/).

Rubrics

- RubiStar is an online tool that helps the teacher who wants to use rubrics but does not have the time to develop them from scratch (http://rubistar.4teachers.org).

- Rubrics for Web Lessons is a collection of resources gathered by Nancy Pickett and Bernie Dodge, San Diego State University (http://edweb.sdsu.edu/webquest/rubrics/weblessons.htm).

- Performance Assessment Rubrics is a collection of resources prepared by SCORE (Schools of California Online Resources for Education) (http://score.rims.k12.ca.us/standards/performanceassessment).

- Kathy Schrock's Guide for Educators is a collection of assessment rubrics and graphic organizers (http://school.discovery.com/schrockguide/assess.html).

References

AAHE Assessment Forum. (1992). Nine principles of good practice for assessing student learning. Retrieved June 27, 2002, from http://www.aahe.org/principl.htm

Anderson, L. W., & Krathwohl, D. R. (Eds.). (2001). *A taxonomy for learning, teaching, and assessment: A revision of Bloom's taxonomy of educational objectives.* New York: Addison Wesley Longman.

Baker, E. L. (2001). Testing and assessment: A progress report. *Educational Assessment, 7*(1), 1–12.

Baker, E. L., & O'Neil, H. F. (1994). Performance assessment and equity: A view from the USA. *Assessment in Education, 1*(1), 11–26.

Bandura, A. (1986). *Social foundations of thought and action.* Englewood Cliffs, NJ: Prentice-Hall.

Bandura, A. (1971). *Social learning theory.* New York: General Learning Press.

Bloom, B. S. (1968). Learning for mastery. *Evaluation Comment, 1*(2). University of California, Los Angeles.

Brown, J. S., Collins, A., & Duguid, P. (1989). Situated cognition and the culture of learning. *Educational Researcher, 18,* 32–41.

Chicago Board of Education. (2000). Why scoring rubrics are important. Retrieved January 8, 2005, from http://intranet.cps.k12.il.us/Assessments/Ideas_and_Rubrics/Intro_Scoring/Rubric_Importance/rubric_importance.html

Cooper, L. (2000). Online courses: Tips for making them work. *The Journal, 27*(8), 87–92.

Cronbach, L. J. (1975). Five decades of public controversy over mental testing. *AmericanPsychologist, 30,* 1–14.

Cyr, T. (1996). Learner assessment. In P. A. M. Kommers, S. Grabinger, & J. C. Dunlap (Eds.), *Hypermedia learning environments: Instructional design and integration* (pp. 255–270). Mahwah, NJ: Lawrence Erlbaum Associates.

Dewey, J. (1938/1968). *Experience and education.* New York: Collier (1968 ed.).

Gearhart, D. (1999). A survey on online course assessment. Retrieved July 18, 2002, from http://www.departments.dsu.edu/instres/papers/assessment_survey.htm

Glaser, R. (1986). The integration of instruction and testing. In E. Freeman (Ed.), *The redesign of testing in the 21st century: Proceedings of the 1985 ETS invitational conference* (pp. 45–58). Princeton, NJ: Educational Testing Service.

Glaser, R. (2001). Conflicts, engagements, skirmishes, and attempts at peace. *Educational Assessment, 7*(1), 13–20.

Hudspeth, D. (1997). Testing learner outcomes in Web-based instruction. In B. Khan (Ed.), *Web-based instruction* (pp. 353–356). Englewood Cliffs, NJ: Educational Technology Publications.

Janesick, V. J. (2001). *The assessment debate: A reference handbook.* Santa Barbara, CA: ABC-CLIO.

Jonassen, D. H. (2003). *Learning to solve problems with technology: A constructivist perspective.* Upper Saddle River, NJ: Merrill/Prentice Hall.

Jonassen, D. H., Peck, K. C., & Wilson, B. G. (1999). *Learning with technology: A constructivist perspective.* Upper Saddle River, NJ: Merrill/Prentice Hall.

Keeves, J. P., & Masters, G. N. (1999). Introduction. In G. N. Masters & J. P. Keeves (Eds.), *Advances in measurement in educational research and assessment,* pp. 1–19. Amsterdam: Pergamon.

Linn, R. L. (1983). Testing and instruction: Links and distinctions. *Journal of Educational Measurement, 20,* 179–189.

Linn, R. L. (2001). A century of standardized testing: Controversies and pendulum swings. *Educational Assessment, 7*(1), 29–38.

McClellan, E. (2001). Assessment for learning: The differing perceptions of tutors and students. *Assessment & Evaluation in Higher Education, 26*(4), 307–318.

Newman, D., Griffin, P., & Cole, M. (1989). *The construction zone: Working for cognitive change in school.* New York: Cambridge University Press.

Office of Technology Assessment. (1992). *Testing in American schools: Asking the right questions.* Washington, DC: U.S. Government Printing Office.

Patton, M. Q. (2000). Overview: Language matters. In *New Directions in Evaluation.* No. 86. San Francisco: Jossey-Bass.

Pea, R. D. (1993). Practices of distributed intelligence and designs for education. In G. Salomon (Ed.), *Distributed cognitions: Psychological and educational considerations* (pp. 47–87). Cambridge, UK: Cambridge University Press.

Salomon, G. (1993). Editor's introduction. In G. Salomon (Ed.), *Distributed cognitions: Psychological and educational considerations* (pp. xi–xxi). Cambridge, UK: Cambridge University Press.

Vygotsky, L. S. (1978). *Mind and society: The development of higher mental processes.* Cambridge, MA: Harvard University Press.

Wiggins, G. P. (1993). *Assessing student performance: Exploring the purpose and limits of testing.* San Francisco: Jossey-Bass.

Wiggins, G. P. (1998). *Educative assessment: Designing assessments to inform and improve student performance.* San Francisco: Jossey-Bass.

PART II

APPLICATION AND IMPLEMENTATION

Chapter 4   **Interacting with Learners**

Chapter 5   **Making Content Interactive**

Chapter 6   **Instructional Hypermedia Design**

Chapter 7   **Multimedia for Web-Based Instruction**

Chapter 4

Interacting with Learners

CHAPTER INTRODUCTION

Interaction is an essential component of education and is particularly important in Web-based instruction (WBI) because of the lack of face-to-face contact. Interaction in a Web-based learning environment can be synchronous or asynchronous. Traditionally, asynchronous interaction has been the primary mode of communication in distance education. With the advancement of telecommunications technology, synchronous communication is becoming increasingly applicable. Web-based asynchronous and synchronous communication have their respective technical requirements and pedagogical implications that are not found in a face-to-face classroom setting. In this chapter interaction includes both interaction between instructor and student and interaction among students. This chapter will:

1. Provide a brief literature review on interaction in learning.

2. Discuss factors that can affect the quality of interaction in learning.

3. Differentiate asynchronous and synchronous communication in terms of technical requirements and pedagogical implications.

4. Discuss appropriate use of communication tools in the Web-based environment.

5. Discuss key issues involved in designing, facilitating, and evaluating interaction in WBI.

LEARNING OBJECTIVES

After studying this chapter, the reader will be able to:

1. Summarize the effects of interaction on learners from affective, cognitive, and social perspectives.

2. Summarize the benefits of collaborative learning.

3. Summarize various factors that can affect the quantity and quality of interaction in teaching and learning.

4. Compare and contrast asynchronous and synchronous communications in terms of potential benefits and constraints from pedagogical, psychological, and technological perspectives.

5. Summarize the primary functions and limitations of online communication tools including e-mail, discussion boards, Usenet, mailing lists, Internet chat, and multimedia conferencing, and be able to make informed decisions about selecting the right tool or tools for a given instructional need.

6. Present various issues that should be addressed in designing and coordinating online interaction, including time flexibility and time management, group formation, task analysis, instructor involvement, learner engagement, resource utilization, and performance assessment.

IMPORTANCE OF INTERACTION IN LEARNING

Interaction has long been considered by educational theorists to be a key to success in learning (Dewey, 1966; Piaget, 1926; Vygotsky, 1978). According to Vygotsky, a child does not develop in a vacuum, but in collaboration with others. The guidance of others helps the child perform at higher levels than she or he would manage autonomously. The difference between autonomous and guided performance is called the zone of proximal development (ZPD). Vygotsky believes that "what a child can do with assistance today she will be able to do by herself tomorrow" (p. 87). Learning is thus fostered by identifying the range of ZPD and helping a learner advance the ZPD. Interaction has also been recognized as complex, multifaceted, and critical to promoting effective learning (Anderson, 2002; Hirumi, 2002).

In a national survey involving 57 public higher educational institutions and 480 faculty members, 44% of the respondents answering the question "What is

C A S E S T U D Y

The IS program of Mid-State University used to rely heavily on the ITV system in the state. Class communication and interaction was mostly in real time and based on a fixed schedule. Moving from ITV to the World Wide Web as the primary medium of course delivery and class interaction involves a major shift from synchronous to asynchronous communication. What technological changes are required with the change in course delivery mode? What type of impact will the technological requirements have on teaching and learning? What pedagogical adjustments do we need to make? How are we going to make asynchronous and synchronous communication complement each other? Are there any new issues to address in organizing group work and collaborative learning in the virtual environment? Let's keep these issues in mind as we move along in this chapter.

FIGURE 🔲 4.1   **Importance of Interaction**

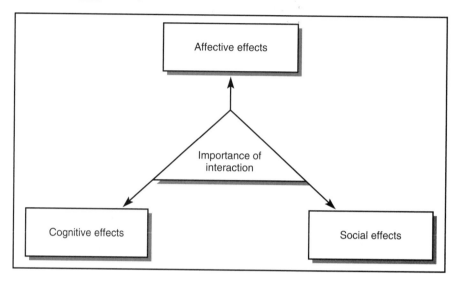

your major concern in the educational process?" mentioned concerns about the quality of interaction (Clark, 1993). Reviewing decades of undergraduate research, Chickering and Gamson (1987) proposed seven principles for good practice in undergraduate education. Among the seven principles, three focus on promoting interaction among students and between student and instructor. The three principles are: (a) encouraging contacts between students and faculty, (b) developing reciprocity and cooperation among students, and (c) giving prompt feedback. In WBI, rich interaction can help the learner overcome the sense of alienation caused by geographical separation from the instructor and peer learners. But the function of interaction is not just that of overcoming a sense of alienation. The benefits of interaction can be further examined from cognitive, affective, and social perspectives (see Figure 4.1).

Cognitive Effects

To be cognitively constructive, interaction must provide informative feedback to learners. Feedback, whether from the instructor or peer students, can facilitate learner comprehension and knowledge retention (Goodwin, 1993; Gorham & Zakahi, 1990; Hunkins, 1989). Constructive feedback can help to reveal gaps or inconsistencies in learners' existing knowledge and prompt learners to refine their understanding and acquire new knowledge (Pilkington, Bennett, & Vaughan, 2000; Webb, 1989). In collaborative learning, students benefit from alternative perspectives and are encouraged to reflect on and revise their own conceptions (Littleton & Light, 1998). Computer-mediated collaboration can help students work more effectively on higher order learning tasks that involve ill-defined problem solving (Hall, 1997; Uribe, Klein, & Sullivan, 2003).

Affective Effects

In addition to cognitive facilitation, interaction can have an impact on learners' attitudes toward learning and can promote learners' motivation and satisfaction (Dillon, 1990; Hackman & Walker, 1990; Nussbaum, 1992). Many educational researchers and theorists consider motivation to be a primary concern of education, not only because of the contribution it makes to academic achievement, but also as an educational outcome in its own right (Ames, 1990; Richmond, 1990), particularly for adult learners (Wlodkowski, 1984; Zvacek, 1991).

Social Effects

Learning can be seen as a continuous interaction between the learner and what surrounds her or him. Many researchers support the argument that meaning should be socially defined and acquired (Salomon, 1981; Vygotsky, 1978). Social interaction promotes cognitive development as well. Constructive peer interaction generally leads to collaborative learning. In collaborative learning, each participant can argue for her or his standpoint, clarify, justify, negotiate, and attempt to convince, rather than impose her or his individual view on the sole basis of personal power or authority (Dillenbourg, 1999; Vygotsky, 1978).

COLLABORATIVE LEARNING

Collaborative learning has its theoretical ground in Vygotsky's (1978) emphasis on social construction of knowledge and Bandura's (1969) peer modeling. Vygotsky believed that learners are capable of performing at higher intellectual levels when working with peers than when working alone. Their new competence is then applied to their individual work; thus collaborative learning benefits the whole group. In their book *Knowledge Web,* Moe and Blodgett (2000) observe that lecture-style instruction results in only 5% of knowledge being retained, while retention rates become increasingly higher with audiovisual presentation, demonstration, and learning by doing, and finally are highest by teaching others.

Reciprocal help in collaborative learning can be both affective and cognitive, and can take the form of exchanging ideas, sharing resources, encouraging one another, providing mentorship and tutoring, and providing reciprocal scaffolding in a zone of proximal development (Brown & Palincsar, 1989; Bruner, 1985; Vygotsky, 1978). Compared with lecture-style teaching, the collaborative learning environment provides relatively realistic, cognitively motivating, and socially enriched learning contexts. While collaborating with peers, learners often encounter fresh ideas, diverse interpretations, and varied learning strategies that may not be congruent with their own prior knowledge and experiences. Confronting different views would encourage them to challenge their own existing knowledge, and resolving conflicts would foster reflection, metacognitive development, and cognitive restructuring.

Exchanging ideas requires the author or speaker to defend, clarify, elaborate, and refine her or his views. Self-critiquing reflection is far more likely to occur in collaborative learning than learning alone (Miyake, 1986). In collaboration, students learn to appreciate the value of teamwork, which is becoming increasingly important in today's working environment. Positive interdependency is an essential element of collaborative learning; each team member is related to other members in such a way that individuals cannot succeed unless the group does (Nelson, 1999). When reciprocal dependencies exist, people grow more individually and perceive greater self-efficacy than they do in competitive and individualistic settings (Johnson & Johnson, 1996; Johnson & Johnson, 1997; Johnson, Johnson, & Smith, 1991; Lou, Abrami, & d'Apollonia, 2001).

Although interaction has potential affective, cognitive, and social benefits, these benefits can be reaped only when we are aware of factors that can constrain or promote interaction and collaborative learning. In the next section, we will examine these factors.

⊙ASE STUDY **Preparation for Group Work**

- To promote collaborative learning, several instructors in the IS program of MSU plan to form study groups in their classes and assign group projects. After a few rounds of discussion, the instructors agree on some fundamental issues that they feel have to be addressed to have effective student group work.

  1. First, how should the groups be formed? By the students or assigned by the instructor? Realizing that many students do not know one another well enough to make informed decisions in selecting group partners, the instructors decide they should assign students to form groups based on geographic location, professional background, and personal preferences. The demographic information can be obtained through an initial online survey that can be implemented in the course management system.

  2. Second, how can instructors ensure reliable communication channels that are available to the students 24/7 and that students can deploy on their desktop without the excessive cost of additional hardware or software installation? For asynchronous communication, the instructors find the discussion board and e-mail tools fit their needs. For synchronous communication, the chat tool that comes with the course management system is rather limited in functionality. The instructors want to enable the students to use multimedia net conferencing in addition to text chat. So they decide to use Microsoft NetMeeting as the primary synchronous communication tool, since MSU has a server that provides the NetMeeting service.

  3. Third, how can course work and assignments be designed to foster communication among students and encourage diverse views and multiple perspectives? Assessment of student work should be process oriented as well as product based. To successfully accomplish the assignments, students must communicate and collaborate with one another on a regular basis.

FACTORS THAT AFFECT INTERACTION IN LEARNING

The quantity and quality of interaction can be constrained by a wide range of contextual factors, including: (a) beliefs and perceptions, (b) teacher direction, (c) learner motivation, (d) learning styles, (e) nature of the task, (f) media, (g) technical support, and (h) immediacy of feedback (see Figure 4.2).

Beliefs and Perceptions

In interpersonal communication, the presumptions a person brings to a situation colors his or her initial perceptions and expectations of the upcoming communication. Teachers' expectancy of students' abilities can influence the frequency of their interaction, type of interaction, and duration of their interaction with students (Cooper & Good, 1983). Reciprocally, what students perceive to be occurring in teaching and learning can also affect their motivations and learning outcomes (Fulford & Zhang, 1993; Furio, 1987; Zhang & Fulford, 1994). For interaction to have a perceived beneficial effect on students' attitudes toward learning and subsequent learning outcomes, we need to make sure that students are conscious of the process of interaction. There are many

FIGURE 4.2 Factors Affecting Interaction

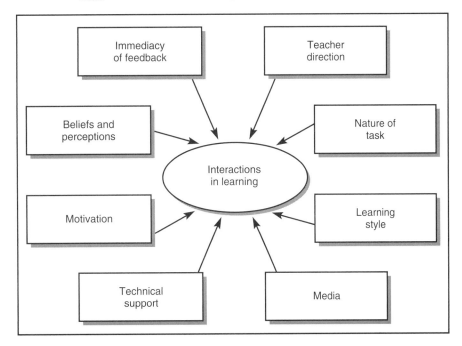

ways to enhance learners' awareness of ongoing peer interaction, such as self-introduction and socialization at the beginning of the course, asking students to form study groups, assigning group projects, or posting questions in a discussion board so students can exchange views, share experiences, or negotiate solutions.

Teacher Direction

In addition to teacher beliefs and perceptions, teacher direction can also have a significant influence on interaction. The learner's perception of interaction between instructor and learner is very much determined by whether the instructor is available when the learner needs help, and whether the instructor responds to learners' e-mails and questions in a timely manner.

In a one-to-one tutoring session with an individual learner, the teacher's role may be more directional. However, if the instructional approach is based on constructive and collaborative learning, the teacher's direction should be exercised more in the role of a facilitator than that of an answer provider. If the course work is based on a group project, the instructor's principal role would be guiding students in a productive direction and monitoring to make sure no members are left out.

In directing learner interaction, questioning plays an important role (Dillon, 1983, 1990). Effective questioning requires the instructor to have a good understanding of learner characteristics, learning needs, required cognitive processes for the instructional content, and strong communication skills. We will further discuss effective questioning later in this chapter.

Learner Motivation

The level of learner motivation can significantly affect the quality of interaction. Many things can affect learner motivation, among them content relevance, learner confidence, task challenge, learner curiosity, learner control, and learner satisfaction (Keller & Suzuki, 1988; Malone & Lepper, 1987). Other variables include learner demographic characteristics such as age, gender, professional background, and interest. When group work is involved, group composition and size can be important factors affecting the quantity and quality of interaction. A very homogenous group tends to converge on most of the issues discussed and is less likely to benefit from sharing experiences and exchanging views. A heterogeneous group with rather incompatible professional backgrounds may have difficulty finding a "common language" of communication. For group interaction and collaboration to be constructive and productive, group members need to have varied individual experiences as well as common core knowledge and background that constitute a shared reference base called "grounding" in collaborative learning (Baker, Hansen, Joiner, & Traum, 1999).

Learning Styles

When we talk about learning style, some of the common terms that come to mind might be field dependence versus field independence, inductive versus deductive learning, and visual thinking versus verbal thinking. Web-based instruction often involves learners from different regions who have very different cultural and educational backgrounds. If learners exhibit a significant level of cultural diversity, we may need to be wary of learning style variations. For example, while viewing the teacher as a facilitator in the classroom may be quite common now in Western educational philosophy, such a view is much less acceptable in Native American and Asian cultures. To create a democratic collaborative environment with group members of culturally diverse backgrounds, participants may need to become acculturated to the value of being on equal terms, sharing the floor in course discussions, and making individual contributions to teamwork.

Nature of Task

Some learning tasks require more interaction among learners than others, particularly those that require task analysis, concept clarification, process adjustment, solution negotiation, and peer evaluation. To engage learners, tasks need to have a certain degree of challenge and uncertainty to stimulate discussion or negotiation (Dillenbourg, 1999). A learning context that encourages productive interaction would be one in which learners have shared interests, but not shared views (Ragoonaden & Bordeleau, 2000). In other words, learners need to have a common core ground for the task in question, but the task should not have a clear-cut "correct" answer so that diverse views and multiple perspectives are encouraged, and discussion and negotiation become a natural requirement (Carroll, 1991).

Media

Education is always closely related to media and technologies (Dede, 1992; Shih & Alessi, 1996). Advocates of media importance consider media to be extensions of man (McLuhan, 1965) and perceive different media as carrying different information attributes (Salomon, 1974, 1979). Olson and Bruner (1974) suggest that media may converge in the content conveyed, but they diverge in the specific processing skills assumed and developed. Salomon (1979) proposes the media attributes theory and argues that the closer the match between the communication system and the mental images, the easier the instructional message is recorded and comprehended. Reviewing the effects of media on learning, Dede and Palumbo (1991) predict that how the medium shapes the message is emerging as a central issue for educational psychology research and information technology development. Gardner (1999) believes that information technologies today play a critical enabling role for the information-age paradigm of instruction, allowing students to articulate their understandings in a range of symbols (audio, graphic, verbal) and allowing teachers to interact with students and assess student performances in more flexible and efficient ways. We will further discuss media-related issues in the section on communication tools later in this chapter and in chapter 5 and chapter 7.

Technical Support

Web-based instruction is technology dependent. Reliable technical support is crucial to the success of communication and interaction. Technical difficulties and breakdowns are a frequent hindrance to online communication (Landis, 2001). In audio conferencing, a breakdown in data transfer for only a few seconds can make the message hard to follow. When net conferencing is used, it is usually necessary to have some alternative backup channel of communication in case the primary channel of communication breaks down. Because of the technical constraints, real-time audio and video conferencing is generally limited to those with a broadband Internet connection. For users with a dial-up modem connection, text chat remains the most reliable method of synchronous communication until better data compression and faster network connection are available to the general public.

In addition to reliable network connectivity, a help desk or service support center is generally needed to provide technical consultation and troubleshooting. To provide consistent and systematic support service, it is a good idea to build a knowledge base to provide online help for all users. The knowledge base would be built through a comprehensive analysis of user needs and would contain descriptions of common problems and typical solutions. Ideally, the knowledge base should have a back-end database support and a front-end Web interface so that both support staff and users can access the knowledge base from anywhere with an Internet connection and a browser.

Immediacy of Feedback

In Web-based instruction, learners generally expect the instructor to respond to their messages as soon as possible, even in asynchronous communication such as e-mail and discussion board. When feedback is delayed or withheld, learners often send e-mails to the instructor to check if the instructor has received their messages or not. If the instructor does not respond to learners' follow-up messages, learner expectation can easily turn into frustration, and motivation for further learning could be seriously affected (Owusu-Sekyere & Branch, 1996). Prompt feedback not only promotes learner motivation, but more importantly helps learners to adjust or reconstruct their thoughts along the learning path and leads to the mastery of skills (Horn, 1994). Immediate feedback can also help avoid or solve possible conflicts in a timely manner because ill feelings may develop if an individual's interpretation of a message is not immediately responded to with feedback.

Despite the importance of prompt feedback, it is not always practically possible or pedagogically desirable. For example, real-time synchronous communication requires participants to be online at the same time to interact with each other, which may be difficult to arrange for nontraditional students with full-time jobs and other commitments. From an instructional point of view, some learning tasks may require reflection and revisions, so feedback immediacy may be unnecessary and even unproductive. To discuss the need for immediate feedback, we need to distinguish between synchronous and asynchronous communication.

ASYNCHRONOUS AND SYNCHRONOUS COMMUNICATION

Immediate feedback is the primary distinction between asynchronous and synchronous communication. In synchronous communication, as we have seen, participants are simultaneously online and interact with each other in real time. Internet-based synchronous communication tools include text chat, net conferencing, whiteboard, file transfer, and application sharing. In asynchronous communication, participants do not have to be online at the same time. The message sender does not expect the recipient to be able to respond immediately. Therefore, asynchronous communication gives participants time flexibility in responding, which is valuable for adult learners with a busy schedule. Time flexibility also allows participants to reflect and to take the time to organize and revise their thoughts. Tools for asynchronous communication include e-mail, discussion board, file sharing, mailing list, and newsgroup.

In the early days of distance education, all communication was asynchronous because of the constraints on message delivery speed. It was the advent of telecommunications that has made it possible to have synchronous distance education. The growth of the Internet and World Wide Web makes it more technically feasible to offer real-time distance education in a virtual environment. However, just because we have the technology available for synchronous communication does not mean that it is always the best choice for class communication. In many cases, asynchronous communication is more effective and efficient. The benefits and constraints of the two modes can be examined from pedagogical, psychological, and technological perspectives (see Figure 4.3).

From a Pedagogical Perspective

In a real-time chat, a conversation often takes on its own life as different topics pop up. Unless controlled by an experienced coordinator or group leader, a live chat can follow spontaneous paths away from the planned track. In asynchronous

FIGURE **4.3**   **Asynchronous versus Synchronous Communication**

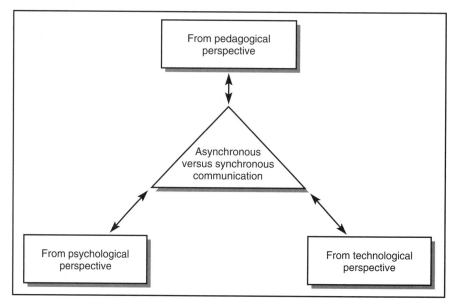

communication, such digression is less likely to occur, since responses are usually targeted and keeping the discussion on track is easier than in real-time conversation.

Asynchronous communication is more learner-centered in that participants have more control over what to say and when to say it. The learner-centered nature of asynchronous communication allows learning to be more inductive, explorative, and oriented to problem solving in the virtual learning environment (Berge, 1999). In contrast, a group-based synchronous approach is more often presenter centered, instructor led, and lecture oriented, largely to replicate traditional "teaching by telling" across distance (Dede, 1996). The latter approach is generally considered more appropriate for tasks that are instructor guided, deductive, introductory, and informing.

For constructive learning to take place, an asynchronous approach is often more appropriate since it gives the learner more control over the learning process and more time to reflect and revise. As Dede (2002) observes, peer learning is hard to foster when the instructor is always right in the middle of things, as in a classroom setting or synchronous chat or conference session. Even when the instructor tries to step off the stage, students still feel the presence of the instructor and are more or less constrained by this feeling.

The dichotomy presented here may help in analyzing the mode of communication in relation to instructional approach. In reality, we more often find an integration of both modes of communication, with interaction varying somewhere along a continuum between the teacher-controlled and student-centered approaches (Berge, 1999; Gilbert & Moore, 1998; Landis, 2001).

From a Psychological Perspective

With different communication modes, participants have different perceptions of their interrelationships and feel obliged to participate at different levels. Jonassen (2000) observes that while they are in synchronous communication, participants are more focused on establishing identity, whereas in asynchronous conferences, participants tend to reflect more on the issues being discussed. In a survey of student perceptions of asynchronous communication in e-education, Wang (2001) has found that 50 out of 103 respondents indicated that conversing via a discussion board allows individuals to be known for their thoughts rather than looks. Without hearing or seeing each other in real time, participants tend to focus on ideas rather than on appearance. Additionally, introverted or shy students generally feel less inhibited and are more willing to express their views on discussion boards where there is no face-to-face presence or time pressures for instant responses. In fact, many introverted students often make more insightful observations than their more vocal peers when they do speak up (Wang, 2001). Web-based discussion forums also seem to lead to more distributed participation. Because it is easy to see who has and has not contributed in an online discussion forum, students tend to feel more obliged to participate and contribute.

From a Technological Perspective

Synchronous communication in Web-based instruction requires a stable, continuous network connection between participants. For audio and video communication, dedicated **bandwidth** is usually necessary to ensure the continuous smooth flow of data. Sporadic delay or loss of data in audio communication can make a speech hard to comprehend. Technical difficulties and breakdowns are major hindrances to online communication and lead to a fragile quality of interaction (Landis, 2001). Technical and practical constraints in synchronous communication can often drive people to choose asynchronous communication for viability. For example, e-mail can be more "immediate" than the telephone or net conferencing because the learner can usually expect a reply within a day or two when a question is sent via e-mail, whereas using the telephone cannot guarantee the establishment of an instant contact (Thomas & Carswell, 2000). Nevertheless, when an e-mail inquiry falls on deaf ears, it can be frustrating for the message sender. However, text chat requires participants to be able to type with generally acceptable speed and accuracy. If a person cannot type as fast as the others, he or she may feel inhibited from participating.

Summary of Tips

1. Keep students aware of ongoing interaction to promote their motivation to learn.

2. Always have alternative communication channels available as backup for real-time communication tasks in case of technical breakdown.

3. Provide prompt feedback to help alleviate learners' sense of alienation, correct misconceptions, and adjust learning progress in a timely manner.

4. Use real-time communication for socializing and communication tasks that require spontaneity and immediate feedback.

5. Use asynchronous communication to encourage reflection and revision in learning.

6. Avoid discussion tasks that have a clear-cut "correct" answer to encourage diverse views and multiple perspectives.

7. Use asynchronous communication to provide more distributed opportunities for shy participants to contribute in class discussion.

8. Use synchronous chat and conferencing for initial brainstorming and planning for a group project, then asynchronous discussion and e-mail for clarification, negotiation, modifications, and revisions.

9. Choose asynchronous mode to give students more control over speed and time.

10. Set up timeframes for most discussion tasks so that discussion does not drag.

11. Avoid large group size for real-time, synchronous, online interactive tasks.

12. Avoid setting assignment deadlines on Friday evening because adult learners often work on their courses over the weekend. Monday morning is usually a more considerate due time for most adult students.

USING THE RIGHT TOOLS

Asynchronous and synchronous communications generally have different technical requirements and pedagogical implications. Understanding the strengths and limitations of the different communication tools (see Figure 4.4) can help us make better decisions in selecting the right tools and using them appropriately for given tasks.

E-Mail

E-mail can be one-to-one or one-to-many (Listserv or mailing list). As a one-to-many tool, e-mail can be an effective way to distribute information among a group of selected members. As a one-to-one tool, e-mail can be an effective means of providing individual guidance and mentoring. E-mail is generally perceived to be more personal than discussion board or mailing list messages. It is therefore a better tool to promote interpersonal relationships. When a student sends an e-mail to the instructor, the student usually expects a timely response. Answering student e-mails typically takes up a large chunk of an instructor's time when teaching online courses. One way to save time is by anticipating or identifying students' common concerns and issues and posting

FIGURE 4.4   Online Communication Tools

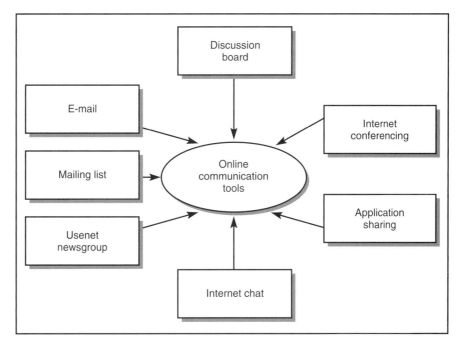

answers to these anticipated questions in the form of FAQs. The FAQs can be distributed through a mailing list or posted on a discussion board.

E-mail user interfaces can come in various forms. An e-mail user agent can be a stand-alone application such as Eudora and Microsoft Outlook, or be included in an application suite such as Netscape Messenger in Netscape Communicator. Stand-alone e-mail applications generally have more functions, such as spelling check and archiving, than browser-based user agents such as HotMail.com and Yahoo!.

Discussion Boards

A **discussion board** system is essentially an electronic message database with a Web interface where people can log in and post messages. A discussion board system is an effective way to provide online discussion forums as communal working space for learners to exchange views and share experiences. The name "discussion board" may make some people assume that a discussion board is a good place for posting announcements to a class. In practice, this is often not true. We have found that students generally check discussion board messages far less frequently than they check e-mail messages. If the instructor has an urgent message to announce to the class, the best option is usually to send an e-mail to the class mailing list. A discussion board is more effective for discussions that require clarification, elaboration, exploration, negotiation, reflection, and revision.

Messages in a discussion board are generally topic-headed or threaded. In a threaded board, messages are organized in an outline format with responses indented and listed directly under the message to which they are replying. The head of the thread is the first message posted. This threading feature is a major advantage of discussion boards since it helps users focus on a topic, keep the conversation on track, and maintain a coherent discussion. However, the threading feature may not be immediately obvious to some novice users. One common problem with a threaded discussion board is that learners sometimes post their responses in the wrong place in the cascading hierarchy, making their responses appear to be dangling or "orphan" messages. Some initial instruction or training may be necessary to help students learn to utilize this threading feature.

A discussion board can be managed at varied levels. Access to a discussion board can be made public or private. A public board allows anyone with a system log-in to post and respond. A private board is accessible only to those who have been registered and accepted by the board manager. Message posting can be immediately released to the board or controlled by a moderator who screens each message submitted before the messages are actually released for posting.

Some discussion board applications allow the board manager to set up multiple conferences within one board, organize students into groups, and assign each group to a separate conference. Since students can participate only in the assigned conference, intergroup sharing of information is not allowed. This can be useful if we want to encourage students to work in a small group. Grouping students into separate conferences is also helpful for a large class with dozens of students, because conversations in a large group of participants can be very difficult to keep on track. What is an optimal group size? It depends on variables such as task nature and learner characteristics, including personal and professional background, shared concerns and interests, level of sophistication, and adaptability.

Mailing Lists

Listserv is one of the best-known mailing list software systems. It is an automated mail distribution service for a group of subscribers. To join and participate in such a group, users send a subscription message. Subscription services are generally automated, but can be moderated by a manager. Moderated services are typically used by professional organizations that wish to have control over their membership. Messages posted in such mailing list groups are generally more professionally oriented.

Participating in professional mailing list groups is a good way for students to keep themselves informed about current development in their field of interest, get involved in professional exchange activities, and get acquainted with other professionals in the same field. The Distance Education Online Symposium (DEOS) is one of the well-known lists for education professionals interested in distance education. You can find its archives and membership information at http://lists.psu.edu/archives/deos-1.html. To find out what mail message groups are available in a particular field, we can use search agents or

ⓒ A S E   S T U D Y   **A Mailing List Group for IS Students**

For students in the IS program at Mid-State University, ACCESS-L is a popular group for anyone working with Access, offering introductory advice as well as professional tips. The group has over 3,500 subscribers (as of January 2005) and has spam filter and virus protection. It is available by free subscription from LISTSERV@PEACH.EASE.LSOFT.COM. The archives are stored at http://peach.ease.lsoft.com/archives/access-l.html.

dedicated resources such as L-Soft Listserv List (www.lsoft.com/catalist.html) and www.listtool.com to browse and search.

Usenet (Newsgroups)

Usenet, which is sometimes confused with Listserv, differs from Listserv in that Usenet does not send messages to subscribed users. Instead, users have to access a Usenet newsgroup to read the posted messages, as in a discussion board system. Unlike a discussion board system, however, many newsgroups are not moderated and allow anyone to subscribe as long as the user's Internet service provider has access to the newsgroups. In moderated newsgroups, the articles are first sent to a moderator for approval before appearing in the newsgroup. Moderated newsgroups are often sponsored by government agencies, educational institutions, and businesses.

Usenet newsgroups are classified hierarchically by subject; for example, sci.bio.ecology, soc.culture.celtic, and comp.lang.java are three newsgroups. The first part of the name (sci, soc, comp) indicates a general category; the second part (bio, culture, lang) specifies a subcategory; and the third part (ecology, celtic, java) usually narrows down to a particular field or subject matter. New categories have been added to the list over the past few years and there are now over 20 top categories. You can visit the Usenet Info Center Launch Pad (www.ibiblio.org/usenet-i/) to view an updated list of categories of newsgroups.

When you post a message to a newsgroup, the message does not show up immediately even if the newsgroup is not moderated. You need to run the update command of your newsreader to refresh the message list so you can see the newly posted messages. If your newsreader does not have a command for updating the list of unread messages, you may have to quit your newsreader and restart it to confirm that the new message has arrived. One common error many novice users make is to post the same message repeatedly because the message does not show up immediately after it is submitted.

In the past, you needed a newsreader program to join, post, and read messages in a newsgroup. Now, you can access newsgroups through a Web browser gateway. For example, Google.com offers its newsgroup service at www.google.com/grphp. For many, it is easier to read news in a dedicated newsreader rather than via Web browser.

Why would people want to use newsgroups instead of a mailing list system like Listserv? Some people prefer not to have messages sent to their e-mail box all the time. Others prefer being able to drop in on a particular newsgroup only when they feel like it. Compared with mailing list groups, newsgroups can be more focused on specific subject matter. If students need to seek advice or get clues on a very specific issue in a particular subject area, such as the use of some particular application or technology, they may find help from the newsgroups that deal only with that topic.

Internet Chat

Based on the media involved, synchronous communication can be grouped into two categories: Internet chat and Internet conferencing. Internet chat is primarily text-based, whereas Internet conferencing can be in multimedia. The text interface of Internet chat can be embedded in a Web browser environment. Such a chat interface generally offers less speed and functionality. More often, chat is conducted through a dedicated server and specially designed client software. Popular chat tools include mIRC, ICQ (pronounced I-seek-you), AOL Instant Messenger, and Microsoft Messenger.

Internet chat has been around for quite a few years now and is probably still the most widely used synchronous communication tool over the Web, mainly because it is easy to use and practically free in most contexts. As portable communication devices and wireless technology become increasingly popular, Internet chat is expected to remain a popular synchronous communication tool in the Web environment. With instant responses, Internet chat can be very effective in building interpersonal relationships and addressing issues that require instant exchange of information and immediate feedback.

Most **instant messaging** tools let you create and control buddy lists of designated colleagues, friends, and family members. The tools will notify you when your buddies are logged in. Messenger tools also allow you to control who sees you when you're online, and who can send you instant messages. You can create your own private chat areas. The only requirement is that you and your buddies must use the same chat software and be logged on at the same time.

Although it is technically possible to have group chat, it is usually difficult to maintain a coherent thread of discussion when a chat session involves a large group of participants and each participant can enter a message any time during the conversation. When one participant asks a question, those who respond may not be able to post their responses immediately after the original question. Between the responses and the original question, there may be several other messages irrelevant to the original question but related to other issues. When this occurs, participants can have a hard time tracking responses to their original questions. One common solution is to ask participants to start their message by addressing the original question raiser or indicating the specific issue they are responding to. Another solution is to have a coordinator who manages the discussion. But this can take away the spontaneity of a live conversation.

Some chat tools allow participants to customize the font they are using so each participant's message can be distinguished. This can make it easy to recognize individual participants in a group chat session.

In addition to enabling student discussions, Internet chat can also be a convenient tool for instructors who want to host virtual office hours. Students can log on at scheduled times or set up appointments to meet online with the instructor and ask questions or just chat.

Internet Conferencing

Although Internet chat is generally limited to text content only, **Internet conferencing** can use multimedia. With audio and video support, multimedia conferencing is usually more effective than text chat in getting people acquainted. The multimedia support also allows information to be presented and shared in more flexible and richer format. By using a **whiteboard,** multiple users across a network can work together in a shared graphic interface that is simultaneously displayed and updated on every participant's screen. A whiteboard is a great tool when a team needs to design a project by drafting diagrams or sketching flowcharts.

Internet conferencing also allows participants to share data and applications. Data sharing can be carried out by exchanging files through file transfer protocol (FTP). **Application sharing** requires all participants to have the same application software to process the data shared, and is therefore also called program sharing. Combined with real-time chat, application sharing can be very effective for mentoring learners in using a computer application or debugging a program. For a student who has difficulty in learning about a graphical user interface, a tutor can use application sharing to walk the student through the steps in using the application interface while providing additional notes or tips through text chat or audio conferencing. Application sharing can also allow the instructor or tutor to help a student troubleshoot an erroneous desktop operation because the instructor or tutor can see what is actually taking place on the student's desktop.

Compared with text chat, Internet conferencing is a more powerful tool for the instructor to use to host online office hours, because it enables the instructor to explain and illustrate points in multimedia and through application sharing.

Despite the many good things, Internet conferencing has some constraints. A major challenge with audio conferencing over the Internet is possible loss of data and consequent discontinuous flow of sound. As we know, data are broken into packets to be transferred over the Internet, and the packets are reassembled into their original sequence when they arrive at the destination. Since the packets may take different routes and arrive at different times, with possible loss of data, it is extremely difficult to ensure an uninterrupted flow of data transfer in sequence, which is necessary for the reproduction of a speech. Even in places where dedicated broadband such as Internet2 is available, there can be a bottleneck in data transfer if end users have slow connections.

Video conferencing has similar constraints. To create the visual perception of continuous motion in video conferencing, video images have to be flipped through at a minimum rate of 15 frames per second. How much data need to be transferred? The formula to calculate image file size in bytes is:

image size in pixels × color depth / 8

We divide the number by 8 because digital file size is generally measured in **bytes** and each byte has 8 **bits.** For an image of 320 × 240 **pixels** with a color depth of 8 bits, the image file size would be 320 × 240 × 8 / 8 = 76,800 bytes. To deliver 15 such images per second is equivalent to transferring 1,152,000 bytes or 1 megabyte (MB) per second over the Internet. This data transfer rate is difficult to maintain over the current Internet, so to reduce the amount of data involved, some type of compression has to be applied. The compression mechanism is often called **CODEC** (compression/decompression). CODEC typically searches through image or sound data for repetitive or similar data across frames that can be removed without significantly affecting the overall quality of the image or sound. Such compression generally works fine where little motion is involved. When lots of motion is needed, the result is often unsatisfactory. Common CODECs found in use today include Motion Pictures Experts Group (MPEG), QuickTime (Apple's standard), RealMedia, Audio Video Interleave (AVI), and Windows Media (Microsoft's streaming media). As compression technology advances, image quality in video conferencing is expected to keep improving. We hope that video conferencing will become a feasible solution for Web-based education in the near future.

Given the current stringent demand and relatively high cost of video conferencing, we should plan carefully if we want to use video in our courses. We should consider whether the use of video is really justifiable by the instructional needs and whether the benefits would overweigh the cost. If we need to let multiple participants see scenes at multiple sites that are continuously changing in real time, video conferencing may be a top choice. However, if what we need is one-way video broadcast and there is no real-time need for two-way interaction between the originating and receiving sites, it may work well to record the scenes and deliver the video as streaming media. Streaming media can generally offer higher video quality and is less susceptible to the packet-switching limitation of data transfer over the Internet. Furthermore, on-demand streaming media allows users to access the video at any time and replay any parts if needed. Often, even video streaming may not be needed if what we want to deliver is a series of slides plus some narration. A set of images with narration can be more easily and effectively prepared and delivered by using Microsoft's PowerPoint. We discuss more multimedia applications for WBI in chapter 7.

CASE STUDY Guidelines for Online Communication

- Taking Web-based courses is a new experience for many of the students in the Is program. The instructors find some students do not know how to use the communication tools appropriately and effectively. For example, some students asked the instructor questions in the class discussion board that were about individual issues and had no relevance to the rest of the class. Some students used e-mail to respond to questions the instructor posted on the class discussion board and expected other students to share their responses by posting. The instructors also find that some students often stray from the assigned topic, others tend to overload their messages with essaylike text. The instructors feel that some guidelines are needed to help ensure appropriate and effective use of the online communication tools. Here's what they have agreed upon and distributed to the students:

1. E-mail is the recommended tool if the student feels the question she or he wants to ask is not an issue other classmates would be interested in.

2. The discussion board is the recommended tool if the student feels the message she or he wants to post relates to the class and the rest of the class would be interested.

3. A model discussion board is set up in each course that demonstrates how collaborative and constructive learning is promoted through message exchanges with coherent and concentrated discussion on issues that are of interest to the class in general.

4. The instructors have selected a few mailing lists to recommend to the students, and each student is required to subscribe to one or two lists that focus on topics the students have learned in their courses. The students are required to write a brief report on what they have learned.

5. Each student group is required to set up a weekly online meeting schedule to discuss the assigned group projects. The instructor may "sit in" when invited or needed, but usually does not participate in the discussion.

DESIGNING AND MANAGING INTERACTION IN WBI

Although Web-based instruction is constrained by the lack of face-to-face interaction between instructor and students and among students, WBI has some major advantages to offer too. Here we will discuss the following areas: (a) time and space flexibility, (b) group composition, (c) learning task, (d) instructor's role, (e) learner engagement, (f) external resources, (g) formative evaluation and feedback, and (h) time management (see Figure 4.5).

FIGURE 4.5   Designing and Managing Interaction in WBI

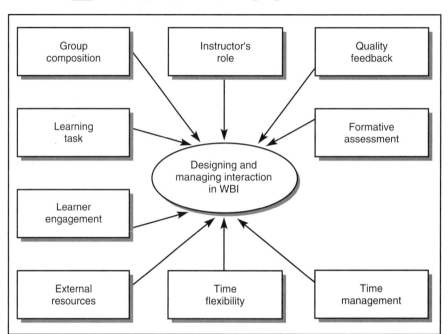

Time Flexibility

For most learners, time flexibility is a primary benefit of WBI. With asynchronous communication, learners do not have to attend each meeting session. Online seminars and discussions are often easier to organize than an actual gathering of dozens of people. In a study that involved 692 online students and 163 on-campus students, Hiltz and Wellman (1997) found that the majority (73%) of students felt the online learning environment is more convenient for communication and interaction. The combination of asynchronous communication and shared virtual work space makes it easy for students to organize and carry out certain learning activities such as debates, case studies, and group projects.

Web-based asynchronous communication also increases the opportunities for each individual to interact with others, since participants do not have to compete with others for the floor and have the options of communicating either individually through e-mail or as a group through mailing lists, a discussion board system, and net conferencing.

Figure 4.6 depicts the options of one-to-one and one-to-many interaction relationships. Each individual can interact with others through e-mail, represented by the inner five-angle star, and each individual can also interact with the rest of the group collectively through a discussion board, a Listserv mailing list group, and net conferencing, represented by the outer circle.

FIGURE 4.6 **One-to-One and One-to-Many Relationships**

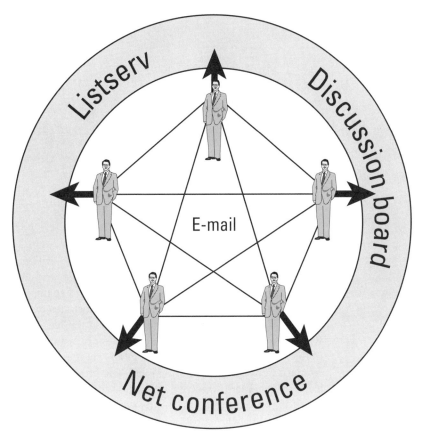

In addition to time flexibility, WBI offers space flexibility. There is no need to find a physical place to meet; each participant can work with the instructor and peers across distance at their own desktops at home or in the office to form a virtual learning community. With the removal of distance barriers, group formation is much more adjustable and flexible. Mentorship and tutorship can be formed between learners regardless of geographic locations. Furthermore, the digital data format makes the Web a convenient medium in which people can coordinate teamwork in a distributed learning environment.

Group Composition

When teamwork is required, group composition and size may affect the effectiveness of interaction. Constructive and productive collaboration requires participants to share a common knowledge base as well as to exchange diverse perspectives. When participants do not have a common core, their interest and motivation to interact with others will be affected. Even if they do interact with each other, the

FIGURE 4.7   **Common Core and Overlapping Among Group Members**

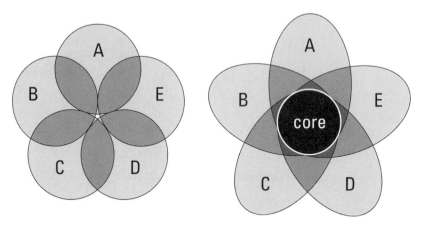

actual exchange of information tends to be superficial because of lack of common ground. However, if group members are homogeneous in background and do not have much diversity in experience and views to share, they are not likely to learn anything new from each other. Figure 4.7 illustrates two examples of overlapping among group members. In the example on the left, each member overlaps only with two adjacent members, and there is no common core for all five members. In the example on the right, all members share a common core in addition to the overlaps between adjacent members. The group composition on the right is more likely to generate productive interaction than that on the left.

It is not easy to form groups with the right composition and size because it requires knowledge of students' backgrounds, interests, and preferences. If the instructor does not know the students well enough to form groups for them, they can form groups by themselves based on their familiarity with one another or anticipated mutual interests. Students send their proposed lists of groups to the instructor for confirmation or approval. Those students who have not formed groups will be assigned to one by the instructor. If the student body is relatively homogeneous, self-formation usually works quite well. However, if teamwork is required for an extensive project, it may be better for the instructor to assign group members. The instructor will need to identify the common core students need to have for constructive and productive interaction to occur. If there is not enough of a preliminary common core among the students, the instructor may need to provide some initial instruction or preparatory resources to help the students establish a basic common core.

Whether the groups are self-formed or assigned by the instructor, it is often necessary to designate a group coordinator or leader to perform logistic coordination, and an editor to take care of gathering group work documentation and drafting and editing group work reports. Each group member should be assigned specific responsibilities and be individually accountable for their contribution to the group work. Individual contribution and accomplishments can be assessed by the instructor through group reports, peer evaluations, and instructor monitoring (Nelson, 1999).

In online collaborative work, group size should be smaller than in face-to-face settings. A large group of eight or more people may work well in a face-to-face setting where taking turns can be managed through nonverbal as well as verbal cues. In an online chat session or net conference, taking turns becomes much more difficult to manage. In addition, it is difficult to engage everybody and keep the conversation on track in an online synchronous chat that involves more than 10 participants. One possible solution is to set up a mechanism to regulate turn-taking so that only one participant can speak at a time. But it tends to suffocate the spontaneity of group conversation.

The size and composition of online groups can vary for different tasks. Project teamwork usually requires a smaller group, whereas discussion can work well with a larger group, particularly asynchronous group discussion. The optimal group size can vary depending on learner maturity and task nature, but a group of four to six members seems to work well in most contexts. When there are fewer members in a group, it is difficult for group members to benefit from diverse views and multiple perspectives.

IN PRACTICE   Tips on Making Group Work Accountable

Professor David Brown of Wake Forest University encouraged collaborative learning in his economics courses. As with many instructors using group work, Professor Brown found that some students can slip through the course without contributing their fair share to the teamwork, and without learning much of the course content. Consequently it was difficult to assign a fair grade to each student. How can we promote collaborative team learning without sacrificing individual accountability and achievement? Professor Brown offered the following tips on making collaborative learning accountable:

1. Keep the team small, preferably two to three people.

2. Assign specific roles to each team member.

3. In addition to submitting a team project (for a team grade), each individual is to submit a critique of the team project.

4. In addition to grading the team project, each individual is to grade his or her individual contribution to the team project.

5. For large, extended team projects, the instructor should periodically contact each team leader to check on the progress of the work.

6. At the end of the course, ask students to name three to five classmates who helped them the most, and give the frequently named students some extra credit.

Source: Brown, D. G. (2002). Accounting for team learning. *Syllabus, 16*(2), 27.

Learning Tasks

As we mentioned earlier, the choice of interaction mode and the effectiveness of interaction are affected by group composition and the nature of the learning task. Peer interaction is usually constructive when learning tasks need support from alternative interpretations, diverse backgrounds, multiple perspectives, peer mentorship, and tutoring. Among other things, the requirement for feedback immediacy in a task determines the choice between asynchronous and synchronous communication modes. For procedural troubleshooting, real-time application sharing plus text chat can be very effective. Synchronous communication is also certainly the choice if the learning task requires participants to negotiate solutions in real time with immediate feedback. If the learning task involves distributed subtasks or requires reflection and revision, asynchronous communication would usually work better. In reality, asynchronous and synchronous tools are often combined to accomplish a series of tasks. For instance, synchronous chat or conferencing can be used for initial brainstorming and planning for a group project. Then asynchronous e-mail exchange and a discussion board can be used for clarification, negotiation, suggestions for modifications, and revisions.

Despite the paramount importance of interaction, interpersonal interaction is not always needed by all learning tasks or at all the stages of a learning task. Some tasks may be better accomplished by individuals rather than teams. Some learners may prefer to do certain tasks by themselves. Some tasks may require initial teamwork to identify and allocate subtasks, and then individual work on the subtasks, and final teamwork to put everything together.

Instructor's Role

Learning in the Web-based environment is generally more learner-centered than in a face-to-face classroom setting. When teaching and learning are mostly asynchronous, students have more control over speed and time. The instructor's role becomes more of a coordinator and facilitator than a lecturer. However, this does not mean that the instructor will have less work to do. The truth is generally the opposite. There is usually a significant increase in the amount of e-mail responses the instructor has to write to answer student questions, particularly on weekends when many nontraditional students are off the job and can spend more time on their course work. It is generally good practice for the instructor to respond to students' e-mails on weekends so that students can get timely feedback and stay on the right track in the course work. In some cases, the instructor may even need to keep office hours during the weekend (Cooper, 2000). In the section on time management later in this chapter, we introduce some time-saving strategies for the instructor.

The discussion board is another area that can take up a considerable amount of management time if students do not know how to use the discussion board effectively. It is a good idea to post a list of general guidelines at the beginning of the course, describing how to post a message and respond to a message, what the essential netiquette is, how to keep postings to an appropriate length, how to cite external resources, and what criteria will be used to assess student participation and performance. Make it clear to students that the value of discussion lies in the process of ongoing clarification and elaboration. The process of clarifying and explaining one's ideas and views promotes metacognitive awareness and social skills. Both instructor and students should avoid posting an elaborate message that is so coherent and comprehensive that further discussion on the issues seems prohibited. Encourage students instead to post their thoughts as they come along and not to try to compose essaylike writings on a discussion board.

Conflicts are inevitable in peer interaction. One of the goals of peer interaction is to negotiate through differences and reach for communally acceptable solutions. However, if conflicts are not resolved in a timely manner, they can impair further collaboration. In an online discussion board, the instructor needs to keep an eye on any frictions and prevent them from escalating into damaging conflicts. For group work that is coordinated by students mainly through e-mail exchanges or other correspondence, the instructor can keep track of students' work progress by asking them to send the instructor periodic reports or team assessments. To make it easy for students to reach the instructor, he or she can hold scheduled or appointed virtual office hours in an online chat or conference room, and students can log in and ask questions or discuss their concerns and needs.

The productiveness of a discussion is often determined by the quality of the questions. Factual questions can rarely stimulate excited talks. Stimulating questions are thought-provoking, encouraging critical and reflective thinking, and allowing students to elaborate by relating to personal experiences and to critique based on diverse perspectives. In general, the instructor should avoid asking too many questions in class discussion forums. When the instructor asks questions, the students feel obliged to answer them. They tend to speak to the instructor's point and refrain from giving any further options beyond what the instructor has asked for (Wang, 2001). Furthermore, students are less likely to speak to one another among themselves (Dillon, 1983). Minimally, the instructor may need to ask only three questions in coordinating an online discussion: one at the beginning to raise the question or define the issue, one in the middle to let the students know if the discussion is on track, and one at the end to help students sum up the discussion. It is beyond the scope of this book to discuss effective instructor questioning in detail. There have been many good writings on the topic. The reader is referred to the books by Dillon (1983, 1990), Hunkins (1976, 1989), and Hyman (1979) for further readings.

The instructor should not be the only person who asks questions in discussion forums. Students should also be encouraged to ask their own questions and express perplexity. In traditional teaching and learning, students are discouraged from asking perplexity questions for fear of exposing themselves as confused or ignorant. Yet perplexity and uncertainty are exactly the conditions that lead to active inquiry and constructive learning (Dillon, 1983). To encourage students to ask questions, the instructor may need to give students credit for asking good questions that indicate active thinking and learning from prior knowledge.

Learner Engagement

Interaction should not be viewed as merely asking a question or two after a certain amount of information is presented. Although important, verbal and nonverbal signal exchange is merely a surface indication of interaction. More important is what is going on in each learner's mind and how that is communicated to others. As Dillenbourg (1999) observes, the quality of interaction among peers should not be measured by the frequency of interactions, but by the extent to which these interactions influence the peers' cognitive processes. Active learning requires the learner to be cognitively engaged. In addition to content relevance and task challenge, explorative learning is often effective in engaging learners. Given the growing popularity of the Internet and students' familiarity with the World Wide Web, they should be encouraged to integrate Internet-based resources to support their discussion. Instructors may also want to provide some Internet resources for students as background materials and give necessary guidance on evaluating and filtering Internet resources. We will further discuss using and evaluating Internet resources in chapter 10.

External Resources

The Internet has removed geographic barriers and made it relatively easy for us to invite guest speakers to participate in chat sessions, net conferences, or discussion forums. Guest speakers can be students from another institution majoring in the same or similar field of study, outside consultants, professional specialists, or field experts in the discipline. Students tend to perceive input from such guest speakers as more authentic and directly applicable in real life. When bringing in guest speakers or participants, it is usually necessary to provide the students with some brief professional background information about the guest speakers so that students can be better prepared to ask questions.

Quality Feedback and Formative Assessment

The quality of feedback on student performances is a crucial aspect of successful online instruction (Thomas & Carswell, 2000). Although instructors do not need to have their presence constantly felt by students in asynchronous communication, instructors may need to monitor student participation regularly and respond to students' needs in a timely manner. Students' remarkable efforts and quality responses need to be acknowledged, and their misconceptions and digressions should be corrected without delay to avoid erroneous reinforcement. For those less active participants, instructors may need to check with them individually through private e-mail to find out if they need any additional help. E-mail is also an effective means of providing individual mentoring and apprenticeship. Since learners tend to check e-mail more frequently than they log on to a discussion board, e-mail would be a better way to send urgent feedback to students.

CASE STUDY Bringing in Guest Speakers

Mid-State University is located in an area where there are a few major government agencies and banking businesses that employ many IT professionals for their information systems. The university often invites IT professionals to talk to the students about the most recent trends and new practices out there in the IT industry. The active link with the IT industry has helped the faculty to adjust the content coverage of the courses and make the curriculum better meet the needs of the IT industry. Students are encouraged to select project topics based on what they have learned from the field experts and to work on authentic projects that can be implemented in real contexts directly or with minimal modification. The authentic nature and application value of their projects have greatly boosted students' motivation to learn and promoted their professional career development.

To make the guest speaker presentations available to distance learners, ITV sessions are set up in which guest speakers can speak either from the university campus studio or one of the statewide ITV studios. Distance learners can participate in the live sessions if they have access to one of the statewide ITV studios. The sessions are recorded on digital video and made available as on-demand streaming video to those who cannot participate in the live session or who need to review the sessions later.

As we mentioned earlier, when participating in discussion, instructors should generally avoid giving their opinions because instructors' opinions tend to stifle students' active thinking and collaborative learning. Students' performances during interaction should be mostly evaluated in a formative manner, based on a combined consideration of both frequency of participation and depth of thought. Credit may also need to be given to students' willingness to share experiences and thoughts with peers. One of the indicators of effective group work is active contribution from each member and negotiation among group members for solutions.

Time Management

Since time flexibility is perceived by most nontraditional students as a primary advantage of WBI, we should allow students to enjoy this advantage. However, time management is equally important in WBI. While giving students some time flexibility, the instructor needs to set up a timeframe for most tasks, in accordance with the types of tasks. In doing so, the instructor can help the students learn to be well-organized and self-responsible learners. For most discussion assignments, each learner should be required to participate at least twice a week. Without a certain degree of timeliness, a discussion topic tends to lose its freshness after being posted out there for a while, and tasks can drag on a discussion board if time is not managed well.

Time management is not just meant for students, but for instructors too. Critics of distance education worried that the virtual classroom would mean less contact between the instructor and the student. Many practitioners now say the opposite is true (Young, 2002). Online instruction has created more opportunities for students to contact instructors, particularly through e-mail. Instructors who have taught Web-based courses have found that it can be overwhelming to answer e-mail that comes by the dozens every day and could arrive at any time. Furthermore, many students seem to expect the instructor to respond to their e-mail in a timely manner. If they don't receive a response within a day, they may send a second message to check. There are some strategies we have found useful in coping with such situations. If an e-mail message requires elaborate explanation and you don't have time to write the answer right away, you can respond with a short note telling the student that you will get back to her or him in a day or two, so that the student at least knows you have received the message and you are going to answer the question soon. If you anticipate or identify some common concerns and questions shared by many students, you can post your answers in the FAQ page on the course site and invite the students to read the FAQ page instead of taking time to answer each student individually.

Another logistic phenomenon we have found is that adult learners mostly work on their courses in the evenings and over the weekend. For that matter, instructors should avoid setting assignment deadlines by Friday evening. Instead, Monday morning is usually a more considerate due time for most students.

Summary of Tips

1. Use e-mail for one-to-one communication and to promote interpersonal relationship.

2. Use e-mail to send urgent messages to students because students usually check e-mail more frequently than they use other online communication tools.

3. Use the discussion board for tasks that require clarification, elaboration, exploration, negotiation, reflection, and revision.

4. Set up a sample discussion forum with exemplary posts and responses as a model for students.

5. Encourage students to post their thoughts as they come along and not to try to compose essaylike writings on a discussion board; elaborate posting in a single discussion message can discourage further discussion on the topic.

6. Encourage students to ask their own questions in online discussion and to express perplexity.

7. Encourage students to join professional mailing list groups to be informed of current developments in their field of interest and to get acquainted with other professionals in the same field.

8. Use text chat only when every participant can enter input fast enough to catch up with others.

9. Use application (program) sharing to monitor and mentor learners in using a computer application or debugging a program.

10. Invite guest speakers to participate in online chat sessions, net conferences, and discussion forums.

11. Post a list of general guidelines at the beginning of the course to inform students how to participate in online class communication and interaction.

12. Post FAQs in anticipation of common concerns and questions students might have.

CONCLUSION

Designing and managing interaction in Web-based instruction is a complex process. The areas we have picked to highlight above are by no means exhaustive. You may find other factors more or less important as contexts vary. The key point is to design your approach and select your strategies based on a good understanding of factors that can affect the effectiveness of interaction in learning, a working knowledge of the communication tools available for WBI and their strengths and limitations, and adjustment of your methods to accommodate the changing needs as teaching and learning move forward.

Chapter Summary

This chapter starts by reviewing the importance of interaction in learning from cognitive, affective, and social perspectives. Interaction is especially important in the Web-based learning environment where learners are physically separate and peer collaboration is crucial to constructive learning. Many factors can affect the quantity and quality of interaction in learning. The chapters highlights the teacher's beliefs and students' perceptions, teacher direction, learner motivation, learning styles, task nature, media, technical support, and feedback immediacy. Feedback immediacy is the defining attribute that distinguishes asynchronous from synchronous communication. The chapter further examines the difference between the two communication modes from pedagogical, psychological, and technological perspectives. To use the two modes of communication effectively and complementarily, it is necessary to have a working knowledge of common communication tools: e-mail, mailing lists, newsgroups, and the discussion board system for asynchronous communication; Internet chat and net conferencing for synchronous communication. Finally, the chapter discusses major issues involved in designing and managing interaction in Web-based instruction. The tasks include identification of learning tasks, selection of appropriate communication mode and tools, formation of productive learner groups, adjustment of the instructor's role, learner engagement, provision of constructive feedback, and time management.

Review Questions

1. What does your personal professional experience tell you about the importance of interaction in learning? What factors, in addition to those described in the chapter, can affect the quantity and quality of interaction?

2. Which communication mode do you feel works better in Web-based instruction: asynchronous or synchronous? Why? How do you think asynchronous and synchronous communication could complement each other in Web-based instruction?

3. What other factors, in addition to those described in the chapter, do you think should be taken into consideration in designing and managing interaction in Web-based instruction?

4. In our case study of the IS program, suppose that you find some students posting messages on the course discussion board discussing the problems they have encountered in the design and development of their individual projects, seeking advice from one another. Do you think such discussion among students should be encouraged? Will the exchange of information affect the validity of assessment? In other words, will the students' final individual projects be true indicators of their competency in database design and development? Why?

Exercises

1. Summarize the effects of interaction on learners from affective, cognitive, and social perspectives.

2. Summarize the benefits of collaborative learning.

3. Summarize various factors that can affect the quantity and quality of interaction in teaching and learning.

4. Compare and contrast asynchronous and synchronous communications in terms of potential benefits and constraints from pedagogical, psychological, and technological perspectives.

5. Create a sample discussion thread that involves several participants and can serve as a model to exemplify constructive and productive participation in online discussion on a topic in your field.

6. Try a synchronous Internet chat with a group of 5 participants, and then with a group of 10 or more participants. Compare the two experiences in terms of quality and frequency of interactions among the participants.

7. Work in a group of three and select a topic of common interest. Each person suggests some discussion questions that are designed to encourage critical and reflective thinking and diverse perspectives.

8. Use a net conferencing tool such as Microsoft NetMeeting to try an application (program) sharing session with a peer learner or friend. Identify the

technical requirements and skills needed for such synchronous online communication.

9. Find a professional mailing list of interest, subscribe to it, and observe the discussions by the subscribers.

Resources on the Web

Collaborative Learning

- Journal of Asynchronous Learning Networks (JALN) (http://www.aln.org)

- The Center for Innovative Learning Technologies (CILT) is a distributed center designed to serve as a national resource for stimulating research on innovative, technology-enabled solutions to critical problems in K–14 learning by fostering and conducting collaborative research and development in areas that are believed to promise significant advances in learning (http://cilt.org/).

- Conferencing on the Web contains a comprehensive list of Web conferencing tools, including discussion board, chat, data conferencing, and audio/video conferencing (http://www.thinkofit.com/webconf/).

- Multimedia Educational Resource for Learning and Online Teaching (MERLOT) is a free and open resource designed primarily for faculty and students in higher education, with collections of links to online learning materials along with annotations such as peer reviews and assignments (http://www.merlot.org).

Discussion Board, Listserv, and Usenet

- Conferencing on the Web is an extensive list of conferencing software packages (http://www.thinkofit.com/webconf).

- L-Soft Listserv List (http://www.lsoft.com/catalist.html).

- ListTool.com is a collection of over 850 Listserv services organized into categories (http://www.listtool.com).

- ACCESS-L focuses on Microsoft Access. It has over 4,000 subscribers as of April 2005. Its archives are accessible (http://peach.ease.lsoft.com/archives/access-1.html).

- The Usenet Info Center Launch Pad is a resource that allows you to browse through Usenet groups organized into categories and search for particular groups by keywords (www.ibiblio.org/usenet-i/).

- Google Newsgroup Service (www.google.com/grphp).

- Microsoft Community Newsgroups is a gathering of various groups covering almost all areas of Microsoft products (http://communities2.microsoft.com/home/msnewsgroups.aspx).

References

Ames, C. E. (1990). Motivation: What teachers need to know. *Teachers College Record, 91,* 409–421.

Anderson, T. (2002). An updated and theoretical rationale for interaction. Retrieved January 9, 2003, from http://it.coe.uga.edu/itforum/paper63/paper63.htm

Baker, M., Hansen, T., Joiner, R., & Traum, D. (1999). The role of grounding in collaborative learning tasks. In P. Dillenbourg (Ed.), *Collaborative learning: Cognitive and computational approaches* (pp. 31–63). Amsterdam: Pergamon.

Bandura, A. (1969). *Principles of behavior modification.* New York: Holt, Rinehart and Winston.

Berge, Z. (1999). Interaction in post-secondary Web-based learning. *Educational Technology, 39,* 5–11.

Brown, A. L., & Palincsar, A. S. (1989). Guided, cooperative learning and individual knowledge acquisition. In L. B. Resnick (Ed.), *Knowing, learning, and instruction: Essays in honor of Robert Glaser* (pp. 393–451). Hillsdale, NJ: Erlbaum and Associates.

Bruner, J. (1985). Vygotsky: An historical and conceptual perspective. In J. Wertsch (Ed.), *Culture, communication, and cognition: Vygotskian perspectives* (pp. 21–34). London: Cambridge University Press.

Carroll, J. M. (1991). The Kittie House Manifesto. In J. M. Carroll (Ed.). *Designing interaction: Psychology of the human-computer interface* (pp. 1–16). Cambridge, MA: Cambridge University Press.

Chickering, A., & Gamson, Z. F. (1987). Seven principles for good practice in undergraduate education. *AAHE Bulletin,* March. Retrieved April 1, 2005, from http://www.aahebulletin.com/public/archive/sevenprinciples1987.asp

Clark, T. (1993). Attitudes of higher education faculty toward distance education: A national survey. *The American Journal of Distance Education, 7,* 19–33.

Cooper, H., & Good, T. (1983). *Pyamalion grows up: Studies in the expectation communication process.* Research on Teaching Monograph Series. New York: Longman.

Cooper, L. (2000). Online courses: Tips for making them work. *The Journal, 27*(8), 87–92.

Dede, C. (1992). The future of multimedia: Bridging to virtual worlds. *Educational Technology, 32,* 54–60.

Dede, C. (1996). Emerging technologies and distributed learning. *American Journal of Distance Education, 10*(2), 4–36.

Dede, C. (2002). Interactive media in an interview with Chris Dede. *Syllabus. 15*(11), 12–14.

Dede, C. J., & Palumbo, D. (1991). Implications of hypermedia for cognition and communication. *International Association for Impact Assessment Bulletin, 9,* 15–28.

Dewey, J. (1966). *Democracy and education.* New York: Macmillan.

Dillenbourg, P. (1999). Introduction: What do you mean by "collaborative learning"? In P. Dillenbourg (Ed.), *Collaborative learning: Cognitive and computational approaches.* Amsterdam: Pergamon.

Dillon, J. (1983). *Teaching and the art of questioning.* Bloomington, IN: Phi Delta Kappa Education Foundation, Fastback No. 194.

Dillon, J. (1990). *The practice of questioning.* London: Routledge.

Fulford, C. P., & Zhang, S. (1993). Perceptions of interaction: The critical predictor in distance education. *The American Journal of Distance Education, 7,* 8–21.

Furio, B. (1987). *The relationship between instructor behaviors and student perceptions of control in the classroom* (Research/Technical Report 143). (ERIC Document Reproduction Service No. ED 291124)

Gardner, H. E. (1999). Multiple approaches to understanding. In C. M. Reigeluth (Ed.), *Instructional-design theories and models: A new paradigm of instructional theory* (Vol. II, pp. 69–89). Mahwah, NJ: Lawrence Erlbaum Associates.

Gilbert, L., & Moore, D. R. (1998). Building interactivity into Web courses: Tools for social and instructional interaction. *Educational Technology, 38,* 29–35.

Goodwin, S. (1993). *Effective classroom questioning.* Urbana: Illinois University Office of Instructional Management Services. (ERIC Document Reproduction Services No. ED 285497)

Gorham, U., & Zakahi, W. (1990). A comparison of teacher and student perceptions of immediacy and learning: Monitoring process and product. *Communication Education, 39,* 354–368.

Hackman, M. Z., & Walker, K. B. (1990). Instructional communication in the televised classroom: The effects of system design and teacher immediacy on student learning and satisfaction. *Communication Education, 39,* 196–206.

Hall, D. (1997). Computer mediated communication in post-compulsory teacher education. *Open Learning, 12*(3), 54–56.

Hiltz, S. R., & Wellman, B. (1997). Asynchronous learning networks as a virtual classroom. *Communications of the ACM, 40*(9), 44–49.

Hirumi, A. (2002). The design and sequencing of e-learning interactions: A grounded approach. *International Journal of E-Learning, 1,* 19–27.

Horn, D. (1994). Distance education: Is interactivity compromised? *Performance and Instruction, 33,* 12–15.

Hunkins, F. (1976). *Involving students in questioning.* Boston: Allyn & Bacon.

Hunkins, F. (1989). *Teaching thinking through effective questioning.* Needham Heights, MA: Christopher-Gordon.

Hyman, R. T. (1979). *Strategic questioning.* Englewood Cliffs, NJ: Prentice-Hall.

Johnson, D. W., & Johnson, R. T. (1996). Cooperation and the use of technology. In D. H. Jonassen (Ed.), *Handbook of research for educational communications and technology* (pp. 1017–1044). New York: Macmillan.

Johnson, D. W., & Johnson, R. T. (1997). *Joining together: Group theory and group skills* (6th ed.). Boston: Allyn & Bacon.

Johnson, D. W., Johnson, R. T., & Smith, K. A. (1991). *Cooperative learning: Increasing college faculty instructional productivity.* Washington, DC: School of Education and Human Development, George Washington University.

Jonassen, D. (2000). *Computers as mindtools for schools: Engaging critical thinking.* Upper Saddle River, NJ: Prentice Hall.

Keller, J. M., & Suzuki, K. (1988). Use of the ARCS motivation model in courseware design. In D. H. Jonassen (Ed.), *Instructional designs for microcomputer courseware* (pp. 401–434). Hillsdale, NJ: Lawrence Erlbaum.

Landis, M. (2001). A comparison of interaction in AV-based and Internet-based distance courses. *Educational Technology & Society, 4*(2). Retrieved March 2, 2003, from http://ifets.ieee.org/periodical/vol_2_2001/landis.html

Littleton, K., & Light, P. (1998). *Learning with computers: Analysing productive interactions.* London: Routledge.

Lou, Y., Abrami, P. C., & d'Apollonia, S. (2001). Small group and individual learning with technology: A meta-analysis. *Review of Educational Research, 71*(3), 449–521.

Malone, T. W., & Lepper, M. R. (1987). Making learning fun: A taxonomy of intrinsic motivations for learning. In R. E. Snow & M. J. Farr (Eds.), *Aptitude, learning, and instruction: III. Cognitive and affective process analysis.* Hillsdale, NJ: Lawrence Erlbaum.

McLuhan, M. (1965). *Understanding media: The extension of man.* New York: McGraw-Hill.

Miyake, N. (1986). Constructive interaction and the iterative process of understanding. *Cognitive Science, 10,* 151–177.

Moe, M., & Blodgett, H. (2000). *The knowledge web.* New York: Merrill Lynch & Co., Global Securities Research & Economics Group, Global Fundamental Equity Research Department.

Nelson, L. M. (1999). Collaborative problem solving. In C. M. Reigeluth (Ed.), *Instructional-design theories and models: A new paradigm of instructional theory* (Vol. II, pp. 241–267). Mahwah, NJ: Lawrence Erlbaum Associates.

Nussbaum, J. (1992). Effective teacher behaviors. *Communication Education, 41,* 167–180

Olson, D., & Bruner, J. S. (1974). Learning through experience and learning through media. In D. Olson (Ed.), *Media and symbols: The forms of expression, communication, and education.* Chicago: University of Chicago Press.

Owusu-Sekyere, C., & Branch, R. C. (1996). Computer mediated communication as a means to enhance interaction and feedback for distance education. *International Journal of Educational Telecommunications, 2,* 199–227.

Piaget, J. (1926). *The language and thought of the child.* New York: Harcourt Brace.

Pilkington, R., Bennett, C., & Vaughan, S. (2000). An evaluation of computer mediated communication to support group discussion in continuing education. *Educational Technology & Society, 3*(3). Retrieved March 2, 2003, from http://ifets.ieee.org/periodical/vol_3_2000/d10.html

Ragoonaden, K., & Bordeleau, P. (2000). Collaborative learning via the Internet. *Educational Technology & Society, 3*(3). Retrieved March 2, 2003, from http://ifets.ieee.org/periodical/vol_3_2000/d11.html

Richmond, V. (1990). Communication in the classroom: Power and motivation. *Communication Education, 39,* 181–195.

Salomon, G. (1974). What is learned and how it is taught: The interaction between media, message, task, and learner. In D. R. Olson (Ed.), *Media and symbols: The forms of expression, communication, and education* (pp. 383–406). Chicago: University of Chicago Press.

Salomon, G. (1979). *Interaction of media, cognition and learning.* San Francisco: Jossey-Bass.

Salomon, G. (1981). *Communication and education: Social and psychological interactions.* London: Sage Publications.

Shih, Y. F., & Alessi, S. M. (1996). Effects of text versus voice on learning in multimedia courseware. *Journal of Educational Multimedia and Hypermedia, 5,* 203–218.

Thomas, P., & Carswell, L. (2000). Learning through collaboration in a distributed education environment. *Educational Technology & Society, 3*(3). Retrieved March 2, 2003, from http://ifets.ieee.org/periodical/vol_3_2000/d12.html

Uribe, D., Klein, J. D., & Sullivan, H. (2003). The effect of computer-mediated collaborative learning on solving ill-defined problems. *Educational Technology Research and Development, 51*(1), 5–19.

Vygotsky, L. (1978). *Mind in society.* Cambridge, MA: Harvard University Press.

Wang, H. (2001). Effective use of WebBoard for distance learning. In T. Okamoto, R. Hartley, Kinshuk, & J. P. Klus (Eds.), *IEEE International Conference on Advanced Learning Technologies.* Los Alamitos, CA: IEEE Computer Society.

Webb, N. M. (1989). Peer interaction and learning in small groups. *International Journal of Educational Research, 13,* 21–39.

Wlodkowski, R. (1984). *Motivation and teaching: A practical guide.* Washington, DC: National Education Association.

Young, J. R. (2002). Online teaching redefines faculty members' schedules, duties, and relationships with students. *The Chronicle of Higher Education, 48*(38). Retrieved June 1, 2002, from http://thisweek.chronicle.com/free/v48/i38/38a03101.htm

Zhang, S., & Fulford, C. P. (1994). Are interaction time and psychological interactivity the same thing in the distance learning television classroom? *Educational Technology, 34*(6), 58–64.

Zvacek, S. M. (1991). Effective affective design for distance education. *Tech Trends, 36,* 40–43.

Chapter 5

Making Content Interactive

CHAPTER INTRODUCTION

"Interactivity" is an appealing buzzword to many learners and educators in the multimedia and Web-based learning environment. Interactive content can engage learners by providing options in learning paths, customizing content selection, responding to learner input, and prompting the learner to further actions. A fundamental attribute of interactivity is content relevance. The key point of content relevance is making the content meaningful, engaging, and challenging to the learner. Meaningful content should be within the learner's knowledge domain; engaging content will stimulate the learner's curiosity to learn; and challenging content will encourage the learner to explore her or his potential to its greatest capacity. However, content relevance is not enough to make content interactive. Truly interactive content should provide opportunities for learners to respond to the instructional content, give feedback accordingly, and adapt to the learner's needs by adjusting the instructional content and learning paths presented to the learner.

This chapter starts by defining interactivity and then examines different levels of interactivity. The chapter then describes important attributes of engaging instructional content and discusses ways of scaffolding to engage learners. Finally, the chapter explores various forms of feedback in programmed instruction and introduces some popular Web technologies that support interactivity.

LEARNING OBJECTIVES

After studying this chapter, the reader will be able to:

1. Distinguish interaction between human interlocutors from interactivity between instructional content and learner.

2. Identify interactivity at perceptual and cognitive levels.

3. Present a range of scaffolding and cognitive navigation structures that can be facilitated by appropriate design of hypermedia.

4. Summarize various ways learners can interact with the instructional source by selecting options, entering input, and receiving feedback.

5. Summarize various client-side and server-side technologies that can support interactivity between the learner and the instructional source.

ASE STUDY

- All the courses in the IS program at Mid-State University used to be taught in face-to-face and synchronous ITV settings. As the Web becomes an alternative medium for course delivery, some instructors are concerned that teaching and learning might become less interactive, because of the lack of face-to-face contact between instructor and students. Without the presence of the instructor talking and walking the students through the instructional content, could the students be engaged in an interactive conversation with the instructional content? What is the nature of interactivity between instructional content and students in a Web-based learning environment? Should Web-based instructional content be organized and presented differently from traditional instructional content? What technology is available to make instructional content more engaging and interactive? What pedagogy adjustments should the instructors make to facilitate interactivity between students and instructional content? Let's keep these questions in mind as we read this chapter.

INTERACTION AND INTERACTIVITY

Interaction can occur not only between human participants, but also between learner and instructional content. Reigeluth and Moore (1999) separate student interaction into two categories: with fellow humans and with nonhuman sources. The second category primarily refers to student interaction with instructional content and the learning environment. In this chapter, we focus on the second category of interaction, and we'll use the term **interactivity** in this text to refer to the interaction between the learner and the instructional source, as is described in many other writings (Kennedy, 2004; Rogers & Scaife, 1998; Schwier & Misanchuk, 1993; Sims, 2000).

How does interactivity between learner and instructional content differ from interaction between human participants? One apparent difference is in the interface of communication. Whereas interaction between human interlocutors can be verbal and vocal, interactivity between learner and instructional content is more often in print and digital form through some electronic input and output interfaces. Another difference is in the type of feedback. Response and feedback in live interaction between human interlocutors are mostly spontaneous, whereas response and feedback from instructional sources are generally predesigned and programmed, thus more or less limited in variability.

Before interactivity actually occurs, instructional content can only have the potential to prompt and engage a learner into interactivity, because what the author intends to convey to the learner via the instructional content may not perceptually and intellectually engage the learner or may even fail to get across to the learner (Jacobs & Ball, 1996; Kennedy, 2004). As Salomon (1981) observes, the actualization of communication is not objectively determined by virtue of the intrinsic qualities of the information source, but rather subjectively determined by what people can attribute, based on their prior knowledge and experience, to the information source (p. 38). In this text, we define **interactivity potential** as any intrinsic qualities of instructional content that are expected to foster interactivity and/or interaction.

FACTORS THAT AFFECT INTERACTIVITY

Effectiveness of interactivity is usually the result of a combination of various factors. These factors include content legibility, content readability, content modality options, content relevance, task challenge, learner control over learning paths, learner input opportunities, and programmed feedback in response to learner performance (see Figure 5.1). Understanding the range and types of interactivity potential can help us explore effective ways to turn the potential into actuality.

Interactivity can also be explored from the perspective of distribution intelligence. The traditional view of cognition is that it is a local phenomenon that is best explored and explained in terms of information processing at the level of the individual. In contrast, **distributed intelligence** theory argues that cognition is better understood as a distributed phenomenon. According to the

FIGURE 5.1   **Factors That Affect Interactivity**

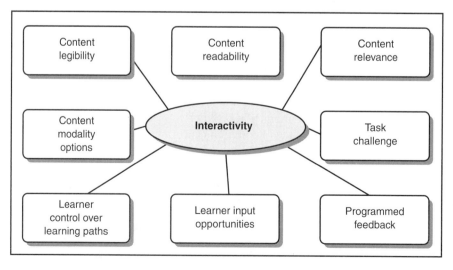

theory, intelligence is not just some mental properties existing only in an individual's mind, but is distributed in the artifacts created by humans (Pea, 1993; Pea & Gomez, 1992; Salomon, 1993).

The manifestation of distributed intelligence is especially notable in computing technology applications such as artificial intelligence and expert systems. The enormous processing power of the computer has brought us interactivity potential not available through older media. A database-supported library of digital materials, for example, can let the user search for desired information in a way far more effective and efficient than searching through the traditional index card system in a library. With programmed instruction supported by artificial intelligence and expert systems digital multimedia can become alive and interactive with users. Computer-enhanced virtual reality allows the learner to explore totally imaginary possibilities, test "wild" hypotheses, and simulate real-life situations. The Internet and the World Wide Web have pooled computer resources around the world and created many new interactivity possibilities, particularly in building connections between distributed content nodes around the world and in establishing virtual learning communities across distance and allowing people to share information resources with truly worldwide scope.

LEVELS OF INTERACTIVITY

Instructional content can be designed to interact with the learner at different levels of learning. Logistically, interactivity usually starts at the perceptual level by getting the learner's attention. The learner's initial attention leads to further examination of particular content. Based on the presence or absence of content relevance and learning objective, the learner may either study more about the topic or move away to search for some more interesting and relevant content. Once the learner is engaged in an interactive conversation with the content, cognitive scaffolding is the key to continuous productive interactivity between the learner and the content (see Figure 5.2).

Attention

John Keller's attention, relevance, confidence, and success model (ARCS; Keller, 1983) proposes that a learning task should start by gaining the learner's attention and activating her or his interest. There are many ways to activate the learner's perceptual curiosity. Graphics tend to get attention more easily than text but should be used with caution and sound instructional objectives. See chapter 7 on multimedia for further discussion about appropriate and effective use of graphics.

Along with graphics, variation in text font can also help direct learner attention. Designers need to be careful not to overuse font variation simply because it is so easy to vary font size, type, and color in digital text. See chapter 6 for a discussion of text font and page layout in instructional hypermedia design.

FIGURE 5.2 **Levels of Interactivity**

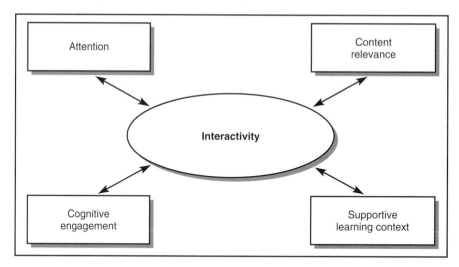

Learner attention can also be caught at a conceptual level with unusual headings and topics, such as two conflicting ideas or phenomena, or a statement that seems to challenge common sense or knowledge, or a problem that calls for a solution. As you would expect, getting the learner's attention at the conceptual level usually works better when there is both content novelty and content relevance.

Content Relevance

Content novelty will stimulate the learner's initial curiosity, and content relevance can help the learner to identify with the content and activate the learner's prior knowledge. Content relevance can occur at both conceptual and procedural levels. The most attractive topic or task would be one about which the learner has some knowledge, but still would like to learn more. Content relevance may also be augmented by allowing the learner to select content modality, sequence, and scope.

Cognitive Engagement

Content relevance is a fundamental attribute to draw learner interest. Additional engagement is needed to bring the learner into further interactivity. For instructional content to be continuously engaging to the learner, the instructional content needs to be cognitively stimulating and challenging, and the instructional system needs to be capable of assessing learner performance, providing formative feedback, giving the learner an ongoing sense of accomplishment, and updating instructional content to move the learner along the

C A S E   S T U D Y   Finding Engaging Topics

Many of the students in the IS program of Mid-State University are adult learners who have full-time or part-time jobs. In deciding on topics that might be engaging and motivating to the students, most instructors conduct a survey or ask the students to list topics and projects that they would like to work on in connection with their personal and professional interests. The following are some engaging topics for the IS students:

1. The Internet provides a vast range of information and resources for an IS student to utilize for her or his studies. However, many skills are required to effectively use the Internet and manage the information and resources available. What skills do you find most crucial and what challenges are still to be met?

2. The use of a database is essential to effective and efficient personal management of Web resources. Do you agree or disagree? Explain your views.

3. A good Web design should be a simple design. Do you agree or disagree? Explain your views.

4. Will digital signatures become a generally accepted means of authorization over the Internet? Describe your expectations and explain your views.

Sometimes, students are allowed to select and work on individual topics. If the instructor finds a topic to recommend to the whole class, but believes background information needs to be provided for a few students, supplementary materials can be prepared either by the instructor or by students for the class to preview. The instructor also uses preview questions to activate possible prior knowledge and prepare background information for the students.

learning path. Bettex (1996) suggests four strategies to make instructional content interactive: (a) Instructional content should confront learners with problem-solving situations; (b) for each activity, several suggestions will be provided to encourage knowledge construction and skill building; (c) instructional content should provide self-assessment activities so that learners can evaluate their own progress; and (d) instructional content should be flexible and allow for ready modifications.

Supportive Context

Hannafin, Land, and Oliver (1999) provide a useful framework that describes an open learning environment and three types of learning context in terms of goal setting, problem identification, task specification, and pursuit of solutions.

TABLE (5.1)   Learning Contexts

Learning context	Externally imposed	Externally induced	Individually generated
Goal and objective setting	By instructor	By instructor	By learners
Topic selection, problem identification, task specification	By instructor	By instructor or learners	By learners
Solutions	By learners	By learners	By learners

Source: Based on Hannafin et al. (1999).

The three contexts are: (a) externally imposed, (b) externally induced, and (c) individually generated (see Table 5.1).

The three learning contexts allow different levels of learner control and encourage different degrees of personal inquiry, divergent thinking, and multiple perspectives. The first context would probably work better when explicit performance requirements are externally imposed with standard assessment measures. The last context is more learner-centered and would probably work better for project-based courses.

Learner Control

Content relevance is usually directly linked to learner familiarity with the topics or tasks. In addition to topic and task familiarity, content relevance can be promoted by giving learners more control over their learning. The methods can include: (a) selecting content modality, (b) selecting sequence of content presentation, (c) selecting content coverage, (d) selecting learning paths, (e) having online help available all the time, and (f) having opportunities to assess learning progress (Merrill, 1975).

A major advantage of increased learner control over learning paths is that the learner becomes more active. Active learning generally leads to greater depth and breadth of processing, which in turn tends to lead to more durable memory (Ausubel, 1966). However, effective learner control depends to a great extent on learner maturity, learning experience, and metacognitive strategies (Jonassen, 1988). Excessive learner control in Web-based instruction can have negative effects, too. For example, free navigation in a complex hypermedia structure can impose considerable **cognitive overload** on the learner, who may become easily disoriented (Dede & Palumbo, 1991). For learners with less experience of a hypermedia learning environment, the course designer needs to be careful to provide options in learning paths that minimize possible learner disorientation.

C A S E   S T U D Y   **Providing an Engaging Project Context**

The second context of the learning framework (Hannafin et al., 1999) may work best when learners have different backgrounds and varied learning needs. An application example could be a database design project for the IS students at MSU. Students are asked to design a database to accommodate their personal or professional needs. The instructor sets the project objectives and evaluation criteria. Each student decides on his or her database application needs and submits a proposal to the instructor, who approves the proposal or suggests alternative choices or other changes. Student choices can vary greatly. Some may want to build a database for their personal collection of music CDs or Web resources; others may choose to work with their company or school to design a database to improve human resources management or inventory management. A K–12 teacher may want to develop a database to keep athletic performance records. With these practically oriented assignments, students are more likely to find relevance and engagement in the instructional content and learning experience.

ADAPTIVE INSTRUCTIONAL CONTENT

Cognitive engagement can be greatly facilitated by adaptive content. Based on well-informed anticipation of learner needs, an adaptive instructional program can provide options in learning paths to meet different learner needs, monitor and assess learner performances, give feedback when desired, and adjust instructional content to meet the changing learner needs. Such an adaptive program would be able to keep the learner moving forward in what Vygotsky (1978) called the zone of proximal development (ZPD) and maintain the learner's motivation to advance.

Developing truly adaptive instructional material can be extremely challenging, requiring extensive analysis of information processing needs for the learning task, well-informed anticipation of learner variations, a well-planned instructional approach, systematic record keeping, and sophisticated programming that can dynamically assess learner performance and provide appropriate feedback and scaffolding. The quality of an adaptive instructional program is a function of several factors, including:

1. How much we know about the information processing needs for a given learning task

2. How well the course designer understands and anticipates learner needs and possible performance variations

3. How much software authoring expertise is available for developing the program

Constrained by the theoretical limitations of our incomplete understanding of human cognition and the technical limitations of intelligent programming, fully adaptive instructional content is still at the research and development stage. There are areas of human mental activities that are beyond the domain of logical information processing, but more under the influence of emotional traits and personality variations. To develop computer programs that can adequately interact with human learners both cognitively and affectively would certainly be a fascinating but daunting task. Despite the difficulty of developing truly adaptive programs, certain level of adaptive capabilities can still be incorporated into instructional hypermedia, particularly in the form of navigational branching and customizing learning paths.

Adaptive Hypermedia

Adaptive hypermedia is a relatively new field that emerged in the early 1990s (Cristea, 2003; Park & Lee, 2004). An **adaptive hypermedia** system is designed to build a model of an individual user, interact with the user, and dynamically customize the content and navigation paths to meet the needs and preferences of that user (Brusilovsky, 2000; De Bra, 2000). Such adaptation and customization is generally made by anticipating user needs based on the system's knowledge of: (a) where the user has been (history based), (b) where the user has been and how those places are related (prerequisite based), and (c) what the user has shown to have understood (knowledge based) (Eklund & Sinclair, 2000). It is possible to initialize the user model through a questionnaire, but an adaptive hypermedia system can do all the adaptation automatically by observing the browsing behavior of the user (De Bra, Brusilovsky, & Houben, 1999).

Adaptive hypermedia systems involve complex programming. However, recent development of authoring tools has made it possible for nonprogrammers to write adaptive hypermedia. Although adaptive hypermedia may hold great promise for interactive individualized learning in the Web environment, empirical research findings are still limited to the actual cognitive benefits of adaptive hypermedia (Park & Lee, 2004). At present, there are very few production-grade authoring tools for educational adaptive hypermedia.

IN PRACTICE   **Interbook: An Adaptive Hypermedia Tool**

InterBook is a tool for authoring and delivering adaptive electronic textbooks on the World Wide Web. Using a knowledge-based approach, InterBook allows the user to develop an electronic textbook from plain text to specially annotated HTML format. InterBook also provides an HTTP server for adaptive delivery of these electronic textbooks over the Web. For each registered user, an InterBook server maintains an individual model of the user's knowledge and navigation support and adaptive help.

Source: http://www2.sis.pitt.edu/~peterb/InterBook.html

Navigation Branching and Learning Paths

Navigation branching is a basic means of providing optional learning paths. In an instructional navigation system, a basic approach can be one that provides optional starting points and lets the learner select among the options to branch off into alternative learning paths. The alternative paths all have instructional values and there is no correct or wrong path. If we want to incorporate a remedial function into the learning path, we can make the hyperlink scheme start with a question statement that branches the learner to two options: one is a remedial page and the other is an affirmative page. The remedial page contains some corrective feedback and will send the learner back to a rephrased version of the original question. The affirmative page will acknowledge the learner's correct choice and move the learner to the next stage of the course (see Figure 5.3). This scheme is, of course, a simplified version of such learning paths.

FIGURE 5.3   **A Simple Branching Scheme**

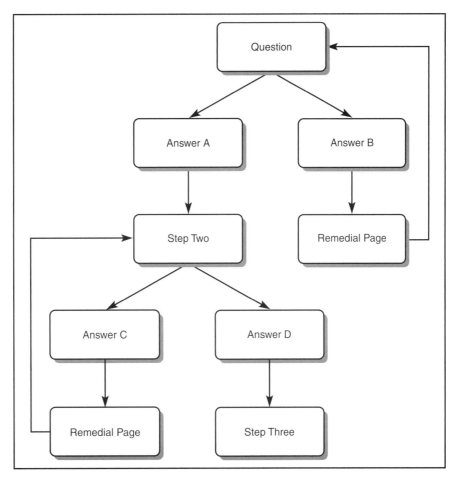

Adaptive instruction can also start by checking the learner's preferences in content modality and learning style, and asking the learner some questions to identify prior knowledge about the subject. Based on learner responses, the instructional program will lead the learner to a set of materials and tasks that are believed to be generally more compatible with the identified needs and preferences. If the learner is found to be in need of some prerequisite knowledge, he or she will be provided with a set of supplementary resources to fill up the gap.

Branching in hypermedia can be strictly procedural, tree structured, case based, or a combination. As the name suggests, procedural branching is typically used in training procedural skills in a step-by-step manner. At each step, the program will assess the learner's mastery of the content. If a deficiency is found, the program will take remedial action either by repeating the previous step or by retraining the step in an alternative approach.

Tree-structured branching generally provides multiple options at each node along a learning path. The learner needs to select the most desirable direction to proceed at each node, but can always return to a higher level to review and select an alternative direction. Tree-branching is usually more appropriate for teaching knowledge and skills that have a hierarchical structure involving multiple levels of content categories.

Unlike a procedure-oriented tutoring module, which is very much instructor led, case-based adaptive content is more learner initiated. Based on the needs analysis, a variety of cases may be provided so that learners can select those that best fit their interests and needs. Case-based branching can be used with the help of an expert system. An expert system is a computer program with artificial intelligence designed to simulate human expert reasoning and problem solving in a particular field of study. The expert system does not usually initiate questions. Instead, the learner comes to the expert system with questions. In responding to the learner's questions, the expert system may raise follow-up questions, analyze learner responses, identify learner needs, query an extensive knowledge base for pertinent data, or present related materials to help the learner elaborate and expand his or her understanding of the issues involved. If there are anticipated learner needs for additional explanations or illustrations at any point along a learning path, we can include a help button on the page to provide context-based help in a just-in-time manner. The content generated from the help link is context-sensitive and varies in accordance with the selection of topics on the page. This type of context-sensitive help also can be found in some interactive computer applications and course management systems.

More sophisticated adaptive content could use embedded remedial loops with multiple branches. Each branch is designed to anticipate a particular range of probable variations in learner performances. Assessing the learner performance, the program will provide appropriate feedback, including correction and elaboration, and let the learner adjust and modify her or his understanding, return to an earlier point to review, and move forward again in the right direction (Jonassen, 1985). Such sophisticated adaptive content would generally require the involvement of an expert system.

Please visit chapter 5 on the Companion Website (**http://www .prenhall.com/wang**) for some samples of hypermedia branching.

The Department of Agricultural & Resource Economics at the University of Arizona has developed a simple expert system that addresses supplemental feeding for range cows. The system is very simple and needs additional knowledge to be incorporated before it would be useful for developing actual range cow feeding supplementation plans. Nevertheless, the example demonstrates the mechanics of developing a fuzzy expert system.

A fuzzy expert system is an expert system that uses fuzzy logic instead of Boolean logic to analyze data. Fuzzy logic is an extension of the conventional logic to analyze the concept of partial truth—truth values between completely true and completely false.

Source: http://cals.arizona.edu/AREC/fuzzy/example.html

LEARNER RESPONSE OPPORTUNITIES AND INSTRUCTIONAL FEEDBACK

Learner response to instructional content is a direct manifestation of interactivity. Learner responses can take many forms (see Figure 5.4), including clicks on hyperlinks to select learning paths, selection of options given by a Web form, mouse or stylus actions on various Web page components, keyboard or stylus data entry into Web form components, and voice message to respond to the user interface.

FIGURE 5.4 **Forms of Interactivity**

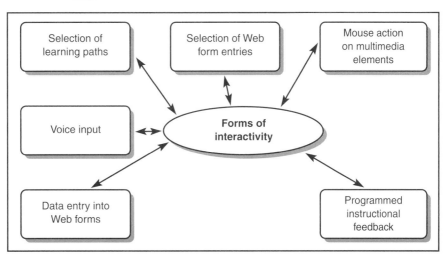

Selection of Learning Paths

The most common and frequent user action in a hypermedia learning environment is probably selecting hyperlinks through a learning path. Learning paths can be linear or nonlinear. A pure linear structure controls the navigation path with two types of hyperlinks: back/previous and forward/next. The learner has to start from the first link and move forward, or move backward and then forward again. A nonlinear navigation scheme gives the learner more than one hyperlink option at most stop points, and the learner needs to decide which option to select at each point in order to proceed. The alternative paths may converge at some subsequent points, though they typically diverge more often than they converge.

Selection of Web Form Items

There are two types of items to select through a Web form: exclusive and nonexclusive. An exclusive selection allows the learner to select only one choice from a group of options. Two types of components allow exclusive choices: radio buttons and drop-down list boxes. A major advantage of using radio buttons to display options is that the user can view all options at once. However, if there are many options, radio buttons can take up a lot of page space. To save space, we can use the drop-down list box. A drop-down list typically shows only one default option and hides the rest until the learner clicks the downward arrow of the box. This feature makes the drop-down list box a popular option when we need to list multiple groups of options, each of which contains a long list of choices, such as course listings for a program or item listings under a category. The drop-down list box is also useful if we need to place a list of choices within a text line, such as a cloze exercise or test (see Figure 5.5).

Nonexclusive choices allow learners to select any or all applicable options given for a group of items. Nonexclusive choices are typically provided through checkboxes in a Web form or hyperlinks that lead to optional paths. Input entered through a Web form can be sent to the instructor's e-mail box or to a processing program, whereas hyperlink options generally lead to different Web pages or send requests to server-side programs.

FIGURE 5.5   Drop-Down List for Cloze Test

Hong Kong draws people from around the world. Tourists come to ind
Others come to [Word #2 ▼] business. Whatever the reason, if you v

| Word #2 |
| (a) trade |
| (b) conduct |
| (c) provide |
| (d) disturb |

Lisa Barron take[   ]he premier hotels in the Asian region.

Data Entry Into Web Forms

When the learner selects among a set of given options, passive reaction or reflexive operation is more likely to occur. In selecting given options, the learner will not make any errors other than what is anticipated in the multiple choices given. In contrast, productive output is in the learner's own language without the constraint of choices given by the programmed instruction. When the learner is required to produce her or his own output, active thinking is more likely to occur, and the learner may make unexpected errors or responses.

Like selective responses, productive output can be sent to an e-mail box (typically the instructor's) or to a processing program. If you recall the distinction we have drawn between interaction and interactivity, you can see that there is a difference between learner output sent to the instructor and learner output sent to a processing program. The former would be interaction between the learner and the instructor, whereas the latter would be interactivity between the learner and the instructional content. Sometimes, the learner output can be sent to both the instructor's e-mail box and a processing program at the same time. We will describe this when we discuss server-side Web technology later in this chapter.

To have the programmed instruction respond to the learner's productive output, a major challenge is to allow for variations in output. Most of these programs can usually take only a limited range of variations, and the text entry has to be relatively short; otherwise a higher level of natural language processing will be required and the program could become extremely complex. The easiest way to handle productive output is probably by keyword match. The processing program will search for some anticipated keywords in the incoming data and then give feedback based on the match findings. If needed, the program can check the sequence of the keywords as well.

Writing a program that can process responses to a question like the seven layers of the OSI model in the accompanying case study would be relatively easy. However, if we want to ask learners to define a concept or describe a phenomenon such as the greenhouse effect, it will be almost impossible to write a program that can take into account all possible response variations and process them accordingly with appropriate feedback. Human instructors can handle this type of processing with far more efficiency and flexibility.

CASE STUDY Keyword Matching and Sequence

- In a computer networking course, we may ask learners to write out the seven layers of the open systems interconnection (OSI) model: (a) physical layer, (b) data link layer, (c) network layer, (d) transport layer, (e) session layer, (f) presentation layer, and (g) application layer. The model is designed to help learners understand computer-to-computer communications in a networked environment. Since the sequence of the layers is important, the processing program would need to check and see if the learner has entered the seven layers in the correct order.

Mouse and Stylus Action

In addition to using the **HTML** text document format, multimedia developers can create Web page components that can respond to a user's mouse actions, such as mouse over, click, and drag. Such interactive components are mostly created in Flash, Shockwave, and Java applets (small Java-language programs). Tablet technology allows the learner to use a stylus pen to interact with the computer screen content. The most prominent advantage of a stylus is its support for drawing and handwriting input.

Voice Input

Voice recognition technology allows the user to interact with a computer through the audio channels of a microphone and speaker. Although accuracy and response time still need to be improved, voice input can be extremely useful for those who cannot use a keyboard and mouse as the interface for interacting with the computer.

Programmed Instructional Feedback

For truly meaningful interactivity to occur, the learner should be involved in active thinking and be engaged in an intellectual conversation with programmed instruction, which can dynamically adapt and update to meet the learner's progressive learning needs. The reciprocal process keeps the learner aware of the ongoing interactivity. This awareness is positively related to learner affective and cognitive growth (Decharms, 1968; Furio, 1987; Willis & Brophy, 1974). To the learner, the quality of interactivity is often evaluated based on the type of feedback the instructional program can provide. Schimmel (1988) classifies instructional feedback into three categories: (a) confirmation, (b) correction, and (c) explanation. We would further categorize programmed

---

IN PRACTICE   **The Semiconductor Applet Service**

Educational Java Applet Service (JAS) is a collection of educational Java applets (small programs) and associated educational materials (such as exercise and quiz questions, tutorials, etc.) in the area of solid state materials and devices. The applet resources are developed and maintained by Professor Chu Ryang Wie's group at SUNY–Buffalo. JAS won a MERLOT Classics Award in 2003. The applets have been used by trainers and educators in composing instructional Web content, presentation materials, classroom exercises, and quizzes.

Source: http://jas.eng.buffalo.edu/

feedback into the following categories: (a) acknowledgment, (b) elicitation, (c) guidance, (d) remedial action, and (e) evaluation.

Acknowledgment can be a simple return message indicating the receipt of input from the learner. Elicitation can be given in two situations: encouraging the learner to try again after a failed attempt at a task, or presenting the learner with a more challenging task after successful completion of the current task. Guidance is usually given as optional help or supplementary resources in places where possible learner uncertainty is anticipated or detected, or alternative interpretation is believed to be helpful. Remedial feedback is provided when the learner makes an error in accomplishing a task. Remedial feedback can suggest possible causes of the error, direct the learner to relevant reference materials, recommend additional resources, and request corrective actions. Compared with other forms of feedback, remedial feedback usually demands the most design and programming expertise, involving knowledge base support and a certain level of artificial intelligence.

Feedback as evaluation is probably the most popular form of feedback given in programmed instruction. Evaluative feedback is typically found in three forms: right/wrong judgment, correction, and grading. If the instructor does not need to see the learner's performance, correct answers can be embedded in a Web page, hidden in a drop-down list box. The learner simply clicks the drop-down button to see the correct answer (see Figure 5.6).

In addition to the simple use of a drop-down box, other technologies are available to create self-assessment exercises, such as JavaScript, Java applets, and Shockwave programs. **JavaScript** is probably the easiest to use since it can

FIGURE 5.6 **Drop-Down Box for Self-Test Answers**

Question 1: What's the capital of Egypt?

1. Beirut
2. Cairo
3. Baghdad
4. Madrid

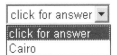

Please visit chapter 5
on the Companion
Website (**http://www
.prenhall.com/wang**)
for some interactive
JavaScript, applet, and
Shockwave
examples.

be integrated with HTML code and can read user input from any Web-form components. In addition, JavaScript can run in any major **browsers** without the need for any additional **plug-in.** Java applets and Shockwave programs are better suited to applications that require multimedia support, particularly dynamic and interactive graphics display.

Self-assessment exercises can be very important in helping the learner to be aware of how well she or he is learning. However, self-assessment programs usually do not store the learner's performance records in a database for the instructor to review, since these programs typically run on the client side only. To make learners' performance records available for instructor review, we need server-side programs with database support and other server resources.

SERVER-SUPPORTED INTERACTIVITY

When the user selects options provided by a Web form or enters text input through a Web form, responses have to be processed by a program. The processing program can reside on the very same page where the user enters responses. The processing program can also reside on the server side, in which case the user responses will be sent over the Internet to the server to be processed.

Client-Side Programs

A major advantage of **client-side programs** is the shift of processing workload to the client, thus reducing the burden on the server. Because a client-side program processes everything by itself without communicating with the server, network traffic is reduced and response is almost instant. This feature makes client-side programs ideal for input verification, self-tests that do not need to store learner performance in a database for record keeping, or other small programs that do not require server resource support. However, there are some major limitations with client-side programs. Because client-side programs are downloaded to be run in the client browser, these programs are generally simple and small, limited in functionality. For security reasons, client-side programs are generally allowed to access only the computer resources permissible by the browser environment. If an object embedded in a Web page needs to access any other resources than the browser environment on the client machine, a request window will usually pop up asking for user permission to allow the object to be downloaded and installed on the user computer. The user can either allow it to be installed or reject it. Finally, the source code of a client program is open to Web page source view. Therefore, client-side programs cannot contain information that should not be viewed by the client.

Most of the client-side programs currently found on the Web are probably written in JavaScript, Java applets, and Shockwave. A Java applet is a short program written in the **Java** language, compiled into a class file, embedded into a Web page as an object, and run in a browser environment. A Java applet can do most of the things a stand-alone Java application can do. You can find many Java applet samples on the Web at http://javaboutique.internet.com and from Sun Microsystems at http://java.sun.com/applets/.

A Shockwave movie is a small program created with Macromedia Director or Flash and embedded in a Web page as an object, like a Java applet. A primary strength of Java applets and Shockwave movies is that they can integrate multimedia. Java applets have been popularly used to illustrate concepts that require visual support, such as atom structures, cell division, and mathematical models. The interactive graphics capability makes Shockwave a very popular technology for developing online games. Because Flash uses line-based vector drawing instead of pixel-based raster painting, Flash movies are relatively small in file size and the graphic interface can shrink or expand to fit the browser window without loss of detail or image distortion. The scalability of the Flash interface makes it a preferred technology for data display on portable devices. Flash Player is now available for more and more handheld Internet-enabled electronic communication devices.

You can find many sample Flash movies from the Macromedia Web site and at www.shockwave.com. A growing number of Web sites are using Flash movies to create their homepage interfaces. To determine if a Web page contains a Flash movie interface, you can right mouse click (hold down the command key if you're using Macintosh) the object in the page. If a context window pops up with a menu item "About Macromedia Flash Player," you know that the object is a Flash movie.

Server-Side Programs

If you need to develop a major program that involves elaborate and sophisticated data processing and requires server resources, particularly database support, a server-side program is usually a better solution. Because a **server-side program** runs on the server and delivers back to the client browser only text data as an HTML page, you can be assured of the protection of the program source code. As an integral part of the server software collection, a server-side program can access and use most of the computing resources on the host server. Given access permissions, a server-side program may also access resources on other servers. For example, using Open Database Connectivity (ODBC), a server-side program can access a database that resides on another server regardless of the physical location of the database server, as long as it is accessible through the network.

The support of a database is important for adaptive instructional content development. Using a backend database integrated with a knowledge base, we can store learners' performance records, modularized course content, and an extensive library of course-related resources in the database and develop adaptive programs that can generate dynamic content, customize learning paths for individual learners, and keep the learning experiences constantly refreshing and updated.

TABLE 5.2   Server-Side Languages and Required Support

Language	Server support required
Active server pages	Microsoft Internet Information Server or UNIX-based server with ASP support, such as ChiliSoft
Java server pages	Any server with Java Servlet support, platform independent
Perl	Any server with Perl installed, typically run through Common Gateway Interface (CGI)
PHP	Apache Web server with PHP engine installed

Server-side programs can be developed in almost any programming language. Many of the software and server components needed for server-side scripting are readily available from the Web, including Java Servlet, Java Server Tomcat, Perl, and PHP. Compared with compiled languages such as C/C++ and Java, **scripting languages** hide many lower-level tasks and are therefore relatively easier to work with. Table 5.2 lists some popular server-side scripting languages and their required server support.

How does a server-side program work? An **HTTP** Web server primarily hosts a collection of static Web pages coded in HTML. HTML cannot generate much dynamic content or allow interactivity between the client and the server. To allow a Web page to communicate with other server resources, a bridge or gateway is needed to link executable programs to the HTTP server. A common gateway interface (CGI) has been one of the popular solutions. CGI specifies how to pass arguments (data parameter values) from a Web page to an executing program on the server as part of the HTTP request. CGI also defines a set of environment variables, which include the HTTP server name, server operating system, client browser type and version, cookie values, remote user name, and IP address. These environment variables are important for client-server communications and appropriate Web content delivery and processing. Perl has been a popular scripting language for developing CGI programs. Other scripting languages available for server-side programs that do not use CGI include Active Server Pages and Java Server Pages.

Which language is best? The choice is usually based on what server support is available and what other resources need to be incorporated. Perl has long been a popular scripting language for developing programs on UNIX-based servers. Support for Perl comes with many UNIX installations, and the integration of Perl with the Apache server is very easy. Perl can also run on Windows servers. Perl software can be downloaded free from a variety of sources, including www.perl.com and www.activestate.com. Because Perl is an

open-source technology, many developers are actively involved in creating freely distributed modules to extend Perl's functionality. Perl has been designed to include elaborate support for regular expression matching and substitution for text string processing and manipulation, making it particularly capable of natural language processing.

If your HTTP server is Microsoft Internet Information Server (IIS) running on a Windows platform, Active Server Pages (ASP) is probably a better choice since the support for ASP is built into the IIS. If a program residing on a Windows server needs to communicate with a Microsoft SQL Server database or an Access database on the same Web site, there are more reasons for you to choose ASP, since ASP can easily integrate with ActiveX Data Object (ADO), which serves as a bridge between a Web-accessible database and a server-side program. Microsoft Access is included in Microsoft Office Suite Professional, so it is widely available without additional cost. However, if your Web server is Apache on a UNIX machine, additional software will have to be installed on the server to provide a runtime environment if you want to implement ASP.

In recent years, Java Server Pages (JSP) has emerged as another popular server-side scripting language. JSP allows Web developers to insert snippets of Java code inside HTML tags. The document is then saved with the file extension .jsp. When the server receives a request for a .jsp file, it will read through the file and convert the embedded JSP code into a Java servlet. The servlet is executed by the Java engine on the server, returning output in HTML format back to the client. JSP can also access Web databases through Open Database Connectivity (ODBC) and Java Database Connectivity (JDBC). Java-enabled servers include Apache Tomcat, Sun's Java Web Server, Netscape Server, and Macromedia JRun. JRun can be installed as a component to support Microsoft Internet Information Server.

Another server-side scripting language is PHP. PHP is to a great extent derived from C, Java, and Perl. PHP is designed for close integration within HTML with the performance goals of quicker response time, improved security, and transparency to the end user. PHP can communicate with most of the common databases, including Informix, Oracle, Sybase, MySQL, and Microsoft SQL Server. Like Perl, a major advantage of PHP is that it is open source and platform independent, which is an important attribute for today's heterogeneous network environments. The PHP server component comes with most Linux distributions. For Windows, Mac, and other platforms, PHP can be downloaded for free from www.php.net.

Although server-side programs are more powerful and resourceful than client-side programs, a major disadvantage of running server-side programs is the workload added to the server and thus the extra time required for data transfer between the client and the server. In practice, client-side and server-side programs are usually jointly used to complement each other and distribute the workload.

IN PRACTICE   **More Server-Supported Programs**

Java applets and Shockwave used to be client-side programs only, but there have been efforts to add server extensions to allow the utilization of server resources. Sun Microsystems' efforts have been on Jini technology and Web services. Macromedia has recently released the MX series of tools that aim to let Shockwave programs integrate with any application server technology to effectively exchange server-side data between rich client user interfaces. Macromedia is also developing an eLearning Suite that aims to provide a standardized development environment for online instructional material developers that integrates several tools of Shockwave technology and database-enabled server support. The suite is designed to be compatible with open learning standards from the Aviation Industry CBT Committee (AICC), IMS Global Learning Consortium, Advanced Distributed Learning Initiative (ADL), and Sharable Content Object Reference Model (SCORM).

Source: http://www.sun.com/software/jini/ and http://www.macromedia.com/resources/elearning/

C A S E   S T U D Y   **Keeping Legacy Programs**

Please visit chapter 5 on the Companion Website (**http://www.prenhall.com/wang**) for some examples of server-supported programs.

• Some instructors of the IS program have been developing database-driven, interactive Web content for years. A large part of the interactive Web content is developed in Active Server Pages, some for tracking user access to various course modules and analyzing learning paths, some for getting learner input and customizing instructional content for the learner, and some for creating simulations. Because the course management system adopted by the state does not have the runtime environment for Active Server Pages, some of the script programs have to be kept on the original server for student access.

CONCLUSION

Information and communications technology is moving at an ever faster pace, faster than we can catch up in related fields of teaching and learning. As Romiszowski (1993) observes, we are likely to be faced with a situation where technology is leading education and training in directions that may not be pedagogically desirable but happen to be economically or politically expedient (p. 76). Since we are unlikely to be able to prevent such changes, we should probably be proactive and make efforts to utilize the existing and emerging technology to serve our educational needs in ways that are as pedagogically beneficial as possible.

Chapter Summary

This chapter starts by distinguishing interactivity from interaction. Subtopics examine interactivity potential and distributed intelligence. The chapter then describes attaining interactivity at four levels: attention, content relevance, cognitive engagement, and engaging context. A direct manifestation of interactivity is learner responses to instructional content and instructional feedback in return. A distinction is drawn between selective responses and productive output. For true interactivity to take place and meet individual learner needs, instructional content must be adaptive. Branching is a basic approach to provide adaptive instructional content in hypermedia. The last section of the chapter describes interactivity that can be attained through client-side and server-side programs. After explaining some common client-side technologies such as JavaScript and Shockwave, the chapter describes some major server-side technologies: CGI, Perl, Active Server Pages, Java Server Pages, and PHP.

Review Questions

1. Do you agree with the distinctions drawn between interaction and interactivity in this chapter? If yes, do you feel there are any other qualitative differences in addition to those suggested in the chapter?

2. What is your view of the theory of distributed intelligence? In which ways do you think the theory of distributed intelligence can help us understand interactivity and interactivity potential?

3. Are there any other levels of interactivity that you feel are important, but that are not discussed in the chapter?

4. In your educational experience, what variables are important in managing learner control over instructional content and the learning process?

5. What factors should we consider when we use learner selective responses and productive output in a complementary manner to promote interactivity?

6. Adaptive instructional content is often expensive to develop. For what kind of instructional needs do you think adaptive content would be most useful and cost effective?

7. Recalling your Web experiences, what types of client-side programs did you find effective? Were you aware of any data processing by server-side programs? What kind of functions did they usually perform?

Summary of Tips

1. Use unusual headings and topics to catch learners' attention.

2. Enhance content salience by selecting topics that students know something about and would like to learn more about.

3. Use prequestions to foster students' recall of prior knowledge about the upcoming topics.

4. Present content in multiple modes and provide options in learning paths to accommodate different learner needs.

5. Make instructional content coverage flexible and adjustable to changing learner needs.

6. Make students aware of learning objectives to enhance content relevance and cognitive engagement.

7. Use branching in hypermedia navigation design to provide scaffolding in learning.

8. Create opportunities to elicit productive responses from students to encourage active learning and divergent thinking.

9. Make instructional content capable of providing formative feedback to keep students aware of ongoing interactivity and their learning progress.

10. Use client-side programs to provide self-exercises and self-tests.

Exercises

1. Compare and contrast interaction between human interlocutors and interactivity between instructional content and learner.

2. Conduct a group discussion on the differences between interaction and interactivity.

3. Summarize various ways learners can interact with the instructional source by entering input and receiving feedback.

4. Select an instructional unit from an existing Web-based course. Comment on the interactivity potential of the unit, focusing on content relevance and cognitive engagement for the intended learners.

5. Conduct a group discussion on the theory of distributed intelligence, focusing on the relationship between distributed intelligence and interactivity.

6. Design a Web-based content module in your field of teaching. Use the strategies discussed in the chapter to strengthen its content relevance and cognitive engagement.

7. Summarize various client-side and server-side technologies that can support interactivity between learner and instructional source.

8. Check with the server administrator of your college or school district and find out what kind of server scripting languages are employed. Ask for sample applications that you can view and find out what kind of client-server interactions can occur.

Resources on the Web

Web resources are dynamic and change frequently. Please visit the Companion Website for a more inclusive and updated list of Web resources.

- Consortium for Interactive Instruction (http://www.whro.org/education/cii/)
- Society for Applied Learning Technology (Journal of Interactive Instruction Development) (http://www.salt.org/)
- Virtual Resource Site for Teaching with Technology (http://www.umuc.edu/virtualteaching/)
- Educational Modules & Simulations (http://www.phy.syr.edu/courses/modsim.html)

References

Ausubel, D. P. (1966). *Educational psychology: A cognitive view.* New York: Holt, Rinehart & Winston.

Bettex, M. (1996). Textbooks: Prospects for the technological era. *EMI: ICEM conference report, 32,* 47–50.

Brusilovsky, P. (2000). Adaptive hypermedia: From intelligent tutoring systems to Web-based education. In G. Gauthier, C. Frasson, & K. ValLehn (Eds.), *Intelligent tutoring systems. Lecture notes in computer science* (Vol. 1839, pp. 1–7). Berlin: Springer Verlag.

Cristea, A. (2003). Adaptive patterns in authoring of educational adaptive hypermedia. *Educational Technology & Society, 6*(4), 1–5.

De Bra, P. (2000). Pros and cons of adaptive hypermedia in Web-based education. *Journal of CyberPsychology and Behavior, 3*(1), 71–77.

De Bra, P., Brusilovsky, P., & Houben, G. (1999). Adaptive hypermedia: From systems to framework. *ACM Computing Surveys, 31*(4). Retrieved January 9, 2004, from http://www.cs.brown.edu/memex/ACM_HypertextTestbed/papers/25.html.

DeCharms, R. (1968). *Personal causation.* New York: Academic Press.

Dede, C. J., & Palumbo, D. (1991). Implications of hypermedia for cognition and communication. *International Association for Impact Assessment Bulletin, 9,* 15–28.

Eklund, J., & Sinclair, K. (2000). An empirical appraisal of adaptive interfaces for instructional systems. *Educational Technology and Society Journal, 3*(4), 165–177.

Furio, B. (1987). *The relationship between instructor behaviors and student perceptions of control in the classroom* (Research/Technical Report 143). (ERIC Document Reproduction Service No. ED 291124)

Hannafin, M., Land, S., & Oliver, K. (1999). Open learning environments: Foundations, methods, and models. In C. M. Reigeluth (Ed.), *Instructional-design theories and models: A new paradigm of instructional theory* (Vol. II, pp. 115–142). Mahwah, NJ: Lawrence Erlbaum.

Jacobs, G. M., & Ball, J. (1996). An investigation of the structure of group activities in ELT coursebooks. *ELT Journal, 50,* 99–108.

Jonassen, D. H. (1985). Interactive lesson designs: A taxonomy. *Educational Technology, 25*(6), 7–17.

Jonassen, D. H. (1988). Integrating learning strategies into courseware to facilitate deeper processing. In D. H. Jonassen (Ed.), *Instructional designs for microcomputer courseware* (pp. 151–181). Hillsdale, NJ: Lawrence Erlbaum.

Keller, J. M. (1983). Motivational design of instruction. In C. M. Reigeluth (Ed.), *Instructional design theories and models: An overview of their current states* (pp. 383–484). Hillsdale, NJ: Lawrence Erlbaum.

Kennedy, G. (2004). Promoting cognition in multimedia interactivity research. *Journal of Interactive Learning Research, 15,* 43–61.

Merrill, M. D. (1975). Learner control: Beyond aptitude/treatment interaction. *AV Communication Review, 23,* 217–226.

Park, O., & Lee, J. (2004). Adaptive instructional systems. In D. Jonassen (Ed.), *Handbook of research on educational communications and technology* pp. 651–684. Mahwah, NJ: Lawrence Erlbaum.

Pea, R. D. (1993). Practices of distributed intelligence and designs for education. In G. Salomon (Ed.), *Distributed cognitions: Psychological and educational considerations* (pp. 47–87). Cambridge, UK: Cambridge University Press.

Pea, R. D., & Gomez, L. (1992). Distributed multimedia learning environments. *Interactive Learning Environments, 2*(2), 73–109.

Reigeluth, C. M., & Moore, J. (1999). Cognitive education and the cognitive domain. In C. M. Reigeluth (Ed.), *Instructional-design theories and models: A new paradigm of instructional theory* (Vol. II, pp. 51–68). Mahwah, NJ: Lawrence Erlbaum.

Rogers, Y., & Scaife, M. (1998). How can interactive multimedia facilitate learning? In J. Lee (Ed.), *Intelligence and multimodality in multimedia interfaces: Research and applications.* Menlo Park, CA: AAAI.

Romiszowski, A. J. (1993). Developing interactive multimedia courseware and networks: Some current issues. In C. Latchem, J. Williamson, & L. Henderson-Lancett (Eds.), *Interactive multimedia: Practice and promise* (pp. 79–96). London: Kogan Page.

Salomon, G. (1981). *Communication and education: Social and psychological interactions.* Beverly Hills, CA: SAGE Publications.

Salomon, G. (1993). Editor's introduction. In G. Salomon (Ed.), *Distributed cognitions: Psychological and educational considerations* (pp. xi–xxi). Cambridge, UK: Cambridge University Press.

Schimmel, B. J. (1988). Providing meaningful feedback in courseware. In D. H. Jonassen (Ed.), *Instructional designs for microcomputer courseware* (pp. 183–196). Hillsdale, NJ: Lawrence Erlbaum.

Schwier, R. A., & Misanchuk, E. R. (1993). Interactive multimedia instruction. Englewood Cliffs, NJ: Educational Technology Publications.

Sims, R. (2000). An interactive conundrum: Constructs of interactivity and learning theory. *Australian Journal of Educational Technology, 16*(1), 45–57.

Vygotsky, L. (1978). *Mind in society.* Cambridge, MA: Harvard University Press.

Willis, S., & Brophy, J. (1974). Origins of teachers' attitudes toward young children. *Journal of Educational Psychology, 66,* 520–529.

Chapter 6

Instructional Hypermedia Design

CHAPTER INTRODUCTION

Web-based instructional text is primarily developed and delivered in hypermedia. Hypermedia can be a combination of different types of documents including digital audio, graphics, animation, video, and text, all interconnected through nodes represented by hyperlinks. Hypermedia design is a complex process that involves combined knowledge and skills in digital graphics, information processing, writing, and scripting. The primary goal of this chapter is to provide some general guidelines on instructional hypermedia from the perspective of accessibility, usability, and information processing. The chapter will:

1. Explore the use of hypermedia for knowledge construction.

2. Discuss navigation structure and user guidance in instructional hypermedia.

3. Introduce some general methods of promoting Web accessibility.

4. Introduce basic ways to enhance Web content legibility, content salience, and readability.

LEARNING OBJECTIVES

After studying this chapter, the reader will be able to:

1. Explain the information attributes of hypermedia and their potential benefits for learning.

2. Identify difficulties learners typically experience in navigating hypermedia.

3. Describe how hyperlink navigation can be both linear and nonlinear.

4. Summarize the use of various navigational cues to facilitate user orientation in hypermedia.

5. Summarize the basic requirements of Web accessibility and the methods to meet the basic requirements.

6. Summarize and apply various ways to enhance content legibility and reader perception, including font variations.

7. Describe how interactivity can take place between frames.

ASE STUDY

● As we know from the previous chapters, Mid-State University is moving the IS program online to make it accessible to out-of-state students. At this time, the university is using a combination of online communication and Web development tools to deliver its courses. Since many of the instructors of the IS program do not have much experience in teaching Web-based courses, it is necessary to provide guidance, training, and assistance for the instructors in adapting to the online instructional environment, particularly the use of hypermedia to prepare and present instructional content. The faculty support team believes that instructors need to have some fundamental knowledge of the information attributes of hypermedia and their potential benefits for instructional material development. Instructors also need to understand how appropriately designed hypermedia might facilitate learning and how poorly designed hypermedia might hinder learning. In addition, instructors need to be aware of the key issues and requirements of Web accessibility.

HYPERMEDIA DEFINED

Hypermedia information architecture is often described as nonlinear. However, to define hypermedia as essentially nonlinear is inaccurate, because hypermedia can be strictly linear. The power of hypermedia is its associativity, or capability to link nodes and lay out paths that allow multiple ways of traversing information. A **node** is a digital file hosted by a Web server and represented and accessed through a Uniform Resource Locator (**URL**). A node can be a Web page, a digital audio recording, a digital video clip, a database, a script, or a server-side program. A **hyperlink** is a string of text that indicates a URL. A hyperlink is typically embedded in an HTML page and responds to the user's mouse action. When a user clicks a hyperlink, the browser sends a document request to the host server, which delivers the requested file over the Internet to the user's browser.

Many of our traditional media present information in a linear manner. For example, a book consists of sequentially numbered chapters and pages; a movie runs along a timeline; and a speech is delivered in a stream of sound. The nonlinear attributes of hypermedia represent a radical change in information organization and presentation from most conventional information carriers. Appropriately designed hypermedia that is hierarchical in structure can facilitate training in deductive and inductive learning, permitting the learner to move easily from abstract and general concepts to concrete and specific examples, or the other way around. Chris Dede (1996) succinctly describes hypermedia as user-controlled interactive technologies in which users can select paths in information navigation and data can be delivered in multiple formats, including digital text, images, video, and sounds.

HYPERMEDIA AND KNOWLEDGE CONSTRUCTION

With multimedia capabilities and a flexible navigation structure, hypermedia can be designed to accommodate various information access needs. Primary strengths of hypermedia as a medium of instruction include: (a) providing rich and realistic contexts for multichannel content delivery, (b) allowing nonlinear access to information, (c) focusing attention on the relationship between information nodes, (d) encouraging active, student-centered learning, and (e) promoting collaborative learning (Yang & Moore, 1996). In a study by the Center for Applied Special Technology (1996), an independent research group, students who had access to hypermedia materials and other online communications were found to perform better in key comprehension, communication, and presentation skills, and six other learning criteria. The study involved more than 500 fourth- and sixth-grade students in seven urban districts in Chicago, Ohio, Florida, California, and the District of Columbia.

Hypermedia has great promise for instructional enhancement mainly because its information structure more or less mirrors the human memory system. According to cognitive scientists, learning can be described as building new knowledge nodes, then connecting them to existing knowledge (Norman, 1983), and the essential attribute of the human memory system is not the storage or retrieval of specific units of knowledge, but rather the organizational schemes by which knowledge is associatively related (Rumelhart, 1977; Spiro, Feltovich, Jacobson, & Coulson, 1991). The interconnections of knowledge in a structured associative network allow learners to interconnect ideas, extrapolate, and infer relationships (Norman, Gentner, & Stevens, 1976).

Another related point is the selective nature of the human memory system. Research has demonstrated that the human memory system selectively stores and structures associational schemes to preserve the most important aspects of relationships without preserving every possible association (Bransford & Franks, 1971; Bransford, Barclay, & Franks, 1972). With a nonlinear and multidimensional organization of content nodes, hyperlink structure can be an effective way to promote cognitive flexibility in an ill-structured domain by providing a "landscape crisscrossing" view of the content domain. Hyperlink structure allows learners to traverse the content by selecting what is most relevant from among varied paths and multiple perspectives (Spiro et al., 1991). As a facilitator of knowledge construction, hypermedia allows learners to access a large knowledge base and seek out information that meets their particular needs, in terms of both their prior knowledge and their preferred learning style. In hypermedia, users can not only browse the information base, but also build additional nodes and links (Spiro et al., 1991).

Although there is great potential in hypermedia for designing flexible learning paths, there have also been problems in hypermedia applications. Yang and Moore (1996) have cautioned about some pitfalls in using hypermedia for instruction. Two commonly reported problems are **navigational disorientation** and cognitive overload. For example, Dee-Lucas and Larkin (1992) point out that although accessing extra information while reading a text can compensate for initial deficiencies in vocabulary or background knowledge, continuous comprehension can be disrupted if the reader is frequently led away by external resource links. How to provide supplementary resources and customize learning paths without undue disruptions of continuous comprehension is a major challenge for hypermedia instructional designers.

One of the ways to keep learning on track is to use a navigation structure that consistently keeps the learner aware of the learning context. Learning paths can be represented in what is called a "breadcrumb trail" with hierarchical or linear relations (see Figures 6.9 and 6.10 later in the chapter). When a course management system such as WebCT is used, the learning context and navigation paths are usually maintained by the system interface and may include a top menu bar, a left menu, and a hierarchical path of links for the current context (see Figure 6.1).

Hypermedia is not only a primary tool with which instructors can present and deliver Web-based instructional content, but also a great tool with which students can collect and organize their learning materials, share and critique

FIGURE 6.1   **Navigation Outline of a Course Site**

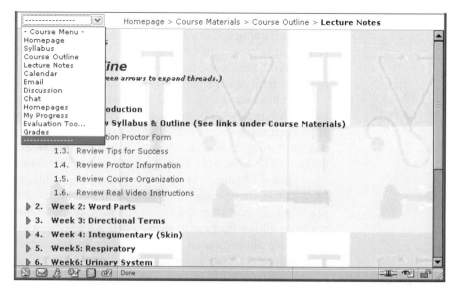

CASE STUDY **A Hypermedia Portfolio**

- For the students in the IS graduate program at Mid-State University, a potentially beneficial application of hypermedia is to develop a Web-based portfolio that consists of a progressive collection of assignments and projects from a particular course or several related courses, with ongoing reflection on the learning experiences. Portfolio development can be individual work or a team project. When a group of students work on a team portfolio, a shared Web space can be set up where team members can contribute to the common portfolio, editing and revising files, exchanging comments, and negotiating solutions. A major advantage of such shared Web space for group work is that everyone can access the work from anywhere at any time, and progress is immediately visible to every member.

information, reflect upon learning experiences, and revise and rebuild their knowledge base. In using hypermedia to present ideas, students will need to apply critical thinking and creative design. Cognitive flexibility, problem solving, and communication skills are all required. Hypermedia enables students to impose some kind of knowledge structure on what they want to present. Working on this structure is often intellectually challenging and engaging to learners (Jonassen, 2003).

NAVIGATION SCHEMES AND CONTENT STRUCTURE

A navigation scheme is a layout showing how nodes are organized and connected through hyperlinks to provide access paths in hypermedia. A basic organizational unit, a node can consist of chunks of text, pictures, audio files, video clips, and so on. A node may present the user with text, graphics, audio, video, and/or hyperlinks that point to other nodes.

There are three primary ways to organize hyperlinks: (a) linear or sequential, (b) hierarchical, and (c) cross-referential. For most course Web sites, the three link structures are integrated rather than used separately.

Linear Structure

Linear structure imposes a strict control on the navigation path for the visitor, who follows a step-by-step route laid out by the designer. A strictly linear structure has only two types of links: previous and next (see Figure 6.2).

Linear structure is often used in presenting procedural knowledge and motor skills where each subsequent content unit must be based on the learner's

FIGURE **6.2**   **A Linear Structure**

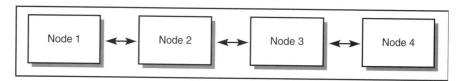

FIGURE **6.3**   **Linear Paths with Alternatives or Options**

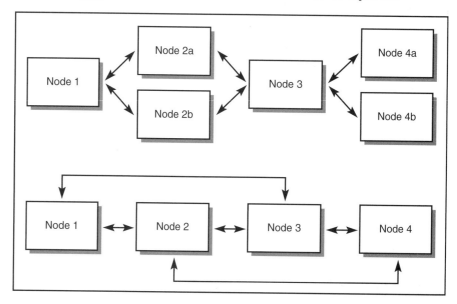

mastery of the preceding parts. In a strictly controlled linear structure, **associative learning** is not encouraged and cognitive flexibility not promoted. Since a pure linear structure could be very limiting, a linear structure with alternatives or options is often more usable (see Figure 6.3). A flexible linear structure is usually more applicable for most courses that require sequential access to course content, material such as evolutionary changes, historic development, a step-by-step operational manual. For the IS students in the accompanying case study, linear hypermedia structure is mostly likely to be used in procedural programming courses.

Hierarchical Structure

Hyperlink associations can be vertical or horizontal. With vertical associations, one content node is conceptually subsumed under another, forming a hierarchical conceptual map of top-down, deductive learning paths (see Figure 6.4).

FIGURE 6.4   A Hierarchical Structure

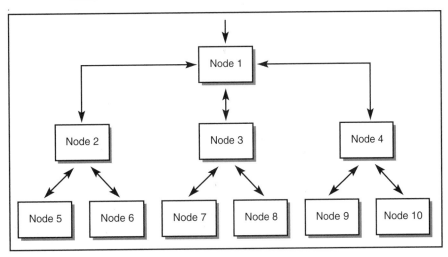

FIGURE 6.5   A Cascading Path

Search Directory ABC

Home > Internet and World Wide Web > World Wide Web > **Web Site Design**

One of the learning theories applicable in designing a hierarchical structure is the elaboration theory proposed by Reigeluth (1999; Reigeluth & Stein,
1983). Based on Ausubel's theory of advance organizers (1966), the elaboration theory states that learning should start with general-level knowledge that
subsumes the information to follow. With reference to both Ausubel's and
Reigeluth's theories, Dee-Lucas (1996) conducted a study on the hierarchical
structure of hypermedia and found that providing an overview structure of
hypertext units facilitates information processing and learning.

In a hierarchical structure, levels of links should not be too deep. When
there are more than four levels, it is difficult for the user to maintain a clear
overview of the content organization (Powell, 2000). If a hierarchical structure
has three or four levels, a breadcrumb trail or cascading path on top of a page
(Figure 6.5) can help the visitor get a clear sense of the current context in terms
of the subsuming nodes (how they are nested), so that the visitor can always
trace back (Fleming, 1998) or go directly to a higher level of the site and check
out more alternative paths (Nielsen, 2000b). Such a structural path can help a
visitor see the higher levels of content if the visitor is brought to the current page
through a search engine or third-party links that bypass the higher level nodes.

Hierarchical knowledge structure is congruent with human cognitive efforts to abstract and classify natural and social entities and phenomena. Hierarchical knowledge structure is particularly common in subject areas where levels of abstraction can be more easily identified. For instance, biology has two major divisions, botany and zoology, each of which can further subsume more specific fields of study, such as ichthyology (the study of fishes), ornithology (the study of birds), and entomology (the study of insects), and subclassifications can go further.

Grid and Mesh Structures

In a pure hierarchical structure, there are only vertical links across nodes. Each node is linked to either higher or lower levels, and there is no direct horizontal link between nodes at the same level. If a navigation structure combines horizontal and vertical links, it would be a grid or mesh structure. A node in a grid or mesh structure can be linked to conceptually related nodes both horizontally and vertically. A grid structure differs from a mesh in that a node in a grid structure is linked to no more than two nodes horizontally and no more than two nodes vertically, whereas a node in a mesh structure can be linked to any number of other nodes in any directions (see Figures 6.6 and 6.7).

Mesh structure can also be called cross-referential structure, because it connects related resources across domains like an extensive cross-section. This

FIGURE 6.6   A Grid Structure

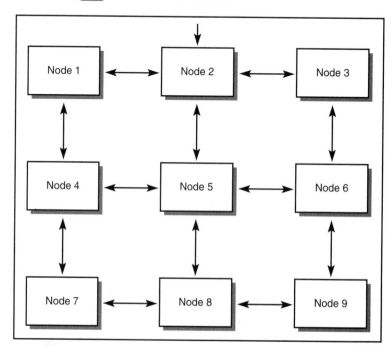

type of knowledge structure is generally applicable in subject areas where key factors and issues do not have clearly definable linear or hierarchical relations, such as in environmental and social sciences.

A complex mesh structure of hyperlinks can be difficult to design and navigate through. In an extreme case where learners are allowed to navigate freely in a mesh navigation scheme, traversing the scheme can impose considerable cognitive overload on the learner, who may become easily disoriented (Dede & Palumbo, 1991). In deploying a meshlike hierarchical structure, it is therefore generally a good idea to link only to those nodes that are of immediate and important relevance.

Figure 6.8 depicts a possible navigation structure of a course site. For the purpose of description, the hyperlink structures depicted here are simplified in terms of number of nodes and possible paths. In reality, we are more likely to find a combination of more than one hyperlink structure employed with far more complex and extensive paths in the navigation scheme of a Web-based course site.

The course home page has six top-level links: syllabus, course units, discussion board, assignments, resources, and instructor contact information. These top-level links may be placed on each lower-level page of the site so that the user can jump directly to any of the top-level nodes no matter where the user is. If the top-level links are not placed on every lower-level page, a

FIGURE 6.7   A Mesh Structure

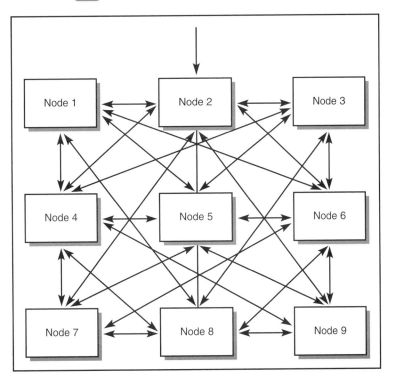

FIGURE ❻.❽   **A Course Site Navigation Scheme**

```
┌──────────┐        ┌──────────────┐        ┌──────────────────┐
│ Syllabus │◄──────►│ Course home  │◄──────►│ Contact Instructor│
│          │        │    page      │        │                  │
└──────────┘        └──────────────┘        └──────────────────┘

┌──────────┐   ┌──────────────┐   ┌──────────────┐   ┌──────────────┐
│ Course   │   │ Discussion   │   │ Assignments  │   │ Resources    │
│ units    │   │              │   │              │   │              │
└──────────┘   └──────────────┘   └──────────────┘   └──────────────┘

┌──────────┐                      ┌──────────────┐
│ Unit 1   │                      │ Unit 1 Work  │
└──────────┘                      └──────────────┘

┌──────────┐                      ┌──────────────┐
│ Unit 2   │                      │ Unit 2 Work  │
└──────────┘                      └──────────────┘

┌──────────┐                      ┌──────────────┐
│ Unit 3   │                      │ Unit 3 Work  │
└──────────┘                      └──────────────┘
```

course home page link, at least, should be placed on every lower-level page so that the user can always return to the home page hub from anywhere within the site. The node of course units branches off into sequentially organized individual units. To save space, only three units are included here. In parallel, the node of assignments branches off into individual assignments. Each course unit is linked to the corresponding assignment and related resources. Inversely, each assignment page is linked to the corresponding course unit and related resources. The discussion board is accessible from each course unit and each assignment page. When the user logs off the discussion board, she or he will be directed back to the course home page.

The structure depicted here is only one possible configuration of a Web course navigation scheme. There can be many alternative configurations, depending on instructional needs. For example, any course unit may branch off into subunits, and each assignment page may contain links to more specific resources and reference materials.

Please visit chapter 6 on the Companion Website (**http://www.prenhall.com/wang**) for online demonstrations of navigation structures.

CASE STUDY   What Navigation Structures to Use?

The courses in the IS program of our case study vary considerably in their knowledge structure and information-processing requirements. Some of them, such as programming courses, may require a more linear approach. Others may use a more hierarchical structure if a top-down or bottom-up approach is more appropriate, such as in courses of System Analysis and Design, Decision Support Systems, Information Systems Planning and Management, and Project Management.

Despite the differences made above, a combination of linear, hierarchical, and mesh structures is probably more often the case with most of the courses. No matter what scheme is used, there are some general principles to observe in building a manageable hypermedia navigation scheme. These principles include: (a) a modular approach to content development, (b) use of navigational aids and cues to help the learner navigate, and (c) a balance between breadth and depth in navigation structure.

Balance Between Breadth and Depth

The balance between content breadth and depth requires us to provide the learner with adequate freedom and options in exploring the content domain while keeping the cognitive load at a manageable level. Specifically, the balance is achieved through careful deployment of horizontal and vertical links on each page. This issue is particularly important in designing hierarchical and cross-referential structures. Some people suggest that there should be no more than six links in a page to avoid cognitive overload, but such a limit is evidently impractical in reality. Grouping and categorization of links can help reduce the cognitive load. When the links are organized into clear headings and sub-headings in a hierarchical scheme, the user should be able to browse through dozens of links with little difficulty. However, a list of 20 or more links presented without any logical order would probably be hard for the user to sort through. Therefore, the balance between breadth and depth is based on the nature of the content and can be enhanced by appropriate organization of links.

Content Modularity

To maximize the number of possible configurations in linking different components of the course content, a modular approach is usually recommended. When the course content is prepared and stored as modules, it is easy to cross-reference different parts of the content, because each module can focus on a specific topic, and it is easier to reuse the modules in different contexts by simply setting or resetting hyperlinks to the modules.

However, modularity is not just for reusability and ease of cross-referencing. We know that Web users are inclined to scan text in the Web

ⓒ A S E   S T U D Y   **Help Instructors Learn the Modular Approach**

- At Mid-State University, initial training sessions are believed to be helpful for instructors to see the importance of a modular approach toward content development in hypermedia, and some examples of course content modules can be illustrative. A demo site with a navigation structure that interconnects content modules on a particular topic is set up to show instructors how modules can be interconnected to develop a thread of description and discussion. Each module is also viewable as a separate unit with a brief description so that instructors can see how modules can be prepared.

browser environment. To accommodate this inclination, Web designers may need to change their writing styles. The general guidelines are: (a) keeping text short and concise, (b) breaking long text into more readable chunks, (c) using headings and subheadings to facilitate scanning, (d) getting to the point directly, (e) highlighting key points, and (f) using lists to summarize.

NAVIGATIONAL GUIDANCE

As evidenced in many studies, a common user problem in Web browsing is the lack of navigational guidance and organizational cues (Rouet & Levonen, 1996). In a survey by Kommers, Grabinger, and Dunlap (1996), 56% of the subjects answered that they tend to get lost in hypermedia because of the freedom to choose paths and the subsequent lack of guidance. To keep the user well oriented in site navigation, a good navigation scheme should always give the user a sense of context within the site, providing links to allow the user to move on to both higher and lower levels in site content structure. Navigational design is about identifying and predicting the needs of the user and building paths that can lead the user to the desired information through a successful interaction with the hyperlink structure. Depending on the site goals, content nature, and user needs, there are many strategies to facilitate navigation. Some are generally applicable; others should be used with discretion.

User Orientation

User orientation basically means letting users know where they are currently located in the course Web site. The first rule to observe is the most basic one: Every course site should have a home page that serves as the hub and point of origin for all traffic coming into your site. From the home page, you set up the online equivalent of road signs telling your visitors where to go and how to get there. There should be a home page link on every other page so that users can return to the hub of traffic at any time.

Jonassen (1982) contends that it is important to present explicit structures in your text to prompt the reader to go to the main pages of the site. Fischer and Mandl (1990) propose that learners should be able to answer the following five questions in a good hypermedia environment:

1. Where am I?
2. How did I get here?
3. What can I do here?
4. Where can I get to from here?
5. How do I go there?

If a course management system like WebCT is used, as in the case of Mid-State University, a general overview of course site structure is usually easy because the course tool has a user interface with a top menu bar and a side menu of links to major course components. The top and side menus are consistently there for the user to use to jump to any major course components or tools. However, if no such prescriptive course tool is used, it is very much up to the designer to set up the course site structure and provide navigation cues. What can we do to help the user get oriented? There are a few common strategies and navigation cues to use.

Navigational Cues

A menu bar is a common navigation aid when the content of a site consists of several primary categories. A navigation bar, also known as a nav bar, is conventionally placed on the left or top of a page. With varying label lengths, a top nav bar usually contains no more than 10 items. In contrast, a nav bar as a vertical list can contain more menu items. If the site content has a hierarchical structure, it is common to combine a top nav bar with a left nav menu. In course management systems such as WebCT and Blackboard, both a top menu bar and a left menu are used to set up the navigation context. By convention, the top nav bar has the top-level links. Clicking on each of the top-level links can optionally change the sublevel links in the left nav menu. If so, the left submenu can be called a context menu.

Navigation menus can simply be a vertical list of text items or a horizontal line of text links delimited with a vertical bar. Decorative menus can be created in simple graphics. Graphics tend to catch attention better than plain text and can therefore help direct user attention. Used appropriately, simple graphics can be effective cues to facilitate user navigation. Directive use of graphics includes directional arrows, signs, dividing lines or bars, and progress status indicators. Figure 6.9 is an example of directive graphics that visually indicates

FIGURE **6.9**   **A Visual Breadcrumb Path**

FIGURE **6.10**   **A Numerically Ordered Breadcrumb Path**

FIGURE **6.11**   **Page from Digital Laboratory Manual**

Note: Screen shot reprinted with permission from Stephen Gallik, University of Mary Washington.

Please visit chapter 6 on the Companion Website (**http:// www.prenhall.com/ wang**) for some samples of navigation cues.

the location of the current page in a series of seven sequential pages. Each of the left and right arrows is linked to a previous or following page.

When a large number of items (more than 10) need to be listed sequentially, a numerically ordered breadcrumb path can be helpful too (see Figure 6.10).

With the help of some Web page authoring tools and JavaScript, we can create more dynamic and interactive menus, with special effects such as rollover, popup submenus, or expandable submenus. There are some examples of such dynamic interactive menus on the Companion Website of the book.

IN PRACTICE   A Digital Laboratory Manual

The Digital Laboratory Manual, developed by Dr. Stephen Gallik at University of Mary Washington, is an online digital laboratory manual to accompany the microscopic study of mammalian and human tissues. The manual consists of 15 chapters with detailed text, more than 200 labeled images, and background information. Most of the images can be enlarged 4, 10, 40, and 100 times to simulate what the student can see under a microscope. The manual has very easy-to-use navigation with a menu bar and a table of contents available at a single click. Page navigation buttons and a visual breadcrumb path are also always visible to let the student move backward and forward (see Figure 6.11).

Source: http://www.gallik.umw.edu

INTERFACE CONSISTENCY AND VARIATION

Navigation in hypermedia is facilitated by a balance between consistency and variation in interface. Consistency means predictability. In a site with a consistent interface design, visitors can quickly become familiar with the site organization and find their way around. However, the need for consistency does not mean that all the pages in a site should have a uniform look and layout. Undistinguishable page appearances can make it hard for visitors to tell they have moved from page to page. A monotonous page appearance may become boring. Generally, a site should be consistent and recognizable in its overall design of page layout and menu locations, but have cross-page variations in color, text font, and graphic decoration. Such variations can help refresh visitors' attention and interest. Of course, color and font variations should not be overused. It is generally recommended that no more than three different colors or font types should be used within one page (Nielson, 2000a; Powell, 2000). When designing navigation bars, we need to maintain a certain level of consistency across the site, including label names, color scheme, icons, and location of navigation bars. Excessive variation in navigation scheme can lead to unfamiliar interfaces for the visitor (Fleming, 1998).

There are several methods of maintaining site interface consistency and achieving page variations. For site-level consistency, we can create header and footer files and include the header and footer in pages where they are needed. Any change made in the header or footer file will be reflected in any pages that include the header or footer. The Cascading Style Sheet (CSS) is another great tool for achieving a balance between site consistency and page variation. CSS was introduced by the World Wide Web Consortium (W3C) in 1996 as a standard means to allow Web designers to have balanced control over consistency and variation in Web page format.

CSS can be specified and applied at cross-site, cross-page, single-page, block, and inline levels. Because the format style can be extended top-down from any higher level to lower levels, the word "cascading" is used to describe it. At the site level, we can specify CSS in a text file that is saved with the .css file extension. The CSS file can be placed anywhere within the site. To use the specified style in a Web page, include a link to the CSS file in the header section of the page, and the page will inherit the style features specified in the CSS file. For example, if you have a CSS file saved as mycss1.css, a link to this style sheet can be included in the head section of any HTML page so that this page can inherit the style, like the following:

```
<haed><title>sample page 1</title>

<link rel="stylesheet" href="mycss1.css" type="text/css">

</head>
```

Although a page can inherit format from a style sheet file, we can also set style at the page level. If the style specified at the page level conflicts with the inherited style, the page level style will overwrite the inherited style. CSS can be enforced even at the text block level. Text block–level CSS is contained in a pair of <SPAN></SPAN> or <DIV></DIV> tags and affects a particular text block only. The two pairs of tags are for text-grouping purpose only and are particularly useful in formatting a block of text with special features, such as citing quotes. The tags are frequently generated when you save a Microsoft Word document as a Web page.

WEB CONTENT ACCESSIBILITY

When designing hypermedia, one important consideration you need to keep in mind is user **accessibility.** For general Web users, accessibility often means access speed: How fast can a page be retrieved over the Internet and loaded into the user's browser? Accessibility can also include compatibility: Can the content of a site be displayed trouble-free in different browsers with different operating systems? For example, some content developed in FrontPage may show up very nicely in Internet Explorer, but not in Netscape or other browsers.

Speed

Users' patience in Web browsing is usually proportional to their expectation of the site content. If users believe the content they are expecting will be worth the wait, they will be patient. Learners are usually patient since they know in-structional content is important and should not be missed. Nevertheless, Web designers should avoid including unnecessary graphics or other multimedia content which only increases download time with little information benefit. In general, for any large-size (more than 50 kilobytes) graphic file, it is a good practice to present it as a hyperlinked thumbnail first and let the visitor choose whether to click on the linked thumbnail to get the full view. For large multimedia files, you should indicate the file size in bytes to give the user an idea of how long it will probably take to download the file.

Section 508

Apart from the broad sense of accessibility to the general public, the term *accessibility* can refer specifically to making Web content accessible to people with disabilities, particularly those with vision and hearing impairments who rely on assistive technology to access and process digital information.

For Web-based instruction, the accessibility requirement is not just a matter of user consideration, but a legal obligation in the United States. Section 508 of the Rehabilitation Act of 1998 mandates that all federally funded agencies and institutions make their Web site content accessible to individuals with disabilities. Private sector Web sites do not have to follow the standards prescribed by the Act, unless a site is provided under contract to a federal agency or institution.

The criteria for Web content accessibility are based on access guidelines developed by the Web Accessibility Initiative of the World Wide Web Consortium (www.w3.org/WAI). A complete list with a detailed description of the standards given by Section 508 is available from the Web site of the Access Board (www.access-board.gov), a federal agency devoted to accessibility for people with disabilities. For Web developers, one of the most important technical requirements to follow is to attach text tags to graphics or other embedded nontext elements so that screen readers can interpret them. HTML has an ALT attribute for the <IMG>(image) tag that can serve as a verbal descriptor for an image. The ALT attribute can also be applied to an applet, image map region, and plug-in. Other important standards of the act include the following:

1. If any information is conveyed with color, the page designer should make sure that it is also available without color, for example, from context or markup.

2. Frames shall be titled with text that facilitates frame identification and navigation.

3. Row and column headers shall be identified for data tables.

4. A text-only page, with equivalent information or functionality, should be provided parallel to a graphics-loaded page. The content of the text-only page should be updated whenever the primary page changes.

5. When a page utilizes scripting languages to display content or to create interface elements, the information provided by the script shall be identified with functional text that can be read by assistive technology.

6. When a Web page requires that an applet, plug-in, or other application be present on the client system to interpret page content, the page must provide a link to a plug-in or applet.

7. When electronic forms are designed to be completed online, the form should allow people using assistive technology to access the information, field elements, and functionality required for completion and submission of the form, including all directions and cues.

8. Client-side image maps should be preferred over server-side image maps. If a server-side image map is used, redundant text links shall be provided for each active region of the map.

Total accessibility is difficult to attain because users may have different types of disabilities, different language needs, and various hardware and software configurations. Nevertheless, a high level of accessibility is certainly possible. To determine which level of accessibility is feasible for a particular context, visit the Web Content Accessibility Guidelines (WCAG) 2.0 at the World Wide Web Consortium (www.w3.org).

Assistive Technology and Tools

There are quite a few assistive tools available now to enhance accessibility. A well-known screen reader on the market is JAWS, developed by Freedom Scientific (www.freedomscientific.com). In addition to its ability to recognize most standard HTML tags, JAWS supports Braille and recognizes some dynamic HTML events such as onMouseOver that are used to run script code such as JavaScript or Visual Basic Script. There is a free talking browser by WeMedia.com that features large buttons and keystroke commands for easy navigation and can speak the text the user selects within the browser. The user can go from link to link using the up and down arrows on the keyboard and select the text for the browser to read, or let the browser read the entire page.

Microsoft Windows 2000 and XP have an accessibility wizard to help adjust a user system for optimal screen display and keyboard access, including selecting the minimal size of viewable text, window border size and icon size, mouse movement preferences, keyboard operation preferences, and sound support to guide computer operations. Windows 2000 and XP have an on-screen keyboard that allows the use of the mouse to enter input (see Figure 6.12) and a magnifier that can enlarge the display on the screen. Windows 2000 and XP also include a Narrator, which can read window menu content and speak character input by the user (see Figure 6.13).

Examples of more advanced assistive technology and tools include the Camera Mouse and EagleEyes developed by Boston College (http://www.bc.edu/schools/csom/eagleeyes/). The former allows a person to control the computer

FIGURE 6.12 On-Screen Keyboard

Note: Screen shot reprinted by permission from Microsoft Corporation.

FIGURE 6.13 Configuration Screen of Windows Narrator

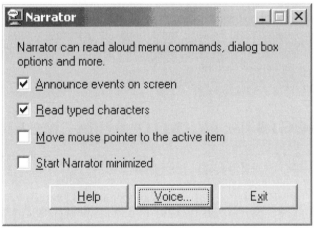

Note: Screen shot reprinted by permission from Microsoft Corporation.

with slight movements of the head, thumb, or toe, and the latter allows a person to control the computer through electrodes by moving his or her eyes.

Browser Compatibility

Different browsers may not have the same capability to display a particular type of document, and the same document may be displayed differently in different browsers. Some proprietary tools allow you to save a non-HTML document as a Web page. Such Web pages may be displayed as expected in some browsers, but appear distorted or even not appear at all in other browsers.

C A S E S T U D Y **Browser Differences Matter** ⋯⋯⋯⋯⋯⋯

● Instructors at Mid-State University have had some lessons in posting different types of HTML and non-HTML documents for Web access. Some instructors occasionally work on documents in Microsoft Word and then save the documents directly as Web pages and post them on the Web. The shortcut saves the instructor time and the documents usually show up fine in the major browsers, especially Microsoft Internet Explorer.

Microsoft Word XP also provides the option to save a document with images embedded as a single Web page (with the .mht extension). An MHT document will have the text and all the embedded images contained within one document, which is especially convenient if you need to show such pages in presentation at a conference or seminar without an Internet connection. One instructor placed an MHT document in WebCT for students to access. Those who used Microsoft Explorer were able to view the document without any problem. However, those who used Mozilla Firefox and Netscape saw the document displayed as a long scroll of text with markup tags. The two browsers couldn't recognize the MHT file extension and displayed the document as plain text in source view. The lesson learned is: Be careful in posting "Web pages" that are not created or saved in a standard HTML form.

CONTENT LEGIBILITY AND SALIENCE

To be of any instructional value, Web content must be legible to the learners. Learner perception of page content can be influenced by several factors: (a) type of objects, (b) color of page components, (c) size of page components, (d) location of page components, and (e) division of page layout. There are many ways to enhance legibility and content salience, including the use of colors, graphics, and text fonts. The use of graphics will be covered in chapter 7. In this chapter, we will focus on the use of color and text fonts.

Foreground and Background Contrast

A primary use of color in Web pages is to achieve a foreground and background contrast to enhance text legibility. In general, dark text against a light background usually provides better content legibility than light text against a light background. Light text against dark backgrounds may offer acceptable legibility, but do not print well.

In addition to enhancing legibility, background and foreground contrast is also used to highlight key points, distinguish certain parts of the page, and direct learner attention. Used appropriately, color can be an easy and effective method to make important parts of page content stand out. For example, we can color text to distinguish headings, titles, and keywords. When data are dis-

FIGURE 6.14 **Colors Used to Delimit Data Boundaries**

Colleges	2000	2001	2002	2003
BIS	1,320	1,380	1,360	1,350
Education	1,200	1,230	1,250	1,250
Engineering	860	900	930	910
Liberal Arts	1,100	1,170	1,190	1,200
Natural Sciences	810	860	880	870

played in tabular format, we can set different colors for table columns, rows, or even cells to separate one part from another (see Figure 6.14).

Color Associations

Colors of text and page background are very easy to set and adjust. Many authors like to use a variety of colors to enhance the perception of Web page content. But colors also have meanings. Throughout human evolution, color has acquired perceptive, affective, and cultural associations with the natural environment and social activities. For example, the association of cold with blue and the association of warm with orange or red are most likely to have derived from our perceptions of the natural environment. Color preferences can also vary with other factors such as age, gender, seasons, and geographic locations. Children generally prefer warm, bright colors. As one becomes more mature, cooler colors with less saturation and more subtlety tend to be preferred (Heinich, Molenda, Russell, & Smaldino, 2002). When designing color schemes for instructional materials, you should consider the affective and cultural influences different colors might have on learners in relation to instructional context. For example, a warm color scheme may be more appropriate for active, dynamic, intense learning activities, whereas a cool color scheme might better fit more contemplative, reflective, thoughtful learning activities.

In **hypertext,** the default color scheme for hyperlinks is: (a) bright blue for an unvisited link, (b) red for an active link (when the mouse moves over it and clicks), and (c) dark purple for a visited link. Since this color scheme is a convention that almost every Web user knows, we should be cautious if we want to use an unconventional color scheme of hyperlinks since that may make it difficult for some users to recognize the hyperlinks. Another caution to keep in mind is the visibility of hyperlinks against the background. If a Web page has a dark background, visited links in default color (dark purple) can become very hard to see. Some Web developers choose to make the visited links on their pages appear grayed out. This is not user-friendly, because it makes it harder for users to see what content they have previously visited. Because hyperlinks are underlined by default, we should avoid underlining nonlinked text. The Companion Website of the book has some examples of color usage in hypermedia.

TEXT LAYOUT AND LEGIBILITY

Even with the increasing use of graphics in Web development, text is still more important than graphics in Web-based instructional content. Appropriate choice of text font and layout can help enhance text legibility, direct attention to different parts of text, set a tone (such as serious or lighthearted), and suggest an image (such as conservative or progressive) (Shuman, 2001). Figure 6.15 illustrates factors to consider in Web page design.

Text Line Length

Because Web pages are viewed in a browser window, Web page size must be examined in relation to the browser window size. By default, an HTML page is displayed to the full width of a browser window. Users' computer display screen resolution can vary, however, so the actual page width they see also varies accordingly. At this time, the resolution of some computer screens can

FIGURE 6.15   Text Layout and Legibility

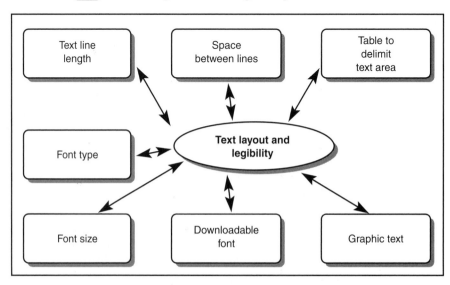

be as wide as 1,600 pixels. Horizontal reading of continuous text lines across such a page width can be very tiring for the eye. A text line across a 1,400-pixel screen can contain over 110 characters or about 25 words. This is far more than the generally recommended text line length, which is between 50 and 70 characters; or roughly between 7 and 15 words (Powell, 2000). Exceedingly long lines of text can make it hard for the reader to scan text or to correctly pick up the next line of text. If the pages are intended to be printed out and read, the browser window width is usually not an issue, because the print page width can adjust automatically to fit the width of the paper. However, if the pages are intended to be read on the screen, we should control the text line length.

A popular method of controlling the length of text lines is to put text in an HTML table and adjust the width of the table or the table cells. HTML table width can be relative or fixed. You set the relative table width by specifying a percentage value (such as 90%) relative to the browser window width. A table with relative width will expand and shrink in accordance with the browser window width. This is therefore not an effective method of controlling text line length, because the line length can vary with the browser window width. In contrast, fixed table width is set by specifying the number of pixels for the width property of the table. A table with fixed width will retain its width regardless of the browser window size. If the table width is set to be 900 pixels and the user browser window is only 800 pixels wide, the table will extend beyond the right border of the browser window, and the reader will have to scroll to the right to see the complete table. To avoid the horizontal scrolling problem, set the table width no wider than the browser window that the majority of your readers have.

Currently, the trend in computer screen size is to move from 800×600 pixels to 1024×768 pixels. However, many people are still viewing Web pages at a resolution of 800×600 pixels. In many less developed rural areas, smaller screen size is not uncommon. If you want to have your pages viewed by the majority of your readers without scrolling, you may need to cater to the lower end of resolutions. You can also conduct a survey to find out what kind of screen resolution your users have. If you have team members who know JavaScript, you can use JavaScript to detect your readers' screen resolutions and adjust your page display accordingly. Because browser window borders take up some space, you should set your Web page to about 760 pixels wide if you want the pages to be displayed without the need to scroll on a 800×600 pixels screen.

Table to Delimit Text Area

A table is a common tool for allocation content in a Web page. When you place text in a table cell that has visible borders, you may need to control the space between the text and the table borders. By default, the border of a table is usually visible and cell padding value (empty space inserted between the border and the text) is usually zero when a table is created. This setting will cause text to stick to the left border of the table, making reading difficult (you can see an example in Figure 6.16). This issue is important for the instructors authoring Web courses in the MSU IS program, since tables are used frequently in many of their courses to organize and present data.

We can make the table border invisible by setting the table border property to zero, but often this is not enough because the text can still stick to the contents in the neighboring cells. To fix the problem, we need to have some padding between the contents of a cell and the cell border. Figure 6.17 gives an example.

Space Between Lines

Text display on a computer screen is harder to read than in print, especially long paragraphs. Breaking a long text into short paragraphs has been found to make reading easier. In addition, it is usually helpful to provide some extra line spacing (leading) in text in a Web page. The print convention is to set line spacing to about one-third to one-half over the type size. If you use a 12-point font, the line spacing should be at least 18 point. In Web pages, we can use Cascading Style Sheet (CSS) to set line spacing through the line-height property. CSS also supports adjusting letter spacing and word spacing, which can be useful in large headings or titles with gaps between certain letter combinations. However, reducing letter spacing generally is not recommended for body text.

FIGURE 6.16   Text Stuck to Table Border

Table border and cell padding. When you set up a table in a Web page editor, the border of the table is usually visible by default and cell padding value is usually zero. This setting will cause text to stick to the left border of the table, making reading difficult. We can make the table border invisible by setting the table border property to be zero, but this is often not enough because the text can still stick to the content in neighboring cells. To fix the problem, we need to have some padding between the content in a cell and the cell border.

FIGURE 6.17   Padding Moves Text Away from Table Border

Table border and cell padding. When you set up a table in a Web page editor, the border of the table is usually visible by default and cell padding value is usually zero. This setting will cause text to stick to the left border of the table, making reading difficult. We can make the table border invisible by setting the table border property to be zero, but this is often not enough because the text can still stick to the content in neighboring cells. To fix the problem, we need to have some padding between the content in a cell and the cell border.

Font Type

Legibility can be affected by the choice of particular fonts. Because Web text is displayed in a users browser window, if a font specified in a Web page is not available on the client's system, the user's browser will use a substitute. A substitute font can have unexpected effects on a Web page display, such as taking up more line space, causing different wrapping of text, distorting content arrangement, and so forth. Here are a few guidelines generally recommended for ensuring appropriate text font display:

1. Specify a font set that lists several fonts in sequence so the browser can select the next one if the previous font is unavailable. For example <FONT FACE="Verdana, Helvetica, Geneva">. . . </FONT> or <FONT FACE= "Times New Roman, Times, serif">. . . </FONT> or <FONT FACE="Courier New, Courier, mono">. . . </FONT>.

2. Avoid specifying uncommon fonts. Common fonts that are installed on most computers are Times Roman, Arial, Verdana, and Helvetica.

3. Specify a font family to be used just in case none of the specified fonts are available. For example: <FONT FACE="Verdana, Helvetica, sans serif">. . . </FONT>. Almost any computer will have at least two font families: serif and sans serif.

4. Use GIF or JPEG graphics to display certain text, because graphics are independent of the font support of client browsers.

Downloadable Font

To make sure that a specified font is used in a Web page, the major browser vendors have developed their own versions of downloadable fonts. Microsoft's solution is called OpenType, an extension of the TrueType format that has been jointly developed by Microsoft and Adobe. It allows fonts to contain either TrueType or PostScript data, or both. OpenType promises to make font development and use much easier. You can visit Microsoft's typography site (www.microsoft.com/typography) to learn more about OpenType. To help users implement Microsoft's dynamic fonts, Microsoft has developed a tool called Web Embedding Fonts Tool (WEFT). You can get the tool and relevant usage information from Microsoft's typography site.

Netscape's solution, called Dynamic Fonts, is based on TrueDoc (www.truedoc.com). To use Netscape's downloadable fonts, we need to include a link to a Netscape font definition file in Portable Font Resource (PFR) format. Use the <LINK> tag to set the REL attribute to fontdef and the SRC attribute to the URL where the font definition file is located. The <LINK> tag is placed within the head section of the HTML document.

```
<LINK REL="fontdef" SRC="http://www.myschool.edu/fonts/customfont.pfr">
```

Graphic Text

Graphic text is an option when strict control of text font type and size is needed. Graphic text is often appropriate for headings and buttons. Even when downloadable font technology becomes mature, graphic text will be still useful to achieve some special effects, such as dynamic rollover in response to mouse movement or action. When using graphic text, we need to be aware that the same size of text font is usually not as sharp in graphic as in plain text, especially when antialiasing (edge smoothing) is applied.

Font Size

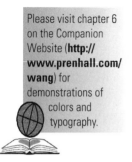

Please visit chapter 6 on the Companion Website (**http://www.prenhall.com/wang**) for demonstrations of colors and typography.

There are seven font sizes in HTML ranging from 1 to 7. If not specified by the page author or customized by the user, the default font size in an HTML page is 3, and the size range will roughly correspond to the point sizes shown in Table 6.1.

However, font size may not be displayed exactly as specified because the user can change his or her browser setting to increase or decrease font size when viewing the text. In Microsoft Internet Explorer 6, the font size can be changed by selecting one of five text sizes (largest, larger, medium, smaller, and smallest) from the View menu. In Mozilla Firefox, the user can also increase or decrease font size from the menu bar as shown in Figure 6.18.

TABLE 6.1   **Font Sizes Compared with Point Sizes**

<FONT SIZE="n">	Point size
1	8
2	10
3	12
4	14
5	18
6	24
7	36

FIGURE 6.18   Font Size Adjustment in Mozilla Firefox 1.0

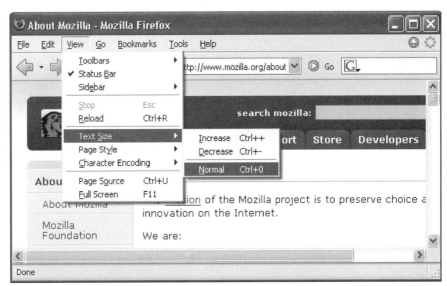

Note: Screen shot reprinted by permission from the Mozilla Organization.

PAGE LAYOUT AND NAVIGATION

Some page layout conventions have evolved since the birth of the World Wide Web. If a page is left and top aligned, the top is usually reserved for placing a title banner, plus some top-level links. If there are no top headings, the left side of the screen is often the place for headings. When there are two or three levels of content, the top and left sides of the page are commonly used to present headings and subheadings, respectively.

Frameset and Frames

A hierarchical content organization can be conveniently structured in hypermedia by using frames. A frameset is a framework that contains two or more frames and takes up the complete browser window space. Each frame contains a Web page. You can include any single Web page in a frame, whether the page is stored locally or on a remote server, by specifying the URL of the page. The frameset in Figure 6.19 contains three frames.

One useful characteristic of frames is that a hyperlink in a frame can retrieve and display the target document in any frame within the frameset or in a new browser window. The frame tag has the attribute TARGET that lets you specify in which frame the linked document should be displayed. To display a page in any other frame within the same frameset, each frame must have a

FIGURE 6.19 **A Frameset of Three Frames and Sample Script**

Top Frame	
Left Frame	**Main Frame**

```
<FRAMESET ROWS="50,*" >
   <FRAME NAME="top" TARGET="leftMenu"
   SRC="http://www.homepages.dsu.edu/mysite/frameset1.htm">
   <FRAMESET COLS="150,*">
      <FRAME NAME="leftMenu" TARGET="main" SRC="menu1.htm">
      <FRAME NAME="main" SRC="content1.htm">
   </FRAMESET>
</FRAMESET>
```

name different from the names of other frames. The name will be used as the value for the TARGET attribute. Figure 6.19 displays the sample script for the frameset shown in the figure.

In a frameset environment like that of Figure 6.19, the top frame page typically remains unchanged. Each link in the top frame will send a new page (most likely a submenu) to the left frame. In turn, each link in the left frame will send a new document to the main frame.

Using frames in hypermedia has been controversial. There are advantages and disadvantages in using frames. As we mentioned earlier, the primary advantage is that a hierarchical navigation scheme can be maintained wherever the visitor goes within the site. The consistent presence of a content overview and the ease of navigating through the levels and parts of the whole structure are particularly helpful in presenting complex topics that involve many levels and many facets, such as the topic of environmental protection.

Apart from navigation concerns, in some situations we may not want to encourage our users to bookmark some of our URLs. For example, more and more Web content today is dynamically generated based on updated data and user input. If this is the case with your course site, you may not want people to bookmark these URLs, since these URLs are pointing to scripts that are expected to return different content each time they are requested, or they may even return error messages if the scripts require some user input and the bookmark does not contain the required input. In addition, users may have difficulty

Please visit chapter 6 on the Companion Website (**http://www.prenhall.com/wang**) for demonstration of the use of frames to facilitate navigation.

FIGURE 6.20   Bookmark Options in Internet Explorer 6

Note: Screen shot reprinted by permission from Microsoft Corporation.

in bookmarking a frame page, because the URL displayed in the site address box of the user's browser is that of the frameset, rather than that of a content page.

Another complaint is about the difficulty in printing a content page. What is printed is often the frameset, which contains nothing but the frameset information.

There are easy solutions to get around these constraints. To bookmark a frame page in Microsoft Internet Explorer 6 and Netscape Navigator 7, right mouse click on the frame and select the appropriate option from the context menu (see Figure 6.20).

To print a frame page, you can simply select the frame page by clicking anywhere on the page and then click the print button on the browser. In Microsoft Internet Explorer, you can right mouse click on the frame page and select Print from the popup menu.

These little tricks for manipulating frame pages may not be well known, and some learners may not like taking extra steps to file bookmarks or print. So as Web designers, you need to be cautious about using frames. First, remember that a frameset should be used for facilitating navigation, not for page layout. For page layout, use CSS or HTML tables instead. Second, remember that frameset convention is that hyperlinks in smaller frames send the linked documents to larger frames. Conventionally, the top frame sends linked documents to the left frame, and the left frame sends documents to the central main frame. Finally, avoid including a third party page in one of your frames, making it appear as if it is your own page, because this can violate copyright and intellectual property laws unless you have permission from the page owner.

Grouping and Listing

Grouping is an important method of content allocation and organization in hypermedia, because a Web page often contains more than one group of content. With headings and subheadings, grouping also facilitates content scanning. Grouping can be based on (a) topics or subject areas, (b) organizational units (such as departments or offices), (c) functions or tasks (such as search by e-mail, name, or location), and (d) types of audience. Gestalt theory (Wertheimer, 1959) offers us a useful framework in grouping content in a Web page.

Page Length

According to Nielsen (1999), 90% of users do not scroll pages; instead, they simply pick from the visible options. This tendency has somewhat changed since Nielsen's study because Web users have become more experienced and know that there are sometimes important links further down the page. Nevertheless, it is evident that users still tend to evaluate the content of the initial screen first before moving on to read more of the page. If you want to let a page scroll, make sure that the important items are displayed on the initial screen either as a list of headings or a list of links with internal anchors.

However, acknowledging users' tendency to avoid scrolling does not mean that we should not have long pages at all. The decision about page size should be based on the nature of page content and user needs. In their *Web Style Guide,* Lynch and Horton (1999) suggest that short pages work well for the home page and menu pages that users scan for hyperlink choices, and longer pages may work well for destination pages where related content can be read with more coherence and better continuation.

Chapter Summary

In this chapter, we have explored utilizing hypermedia for knowledge construction. We have also described common navigation structures and their possible applications for different subject matters. Some guidelines are offered for providing navigational guidance in instructional hypermedia. The issues of Web accessibility are discussed with reference to both general user needs and legal requirements. A few basic methods are introduced that can help improve accessibility of Web content. The chapter finally elaborates on using color, text font, and page layout to enhance the legibility and readability of Web content.

Review Questions

1. Do you think designing and providing a template is a good approach for helping less experienced instructors start learning instructional hypermedia design? Why?

2. Hypermedia can let us organize the knowledge of a subject domain with great flexibility. Pick a subject domain that you are knowledgeable about and draft an organization structure that would be most appropriate for presenting content in that domain.

3. Accessibility is not only a usability issue but also a legal issue for Web-based instructional content provided by any federally funded institution. However, achieving and maintaining a satisfactory level of accessibility for all course content can consume a lot of resources. What approach do you think we should take in following the accessibility requirements?

4. Spacing and paragraphing is necessary for facilitating text reading and scanning on the computer screen. However, spacing and paragraphing can make text appear "chunky" or fragmented. What can we do to avoid or reduce possible fragmentation?

Summary of Tips

1. Encourage students to use hypermedia as a learning tool to search for information, organize data, and present ideas.

2. Combine linear, hierarchical, and referential link structures to form an optimal navigation scheme in instructional hypermedia.

3. Avoid having more than four levels in a hierarchical navigation scheme.

4. Use cascading paths to help learners see and trace their learning paths.

5. Use context cues in hypermedia to help learners find their way in navigation.

6. Use Cascading Style Sheet (CSS) to promote interface consistency and variation in hypermedia.

7. Use a modular approach in content development to facilitate connectivity among modules and promote module reusability.

8. Use a light background and dark foreground for optimal text legibility.

9. Provide more space between lines for reading text displayed on the computer screen.

10. Provide more paragraphing for easier reading and scanning of text on a computer screen.

11. Control text line length on the computer screen to less than 80 characters.

12. Use browser frames to facilitate hierarchical content organization and navigation. Avoid using frames for page layout.

Exercises

1. Explain the information attributes of hypermedia and their potential benefits for learning.

2. Identify difficulties learners typically experience in navigating hypermedia.

3. Summarize the use of various navigational cues to facilitate user orientation in hypermedia.

4. Summarize the basic requirements of Web accessibility and the methods of meeting the basic requirements.

5. Summarize and apply various ways to enhance content legibility and reader perception.

6. Suppose you are assigned to teach a freshman English composition course (or a course in your field of teaching) online. Think about the navigation scheme you would use for the course site and draw a diagram of your design. Are you going to organize the course content in a chronological line and let students access the materials strictly in that time sequence? Does any of the course content have a knowledge structure that requires hierarchical organization and presentation? Should each subsequent unit be based on the mastery of previous units? Should the students be allowed to preview forthcoming units? Should there be cross-references between content units? If external resources need to be linked from within the course content, where should they be placed?

7. For the course you have chosen to teach online, develop a plan to break the course content into modules of appropriate scope and size for optimal linkage in the hypermedia environment.

8. Develop a few Web pages with graphics and tables. Ask someone with knowledge of the Americans with Disabilities Act (ADA) or someone who is visually impaired to test the pages with a screen reader.

9. Play with different combinations of text and page background colors and record your perceptions of their legibility. Invite your colleagues and friends to view the pages and tell you their perceptions.

10. Create a few Web pages with different paragraph lengths and different lengths of text line. Invite your colleagues and friends to view the pages and tell you which pages are easier to read, including scanning.

11. Design an instructional content module in hypermedia that describes an object or phenomenon, illustrates a procedure, or introduces a concept or organization. The module should have at least nine pages, organized into three levels, with a top-level home page, at least two second-level pages, and at least four third-level pages. The top-level page has links to all second-level pages. Each second-level page has links to the top-level home page and related third-level pages. Each third-level page has links to the top-level page and related second-level pages. The links on the third-level pages should be in breadcrumb trail (path) form.

12. Use a frameset to develop a content module focusing on a complex topic such as environmental protection. The frameset should consist of three frames: top banner, left menu, and main content frame. The top banner frame has top-level topic links, such as air pollution, land erosion, and water pollution. Each topic link in the top banner opens a corresponding menu page in the left menu frame. For instance, the link on air pollution opens a menu page that has subtopics such as global warming, ozone layer depletion, auto emissions, and so on. Each subtopic in the menu pages is a link that opens a content page about that specific subtopic in the main content frame.

Resources on the Web

Hypermedia design is difficult to describe on paper. In the Companion Website (www.prenhall.com/wang) for this book, we have included some samples to illustrate issues involved in instructional hypermedia. Web resources are more dynamic and change frequently. Please visit the Companion Website for a more inclusive and updated list of Web resources.

- Style Guide from the World Wide Web Consortium (www.w3.org/Style/).

- WWW Style Manual from Yale Medical School (info.med.yale.edu/caim/manual/).

- Section 508 of the Rehabilitation Act: Electronic and Information Technology Accessibility Standards (www.access-board.gov/508.htm).

- The usability site from the National Cancer Institute (www.usability.gov), which has sections on usability and accessibility basics and on how to design usable Web sites.

- Visualization and Usability Group from the National Institute of Standards and Technology (www.itl.nist.gov/iad/vvrg/index.html).

- The Usable Web (www.usableweb.com), which contains many links on Web usability.

References

Ausubel, D. P. (1966). *Educational psychology: A cognitive view.* New York: Holt, Rinehart & Winston.

Bransford, J., Barclay, J., & Franks, J. (1972). Sentence memory: A constructive versus interpretive approach. *Cognitive Psychology, 3,* 193–209.

Bransford, J., & Franks, J. (1971). The abstraction of linguistic ideas. *Cognitive Psychology, 2,* 331–350.

Center for Applied Special Technology (1996, October 17). On-line use is pupil's gain. *USA Today,* p. 1D.

Dede, C. (1996). Emerging technologies and distributed learning. *American Journal of Distance Education, 10*(2), 4–36.

Dede, C. J., & Palumbo, D. (1991). Implications of hypermedia for cognition and communication. *International Association for Impact Assessment Bulletin, 9,* 15–28.

Dee-Lucas, D. (1996). Effects of overview structure on study strategies and text representations for instructional hypertext. In J. F. Rouet, J. J. Levonen, A. Dillon, & R. J. Spiro (Eds.), *Hypertext and cognition* (pp. 73–108). Mahwah, NJ: Lawrence Erlbaum Associates.

Dee-Lucas, D., & Larkin, J. H. (1992). *Text representation with traditional text and hypertext.* Pittsburgh: Carnegie Mellon University.

Fischer, P. M., & Mandl, H. (1990). Towards a psychophysics of hypermedia. In D. H. Jonassen & H. Mandl (Eds.), *Designing hypermedia for learning.* NATO ASI Series, Vol. 67. New York: Springer-Verlag.

Fleming, J. (1998). *Web navigation: Designing the user experience.* Sebastopol, CA: O'Reilly.

Heinich, R., Molenda, M., Russell, J. D., & Smaldino, S. E. (2002). *Instructional media and technologies for learning.* Upper Saddle River, NJ: Prentice Hall.

Jonassen, D. H. (1982). *The technology of text, principles for structuring, designing and displaying text.* Englewood Cliffs, NJ: Educational Technology Publications.

Jonassen, D. H. (2003). *Learning to solve problems with technology: A constructivist perspective.* Upper Saddle River, NJ: Merrill/Prentice Hall.

Kommers, P., Grabinger, S., & Dunlap, J. (Eds.). (1996). *Hypermedia learning environments: Instructional design and integration.* Mahwah, NJ: Lawrence Erlbaum Associates.

Lynch, P. J. & Horton, S. (1999). *Web style guide: Basic design principles for creating Web sites.* New Haven, CT: Yale University Press.

Nielsen, J. (1999). *The top ten new mistakes of Web design.* Retrieved March 16, 2002, from http://www.useit.com/alertbox/990530.html.

Nielsen, J. (2000a). *Designing web usability.* Indianapolis, IN: New Riders.

Nielsen, J. (2000b). *Is navigation useful?* Retrieved March 16, 2002, from http://www.useit.com/alertbox/20000109.html.

Norman, D. (1983). Some observations on mental models. In D. Gentner & A. Stevens (Eds.), *Mental models.* Hillsdale, NJ: Lawrence Erlbaum Associates.

Norman, D., Gentner, S., & Stevens, A. (1976). Comments on learning schemata and memory representation. In D. Klahr (Ed.), *Cognition and instruction.* Hillsdale, NJ: Lawrence Erlbaum Associates.

Powell, T. A. (2000). *Web design: The complete reference.* Berkeley, CA: Osborne.

Reigeluth, C. M. (1999). What is instructional design theory and how is it changing? In C. M. Reigeluth (Ed.), *Instructional-design theories and models: A new paradigm of instructional theory* (Vol. II, pp. 5–30). Mahwah, NJ: Lawrence Erlbaum Associates.

Reigeluth, C. M., & Stein, F. S. (1983). The elaboration theory of instruction. In C. M. Reigeluth (Ed.), *Instructional-design theories and models: An overview of their current status* (pp. 335–381). Mahwah, NJ: Lawrence Erlbaum Associates.

Rouet, J. F., and Levonen, J. J. (1996). An introduction to hypertext and cognition. In Rouet, J. F., Levonen, J. J., Dillon, A., & Spiro, R. J. (Eds.), *Hypertext and cognition,* p. 10. Mahwah, NJ: Lawrence Erlbaum Associates.

Rumelhart, D. (1977). *Introduction to human information processing.* New York: John Wiley & Sons.

Shuman, J. E. (2001). *Multimedia concepts.* Boston: Course Technology.

Spiro, R., Feltovich, P., Jacobson, M., & Coulson, R. (1991). Cognitive flexibility, constructivism, and hypertext: Random access instruction for advanced knowledge acquisition in ill-structured domains. *Educational Technology, May,* 24–33.

Wertheimer, M. (1959). *Productive thinking* (Enlarged Ed.). New York: Harper & Row.

Yang, C. S., & Moore, D. M. (1996). Designing hypermedia systems for instruction. *Educational Technology Systems, 24,* 3–30.

Chapter 7

Multimedia for Web-Based Instruction

CHAPTER INTRODUCTION

Media have always been closely related to instruction, whether classroom-based or online. The new medium of the Web makes it possible to provide learning opportunities for those learners who otherwise cannot attend campus classes due to location and time constraints. When the World Wide Web first came into being, there was little multimedia use over the Internet because of bandwidth constraints and limited computer processing power. As broadband Internet connection becomes increasingly available and data compression technology advances, multimedia applications are becoming more feasible in Web-based instruction (WBI). However, even with the increasing accessibility, multimedia applications are still costly to develop and deliver. To use reasonably affordable multimedia for instructional purposes, we need to have a good understanding of multimedia attributes and the basic requirements and constraints for implementing multimedia in WBI. This chapter will:

1. Briefly review the literature on media attributes and the debate on media effects on learning.

2. Inquire into the functions of visuals and their possible instructional applications.

3. Discuss the appeals and constraints of audio for WBI.

4. Explore the instructional functions of video.

5. Introduce some popular technologies for making digital video and creating virtual reality.

LEARNING OBJECTIVES

After studying this chapter, the reader will be able to:

1. Present the information attributes of media in light of their effects on information processing and learning.

2. Identify possible hindering effects of inappropriately combined multimedia, taking the instructional context into consideration.

3. Classify the use of visuals from their functional perspectives.

156

4. Identify potential benefits and common constraints in using audio for Web-based instruction.

5. Outline the common digital audio formats currently available.

6. Summarize the primary benefits and common constraints in using video for Web-based instruction.

7. Outline the common digital video formats currently available.

8. Explain the concept of streaming media and understand the common streaming technologies currently available.

9. Present the basics of common technologies for creating digital animation and virtual reality.

10. Recognize the value of print text and appropriate ways of delivering printable content for Web-based instruction.

DO MEDIA MATTER?

The question about interaction between media and learning is not new. Artists and scholars have observed the human perception of media effects on learning over the centuries. The Roman poet Horace (65 B.C.–8 B.C.), in his *Art of Poetry,* observed that "the mind is more slowly stirred by the ear than by the eye." A chief advocate of media, Marshall McLuhan (1967), argued that all media are extensions of some human faculty, psychic or physical, and societies have always been shaped more by the nature of the media than by the content of the communication. The modern behaviorist views learning as reaction to external stimuli and therefore believes in the availability of "one best medium" for learning tasks in general. In language teaching, the audio-lingual and direct methods are heavily influenced by the behaviorist view. But behavioral learning is criticized for its inadequate attention to the information attributes of content, the role of the learner's prior knowledge, and the learner's ability to apply knowledge and skills to new contexts. This dissatisfaction with the behavioral approach to learning has led to the growth of the cognitive approach.

Opponents of media importance do not believe that media affect learning. This extreme view holds that media do not have any effects on learning under any conditions; it is the instructional method that counts (Clark, 1983). Jamison, Suppes, and Wells (1974) conducted an extensive survey of studies that compared traditional instruction with instruction via computers, television, and radio. Their survey concluded that "no significant difference" was the typical outcome of the comparison of the two forms of instruction. However, confounding variables and design problems have been identified in these media comparison studies. It was found that the typical experiment comparing the effectiveness of one medium with another was actually a study of different technologies (Salomon, 1974). The media were used as mere "conveyances for the

C A S E   S T U D Y ···

> ● The MSU Information Systems master's program used to deliver its courses to distance students through a statewide interactive videoconferencing network (IVN) with satellite sites distributed across the state, linking all higher educational institutions and K–12 school districts. As MSU moves courses online to make the program Web based, the program administrators and faculty would like to retain as much of the multimedia interactivity offered by the IVN as possible. The faculty would also like to explore additional multimedia capabilities offered by current technologies to enhance content presentation, class communication, and student comprehension, including data-driven graph, digital audio, digital video, computer simulations, digital moviemaking, and asynchronous video streaming. In planning and designing the Web delivery of the IS courses, instructors may ask:
>
> 1. Would the use of visuals be helpful in presenting the course content? If yes, what kind of visuals, realistic representations or selective, symbolic drawings? Will static images be adequate? Is animation needed?
>
> 2. Does any course need the support of charts and diagrams? If yes, what types of tools are available?
>
> 3. Does any course involve procedural knowledge that would be better demonstrated through computer screen action capturing?
>
> 4. Are there any publicly available videos that can be used as primary or supplementary course content?
>
> 5. Are any instructors planning to use digital video for their courses? If yes, is video really necessary? Will audio recording plus some still images meet their needs?
>
> 6. If digital video is going to be used, should it be streaming video, on-demand download, or CD-R to distribute the video?
>
> 7. Is any computer simulation needed?

treatments" (Clark & Salomon, 1986). In other words, most media comparison studies were done with a particular medium as a tool, not on the information attributes and cognitive effects of the medium (Clark & Salomon, 1986). In a more recent report by Tom Russell (1999) based on an extensive metadata analysis, learning outcomes from technology-supported alternative forms of education were found to be similar to the learning outcomes of traditional on-campus learning. However, similar confounding problems were also found in these studies.

In discussing media applications in learning, we need to ask some important questions: Do different media have different effects on learning? How does the use of multimedia differ perceptually and cognitively from the use of a single medium? And how does simultaneous use of multimedia differ from separate use of multimedia?

Media Attributes and Effects on Learning

Cognitive researchers observe that different media have different symbolic attributes (Mayer, 2001; Moreno & Mayer, 1999; Salomon, 1979) or information "bias," which can play a crucial role in revealing and communicating unique aspects of reality (Carpenter, 1960; Meringoff, 1980). Information bias can be so unique that information coded within one medium may not be fully recoded in another without losing some of its features. A simple demonstration is to challenge anyone who doubts this proposition to convey the content of a musical performance in verbal expression. The proposition can be demonstrated in other daily experiences. For example, what we can perceive from a weather forecast on television is not the same as what we get by listening to the same message on radio. Similarly, the perceptions we have when watching a movie based on a novel are usually different from the perceptions we have when reading the book. Such differences in perception are believed to be due to the different mental processes and skills involved in the information encoding and decoding processes (Salomon, 1974). From an instructional perspective, these information attributes or biases can suggest important guidelines in developing course materials and designing learning activities. If information encoded into different media requires different decoding activities, then relevant cognitive skills would be needed and training required for extracting the embedded information (Clark & Salomon, 1986; Olson & Bruner, 1974).

Multimedia versus Single Medium

Rather than focusing on differentiating effects of different media, some educators call attention to the use of multimedia versus a single medium. General findings indicate that appropriately combined media can enhance learning, whereas inappropriately combined media can hinder learning. What determines appropriate versus inappropriate is usually based on whether visual, verbal, and audio sensors work together in a complementary or competing manner. If two media that require the same channel of sensory perception, such as image and text, are used simultaneously to present the same message in a redundant way, split attention can occur to hinder information processing. However, if two media are used in a way that complements perception rather than competes for attention, information processing may be facilitated. Moreno and Mayer (2002, 1999) found that the combination of pictures and audio narration is more effective than that of pictures and print (on-screen) text.

Media and Context

Many educational theorists and researchers argue that it is practically impossible to determine whether differences in learning outcomes are caused by the differences in media or methodology, considering the fact that media and methods are inseparable. In a well-designed instructional situation, a medium's capabilities enable the chosen methods and the methods that are used take advantage of the medium capabilities (Mayer, 2001). To understand the role of media in learning, we must conduct our studies in the contexts of the cognitive and social processes by which learning takes place (Kosma, 1994). From an instructional point of view, Salomon (1974) describes four interacting factors that could determine the effectiveness of an instructional event with a particular medium, and observes that it is in the overlapping area of the four factors that instructional effectiveness of media can be maximized. The four factors are:

1. The extent to which the medium affects particular mental activities

2. The extent to which the event leads to the extraction of the critical information from the medium

3. The match between the medium and the requirements of the instructional task

4. The match between the medium and the characteristics of the learner

Media capabilities have greatly evolved since the time of the studies reviewed by Clark (1983), particularly since the birth of the World Wide Web. Chris Dede (1996) contends that how a medium shapes its users and its message is a crucial issue in understanding the transformation of traditional distance education into hypermedia-based distributed learning.

FUNCTIONS OF VISUALS

A visual representation is more likely to catch our attention because our eyes are more easily drawn to an image than by a line of text. The visual aspect of information processing is so pervasive in our perception of the world that we use the word "see" in English to mean comprehension or knowledge. We place so much trust in our visual perception that we use it as a truth judgment criterion: "seeing is believing." Such a trust is not language-specific; similar sayings can be found in other languages as well.

The advent of the electronic age has fundamentally changed the role visual media play in our life. Television has greatly advanced the popularity of visual information dissemination. The advancement of personal computers has

FIGURE 7.1   Functions of Visuals

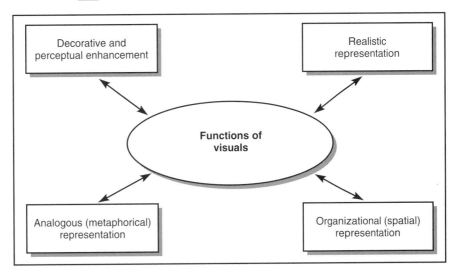

given us increasingly powerful and user-friendly applications for graphic creation and distribution. With some training, anyone can manage to use graphic
tools to create and edit digital images, generate data-driven charts and diagrams, create publishable drawings and paintings, and produce digital videos.
On top of all, the World Wide Web has made the distribution of visual data easier than ever before, across the world to large groups of audiences.

We all know that visuals are often more effective than words to express an
idea or arouse emotion. All visuals bear some resemblance to what they represent. The resemblance ranges from true-to-life realism to simplistic abstraction or metaphorical association. The fundamental nature of visuals is that they
are iconic; and the primary value of visuals is their capacity to convey information that cannot be coded verbally (Gombrich, 1974).

Functionally, visuals can be categorized into four groups (see Figure 7.1):
decoration and perceptual enhancement, realistic representation, analogous
and metaphoric representation, and organizational representation.

Decoration and Perceptual Enhancement

The most elementary use of visuals is for decoration and perceptual enhancement. Common techniques include appropriate color contrast between figure
and ground (foreground and background) to make content stand out; and
combined use of colors, lines, shapes, and space to orient attention and interconnect or separate parts of content through alignment, allocation, contiguity,
and orientation. Figure 7.2 is an example of using gradient and shape to direct
attention to the title of the page.

FIGURE 7.2 Using Gradient and Shape to Direct Attention

New Employee Orientation

Start

FIGURE 7.3 Icons of Direct Resemblance

Note: Screen shot reprinted by permission from Microsoft Corporation.

Chapter 6 has a detailed discussion on the appropriate use of colors and directional visuals to enhance digital text legibility and facilitate learner navigation of Web content.

Realistic Representation

Realistic paintings and photographs are mostly used to represent context, environment, and scenes from real life. Realism not only enhances content authenticity, but also facilitates content mapping. Most of us have experienced viewing a photo that was taken years ago on vacation and recalling many details of the trip. Such recollections usually do not occur as easily with verbal stimuli. The matching between realistic depiction and what is stored in the brain as visual memory activates quick responses and associations. Invoking quick response and association with realistic visuals is similar to using icons as shortcuts to represent frequently performed functions and tasks in the computer-user interface, such as selecting paragraph alignment, bullet lists, or boldface type (see Figure 7.3).

Realistic visuals generally need to include enough details to make the representation look real, like what you see in daily life (see Figure 7.4).

With the increasing popularity of digital cameras and scanners, realistic capturing and representation of scenes from real life has become very easy. Activities and events captured from student activities, field trips, or daily life can serve as authentic materials to provide contexts or present scenarios for varied instructional tasks. Some students in the MSU IS program use digital cameras to capture scenes of the workplace where they complete their internships and use the photos in their reports and presentations.

Although realistic depiction can give the viewer a feeling of authenticity, excessive realistic details can be a major hindrance in some cases. Irrelevant details tend to distract attention and obscure the focus of information. Extra-

FIGURE **7.4** **A Realistic Representation**

FIGURE **7.5** **Selective Encoding to Show the Bone Structure**

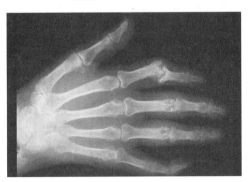

Please visit chapter 7 on the Companion Website (**http://www.prenhall.com/wang**) for some visual examples of color and action.

neous details in realistic representation can add to the cognitive load. To highlight important points and minimize possible distractions, it is often necessary to be selective in graphic encoding. Selective encoding can make the most relevant parts stand out, remove coverings, eliminate interfering details, and highlight or even exaggerate characteristics (see Figures 7.5 and 7.6).

Selective encoding and representation can be found in all fields of study. However, be careful when using selective encoding because oversimplified representation can make recognition difficult. Dwyer (1978) proposes a curvilinear

FIGURE 7.6 **A Selective Drawing versus a Realistic Picture of a Computer Hard Drive**

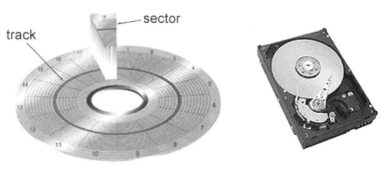

FIGURE 7.7 **Icons of Metaphoric Representation**

Note: Screen shot reprinted by permission from Microsoft Corporation.

continuum to describe the relationship between the amount of realism and the ease of recognition, and suggests that either too much or too little realism can affect recognition and information processing. Horn (1999) notes that recognizing a graphic representation depends on context, frequency of usage, and scope of usage. This observation is particularly relevant when we use analogous and metaphorical graphic representations.

Analogous and Metaphorical Representation

In some cases, direct resemblance may not be applicable or conducive to visual perception and cognition, particularly in situations where easy recognition is needed. Using an analogous or metaphorical representation can usually speed up recognition and response by removing less relevant details and highlighting the prominent characteristics of an object or phenomenon. Examples of such usage include traffic and road signs, icons in the computer-user interface, badges, emblems, flags, and logos. Figure 7.7 shows the icons in the computer-user interface that signify the functions of hyperlink, refresh, undo and redo.

Sometimes, it may be hard to tell whether an image is more realistic or more metaphorical, particularly in graphic representations that are designed to appeal to emotions, such as advertisements and posters (see Figure 7.8).

FIGURE 7.8 Metaphorical and Realistic Image

Source: National Archives and Records Administration.

FIGURE 7.9   **Line Chart, Pie Chart, and 3-D Charts**

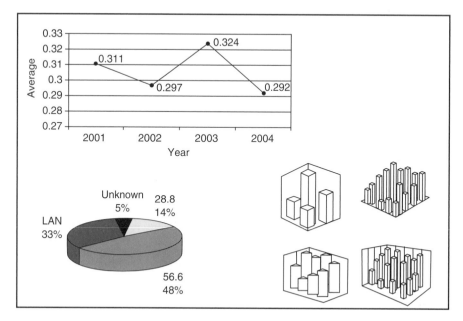

Organizational (Spatial) Representation

Analogous representation is often found in the form of charts and diagrams to focus on spatial resemblance and to illustrate procedural and quantitative relationships. Application examples include:

1. Pie chart to show proportional differences among comparable groups (Figure 7.9)

2. Line chart to show changes or developmental trends along a timeline (Figure 7.9)

3. 3-D chart to show multidimensional relationships (Figure 7.9)

4. Bar chart to show organizational or quantitative differences (Figure 7.10)

5. Flowchart to illustrate procedures

6. Diagram to describe organizational structures

As can be seen from the chart and bar examples, a minimal amount of text is usually integrated into organizational graphics to identify components and clarify relationships.

FIGURE 7.10 Bar Chart and Tabular Data Representation

Multiple Choice Questions | Quiz >> **midterm** | Student Count: 24 | **help**

cate	#	error frequency (red indicating error)	choices A	choices B	choices C	choices D	choices E	✔
1	1	1 — 23	23		1			A
1	2	24		24				B
1	3	12 — 12	12			12		D
1	4	24		24				B
1	5	3 — 21	3		21			C
1	6	14 — 10	9	5		10		D
1	7	3 — 21		1	21	2		C
1	8	24		24				B
1	9	2 — 22	2		22			C
1	10	24		24				B
1	11	5 — 19	3	19	2			B
1	12	24				24		D
1	13	17 — 7	4	6	3	7	4	D
1	14	8 — 16		8		16		D
1	15	4 — 20	1	1		20	2	D

Ⓒ A S E   S T U D Y   Diagrams as Visual Learning Aids ·············

For the students in the IS program at MSU, chart and diagram creation is one of the most needed visual applications in many of their courses. Charts are useful in analyzing and presenting data with quantitative differentiations. Diagrams are often effective visual aids to depict procedural and organizational relationships. These visuals are not only valuable instructional aids for the instructor but also great learning tools for the students to help them visually master instructional content and communicate their thoughts and ideas to others.

Many software tools are available for creating charts and diagrams. Microsoft Office Word includes a drawing tool that can be used to draw diagrams. Microsoft Excel can easily generate charts based on the data in a worksheet. When you select "Save as Web Pages" from the File menu, charts in Excel will be automatically converted to GIF images ready for Web use. More specialized graphic tools are also available for sophisticated drawings and chart or diagram creation, such as Adobe Illustrator, Microsoft Visio, and Inspiration. Visio is the selected high-end visual design tool for the IS program because of its IT-related features (see Figure 7.11).

FIGURE 7.11   Microsoft Visio

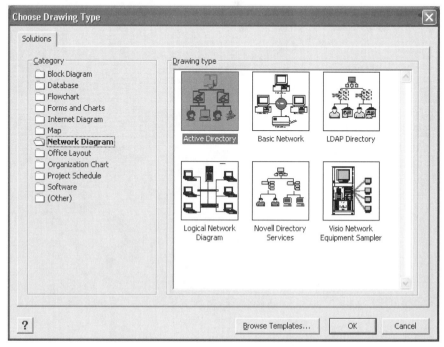

Note: Screen shot reprinted by permission from Microsoft Corporation.

AUDIO FOR WEB-BASED INSTRUCTION

Audio and video are often integrated, but audio can be used independently of video. Audio input is an important part of life. We listen to news, weather forecasts, and sports events on radio or television; we attend meetings, lectures, seminars, and social gatherings; we watch movies and television programs; and we keep in contact with others by telephone.

The Appeals and Constraints of Audio

A primary difference between listening and reading is obviously the auditory attribute of sound. This unique attribute makes audio an unsubstitutable medium for music and language training and for providing content for the visually impaired or those who cannot read text for others reasons. When instructors and students are separated by physical distance, hearing the instructor can also help alleviate the alienation perceived by some students who are not used to distance learning over the Internet.

Because listening in one's native language is as automatic as breathing, we can combine audio messages with text or visuals to enhance comprehension and learner-content interactivity without causing much cognitive overload. For example, audio signals can be used to keep the learner informed of various computer operations and task accomplishments, such as application launching and closing, data transmission, and task completion. As digital recording becomes increasingly easier to use, adding narration to the text outlines in a slide show is often an effective means of presentation. To let audio and text complement each other rather than compete against each other, however, some recommend that we should avoid echoing text display with audio (Gibbons & Fairweather, 1998), because simultaneous presentation of audio with redundant text may not be beneficial to information processing and retention (Kalyuga, Chandler, & Sweller, 1999; Barron, 2004).

Because listening is usually not a conscious effort, it is hard for most people to remain concentrated on a listening task for an extended period of time. In fact, concentrated listening can be extremely grueling if it extends for too long, especially when the speaker is not in front of the listener. If we need to deliver a long recorded speech over the Web, we may want to break the speech into several segments, each a few minutes long. This would allow students to take short breaks between segments, and students can select particular parts of the speech to listen to or replay.

The appeal and effectiveness of speech come largely from the nonverbal expressiveness and colloquialism that are available in speech, but hardly replicable in writing. The nonverbal expressions include variations in vocal pitch, sound volume, intonation, tone, rhythm, and stress. Such variations can express attitude, feeling, and mood in ways that are difficult to achieve or describe in writing.

Another constraint in listening to a speech is linearity. Because of the linear nature of speech, many information processing strategies applicable in reading are inapplicable in listening. For example, scanning and skimming are effective ways to get main ideas when reading, but not when listening, since the complete text is not available for perusal. Consequently, prediction plays a more important role in listening than in reading. The ability to predict in listening is partly based on the listener's prior knowledge of the subject matter and partly on the listener's familiarity with idiomatic expressions, including common colloquialisms, collocations, clichés, proverbs, idioms, and so on. To help the learner better comprehend a speech and reduce learner anxiety, we may need to provide a text introduction with necessary background information to facilitate prediction and comprehension. For extended messages, providing prelistening questions can guide the learners, help them focus on major points, and prevent the problem of "not seeing the woods for the trees." If there are many colloquial expressions or jargon in the speech that are unfamiliar to the students, we may need to define or explain these items in the prelistening activities. For language and speech training, transcripts of the speech can be a valuable learning aid too if provided in advance. However, as mentioned earlier, reading transcripts while simultaneously listening to a speech can add to cognitive load and generally is not advisable.

Finally, because sound is ephemeral, follow-up access and information retrieval can be an issue. Typical solutions are to make the recording available for replay or provide scripts as redundant copy of the content. The recordings and scripts should be provided as options so that learners can selectively use them in a complementary or supplementary manner (Allesi & Trollip, 2001).

Digital Audio Production

Digital audio recording and editing have become very affordable and applicable on most personal computers today. With an easy-to-follow graphic user interface, we can crop, cut and paste, insert, and rearrange components of an audio clip by visually selecting, dragging, and dropping (see Figure 7.12).

Digital audio delivery over the Internet is becoming increasingly easier thanks to growing Internet accessibility and computer processing power. However, digital audio files are still large compared with text and still images and take more time to download. Compression, which basically means removing some less than necessary data, is generally needed to reduce the file size. Compression rates vary in accordance with the choice of audio quality and intended bandwidth. The file size reduction ratio can be as much as 10 to 1. For example, a Windows standard audio WAV file of 100 MB can be reduced to around 10 MB or less when converted to RealMedia.

The way in which data are compressed (encoded) and decompressed (decoded) is called CODEC (compressor and decompressor). Table 7.1 lists some popular digital audio formats.

FIGURE 7.12 **Editing Interface of Adobe Audition**

Note: Adobe Audition screen shot reprinted with permission from Adobe Systems Incorporated.

TABLE 7.1 **Popular Digital Audio Formats**

Format	Platform	Compression	Applications
WAV	Windows	Less compressed	For any audio
AIFF	Mac	Less compressed	High-quality audio
MIDI	Both Windows and Mac	More compressed than WAV, AIFF	Requires special hardware and software to create and convert
MP3	Windows, Mac, Unix	Highly compressed	For music, easily distributed
Windows Media	Windows	Highly compressed	For streaming over the Internet
RealMedia	Windows, Mac, Unix	Most highly compressed	For streaming over the Internet

C A S E   S T U D Y   **Audio Recordings**·················

- Listening to a speech often gives the listener a feeling of the presence of the speaker, bringing the speaker closer to the listener. Some MSU instructors record a greeting message every week and encode the message in RealMedia to be streamed on demand or downloaded by students for offline listening. Because the recorded audio messages are quite small in size, they are easy to download over the Internet. The messages generally do not contain detailed instructional content. Instead, they are mostly quick reviews of last week's activities and briefings of the coming week's work. Many students report that the audio messages add a personal touch to the communication between the instructor and students and make the students "feel" less "distant" from the instructor.

The choice of format is mostly constrained by the recording device, the need for future editing, and considerations of user accessibility. A highly compressed file is smaller in size and easier to download, but allows less room for further editing. A less compressed format allows more room for editing, but is larger in file size and demands more bandwidth to deliver. The common strategy is to encode the original sound file in a format that allows more room for editing. Once the editing is done, we convert the edited file into a more compressed file format for easy delivery and downloading.

Following a speech over the Internet can be hard due to the lack of visual support such as body language and facial expression. This is where digital video can help.

INSTRUCTIONAL USE OF VIDEO

Video production used to be a highly professional business. With the advancement of the camcorder and digital video technology, video making has now become something that people can do at home, on vacation, and in places such as auditoriums, classrooms, science labs, business offices, athletic fields, and workshops. Because video can integrate sound, action, and scene, it can be a great tool for students to record their lab experiments, field trips, debate sessions, or seminar presentations, and review the events with follow-up discussion and evaluation.

Action and Motion

The primary advantage of video is to let us see and hear the action and motion of a scene. Compared with static photographs, the distinctive power of video is to show continuously changing scenes or evolving events. Video is therefore a good tool to demonstrate highly procedural and context-based events such as hardware installation, lab experiments, and field observations.

Affective Impact

The capability of showing a scene as it appeared in real life makes video a powerful medium of attitudinal and emotional impact. Documentary movies generally have more influence on the audience's attitudes and emotions than text documents have on readers. In the movie *Nuremberg,* for example, the prosecutor of the Internal Military Tribunal started by presenting the numbers of Jewish people who were persecuted or murdered by Nazis, but did not seem to be able to speak strongly with those figures. However, when the prosecutor presented a video that captured the scenes of the horrible war crimes committed by the Nazi forces, the emotional impact on the audience was far more shocking than those numbers and verbal descriptions.

Accessing the Inaccessible

Because the viewer of a video can be physically separate from the actual scene, we can use video to capture and represent scenes from remote or restricted areas, or scenes of hazardous or risky events. Video makes it possible for us to see on the screen what expeditions saw in the rain forests along the Amazon River, under the blue oceans, or in deep outer space. Video also allows us to see the launch of a spacecraft, the explosion of a nuclear bomb, or the operations of a space flight control center. Through video, we can let students see objects that are large to bring into the classroom or too small to see with the naked eye. In this sense, video really becomes an extension of human perception sensors.

Manipulating Time and Space

Capturing and presenting scenes from remote or restricted areas is not the only power of video. The more useful functions of video are to use techniques such as montage, microscope, fast or slow motion, and zooming to re-create scenes that we do not normally see in daily life, even as a spectator on the spot. For example, microscopic video can let us examine the structure of a microcomputer chip or the process of cell division. Zooming can let us view an object or phenomenon from a micro level to a macro level, and vice versa. NASA had a video that starts with a close-up look of part of the city of Orlando and gradually zooms out all the way to the height of a satellite view of the globe. New video technology also allows us to capture and present scenes from multiple sites on the same screen simultaneously, creating a virtual community with multimedia communication channels.

CASE STUDY **Video for the IS Students**········

- For the IS program of Mid-State University, video is an effective tool to present scenarios for case studies, which are often used as a basis for group discussions and team projects. Students have used digital video cameras to record interviews with subjects of their research study, their field trip experiences, and group project presentations. The videos have enabled the students to bring authentic scenarios and stories from the business and education fields into class to provide application contexts for the course content. Most of the videos are archived on DVD-R and are included by many students in their multimedia portfolios for future reference.

Video can compress time by taking snapshots, in intervals, of a long process, such as the formation of a hurricane or the growth of a plant. When the movie is played, the viewer can see the complete process in just a few seconds or minutes, whereas the actual process may have taken hours, days, or months. Video can also expand time by photographing a scene at high speed and then playing the movie at normal speed. When the video is played, the effect is slower than normal motion. We are all familiar with slow motion in coverage of sport events. With the capabilities of compressing and expanding durations, video can be very effective in demonstrating motor skills, even more effective than by having learners observe the actual performance in real life, because video can skip trivial parts and slow down to focus on important details for the learners.

Capturing Screen Action

Please visit chapter 7 on the Companion Website (**http://www.prenhall.com/wang**) for some examples of screen action capturing video.

Another type of video that many instructors find helpful is the capturing of screen actions while going through the user interface of an application running on the desktop. Video of this type is most useful for illustrating procedural operations of a desktop application that involves visual details, such as digital graphic creation, application troubleshooting, program debugging, and manipulation of a graphic user interface. There are several software packages available for screen capturing. One of the tools available is Camtasia, developed by TechSmith. The tool can capture screen action and sound from the desktop screen and save the data into an AVI movie or Shockwave file. The Shockwave file is relatively small in size and easy to download over the Internet. Additional features of the tool include adjusting the screen area for capturing; zooming in and out; adding annotation, voice narration, callouts, logos, and graphics; and applying effects like cursor and object highlighting, watermarks, time stamps, and audible mouse clicks.

CASE STUDY **Screen Action Capturing Video**

- Screen action capturing videos are extensively used in teaching and training at Mid-State University. The faculty development team has also used Camtasia to create online tutorials that demonstrate the use of various components of WebCT for both instructors and students who are novice users of the course management system. The instructors of the Visual Basic programming course have used Camtasia to record and illustrate the procedures that involve various visual elements of the graphic user interface of the Visual Basic application. The instructors of the systems design course have used the screen capturing software to show how different components of the tool can be used to create organizational and structural diagrams.

DIGITAL VIDEO PRODUCTION

The visual illusion of continuous motion in video is based on the optical phenomenon called persistence of vision. As we know, the eye can retain an image cast on the retina for a fraction of a second after the image is out of view. If a second image is presented before the trace of the previous image fades, the perceived visions blend into each other. The perception of smooth continuous motion requires related images to be successively presented at a rate of 30 frames per second (fps), which is the frame rate used on a home TV. The eye can start to see discrete frames (jerky motion) at about 12 fps. Therefore, digital video generally requires a minimal 15 fps to make motion appear smooth.

Most of the video cameras available on the market today are digital. If you use a nondigital, analog video camera, you'll need to convert the analog video to digital in order to deliver it via the Internet. Digitization can be easily done on current Apple computers because the necessary hardware and software are built into the system. For the PC environment, additional items may be needed. The first thing to have is a video capture card, which looks like a regular video card or modem card, plugged into a PCI slot of your computer. The video capture card is then connected through a cable to the analog video output device such as a VCR or video camera. When you play the tape in the VCR or video camera, the data will be fed through the video capture card into your computer and encoded into digital data with the help of some software.

Advantages of Digital Video

Compared with analog recording, digital video capturing has many advantages. The most popular digital video format used today is Mini DV. The advantages of Mini DV include:

1. Much higher resolution than VHS
2. CD-quality audio

FIGURE 7.13 **Working Interface of Adobe Premiere**

Note: Adobe Premiere screen shot reprinted with permission from Adobe Systems Incorporated.

3. Component color sampling to retain three times as much color information as analog VHS and S-VHS video

4. Easy data transfer without loss of data

5. Nonlinear editing

6. Smaller camera and tape

For nonprofessional video producers, the biggest advantage of digital video is probably that of nonlinear editing. Most video editing tools provide a nonlinear, graphic user interface. With a certain amount of training, a novice can easily learn to use such an editing tool to cut, paste, insert, and reorganize video clips into a presentable movie. Editing techniques include slice, crop, merge, transition, superimposing, and filters. Figure 7.13 shows the editing interface of Adobe Premiere 5.1 with a frame-based timeline and multiple tracks for audio, video, and transition.

TABLE 7.2 **Popular Digital Video Formats**

Format	Compression	Applications
MPEG-1	Less compressed	VHS movie quality at CD-ROM data rate
MPEG-2	Less compressed	For digital TV and DVD encoding
MPEG-4	Moderately compressed	Low bandwidth video for the Web and telephony
MPEG-7	Moderately compressed	For a broad range of multimedia applications
QuickTime	Less compressed	Apple standard for digital audio and video; supports 360-degree virtual reality
AVI	Less compressed	Default Windows-based video; easy to edit and convert to other video formats
Windows Media	Highly compressed	For streaming over the Internet with near-VHS quality
RealMedia	Most highly compressed	For streaming over the Internet with low bandwidth

Digital Video Formats

Digital video has different compression schemes. Like digital audio file compression, digital file size becomes smaller as the compression rate goes higher, but more highly compressed video leaves fewer editing possibilities. Furthermore, compression is usually a one-way operation. You can easily convert less compressed or uncompressed digital video such as Windows AVI into more compressed video such as RealMedia, but not the other way around, because the data that are cast away during compression are not recoverable. In producing a video, it is generally a good idea to prepare the original clips in a less compressed format such as AVI so that you can edit the clips later. When the video is ready for delivery, you can convert it to RealMedia or Windows Media. Table 7.2 lists some popular digital video formats.

What to Consider When Using Video

Even with the easy-to-use camcorder and user-friendly editing tools, videos are resource-intensive and time-consuming to produce. To produce a video that can qualify for instructional applications generally requires careful planning and some expertise in instructional material development, photography, and video editing. Before we decide to use video for Web-based instruction, we may want to ask ourselves whether the amount of investment to make can be justified by our instructional needs. For example, if what we want to deliver is

⦿ASE STUDY   Breaking Long Videos Into Short Segments ·······

• Earlier in the chapter, we mentioned that students do not like listening to extended audio recordings. The same is true of video recordings. Some of the IS instructors at MSU record their lectures or seminars in digital video and encode the video into streaming media to be viewed by those students who cannot make it to the real-time sessions. To make the viewing experience less tiring, many instructors break the recordings into modules with subtopics so that students can selectively view the recorded videos at different times.

a professor's lecture without much action or motion, an audio recording with a still picture of the speaker might be more cost-effective.

A major issue in distributing video over the Internet is file size. Video files are larger in size than any other media and require a considerable amount of storage space and user download time. For Web delivery, regular digital video file formats such as Apple QuickTime and Windows AVI are often not easy to use because of their relatively large file size. Typically, one minute of AVI video takes up over 10 MB, and 60 minutes of AVI video can take up to 1 GB. To make digital video accessible to users with a dial-up Internet connection, higher video compression technology is needed. Currently the best technology to use is RealMedia by RealNetworks. When converted from AVI or QuickTime to Real-Media, a video file can be reduced by more than 90% in size. Furthermore, RealMedia can be streamed, which is discussed in the next section.

Because of the bandwidth and file size restrictions, video delivered online is generally low in resolution. Small text and fine visual details are typically hard to discern. Before making an online video, the designer should plan it carefully and may need to test view the video to make sure that all the important elements are legible when viewed online. If what needs to be delivered is a combination of short text notes, still images, and video, an alternative tool to consider is Microsoft Producer, which can integrate video, text, and still images into one interface that can be viewed in a browser window. Furthermore, compression technology reduces the file size for easy download online.

IN PRACTICE   Chemistry Online via Digital Slides

To improve the teaching and learning effectiveness of UC Berkeley's General Chemistry 1A course and to accommodate an increasing number of students, a series of technologies have been used to reform the course delivery and class participation. In addition to the use of online quizzes and prelaboratory exercises, with automatic grading and immediate feedback, digital slides with graphics and animation are made available online, and lectures are delivered through streaming video and also archived for later on-demand replay.

Source: http://ist-socrates.berkeley.edu/%7Echem1a/

STREAMING MEDIA

The term **streaming media** refers to media data that are delivered from the server to the client in a continuous flow like a stream. The client can start viewing the content shortly after the streaming starts, instead of in the traditional way of downloading the complete file first to the client's local computer before viewing. Audio streaming today can offer very enjoyable sound quality at moderate modem speeds. However, streaming video still tends to be blurry in image, jerky in movement, and sporadic in sound, unless the client and server are connected through a broad bandwidth.

Streaming can be done from a prerecorded media clip (on-demand streaming) or from a live broadcast (real-time streaming). Smooth streaming, especially live broadcast, requires a fast and stable network connection and a client computer powerful enough to decompress the received data in real time. To play RealMedia, a Pentium-class computer is the minimum requirement. Streaming media is particularly useful when an extended audio or video file needs to be delivered over the Internet. Two types of streaming are popular today on the Web: RealMedia and Windows Media. They both have advantages and constraints.

RealMedia can be streamed from either RealServer or a standard Web server. The major advantage of RealServer is its support of multirate "Sure-Stream," which basically means that RealServer can dynamically adjust the data transfer rate based on the user preference settings and network traffic conditions while the data are being streamed. In contrast, data streamed from a standard Web server would be transferred at a single fixed rate.

Although streaming can reduce client waiting time, the quality is very much contingent upon network conditions. For users with dial-up modem connections, streaming video can be jerky and the streaming process can often be interrupted if the network traffic is heavy.

ANIMATION AND INTERACTIVITY

Flash and Shockwave are two popular digital technologies for creating and publishing multimedia materials over the Internet today. Flash Player is included in the latest download of Microsoft Internet Explorer and Netscape Navigator. The two names, Flash and Shockwave, are sometimes used interchangeably, but they are two different technologies. There is some justification for this interchangeable use—and subsequent confusion—since the published file of a Flash movie has the file extension .swf, supposedly standing for "Shockwave file."

For the end user, a major difference is that a Flash movie is authored with Macromedia Flash and played with the Flash Player, whereas a Shockwave program is authored with Macromedia Director and played with the Shockwave Player. You can find out whether an animation in a Web page is Flash or Shockwave or neither by right mouse clicking on the animation. If a window pops up with the menu item "About Shockwave Player," it is a Shockwave program. If a window shows up with the menu item "About Flash Player," it's a Flash movie. Flash movies are delivered as .swf files, whereas Shockwave programs are distributed as .dcr files. Some third-party tools can also generate Flash or Shockwave files, but they are all derivative technologies.

Despite the common confusion about Flash and Shockwave, there are some important differences between the two. Macromedia Director was originally designed for authoring offline multimedia programs and has a longer history than Flash. Many of the multimedia CD-ROMs you see today were created with Director. Because Director was not meant for the Web, the files generated by Director tend to be larger in size than similar Flash files. However, Director is more versatile than Flash in creating 3-D effects and interactive functions.

Flash was first and foremost designed to create Web-based animation with some basic interactivity. To make finished products easy to download, Flash files are small. Flash animation can be 10 times smaller in file size than animated **GIF** and also far more flexible and interactive. It is estimated that over half of the most visited Web sites use Flash to develop their Web interfaces (Geller, 2001). Flash has a built-in scripting language called ActionScript. However, for simple animation that does not involve sophisticated interactivity, no programming is required to create movies in Flash. Figure 7.14 is a screen shot of a simple Flash movie that illustrates the water cycle.

Please visit chapter 7 on the Companion Website (**http://www.prenhall.com/wang**) to see the actual Flash movie.

FIGURE 7.14   A Flash Movie About the Water Cycle with Animation

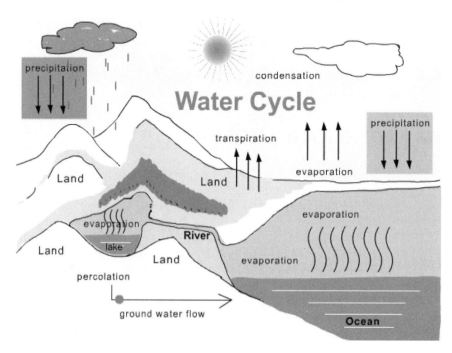

CASE STUDY **Flash Animation**

- Flash animation technology has been used in some of the courses in the IS program of MSU to create simulations and illustrations driven by data the user enters or randomly generated with a specified range. One of the applications is a Flash program that simulates the traffic flow of a computer network that can respond to varying data input and traffic conditions. Another application is a Flash program that simulates the structure and working mechanism of a computer so that students can visually see how information is processed by a computer through the input and output devices.

VIRTUAL REALITY

In digital technology, **virtual reality** (VR) means computer simulations that use 3-D graphics to simulate real-world situations and allow the user to interact with the simulations by moving around, zooming in and out, and interacting with objects in ways similar to what happens in the real world. Virtual reality has application values for many professional fields, including aviation, architecture and interior design, business modeling, city planning, medicine, performing arts, and law enforcement. Functionally, virtual reality can provide educational potentials in the following areas: (a) data gathering and visualization, (b) project planning and design, (c) design and provision of interactive training systems, (d) virtual field trips, and (e) design and provision of experiential learning environments (McLellan, 2004).

Virtual reality used to be rather costly to develop. Now, with the rapid advancement in computing technology and the growth of the World Wide Web, there have been widespread endeavors to put VR into educational use. Virtual reality can be created through a variety of technologies. For the Web environment, some of the common choices are virtual reality modeling language (VRML), QuickTime VR, Shockwave, and Java. **VRML** is the 3-D equivalent of HTML for the Web. VRML documents are text documents with the extension .wrl. To view VRML files, you need a VRML browser or a VRML plug-in to your Web browser. It's beyond the scope of this book to discuss VRML in detail. But you can learn more about VRML and get a list of VRML browsers from the Web3D Consortium's Web site (http://www.web3d.org).

QuickTime VR is Apple's technology for virtual reality. There are two types of QuickTime VR applications: panorama and 360-degree object view. QuickTime VR panorama movies are created by taking a dozen or more overlapping still pictures of surrounding scenes from a central point, and then stitching the pictures together with some special software. The composite picture is then converted into a QuickTime VR movie and placed on the Web.

QuickTime VR 360-degree object movies are created by placing an object on a turntable and taking multiple still pictures of the object as it is turning around. The pictures are put into a linear movie and then a Quick-Time VR movie. The viewer can use the mouse and keyboard to rotate the object and zoom in and out. QuickTime VR movies can run on any platform that has QuickTime Player installed or in any browser with a Quick-Time plug-in. At the University of Texas at Austin, the College of Education has a QuickTime VR tutorial for educators (http://www.edb.utexas.edu/teachnet/QTVR/).

More resources are needed to design and develop 3-D graphics, and they require users to have a special browser or additional plug-in to interact with the content. Because of these constraints, 3-D graphics should be used only when the investment can be justified by instructional needs. In general, 3-D graphics are helpful when we need to present visual objects or phenomena that should be viewed from different perspectives (Nielsen, 1998). Examples might include: (a) biological examinations, (b) medical operations, (c) mechanical and civil engineering designs, and (d) chemical structures.

Please visit chapter 7 on the Companion Website (**http://www.prenhall.com/wang**) to see more examples of virtual reality.

IN PRACTICE

The University at Buffalo's Virtual Reality Laboratory pioneers the use of VR technology in areas such as surgery, remote robotic control, volcanic simulation, and factory design.

Source: http://www.vrlab.buffalo.edu/

East Carolina University has a Virtual Reality and Education Lab that aims to develop applications of VR in education and training, gather information on educational applications of VR throughout the world, and disseminate information about educational VR around the world.

Source: http://www.coe.ecu.edu/vr/vrel.htm

The Institute for Creative Technologies (ICT) of the University of Southern California specializes in creating Experience Learning Systems (ELS) for military training and a broad range of educational initiatives.

Source: http://www.ict.usc.edu/

The University of Michigan Virtual Reality Laboratory (VRL) explores applications of immersive and nonimmersive virtual environments for educational and industrial applications, such as virtual prototyping of engineering designs, simulations, medicine, architecture, archeology, and other areas.

Source: http://www-vrl.umich.edu/

PRINT TEXTBOOKS

Despite the increasing availability of Web-based multimedia applications, so far text remains the primary means of content delivery in Web-based instruction. Digital text offers the benefits of easy distribution, modification, reproduction, and search capability. But digital text is not suited for prolonged reading on a computer screen; text legibility on the computer screen is poorer than that of print in contrast and resolution. Many users tend to scan and skim Web page text, or they print out a page to read. Text content therefore has to be written in a way that is easy for readers to scan (Nielsen, 2000). For extended and systemic coverage of subject matter, therefore, a print textbook is often a better way to organize and present the content. Besides, a print textbook is easy to carry around and can be read anywhere.

A major drawback of using a print textbook is that its content can become outdated quickly. To have a print textbook and Web-based content complement each other, it might be a good idea to use a print textbook to provide focused readings and use the Web to create an online learning environment for content updating, information sharing, and class communication, such as posting the syllabus, study guide, memos, lesson notes, and unit summaries.

E-BOOKS

In recent years, a growing number of **e-books** (electronic books that can be read on a computer or other digital device) have become available from various publishers for distribution over the Internet. Compared with traditional print books, e-books can more easily incorporate multimedia and Internet resources. When learners open an e-book, they will be viewing formatted pages with "bells and whistles" built in. They can highlight important parts of the text, add annotations, search through the text using a search tool, open hyperlinked resources, and look up related references. For authors and editors, e-books make it easier to modify and update content, restructure organization, and search by keyword or metadata. E-books are particularly effective for certain subject areas where information is often structured in relatively discrete blocks and where content needs to be frequently updated (Cox, 2004). Such areas include business, computer science, information systems, technology, law, and political science.

At the time of this writing, the number of e-book titles available is small compared with that of print texts. For e-books to be more widely used, there are some barriers to overcome. As mentioned earlier, readers generally do not like reading extended text on a computer screen because text legibility on the computer screen is poorer than printed text. Another major issue to address is the protection of the digital content from illegal copying and distribution.

HTML and XHTML are not designed for distributing e-books, and they do not have built-in measures to protect author copyright, which is a primary concern for many authors in letting their works be distributed in the Web environment. Among the various alternative formats currently available, portable document format (PDF) is one of the most popular. PDF is the native file format of Adobe Acrobat. Users can convert documents from most other applications to a PDF format that can be displayed in Acrobat Reader, independent of platform and with adjustable resolution. A major strength of Acrobat is its ability to keep the original look of a document when the document is converted to PDF. For multiple page documents, Acrobat also allows users to create a table of contents (called bookmarks in Acrobat) with clickable links to different parts of the document (see Figure 7.15).

Released in January 2005, Acrobat 7 has some new features, making it an even better tool for preparing and distributing e-books. Authors can use it to easily create a single PDF document from multiple sources, including portions of Web pages, videos, photos, and other Adobe PDF documents. The use of standardized metadata makes it easy to search PDF documents for needed materials. Authors can also set access control to protect sensitive and confidential

FIGURE **7.15** **Page of an Acrobat PDF Document with Bookmarks**

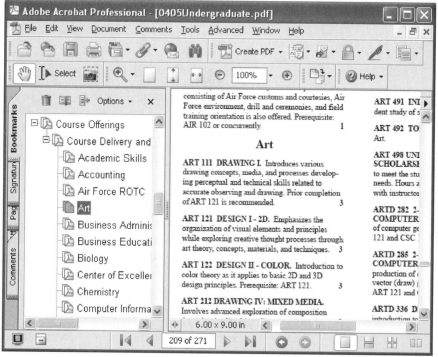

Note: Adobe Acrobat Professional screen shot reprinted with permission from Adobe Systems Incorporated.

IN PRACTICE   Safari Books Online

Owned jointly by Pearson Education and O'Reilly, Safari Books Online offers IT professionals the full text of 2,500 titles in e-book format (as of January 2005), growing at about 50 books monthly.

Safari also has an online reference center available on an enterprise or individual subscription basis, with the latest publications from Adobe Press, Addison Wesley, Cisco Press, New Riders, O'Reilly, Peachpit Press, Prentice Hall, Que, and Sam's Publishing.

Source: http://www.safaribooksonline.com

documents both inside and outside an institution's firewall, online and offline. Additional restrictions can be set on whether the distributed PDF documents can be printed, copied, or modified by the reader so that the copyright of the works can be protected.

However, accessibility can be a problem with some of the digital rights management (DRM) tools currently available, because many of these tools do not allow text-to-speech conversion, thus making the text unreadable to screen readers. The disabling of text-to-speech is reportedly in response to publishers' requests because the publishers' contracts do not include audio performance rights (Coyle, 2003).

Chapter Summary

This chapter starts by reviewing research literature on media attributes and the debate over media effects on learning. The general belief is that different media have different information attributes and require different perceptual and cognitive skills in encoding and decoding the information embodied in the media. Appropriately combined media can be more effective than a single medium in conveying particular messages. However, the use of media should be considered in the context of environmental factors and participant characteristics.

The chapter examines the four primary functions of visuals: decorative and perceptual enhancement, realistic representation, analogous metaphorical representation, and organizational representation. The first and third functions appear to be more relevant for computer user interface design, and the second and fourth are more useful in helping students analyze and communicate information.

Audio can add a personal touch in communication and is relatively easy to implement over the Internet. However, extended recorded speech may not be appropriate in WBI because listeners can easily get bored and stop concentrating. The chapter introduces several common digital audio technologies currently available.

Digital video is probably the hottest multimedia technology right now. The chapter discusses several primary instructional functions of video, including recording action and motion, affective impact, access to the inaccessible, manipulation of time and space, and screen action capturing. The chapter also discusses the advantages of digital video, calls the reader's attention to several things to consider or avoid in using digital video, and introduces some common digital video formats used today.

The chapter concludes with some overviews of streaming media, Flash and Shockwave for animation and interactive multimedia, and Virtual Reality. Examples of how multimedia can be used in our IS program case study are woven throughout the chapter.

Review Questions

1. What's your view of media effects on learning? Do you feel media have information bias? If yes, what kind of information bias?

2. Visit some of your favorite Web sites and categorize the functions of the graphics used there. Do you feel there is any other category of graphics other than the four types given in the chapter?

3. For what type of instructional needs do you think a print textbook would be a better medium of content delivery than hypermedia in Web-based instruction?

4. For what kind of instructional needs do you think audio can work more effectively than text and video?

5. What types of instructional needs would justify the relatively higher cost involved in producing and delivering digital video over the Web?

Summary of Tips

1. Use different media to complement one another in conveying information, not to compete with one another for attention.

2. Use simple decorative graphics to help direct the learner's attention.

3. Use realistic visual representation to present authentic context.

4. Use analogous and metaphorical visuals to facilitate easy recognition and quick response.

5. Use organizational and spatial visuals such as charts and diagrams to show structures, procedures, development, and differences in quantity.

6. Use audio such as recorded messages to add a personal touch to instructional content and class communication.

7. Record audio in less-compressed format for easy editing, and then convert to more highly compressed format for distribution and streaming.

8. Avoid making long audio recordings because listeners lose their concentration easily when listening to long audio recordings.

9. Use preview materials to prepare students before a listening task.

10. Avoid using video for content that involves no more than a talking head.

11. Use video to represent procedural content that requires the support of visual context.

12. Use video to provide students access to what is otherwise difficult or impossible to access.

Exercises

1. List some possible hindering effects of inappropriately combined multimedia, taking the instructional context into consideration.

2. Spend 10 to 15 minutes browsing some of the Web sites that you know have rich visuals. Note and categorize the occurrences of visuals in terms of their functions.

3. If you are teaching a class, teach the same topic or train the same skill using different combinations of media. Assess the effects on students' perceptions and performances.

4. Outline the common digital audio formats currently available.

5. Outline the common digital video formats currently available.

6. Explain the concept of streaming media and the common streaming technologies currently available.

7. If applicable, prepare a short narration that can fit into an instructional content module. Record the narration, and edit the recording with a sound editing software tool. Convert the edited recording into streaming media and test it on the Web.

8. Summarize the primary benefits and common constraints in using video for Web-based instruction.

9. Prepare a PowerPoint presentation that introduces the basics of common technologies for creating digital animation and virtual reality.

10. Interview some of your colleagues and friends and ask them how they feel about media effects on learning. Is there any particular medium that they feel has special information attributes for information presentation? What kind of media combinations do they find particularly helpful for information presentation?

11. Select segments of TV programs from the Discovery Channel, any news channel, and the Weather Channel. Analyze how reality is captured and represented through the various techniques described in the chapter.

Resources on the Web

Multimedia is an extensive topic that cannot possibly be covered in adequate detail in a short chapter. For further reading about multimedia and instructional integration, the following reading list is suggested:

- *Visual Language: Global Communication for the 21st Century,* by Robert Horn (MacRovu, Inc., 1999).

- *Instructional Media and Technologies for Learning,* by Robert Heinich, Michael Moldenda, James Russel, and Sharon Smaldino (Prentice Hall, 2002).

- *Integrating Educational Technology into Teaching,* by M. D. Roblyer (Prentice Hall, 2003).

- *Instructional Effectiveness of Video Media,* by Douglas Wetzel, Paul Radtke, and Stern Hervey (Lawrence Erlbaum Associates, 1994).

Please visit chapter 7 on the Companion Website (**http://www.prenhall.com/wang**) for Web resources on educational multimedia.

Some of the examples presented in this chapter would be better viewed in the actual Web environment, particularly the examples of screen-capturing video, streaming media, and virtual reality. The Companion Website of the book provides a list of examples.

References

Allesi, S. M., & Trollip, S. (2001). *Multimedia for learning: Methods and development* (3rd ed.). Needham, MA: Allyn & Bacon.

Barron, A. E. (2004). Auditory instruction. In D. Jonassen (Ed.), *Handbook of research on educational communications and technology,* pp. 949–978. Mahwah, NJ: Lawrence Erlbaum.

Carpenter, E. (1960). The new languages. In E. Carpenter & M. McLuhan (Eds.), *Explorations in communication.* Boston: Beacon Press.

Clark, R. (1983). Reconsidering research on learning from media. *Review of Educational Research, 53,* 445–460.

Clark, R., & Salomon, G. (1986). Media in teaching. In M. C. Wittrock (Ed.), *Handbook of research on teaching: A project of the American Educational Research Association* (3rd ed.), pp. 464–478. New York: Macmillan.

Cox, J. (2004). E-books: Challenges and opportunities. *D-Lib Magazine, 10(10).* Retrieved December 18, 2004, from http://www.dlib.org/dlib/october04/cox/10cox.html.

Coyle, K. (2003). The technology of rights: Digital rights management. Based on a talk originally given at the Library of Congress, November 19, 2003. Retrieved December 26, 2004, from http://www.kcoyle.net/drm_basics.pdf.

Dede, C. (1996). Emerging technologies and distributed learning in higher education. *American Journal of Distance Education, 10(2),* 4–36.

Dwyer, F. M. (1978). *Strategies for improving visual learning.* State College, PA: Learning Services.

Geller, M. (2001). Sibling rivalry or dynamic duo? Macromedia Flash versus Shockwave. *Macromedia Newsletter,* 2001. Retrieved July 3, 2003, from http://www.macromedia.com/newsletters/edge/december_2001/miriamgeller.html

Gibbons, A. S., & Fairweather, G. B. (1998). *Computer-based instruction: Design and development.* Englewood Cliffs, NJ: Educational Technology Publications.

Gombrich, E. H. (1974). The visual image. In D. Olson (Ed.), *Media and symbols: The forms of expression, communication and education (73rd annual yearbook of the National Society for the Study of Education).* Chicago: University of Chicago Press.

Horn, R. E. (1999). *Visual language: Global communication for the 21st century.* Bainbridge Island, WA: MacroVU.

Jamison, D., Suppes, P., & Wells, S. (1974). The effectiveness of alternative instructional media: A survey. *Review of Educational Research, 44,* 1–68.

Kalyuga, S., Chandler, P., & Sweller, J. (1999). Managing split-attention and redundancy in multimedia instruction. *Applied Cognitive Psychology, 13,* 351–372.

Kosma, R. B. (1994). Will media influence learning? Reframing the debate. *Educational Technology Research and Development, 42,* 7–19.

Mayer, R. E. (2001). *Multimedia learning.* New York: Cambridge University Press.

Moreno, R., & Mayer, R. E. (1999). Cognitive principles of multimedia learning: The role of modality and contiguity. *Journal of Educational Psychology, 91,* 358–368.

Moreno, R., & Mayer, R. E. (2002). Learning science in virtual reality environments: Role of method and media. *Journal of Educational Psychology, 94,* 598–610.

McLellan, H. (2004). Virtual realities. In D. Jonassen (Ed.), *Handbook of research on educational communications and technology,* pp. 461–497. Mahwah, NJ: Lawrence Erlbaum.

McLuhan, M. (1967). *The medium is the massage.* Corte Madera, CA: Gingko Press.

Meringoff, L. K. (1980). Influence of the medium of children's story apprehension. *Journal of Educational Psychology, 72,* 240–249.

Nielsen, J. (1998). *2D is better than 3D.* Retrieved April 2, 2002, from http://www.useit.com/alertbox/981115.html.

Nielsen, J. (2000). *Designing web usability.* Indianapolis, IN: New Riders.

Olson, D., & Bruner, J. (1974). In D. Olson (Ed.), *Media and symbols: The forms of expression, communication and education (73rd annual yearbook of the National Society for the Study of Education).* Chicago: University of Chicago Press.

Russell, T. L. (1999). *The no significant different difference phenomenon.* Chapel Hill, NC: Office of Instructional Telecommunications, North Carolina State University.

Salomon, G. (1974). What is learned and how it is taught: The interaction between media, message, task and learner. In D. Olson (Ed.), *Media and symbols: The forms of expression, communication and education (73rd annual yearbook of the National Society for the Study of Education).* Chicago: University of Chicago Press.

Salomon, G. (1979). *Interaction of media, cognition and learning.* San Francisco: Jossey-Bass.

PART III

MANAGEMENT

Chapter 8   Copyright and Intellectual Property

Chapter 9   Course Management Systems

Chapter 10   Utilizing Web Resources

Chapter 11   Policy and Management for Web-Based Instruction

Chapter 8

Copyright and Intellectual Property

CHAPTER INTRODUCTION

Most faculty members have been on both ends of the spectrum when it comes to copyright and intellectual property. Faculty members have asked permission to use materials and have created materials that they have given permission for others to use. Copyright and intellectual property can be complex issues, which we hope to make a little clearer in this chapter.

LEARNING OBJECTIVES

After studying this chapter, the reader will be able to:

1. Dispel the myths about copyright and intellectual property.

2. Summarize the new issues about copyright and intellectual property in the e-learning environment.

3. Explain what fair use means and how to determine the limit of fair use.

4. Outline the procedures to take in order to obtain copyright permission.

5. Evaluate models and guidelines for policy related to copyright and intellectual property.

CASE STUDY

- As some of the faculty members at MSU work on their online courses, they look at the materials they have used in their classroom courses and wonder how they can use these materials in their online courses. A group of faculty members decides to meet with the director of their online program to find out about copyright for materials to be used online. As you read this chapter, think about whether any of your course materials might require permission to use and how you would go about requesting permission to use those materials. At the end of the chapter you will find several scenarios you can review.

WHAT IS COPYRIGHT?

Copyright gives the creator of a work (written, music, artwork, photography, or audiovisual works) the right to:

1. Reproduce the work—make copies of a protected work
2. Distribute the work—sell or otherwise distribute copies to the public
3. Create adaptations or derivative works—prepare new works based on the protected work
4. Perform and display the work—perform a protected work such as a stage play or display a work in public (Fishman, 2000)

The purpose of copyright is to encourage intellectual and artistic creation. However, there are a few limits to copyright protection. One is that ideas and facts are not protected. What is protected is how the creator of a work expresses the facts and ideas. The second limitation is fair use. The concept of fair use was established to provide a free flow of ideas and is used extensively by educators. The third limitation is public domain. Works that are no longer protected by copyright, such as when the copyright is lost or has expired, and works authored or owned by the federal government are in the public domain (Fishman, 2000).

TRADITIONAL REGULATIONS AND PRACTICES

Copyright laws in the U.S. have been in place since 1790. Most professors are comfortable with the copyright procedures applicable to their traditional classroom courses. For example, a teacher can make a single copy of a book chapter, article, story, poem, chart, or diagram to use in preparation for a class. Multiple copies can be made for the classroom following the guidelines established by the copyright laws.

FIGURE 8.1   Section 107 of the U.S. Copyright Act of 1976: Fair Use

Notwithstanding the provisions of sections 106 and 106A, the fair use of a copyrighted work, including such use by reproduction in copies or phonorecords or by any other means specified in that section, for purposes such as criticism, comment, news reporting, teaching (including multiple copies for classroom use), scholarship, or research, is not an infringement of copyright.

In determining whether the use made of a work in any particular case is a fair use the factors to be considered shall include:

1. the *purpose and character* of the use, including whether such use is of a commercial nature or is for non-profit educational purposes;

2. the *nature* of the copyrighted work;

3. the *amount and substantiality* of the portion used in relation to the copyrighted work as a whole; and

4. the *effect* of the use upon the potential market for or value of the copyrighted work.

The fact that a work is unpublished shall not itself bar a finding of fair use if such finding is made upon consideration of all the above factors.

Most institutions have offices to process copyright permissions. The procedures for obtaining copyright permission for materials used in the classroom have been in place for years. If you are unfamiliar with the provisions of fair use in the Copyright Act see Figure 8.1.

Here is a quick rundown of the fair use guidelines:

1. Students can use portions of others' works in multimedia projects if the work is part of assignments for the course.

2. Faculty can use portions of others' works in multimedia projects if the work is part of course materials for teaching remote courses. There is a two-year time limit.

3. There are fair use limits depending on the form of medium: (a) up to 10% or 3 minutes of a copyrighted motion media work; (b) up to 10% or 1,000 words of text; (c) up to 10% or 30 seconds of music and lyrics; and (d) up to 5 photographic images.

NEW COPYRIGHT ISSUES IN THE E-LEARNING ENVIRONMENT

The digital age, however, has changed the world of copyright permission. The concept of the classroom has reached outside the walls of the institution, causing confusion with established copyright procedures. It is not safe to assume

FIGURE ⑧.② **Copyright Myths: True or False?**

True or False?

A work has to be published and registered with the U.S. Copyright Office to receive copyright protection.

Anything on the Internet is public domain.

A work copyrighted in another country is public domain in the United States.

The doctrine of "fair use" means that copyrighted materials can be used in an educational setting without permission.

Distance education classes can be considered to be an extension of the traditional classroom as far as copyright situations are concerned.

Any type of visual material can be shown over a distance education network.

Similarly, a teacher can use a videotape in a distance education course under "fair use."

The copyright law is clear when it comes to distance education interpretations.

Legal penalties for copyright violations are not very costly.

It is required that the copyright notice be placed on materials; lack of notice means that they are in the public domain.

Faculty members' images and course materials may be freely used and archived for future distribution over a telecourse distribution system without concern for ownership.

It is relatively easy and not time-consuming to seek clearances and permissions from copyright owners.

Would you believe they are all false?

Sources: Bruwelheide, J. H., 1997; Simonson, Smaldino, Albright, & Zvacek, 2000.

that fair use in the classroom has the same meaning for those courses delivered off-campus. Reviewing copyright in the e-learning environment, the first thing to determine is what is true and what is a myth. Figure 8.2 is a representation of the beliefs about copyright of many faculty members and administrators of higher education.

As stated earlier, most instructors are familiar with the copyright procedures for the traditional classroom and understand the copyright laws through 1976. The most recent copyright law, the Digital Millennium Copyright Act (DMCA), was passed in 1998 to address some of the issues facing copyright holders in the digital age.

The purpose of the Act was to update the laws for the digital environment. The Act makes no change to the fair use doctrine, but critics note that the new prohibitions of the Act restrict fair use and favor copyright holders (Vaidhyanathan, 2002). The Act has five areas:

Title I: WIPO Treaties Implementation

Title II: Online Copyright Infringement Liability Limitation

Title III: Computer Maintenance or Repair Copyright Exemption

Title IV: Miscellaneous Provisions (which includes digital preservation and distance education)

Title V: Protection of Certain Original Designs

The distance education section of Title IV specifies eight factors to be considered:

1. The need for an exemption from exclusive rights of copyright owners for distance education through digital networks

2. The categories of works to be included under any distance education exemption

3. The extent of appropriate quantitative limitation on the portions of works that may be used under any distance education exemption

4. The parties who should be entitled to the benefits of any distance education exemption

5. The parties who should be designated as eligible recipients of distance education materials under any distance education exemption

6. Whether and what types of technological measures can or should be employed to safeguard against unauthorized access to, and use or retention of, copyrighted materials as a condition of eligibility for any distance education exemption, including, in light of developing technological capabilities, the exemption set out in section 110(2) of Title 17, United States Code

7. The extent to which the availability of licenses for the use of copyrighted works in distance education through interactive digital networks should be considered in assessing eligibility for any distance education exemption

8. Other issues relating to distance education through interactive digital networks (pp. 31–32 of the Act)

The DMCA is restrictive when it comes to distance education. Another law, signed in November 2002, is designed to ease some of those restrictions. This act is known as the TEACH (Technology, Education, and Copyright Harmonization) Act. Dr. Kenneth Crews wrote an excellent summary of the Act for the ALA (http://www.ala.org/washoff/teach.html). We would like to summarize some key points but recommend that you read the article.

First, Dr. Crews (2003a, p. 4) comments that "the TEACH Act is a clear signal that Congress recognizes the importance of distance education, the significance of digital media, and the need to resolve copyright clashes." The law makes some clear points about how distance education should be administered by institutions: Distance education should be provided in installments over a specific time period. Institutions providing distance education are to be accredited, provide a copyright policy with accurate copyright information, and provide a notice to students that course materials are copyright protected and available only to enrolled students. In addition there must be limited access to course materials by enrolled students, and there must be technological controls so that the material is used and stored no longer than for the duration of the course (Crews, 2003; Lindsey, 2003). There are additional guidelines for technology officials, instructors, and librarians.

Crews (2003b) comments that the TEACH Act also demonstrates that distance education is not as broadly recognized or as flexible as educators would like. The law states that copyright permission is granted in the context of "mediated instructional activities" and this is based on the traditional classroom setting. It is restrictive about most distance delivery forms, particularly online or Web-based instruction.

Among the controversies surrounding copyright for e-learning courses is digital rights management (DRM). DRM includes the hardware and software systems used to restrict the use and reproduction of digital information. According to the Electronic Privacy Information Center (EPIC; 2004), DRM systems restrict the use of digital files in order to protect the rights of the copyright holders. DRM systems are restrictive in that they cannot recognize fair use rights because fair use cannot be defined for the DRM system that may be in place. This is an area to watch in the development of DRM systems.

Dahl (2004) describes how the TEACH Act resolves the basic issues raised by the DMCA:

1. Allowing use of reasonable and limited portions of copyrighted audiovisual and dramatic musical performances (such as audio/video clips)

2. Allowing students to access distance education course materials from any computer at any location

3. Allowing digitizing portions of materials without first obtaining permission, if those materials are only available in analog format

4. Legalizing cache copies of materials

5. Allowing storage of copyrighted materials on servers (p. 1)

Keeping these factors in mind, we will review copyright protection for different types of online works. Digital copies of text files and online versions of images and sounds, photos, graphics, and recordings are fundamentally no different from their printed versions. They are all protected by copyright. For example, it is an infringement to scan a picture and place it on the Internet without permission. It is also an infringement to download text or an image without permission. Downloading an image or sound and modifying it is also a copyright infringement. Copyright owners have the exclusive right to make a derivative work from a copyrighted work, so for someone else to do so requires permission (Fishman, 2000).

Original Web sites are protected by copyright. If a site contains valuable material, it is recommended that the site contain a copyright notice, although it is not necessary. A copyright notice should contain the word copyright or the symbol, the date, the creator's name, and the phrase "all rights reserved."

Are copies in RAM considered copyright violation? This is an unsettled legal question. RAM (random access memory) is where items are stored temporarily until your computer is shut off. Some copyright experts and courts have considered a copy in RAM to be a copy for copyright purposes because a computer can be left on for an extended period of time. However, copyright experts usually do not believe that loading a digital copy in RAM to be copying the work, because it is temporary and is lost when the computer is shut off. Under this view, reading an online work is permissible as long as a permanent copy is not made to the hard drive or a disk or printed out (Fishman, 2000). However, the TEACH Act does allow for legal copies of materials, according to Dahl (2004). In any case, always seeking permission is the best way to resolve any question of fair use.

E-mail is protected the same way as a letter—it is considered to be an original document and is fully protected by copyright the instant it is sent or fixed in a physical medium such as a hard drive. The author of an e-mail owns the copyright, unless it was created in the scope of employment, and then the employer is considered the author for copyright purposes (Fishman, 2000). Modifying an e-mail without the owner's permission would constitute a copyright violation.

It is important to understand that you are liable for copyright infringement whether you know the work is protected or not. Along with that, you don't have to infringe on someone's work yourself to be liable (Fishman, 2000). For example, if you let someone else use your computer and that person violates a copyright, you can be held responsible for contributory infringement.

However, the situation is different for Internet service providers (ISPs). On the whole, an ISP is not held liable if a subscriber commits an infringement, unless the ISP knew about the infringement and did nothing or had the ability to control the infringer's acts and did nothing (Fishman, 2000). What does that mean for an educational institution that serves as an ISP? The DMCA views faculty members and graduate students who are engaged in teaching or research to be covered under the principles of academic freedom. Thus universities that serve as ISPs are exempt from liability if the following conditions are met:

1. The alleged online infringement must have occurred while the faculty member or graduate student was engaged in teaching or legitimate scholarly or scientific research.

2. The alleged infringement does not involve the faculty member or graduate student posting online any course materials that were required or recommended for any course during the past three years.

IN PRACTICE

If you want to learn more about what is required of you and your institution regarding copyright and how to obtain copyright to use materials in a Web-based course, go to the University of Texas copyright crash course at www.utsystem.edu/OGC/IntellectualProperty/admin.htm.

3. The college or university must not have received more than two notifications over the past three years that the faculty member or graduate student was infringing.

4. The college or university must provide all of the users of its system or network with informational materials describing and promoting compliance with copyright law—these can be Copyright Office materials or other materials such as copyright books in the library. (Fishman, 2000)

When it comes to Web sites, there are two main areas of concern related to copyright: unauthorized transfer of information to and from Web sites and linking Web sites. Copying or downloading information from another site to your own site is an infringement. So is uploading copyrighted information to a site of your own creation. Currently permission is not needed for a simple word link between sites, but it is required if the link comprises a trademark from the linked site (Kearsley, 2000; Stim, 2004). Stim (2004) provides several ways to stay out of trouble with Web site permissions. First, assume that the site is protected and seek permission. Second, if someone complains that your site constitutes unauthorized use, investigate the claim promptly and remove unauthorized material if necessary. Finally, when using freeware and shareware, be sure to read the "click to accept" agreements for the conditions of use.

Mckenzie (1996) provides some advice for teachers and students when posting work on the Web:

1. Neither teachers nor students may safely make use of others' materials when they publish on the web unless they have requested and received formal permission to do so.

2. Check the licensing agreements for all software and for freeware and shareware. Most of these agreements require you to print a credit line when using clip art in a document or on a Web site.

3. Student work is intellectual property and deserves protection. Many school districts post copyright notices at the bottom of such pages. It is recommended that student work not be published with both the student's and parent's permission and that the student's full name should not be published.

CURRENT PRACTICES—ESTABLISHING GUIDELINES FOR FAIR USE IN DISTANCE LEARNING

Picciano (2001) stressed the importance of institutions' establishing guidelines on copyright and fair use as it pertains to distance learning efforts. Suggested guidelines include:

1. Identify a person(s) or office at the institution who has and maintains expertise in copyright law.

2. Make the copyright policy and institutional guidelines available in manual or pamphlet form to all faculty.

3. Delineate the differences in fair use between traditional face-to-face instruction and distance learning.

4. Acknowledge and place copyright credit on all legally made copies.

5. Encourage faculty to obtain permission to use copyrighted work.

6. Provide an institutional form letter for seeking permission.

7. Develop awareness and expertise with copyright in academic support offices such as media centers, libraries, and reproduction services.

8. Develop expertise in academic support areas to assist faculty in locating legitimate materials, copyrighted or otherwise.

9. Conduct occasional audits of classes and Web sites to determine if any infringement of copyright is occurring in the institution. (p. 127)

Making Sure You Meet the Fair Use Guidelines

If you are teaching via a password-protected site to which only students or other invited guests may gain access, you probably qualify for fair use rules. In essence, your site may be deemed the equivalent of a traditional classroom (Ko & Rossen, 2001).

If you are concerned that you may refer to a site at a later date only to find that it has disappeared, you may want to seek permission to copy the site into your course materials. That way you will be assured that you will have that information for future use.

A word of caution on fair use of Web sites. Some educators feel that if you have not received permission from the owner, you should not use materials or information from a site. Don't link a site to yours without seeking permission. Our rule of thumb used to be "when in doubt, ask." Now it is "always ask."

Alternatives to standard copyright protection are now being developed. One popular site used by educators is http://creativecommons.org. At this site you can obtain a license to use materials by others, and you can add your creations to the site to allow others to use them. You give up no copyright privileges in doing so.

Finding the Rightful Author

If there is no person or office on your campus that assists with obtaining copyright permission, you can do some Web searching for the rightful owner of a work. Here are two Web sites that are helpful:

The Copyright Clearance Center at http://www.copyright.com

The University of Texas System Crash Course in Copyright at http://www.utsystem.edu/ogc/intellectualproperty/cprtindx.htm

When you send a letter or e-mail to obtain copyright permission, identify yourself and your position. Explain that you would like permission to use the work in your course; then provide the citation of the work you wish to use. If you are writing a letter, ask the author to sign and return the letter giving permission. If you are sending an e-mail, indicate that the reply to the e-mail will be used as the permission. Be sure to thank the author for granting permission to use his or her work.

Figure 8.3 shows a sample letter. It is a good idea to keep a copy of all your correspondence.

FIGURE (8.3)   **A Sample Copyright Permission Letter**

[On your letterhead]
[Date]
[Name and address of copyright owner]
Dear [name]:
I am [your name and institution]. I would like permission to [explain circumstances].

Please indicate your approval of this permission by signing this letter below and returning it to me as soon as possible. My fax number is listed above. Your signing of this letter will also confirm that you are the copyright owner of the material described.

Thank you very much.
Sincerely,

[Your name and signature]
PERMISSION GRANTED FOR THE USE REQUESTED ABOVE:
[Type name of owner below signature line]
Date:

What to Do If the Author Does Not Respond

If no one responds to your request to use material, you can use it knowing that you made a good-faith effort to contact the author to secure permission (Ko & Rossen, 2001).

INTELLECTUAL PROPERTY RIGHTS AND OWNERSHIP OF ONLINE COURSE MATERIALS

Historically, it has been difficult for institutions to exert their ownership rights over course materials (Kearsley, 2000). However, the way that online course materials are created has changed the institutional perspective on ownership of course materials. A good resource on intellectual property, the Pew Learning and Technology Program report put together by Carol Twigg (2000), points out that online course materials are not just the creation of the faculty member, but of a team that includes other institutional employees and that uses institutional resources. Institutions are pursuing intellectual ownership rights for a couple of reasons (Twigg, 2000):

▶ The institution sees the course and course materials as a source of income.

▶ The institution fears that the faculty member will package the course materials and make them available outside the institution, causing competition. (pp. 13–14)

The Pew report also stressed the importance of explaining terms when it comes to intellectual property policy. The symposium participants who developed the Pew report developed the following components of a course:

1. Content—the subject matter such as calculus, biology, Spanish and so on.

2. Course materials—to illustrate or explain the content.

3. A planned program of study—the structure of the course, including learning goals and strategies for achieving them.

4. Planned and spontaneous interactions—between faculty and students, students and materials, students and students.

5. An institution or organization—to offer the course, market it, and award credit. (Twigg, 2000, p. 16)

Clearly defining a course and course materials is important in intellectual property policy because the makeup of an online course involves much more than content. Student-to-student interaction in a course, via a discussion board or e-mail, is the property of the student writing the correspondence; it would not be the property of the faculty member or the institution. It can become a complicated matter.

Changing Your Institution's Intellectual Property Policy and Procedures

Your institution may be comfortable with its existing intellectual property policy. However, if the institution is concerned about its part in the ownership of digital intellectual property because institutional resources were used, it is important to develop a clearly stated contract that spells out the rights of both the institution and the faculty member. Everyone has heard of the KIS principle—keep it simple. Instead of planning for all the exceptions that may arise with the use of a certain set of course materials, an intellectual property policy should state that the faculty member owns his or her course materials. The policy can then provide a list of specific conditions under which the intellectual property would be shared. For a faculty member, knowing up front what the policy is and having the procedures defined through the policy makes a contract for developing course materials clearer and less stressful to create. It becomes a win-win situation for both the faculty member and the institution. If you would like to add a little more definition to your intellectual property policy, here are three models for ownership.

Model 1. The faculty member owns the work. The faculty may assign ownership to the institution, thereby relinquishing management and control of the work (and relinquishing standing to sue for copyright infringement) in exchange for some form of remuneration. The faculty author may also retain ownership but grant the university a nonexclusive license; that is, the right to use the materials when the course is taught by someone other than the faculty author. The author and university may also agree to share profits from commercialization, depending on the university's contribution to the work.

Model 2. The university or college owns the work under the work-for-hire doctrine. The university retains control for distribution and licensing and retains the ability to pursue copyright infringers. The faculty author would be entitled either to royalties for subsequent use of the work and a nonexclusive license or to a nonexclusive license or royalties to use the materials in classes elsewhere.

Model 3. The faculty member creating distance learning materials is an independent contractor, and the creation of the work is outside the scope of employment. Therefore the faculty author would have ownership and the ability to assign or license the work, as in the first model (Hawke, 2001, pp. 34–35).

Scenario: Multimedia Production—Faculty

A professor teaches an art course in a face-to-face classroom setting. She often uses music recordings and video clips in her class under fair use guidelines.

Now, the professor has been asked to teach the same course in a Web-based environment. She plans to use as many of the audio and video materials used in the face-to-face classroom setting as copyright requirements will allow for online use. In addition, she may need to put some of the audio and video clips on CD or DVD for students who have dial-up Internet connections and therefore have difficulty in accessing the online audio and video.

Analysis. Guidelines for copyright of multimedia materials used in the Web environment are currently the subject of negotiations among various groups in the Consortium of College and University Media Center. Some agreed-on general guidelines have emerged.

▶ Use password protection to limit access to enrolled students only.

▶ Make students aware that the audio and video materials used in the course are copyright-protected, and the students may not make copies of them for further distribution.

▶ Remove the multimedia materials from the Web as soon as they are no longer used in the course.

▶ Check the specifications for using reasonable and limited portions of multimedia materials. Specifications vary based on the nature of content and type of media.

▶ When in doubt, ask the copyright owner. Digital recreation and distribution of multimedia material may affect the marketability of the original work, even if only short segments of the original work are involved.

Scenario: E-Mail Copyright and Privacy

An instructor is using both e-mail correspondence with students and a discussion board. During a discussion on the discussion board, one student asks a question that the instructor thought another student explained very well in an e-mail the week before. The instructor posted the e-mail comments to the question on the discussion board, only to have the student who sent the e-mail become very upset. The instructor thought that because the e-mail was course related, it was fine to post the private conversation on the class discussion board. Has he violated copyright by posting the e-mail to the discussion board?

Analysis. Although the instructor was forwarding the e-mail within the context of the course, it is still a copyright violation to forward a student's e-mail message. The author of an e-mail message owns the copyright of that message; it is a violation to modify the content or forward it without the consent of the author. Sharing correspondence between the instructor and the student (not on the public discussion board) with the entire class would often be beneficial. This instructor should have asked the student if it was all right to post, or asked the student to post the comments.

Scenario: Entrepreneurial Faculty

Faculty from an established institution are offering a package of case-based courses sold over the Internet and delivered via the Internet to colleges, universities, and school districts in North America and overseas. The courses can be purchased and repackaged by the purchasing institution; the students can enroll in the courses at the developing institution for credit; or the courses can be used for inservice by school districts. These faculty members are using their institution's continuing education unit to process enrollments and the negotiated fees are being paid to the faculty members' college, where the faculty members then access the funds for their use.

Analysis. In this case, entrepreneurial faculty are running a business from their offices and using university resources to do so. Here are some of the questions that have come up about this case:

▶ Does the institution have an obligation to maintain control of this situation? If yes, how should it go about doing so?

▶ What happens if the products being produced are not of high quality? Will that affect the institution's reputation?

▶ If the case materials generate a substantial revenue stream, how should this be divided among the interested parties?

This case was adapted from case 3 in the Pew Learning and Technology Program report (Twigg, 2000).

Chapter Summary

This chapter has given a brief summary of copyright and intellectual property law. The rule when it comes to copyright is: always seek permission. It is also a good idea to keep track of what is happening with copyright law. This is an area that is continuing to be defined by updates to the copyright laws. Follow lists and newsgroups on this issue and put your two cents in with your legislators when the bills come up.

If your institution has not developed policy for copyright and intellectual property, encourage it to do so. If your institution has policy in place, encourage administration to keep it up-to-date. This will protect both the faculty member and the institution as the laws continue to be defined to accommodate copyright and intellectual property in the information age.

Review Questions

1. What is permitted under the U.S. Copyright Act fair use guidelines?
2. What is the effect of the DMCA and the TEACH Act on educators?

3. How would you seek permission to use a work in a Web-based course?

4. What is the intellectual property policy at your institution or organization?

Summary of Tips

1. Seek the owner's permission before scanning an image and placing the digital copy on the Web.

2. Seek the owner's permission if you want to download a graphic work from the Web and reuse it.

3. Do not skip the "click to accept" agreement when downloading and using freeware and shareware.

4. Append a copyright notice if you have put valuable materials on your Web site.

5. Set up institutional guidelines on copyright policy and provide these materials to all faculty and students.

6. Develop an institutional policy that spells out the contract between the institution and faculty members on course materials that faculty members create.

7. Designate a person in your institution as the consultant on copyright issues.

8. Provide a template of an institutional form letter for faculty to use in seeking copyright permissions.

9. Give seminars to answer questions on copyright issues.

10. Keep a copy of all of your correspondence when seeking copyright permissions.

Exercises

1. Summarize the common myths about copyright and intellectual property.

2. Outline the procedures to take to obtain copyright permission.

3. Visit the Web resources introduced in this chapter and to learn about new developments and publications on copyright and intellectual property for electronic work.

4. Design and conduct a survey at your school to find out how much faculty and students know about copyright and intellectual property.

Resources on the Web

- U.S. Copyright Office, Library of Congress (http://www.copyright.gov)

- Comprehensive site maintained by intellectual property attorney Benedict O'Mahoney (http://www.benedict.com)

- Copyright and fair use site maintained by Stanford University Libraries (http://fairuse.stanford.edu)

- Alternative copyright site (http://creativecommons.org)

References

Bruwelheide, J. H. (1997). Copyright: Opportunities and restrictions for the Teleinstructor. In T. E. Cyrs (Ed.), *Teaching and learning at a distance: What it takes to effectively design, deliver, and evaluate programs.* San Francisco: Jossey-Bass.

Crews, K. (2003a). Copyright and distance education: Making sense of the TEACH Act. *Change,* November/December 2003.

Crews, K. (2003b). *New copyright law for distance education: The meaning and importance of the TEACH Act.* Retrieved August 5, 2003, from http://www.ala.org/washoff/teach.html.

Dahl, J. (2004). Working with—and around—the TEACH Act. *Distance Education Report, 8*(5).

Fishman, S. (2000). *The copyright handbook: How to protect and use written works* (5th ed.). Berkeley, CA: Nolo.

Hawke, C. S. (2001). *Computer and internet use on campus: A legal guide to issues of intellectual property, free speech, and privacy.* San Francisco: Jossey-Bass.

Kearsley, G. (2000). *Online education: Learning and teaching in cyberspace.* Belmont, CA: Wadsworth Thomson Learning.

Ko, S., & Rossen, S. (2001). *Teaching online: A practical guide.* Boston: Houghton Mifflin.

Lindsey, M. (2003). *Copyright law on campus.* Pullman, WA: Washington State University Press.

Mckenzie, J. (1996). Keeping it legal: Questions arising out of Web site management. Retrieved August 22, 2002, from http://www.fno.org/jun96/legal.html.

Picciano, A. G. (2001). *Distance learning: Making connections across virtual space and time.* Upper Saddle River, NJ: Merrill/Prentice Hall.

Simonson, M., Smaldino, S., Albright, M., & Zvacek, S. (2000). *Teaching and learning at a distance: Foundations of distance education.* Upper Saddle River, NJ: Merrill/ Prentice Hall.

Stim, R. (2004). *Getting permission: How to license and clear copyrighted materials online and off* (2nd ed.). Berkeley, CA: Nolo.

Twigg, C. A. (2000). *Who owns online courses and course materials? Intellectual property policies for a new learning environment.* The Pew Learning and Technology Program 2000. Troy, NY: Center for Academic Transformation, Rensselaer Polytechnic Institute.

Vaidhyanathan, S. (August 2, 2002). Copyright as cudgel. *Chronicle of Higher Education,* B7–B8.

Chapter 9

Course Management Systems

CHAPTER INTRODUCTION

Managing Web courses requires more than putting up course materials in a Web space and setting up hyperlinks across pages. Many more tasks are involved. You will have to think about access control, file import and export, content organization and presentation, automated quizzes, grade checking, and online communications. In recent years, many software packages have been developed to facilitate online course delivery and management. These packages, generally called course management systems (CMS), provide a Web browser interface that integrates all the tasks just mentioned. This chapter will examine the functions needed for a Web-based CMS and discuss issues to consider in selecting a system. We hope the discussion can help you make better-informed decisions in selecting tools for Web-based instruction. The chapter can be of value for both administrators and instructors involved in providing Web-based instruction.

LEARNING OBJECTIVES

After studying this chapter, the reader will be able to:

1. Outline the key components and functions of a course management system.

2. Explain the major advantages and constraints of a browser-based working environment for a course management system.

3. Present the key issues and requirements for content portability across different course management systems.

4. Summarize the major efforts made by various organizations and vendors to promote standardization in learning object development.

5. Outline the technical constraints and possibilities of online quizzing and design methods to prevent cheating.

6. Describe some major endeavors in open source course management system development.

C A S E   S T U D Y

- Mid-State University began Web-based course delivery around 1995, and many of the instructors have accumulated a significant amount of experience in developing and delivering Web-based instruction. The university used a combination of tools for hypermedia development and Web-based course delivery. To promote statewide collaboration in Web-based instruction, the state has selected WebCT to be the course management system used by all state institutions. Key issues to address in preparing faculty and students to adopt the new course management system are the following:

  1. Most faculty members know little about this course management system and some have misconceptions about it. A preliminary task is to help the faculty become acquainted with the key components of the system and become informed about the primary benefits of using the system.

  2. The user interface of WebCT is browser based. The instructors need to be aware of the features of the browser-based interface for course management.

  3. Many instructors have existing course materials prepared in FrontPage and wish to port most of the materials into the new system. Helping the instructors transfer the existing materials into the new course environment will be a major challenge.

  4. In anticipation of future content migration, and in light of the standards specified by IMS and SCORM, course designers are encouraged to take a modular approach to the development of course materials.

  5. The new course management system offers a set of online assessment tools that are different from what the faculty used before. Training is needed to help faculty become competent in the new assignment and quiz tools in WebCT. Some faculty may also need to transfer the quiz items from the previous system to the question database in WebCT.

KEY COMPONENTS OF A COURSE MANAGEMENT SYSTEM

A **course management system** (CMS) is typically a software package that integrates a broad range of online course functions into a unified interface. Although some of the functions of a CMS may be provided separately by individual tools with more power and flexibility, the primary advantage of a course management system is its integrated online environment. For example, dedicated Web site management tools such as DreamWeaver and FrontPage may have more flexible and user-friendly file management functions, but file management in a course management system can be linked to student assessment (assignment

TABLE 9.1   Essential Functions of a Course Management System

Category	Function
User management	Access control, record keeping, activity tracking, grouping
File management	File uploading and downloading, folder organization, archiving, backup
Content organization and presentation	Hyperlink structure, navigation scheme, navigation guidance and cues, multimedia support
Assessment	Assignment submission and grading, automated quizzes, gradebook, statistics of students' performance
Online communication	Discussion board, chat rooms, e-mail, whiteboard, file sharing

FIGURE 9.1   Key Functions of a CMS

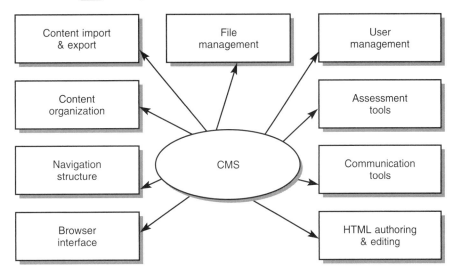

submission and grading) and activity tracking. Table 9.1 and Figure 9.1 list some of the most important functions of a course management system.

Additional functions and tools may be desired, but at the time of this writing they are not available in popular course management systems or are supported only to a very limited extent. Table 9.2 lists some of these additional functions.

Over the past few years, there has been a rapid growth of course management system development and applications. As discussed in chapter 1, a

TABLE ⑨·⑵   **Additional Functions of a CMS**

Category	Function
Interface	Customizable templates for user interfaces
HTML authoring	A truly what-you-see-is-what-you-get (WYSIWYG) HTML page editor
Online communication	Synchronous program sharing, audio/video conferencing
Assessment	Error analysis of students' performance on quizzes

third of all college courses now use course management tools (Green, 2003). Students' perception of course management systems appears to be mostly positive, too. In a survey conducted by the Education Center for Applied Research of 4,374 freshmen and seniors from 13 colleges, 76% indicated that their experience with a course management system was positive or very positive (Young, 2004). As the use of course management systems evolves, some have anticipated the emergence of course creation systems, software packages that can assist in the creation of courses that can be readily imported into a course management system (Strauss, 2004).

Some of the popular course management systems at the time of this writing include WebCT, Blackboard, and Design2Learn. Our experience with course management systems is mostly with WebCT Campus Edition (CE) 4, so we'll primarily use WebCT CE 4 to illustrate CMS features. Course management systems will evolve and change, but we would expect to see their key components remain. The discussion in this chapter about these key functions will continue to have general reference value.

Browser-Based Interface

Before we discuss the key components of course management systems, let's look at the immediate feature you'll notice when you start using a CMS like Blackboard or WebCT: the browser-based user interface. All users, including the system administrator, course designers, and learners, access the CMS through a browser interface (see Figure 9.2). Using a browser-based interface can be both facilitating and limiting. It can be facilitating because a standard browser is the only user software requirement and there is practically no platform compatibility problem.

A major constraint of the browser-delimited working environment, however, is the lack of support of native applications. This is an inherent constraint, since browsers generally are not allowed to run native applications on the client system.

FIGURE 9.2   Designer Interface in WebCT CE 4

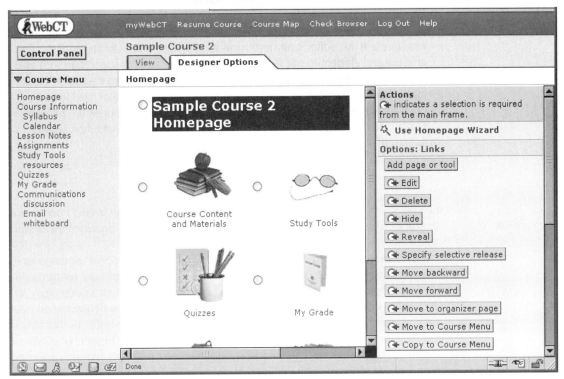

For example, HTML page editing functions in a browser environment are generally not as well supported as in a desktop application. A plug-in or a Java applet is usually required to support HTML page editing to some limited extent. File management in a browser environment is often very constraining, too. For example, you usually have to click several buttons to upload or download a file, or copy or move a file. Usually you cannot move files and folders around by dragging and dropping. Nor can you copy an item from your desktop and directly paste it into the work space of the HTML editor in the browser window.

User Management

Unless your online courses are open to the public, you will need to control access to them. Most online courses provide some general information for prospective students or visitors without requiring log-in, such as a course description or syllabus, but require the user to log in to access detailed course content. Web-based course management systems generally have a central access point for all users. A global account system requires each user to have only one account to access all

CASE STUDY   **Choose an HTML Editor**

- Because the course management system currently available does not have an easy-to-use HTML editor, many instructors at Mid-State University find it more effective and efficient to edit their HTML pages with a desktop application such as DreamWeaver or FrontPage and then upload the edited page into the course management system. When they have a number of documents that need to be uploaded into the course management system, they usually compress or "zip" the files on their desktop first, upload the "zipped" files all at once, and then expand or "unzip" the files in the course management system.

the courses in which the user is registered. This makes course access convenient for students who enroll in more than one course because it provides them with central access to their different courses.

User management is not possible without database support. Some course management systems have a built-in database engine; others may require connection to external databases. A scalable course management system may include not only a built-in database but also external database connectivity. An industry standard database system can significantly increase the performance and scalability of a course management system. Today, higher versions of course management systems can also be integrated with institutional resource management systems such as DataTel, PeopleSoft, and SunGard SCT. Such integration can provide a single sign-on for all users. Users are automatically assigned to courses based on their registration records in the institutional database system.

Although the integration with an institutional resource management system can automate user registration and course assignment, there are many other student management functions that a general resource management system cannot handle. These functions are usually handled by the course management system (see Table 9.3).

Most course management systems support the creation of student groups. Each group can have its own shared work space, discussion forum, chat room, and assignment box. Monitoring student visits to different content modules can keep the instructor informed about students' learning activities to assess their learning needs and progress (Cooper, 2000). WebCT CE 4 can record a student's first access and last access to a course site. Other recording capabilities include the number of pages visited and messages posted by each student (see Figure 9.3).

File Management

Web-based course content files are generally stored (at least for the user's view) and presented in a directory-subdirectory structure. The directory structure is

TABLE 9.3 **User Management Functions**

Functions	Function descriptions
Availability control	Setting up the availability of course content modules or exercises based on student needs and learning progress
Visitation tracking	Tracking student visitation of course modules and participation in discussion
Grouping	Grouping students for different learning tasks
Customization	Customizing a content module, an exercise, or a quiz based on learner needs and learning progress
Record reset	Overriding or resetting student records on exercises or quizzes based on instructional needs

FIGURE 9.3 **Student Tracking in WebCT CE 4**

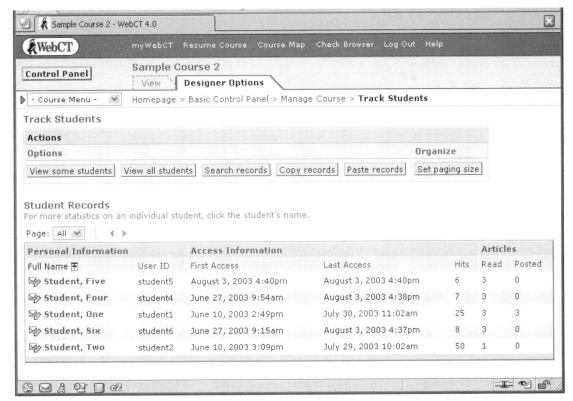

FIGURE 9.4 **File Management Interface in WebCT CE 4**

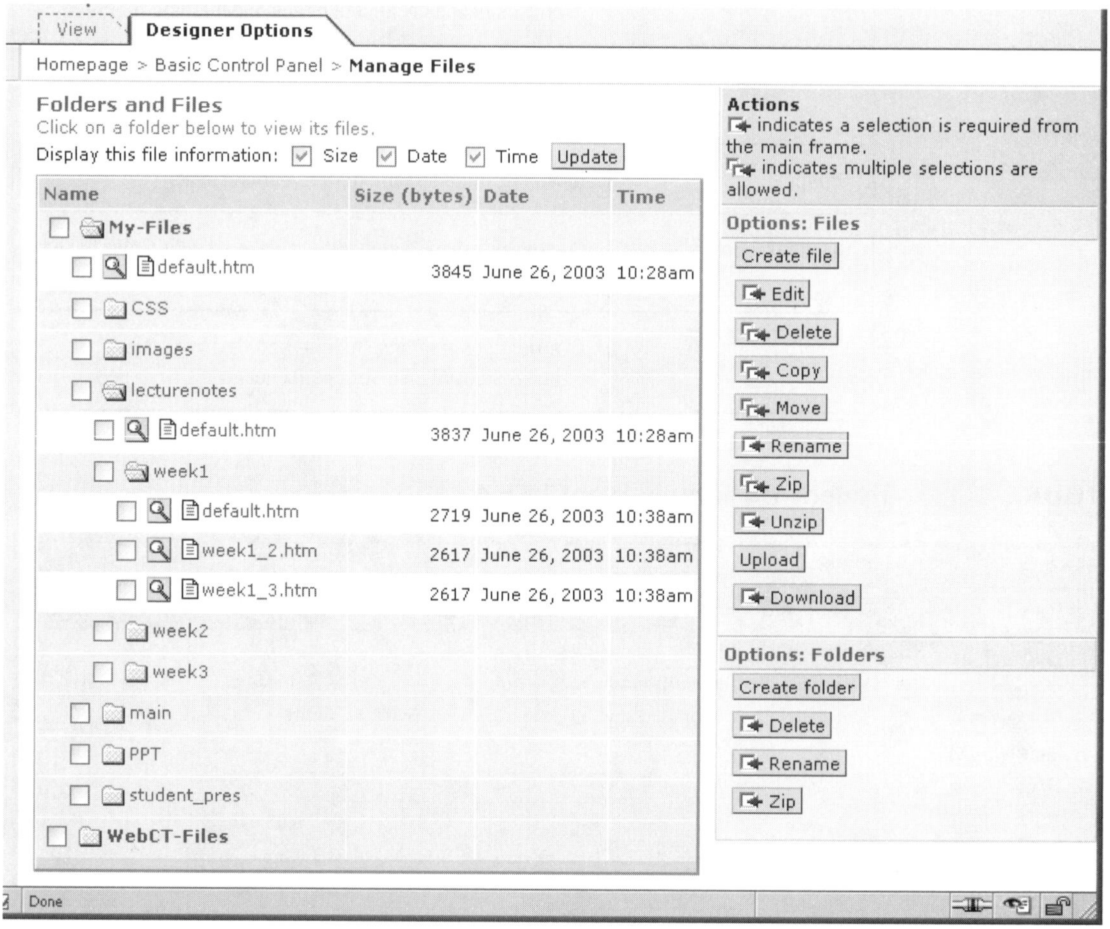

sometimes called a "tree structure" because each node on the structure can branch off into subdirectories. A basic function of the directory structure is to organize files into categories based on functions or topics. This method of file organization is familiar to most computer users, since almost all computer applications now use directories and subdirectories to mange files (see Figure 9.4).

As with any other application, data backup is a crucial function of a CMS. In WebCT CE 4, the course backup function is provided by an archiving tool (see Figure 9.5). WebCT CE 4 can archive the complete course as a zipped (compressed) file. The course designer can either keep the zipped file on the server or download the file to a local storage medium. The latter is generally a safe choice since the backup can be kept separate from the server. The archiving process can keep all the course data and settings, including assignments, quizzes, discussion messages, and student records. When restoration is

FIGURE 9.5 Course Backup in WebCT CE 4

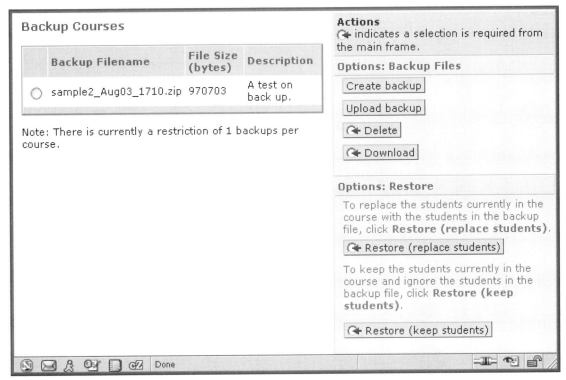

needed, the designer can either restore the course with all existing student records or restore the course without any records. The latter option is handy when it's time to reset the course for the use of a new group of students.

One interesting thing to note about the course backup in WebCT CE 4 is that the zipped file generated by WebCT cannot be opened outside WebCT using a standard zip tool; it can only be restored back into WebCT and unzipped within the course space using the unzip tool in WebCT. This restriction is understandable, given the fact that the backup file includes data other than documents and media files. The additional data include CMS-specific information such as course settings, quiz settings, student assignments, quiz results, discussion board messages, and so on.

Content Organization and Presentation Structure

Files uploaded to a CMS are typically organized in a standard directory-subdirectory structure like that of a desktop file management system. Course management systems may have special ways of content organization and presentation, however. For example, WebCT CE 4 uses an "organizer page"

ⒸASE STUDY   **File Management in a CMS**··········

- In the experience of the MSU instructors, a major inconvenience with a browser-delimited file management interface is that only one file can be uploaded or downloaded at a time. If you need to upload or download multiple files, you need to zip the files first, upload or download the zipped file, and then unzip the file after it is uploaded or downloaded. In addition, moving files by drag-and-drop is not yet supported in most current browser-based course management systems. Quite a few button clicks are involved in a browser interface for a file uploading or downloading operation.

  Another inconvenience the instructors have found is that moving or renaming files in a browser-based course management system like WebCT may break associated hyperlinks, because the course management system is not capable of detecting the associated hyperlinks and updating the links automatically. This requires the course designer to have a careful plan of the course content structure. Once the files are linked and the hyperlink structure is set, moving or renaming files should be avoided.

to group related links on one page. The links added to an organizer page can point to individual files uploaded into the WebCT course space, certain WebCT built-in tools, other organizer pages in the same course space, or external resources outside WebCT. A major advantage of the organizer page is that each link added to an organizer page can have its own release settings. These settings can be specified in terms of date and time, learner characteristics, and learning progress such as student accomplishments of particular assignments or quizzes (see Figure 9.6).

Another feature of content organization in WebCT CE 4 is its use of the "content module." The content module organizes and presents course content units in the form of a table of contents with headings and subheadings (see Figure 9.7). The subheadings are hyperlinks pointing to files that have been uploaded into WebCT course space.

Assessment Tools

In addition to user access control, the most desirable function of a course management system is probably its computer-assisted assessment tools, particularly online quizzing. Course management systems may differ significantly as to what type of quiz questions can be supported, how quizzes can be set up and administered, and what type of feedback can be provided to students.

Question Types. There are roughly two types of questions for computer-assisted quizzing: one supports automated grading by the quiz system and the

FIGURE 9.6 Release Condition Settings in WebCT CE 4

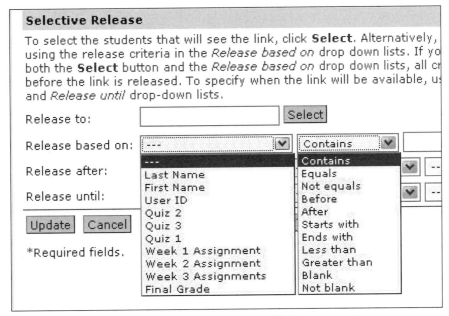

FIGURE 9.7 A Content Module in WebCT CE 4

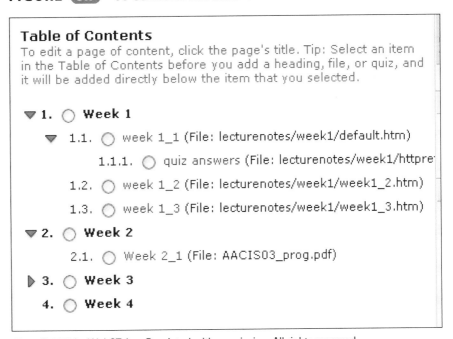

TABLE ⓽.⁴   Types of Questions Used with Automated Grading

Question type	Features
Multiple choice	Minimum of three choices, usually no more than six choices
True/false	A variation of multiple choice with only two options
Matching items	Two columns are given; students pick items from one column to match those in the other
Calculated questions	Designers specify a formula with a range of possible values; the quiz system generates the question with random values within the range for the question and answer selections
Ordering items	A set of items is presented in incorrect order; students rearrange the items into correct order
Short answer	Automated grading is possible if correct answers are short and do not allow much variation in wording or sequence of words

other requires manual grading by the instructor. The types of questions that allow automated grading generally include multiple-choice and true/false selections, matching items, calculated answers, filling in blanks, ordering items into sequence, and short answers without much variation (see Table 9.4).

Multiple-choice questions are probably the most popular form of quiz questions that can be graded with an automated system. Some quiz systems allow the designer to offer more than one correct answer for a question. The scoring options can be cumulative or inclusive. The cumulative option lets the quiz designer distribute weights among the multiple correct answers and gives corresponding credit to all corrected answers. The inclusive option requires the quiz taker to pick all correct answers for the credit. If the quiz taker misses any of the multiple correct answers for the question, no score is given. Carefully designed multiple-choice tests can be used to assess very high levels of analytic and logical thinking skills. (See chapter 3 of this book for further discussion of objective tests in Web-based instruction.)

Calculated questions can be set to allow a range of tolerance for possible correct answers. They are usually designed to test math skills. In addition, calculated questions can help promote question reusability and prevent possible cheating by quiz takers who may spread the correct answers, since the values in the question and possible answers can vary each time the question is generated by the quiz system. Matching items can be particularly useful for assessing students' ability to distinguish a set of related concepts or items.

Question Reusability. All instructors know that it is not easy to design good questions. It can save a great amount of time and resources if questions can be reused from quiz to quiz or even across courses. We can make questions reusable by storing them in a question database. When setting up quizzes, the instructor can simply select questions from the database. Given a good number of questions in the database, the course designer can even let the quiz engine randomly pick questions from the database. The instructor can also add or remove questions as long as the quiz has not been released to the students or no student has taken the quiz yet. Another advantage of having questions in a database is portability. It is generally quite easy to export large numbers of questions from one database and import them into another. WebCT uses a question database to manage all the questions in a course.

Some course management systems do not have a question database. In such systems, the course designer adds questions to a quiz when the quiz is created. All the questions are bound to the quiz. When the quiz is deleted, all the questions tied to the quiz are deleted along with the quiz.

Grading and Feedback. If questions can be reused by more than one quiz, different score weights may need to be assigned to the same question when it is picked for different quizzes. Score weight should therefore be assigned as questions are picked for each quiz, instead of being permanently attached to questions in the question database.

Instant grading is usually a feature that most students like about computer-assisted quizzes. However, instant grading and correct answers may have to be withheld sometimes. In the Web-based learning environment, it is not always possible to require all students to take the same quiz at the same time. Family commitments, job duties, unexpected technical difficulties, and other contingencies may prevent some from taking the quiz at the given time. If instant grading and immediate feedback are provided in such situations, it may create some opportunities for some quiz takers to share answers. To prevent them from spreading the correct answers, an online quiz system should give the instructor the option to withhold instant grading and to release grading and correct answers only when the quiz is over or after every student has taken the quiz.

Unlike score weight, feedback can be permanently attached to each question when the question is created or edited. For multiple choices, feedback can be attached to particular choices. If the instructor has chosen to release correct answers after the students have taken the quiz, students may receive specific comments on errors as well as an explanation of the correct answer, including possible references or suggestions for further study. Additional general feedback on each student's overall performance can be provided at the quiz level too. The instructor should be allowed to override scores generated by the quiz engine to give credit to students' answers or attempts that should be credited.

In addition to grading and verbal feedback, descriptive statistics of student performances should be made available to both instructor and students. For the instructor, a statistic report in tabular form would be helpful, and even better if the report can be exported as a spreadsheet. The statistics may include the number of students who have taken each quiz, length of time for each student to finish the quiz, class average score, highest/lowest scores, and standard deviation. In addition to descriptive statistics, error analysis is a valuable tool for the instructor to view the distribution patterns of students' errors, especially with a visual display of the patterns. Chapter 3 has more discussion of error analysis.

Communication Tools

Major course management systems generally include basic communication tools such as e-mail, discussion boards, and chat rooms. A primary advantage of a built-in e-mail service is that users do not need any additional software, nor do they need to log in again. To send an e-mail to a class member, they simply select a name from a list of class members, compose the message, and send it. The instructor can also send messages easily to everyone in class without using an additional distribution list. Another advantage of having a dedicated class e-mail box is that class messages will not get mixed with spam or commercial e-mail and be accidentally deleted as junk mail. Figure 9.8 shows the e-mail composition screen in WebCT.

FIGURE 9.8   E-mail Composing Interface in a CMS

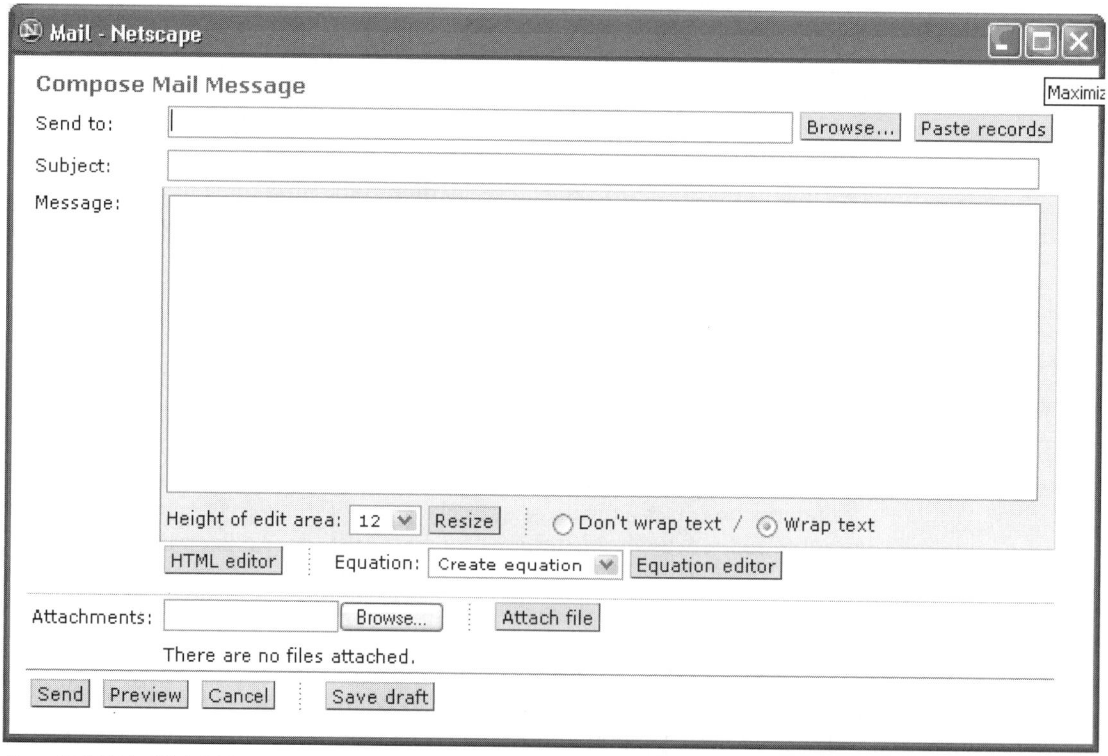

Almost all course management systems have a discussion board tool that supports threaded posting and responding. Some systems allow the user to change or delete messages he or she posted; other systems do not. Not allowing students to change or delete a posted message may help keep information integrity because such change or deletion can make follow-up responses appear off target or pointless.

Discussion can be public and open to all class members, or private to students picked by the instructor to form small groups (see Figure 9.9). This can be effective if students need to be assigned to different tasks without sharing task-related information across groups.

As of this writing, few course management systems support synchronous Internet conferencing as an integrated tool. The only synchronous communication tools supported by most course management systems are the chat tool and whiteboard. If your Web-based courses require real-time Internet conferencing with audio and video interaction, you may need to find a third-party tool. Fortunately, there are many such software packages available on the market, with varied functionality and scalability.

FIGURE 9.9   Discussions in WebCT CE 4

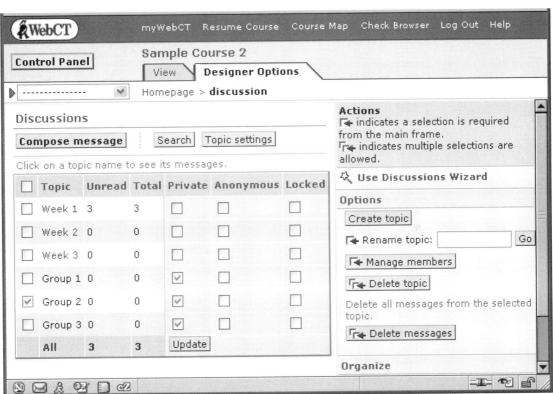

WHAT TO CONSIDER IN ADOPTING A COURSE MANAGEMENT SYSTEM

New course management systems will continue to emerge, and existing ones will keep evolving. Some reviews list all the functions found in existing course management systems in tabular form for comparative evaluation (see Figure 9.10). Such a feature-listing approach has some problems. First of all, it can be misleading to evaluate a CMS by looking at the number of features it has. We feel performance effectiveness and usefulness of the key functions are more important than the number of functions. We would rather have a CMS that has fewer functions but performs well on the essential functions than have a CMS with more functions but that performs poorly on the essential functions.

Second, for users who need to evaluate and select a CMS, the long list of features can be overwhelming. The reader may get lost among all the details. Even more experienced users usually find it necessary to prioritize important functions of a CMS and differentiate essential features from nonessential ones. In this chapter, we will not try to discuss all the possible features. Instead, we will focus on what we have found to be critical components and key issues in adopting a CMS (see Figure 9.11). For those readers who would like to find out more about details of varied additional CMS features, refer to the list of Web resources at the end of the chapter.

Cost and Portability

In selecting a CMS, administrators and instructors generally have different concerns and interests. For the administrator, cost and portability is on top of the list. The cost of adopting a course management system has two levels. The apparent cost includes the one-time purchase payment or the annual license, server setup, and system configuration. For the annual license, the cost can be based on the number of students enrolled per semester or site based (per server) with unlimited access.

In adopting or migrating to a new course management system, the less apparent cost can be far more significant, resulting from user training, course material conversion, and development. Although major CMS vendors have stepped up their efforts to be compliant with open standards such as the IMS Global Learning Consortium (IMS) standards and the shareable content object reference model (SCORM), transferring large amounts of course materials from one CMS to another is still a time-consuming and troublesome task. Course management system vendors generally build proprietary features into their software for market competitiveness and tend to have unique ways of file organization, navigation structuring, and content presentation. These proprietary features can be barriers if users need to move from one system to another.

FIGURE 9.10 **Features Listed in a Comparative Study of CMS**

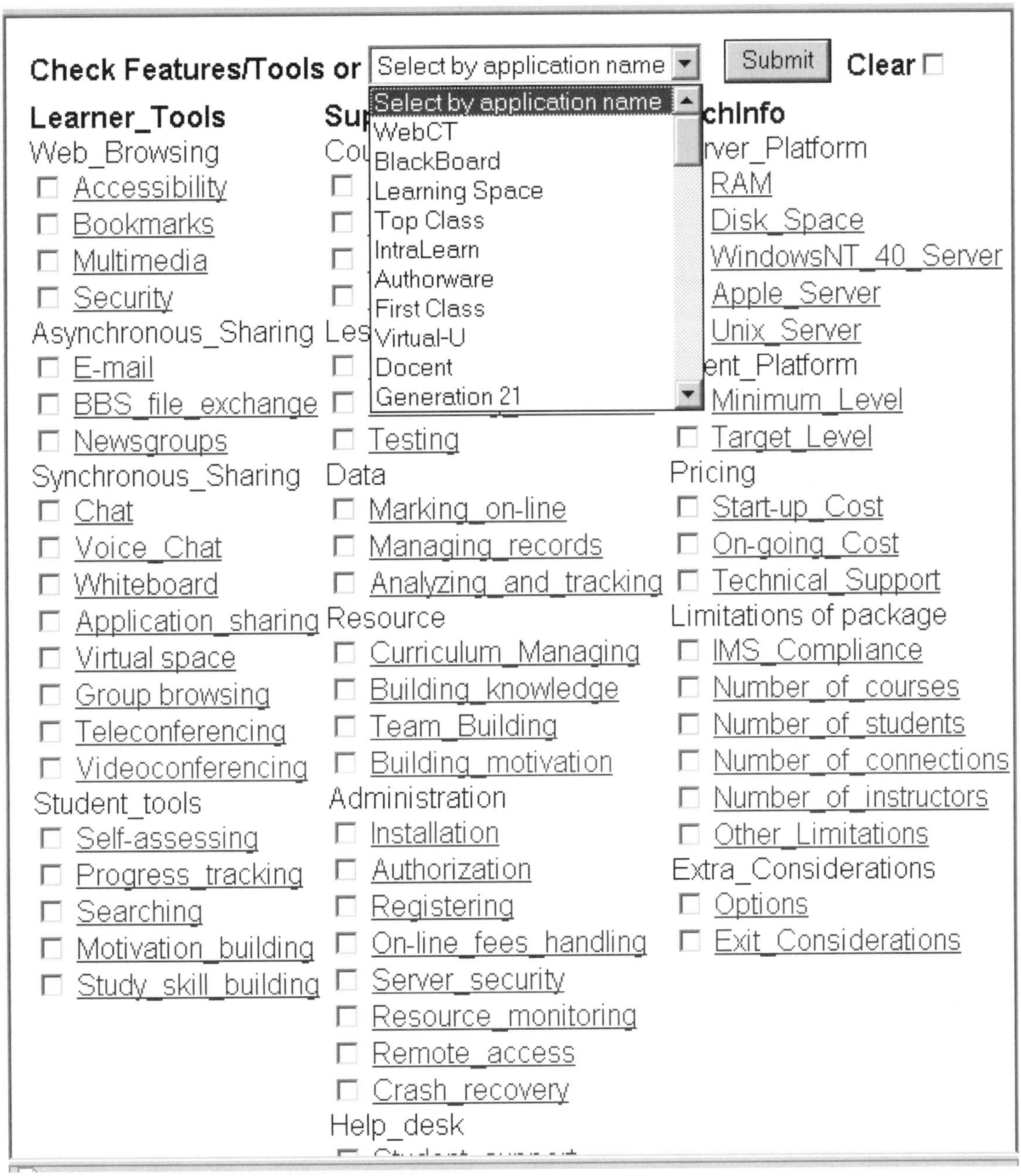

Check Features/Tools or | Select by application name ▼ | Submit | Clear ☐

Learner_Tools	Sup_____chInfo

Select by application name ▲
WebCT
BlackBoard
Learning Space
Top Class
IntraLearn
Authorware
First Class
Virtual-U
Docent
Generation 21 ▼

Learner_Tools
Web_Browsing
☐ Accessibility
☐ Bookmarks
☐ Multimedia
☐ Security
Asynchronous_Sharing
☐ E-mail
☐ BBS_file_exchange
☐ Newsgroups
Synchronous_Sharing
☐ Chat
☐ Voice_Chat
☐ Whiteboard
☐ Application_sharing
☐ Virtual space
☐ Group browsing
☐ Teleconferencing
☐ Videoconferencing
Student_tools
☐ Self-assessing
☐ Progress_tracking
☐ Searching
☐ Motivation_building
☐ Study_skill_building

Sup...
Cou...
☐ ...
☐ ...
☐ ...
☐ ...
☐ ...
Les...
☐ ...
☐ ...
☐ Testing
Data
☐ Marking_on-line
☐ Managing_records
☐ Analyzing_and_tracking
Resource
☐ Curriculum_Managing
☐ Building_knowledge
☐ Team_Building
☐ Building_motivation
Administration
☐ Installation
☐ Authorization
☐ Registering
☐ On-line_fees_handling
☐ Server_security
☐ Resource_monitoring
☐ Remote_access
☐ Crash_recovery
Help_desk
☐ Student_...

...chInfo
...rver_Platform
☐ RAM
☐ Disk_Space
☐ WindowsNT_40_Server
☐ Apple_Server
☐ Unix_Server
...ent_Platform
☐ Minimum_Level
☐ Target_Level
Pricing
☐ Start-up_Cost
☐ On-going_Cost
☐ Technical_Support
Limitations of package
☐ IMS_Compliance
☐ Number_of_courses
☐ Number_of_students
☐ Number_of_connections
☐ Number_of_instructors
☐ Other_Limitations
Extra_Considerations
☐ Options
☐ Exit_Considerations

FIGURE 9.11   **Things to Consider in Adopting a CMS**

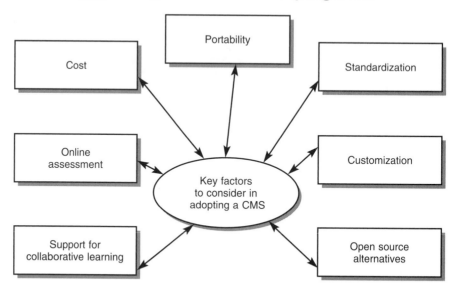

The uniqueness in functions and structures of a course management system can have a pedagogical impact too. Instructors may need to make changes in teaching methodology to fit what is given by a particular course management system. Students will need to make similar adaptations to become comfortable and competent with the new system. Some sample unique features were described earlier in this chapter.

Standardization

For an institution to avoid being bound by one particular proprietary system and crippled from moving to other systems, there should be minimal investment required for transferring course materials from one system to another. Course designers should not be required to spend a great amount of time converting and transforming the materials and rebuilding the courses in the new system. For content modules to be readily interoperable across different systems, a certain degree of standardization is needed. In recent years, there has been a growing awareness of the need for the establishment of standards for content development in online education and training. In their 2001 report, the President's Information Technology Advisory Committee (PITAC, 2001) of the U.S. government recommended that the federal government should work with industry and academia to develop technical standards for extendable component-based technologies and infrastructures that can be widely used in online education and training. Over the past few years, organizations have been established to develop standards with specifications for content developers to refer to in making content modules portable across platforms and systems. Key organizations include Advanced Distributed Learning (ADL) (http://www.adlnet.org), the Open Knowledge Initiative (OKI) (http://www.okiproject.org/), the IMS Global Learning Consortium (http://www.imsglobal.org), the IEEE Learning Technology Standards Committee (http://ltsc.ieee.org/), and the Schools Interoperability Framework (SIF) (http://www.sifinfo.org).

Modular Approach. The modular approach is an essential characteristic of portable content development and of hypermedia. It is a current trend in the e-learning environment. Content modularization essentially means preparing instructional content in **learning objects** that are free-standing and self-contained, reusable in multiple contexts, and transportable across different applications and operating systems.

Web-based course materials generally take a lot more time to develop than printed course materials. It can significantly reduce the cost of material development if content modules can be used by as many users and in as many settings as possible once they are created. In order for content modules to be reusable across different systems, some standardization is necessary.

When content is prepared and stored in modules, each of which focuses on a specific topic or is designed for a specific task, it is easier to reuse the modules in different contexts. From a business point of view, the value of content is increased when content is reused and distributed to a broad audience. In addition to reusability and interoperability, another key advantage of content modularization is flexible connectivity. The key attribute of hypermedia is flexible linkage to join related content modules. To facilitate flexible connectivity, hypermedia content needs to be developed in small independent modules. Small modules are easier to select and link to accommodate different learning paths and facilitate adaptive instruction (Longmire, 2000).

IMS and ADL Specifications. A modular learning object is a conceptually appealing idea, though there are many challenges to meet before standardized learning objects can be widely implemented. Major course management system vendors have become aware of the importance of standardization and are directing their efforts in this direction. Most of the standardization efforts are based on IMS specifications. IMS is a not-for-profit organization that has contributing members from hardware and software vendors, Web service providers, educational institutions, government agencies, multimedia content providers, publishers, system integrators, and others. IMS aims to promote the worldwide adoption of standards that will support the interoperability of distributed learning environments and content from different authors. Standards that IMS is trying to develop begin as specifications. The specifications for modular learning objects are extensive. For example, for content packaging, specifications can cover such attributes as author name, copyright, contact, media

IN PRACTICE   Cisco's Reusable Learning Objects and the MERLOT Project

Efforts are being made to create and promote the use of learning object repositories. Cisco's reusable learning object strategy (Cisco Systems, 2003) is an example of a modular approach to e-learning content development. Based on Merrill's component display theory (1983, 1999), Cisco is trying to develop an approach to building reusable, granular learning modules that can be composed independently of a delivery medium and accessed through a database (Cisco Systems, 2003).

In North America, there is the MERLOT project (Multimedia Educational Resource for Learning and Online Teaching) and Canada's Portal for Online Objects in Learning (POOL). MERLOT is an open resource collection primarily for faculty and students of higher education. Links to online learning materials are collected along with annotations and peer reviews (MERLOT, 2004). Members of MERLOT contribute materials and form virtual communities in their respective disciplines. Attributes of learning objects in MERLOT include author, copyright, peer review ratings, material type (animation, simulation, tutorial, case study, drill/practice, quiz, lecture, reference material), object location, subject categories, description, intended audience, technical format (HTML/text, JavaScript, audio, video, Flash, Authorware, Shockwave, Director file, Java applet, image, PDF, VRML, executable program), CMS compatibility (Blackboard, WebCT, other), technical requirements, language, and cost of adoption.

type, content length, display template, markup definition (XML or Data Type Definition), format definition (CSS or XSL), modularity level, discipline category, topic area, skill area, competency indicator, and the like. Figure 9.12 lists some of the IMS specifications that have been released as of December 2004.

Another pioneer endeavor that has been instrumental in promoting e-learning objects is the Advanced Distributed Learning (ADL) Initiative. ADL was started in 1997 by the U.S. Department of Defense as "a collaborative effort between government, industry and academia to establish a new distributed learning environment that permits the interoperability of learning tools and course content on a global scale. ADL's vision is to provide access to the highest quality education and training, tailored to individual needs, delivered cost-effectively anywhere and anytime" (ADL, 2004b). ADL has specified some functional requirements for designing and developing interoperable and shareable learning objects and tools. The requirements are:

1. Accessible from multiple remote locations through the use of metadata and packaging standards

2. Adaptable by tailoring instruction to individual and organizational needs

FIGURE 9.12 IMS Specifications

Specification	Description
Content Packaging Specification	For easy content transfer across platforms
ePortfolio Specification	Promotes lifelong learning and makes exchanging portfolios from school to work transitions easier
AccessForAll Meta-Data Specification	For identifying resources that match a user's stated preferences or needs
Digital Repositories Specifications	For standard access to any collection of resources that are accessible via a network without prior knowledge of the structure of the collection; . . . intended to utilize schemas already defined elsewhere . . . rather than attempt to introduce any new schema
Learning Design Specification	Provides a generic and flexible language to enable many different pedagogies to be expressed and shared
Meta-Data Specifications	For defining standardized content search parameters
Question and Test Interoperability	For sharing test items and making assessment tools interoperable
Learner Information Package Specification	For the interoperability of Internet-based learner information systems with other systems that support the Internet learning environment
Enterprise Specification	For sharing data with administrative applications and services across different interfaces and platforms
Competency Definition Specification	For defining skills, knowledge, tasks, and learning in terms of key characteristics of a competency independent of its use in any particular context
Reusable Definition of Competency or Educational Objective Specification	For creating common understandings of competencies as part of a learning or career plan, as learning prerequisites, or as learning outcomes, and for exchanging these definitions between learning systems, human resource systems, learning content, competency or skills repositories, and other relevant systems
Enterprise Services Specification	Specifies how systems manage the exchange of information that describes people, groups, and memberships within the context of learning
Accessibility Specification	For developing accessible learning applications

Source: IMS Global Learning Consortium, 2004.

3. Affordable by increasing learning efficiency and productivity while reducing time and costs

4. Durable across revisions of operating systems and software

5. Interoperable across multiple tools and platforms

6. Reusable through the design, management, and distribution of tools and learning content across multiple applications

In January 2000, ADL released the sharable courseware object reference model (SCORM) version 1.0. SCORM is a collection of specifications adapted from multiple sources to provide a comprehensive suite of e-learning capabilities that enable interoperability, accessibility, and reusability of Web-based learning content. One year later, SCORM Version 1.1 became available. With SCORM 1.1, the full name was changed from Shareable Courseware Object Reference Model to Shareable Content Object Reference Model. The name change reflected the fact that SCORM can apply to various levels of content, smaller or larger than an entire course (ADL, 2004a). SCORM 1.2 was released in October 2001, with the addition of content packaging application profiles. Derived from the IMS content packaging specification, these profiles map the content structure format (CSF) from SCORM Version 1.1 into the general IMS specifications. SCORM consists of four distinct "books" that contain the critical elements. The first book, Overview, contains high-level conceptual information, history, current status, and future direction of SCORM. The second book, Content Aggregation Model (CAM), describes the components used in a learning experience, how the components are packaged, and how the components are described to facilitate searching and sharing. The third book, Run-Time Environment (RTE), describes the Learning Management System (LMS) requirements for managing the run-time environment. The fourth book, Sequencing and Navigation (SN), describes how SCORM conformant content may be sequenced through a set of learner-initiated or system-initiated navigation events. Future versions of the four books will include lessons learned and gained from implementing this version of SCORM (ADL, 2004a).

Customization

Although standardization is essential to ensure content portability and reusability across systems, a course management system should also allow course designers to customize the user interface to a certain extent. Different subject domains may have different requirements for content structuring and the navigation scheme. Course designers and instructors may have different needs and preferences for content organization and presentation. Current versions of popular course management systems such as Blackboard and WebCT support some degree of customization. For example, course designers in WebCT 4 can

IN PRACTICE   **CMS Vendors' Efforts**

Standardization and interoperability are concerns not only of government agencies and educational institutions but also CMS vendors who have been seeking to develop portable content modules in a standardized interface for easy interoperability. For example, Blackboard is advocating Blackboard Building Blocks to support users in integrating external tools, systems, and content into the Blackboard e-Education Suite (Blackboard, 2004b). Using Blackboard's building block architecture, QuestionMark and Blackboard have developed a Blackboard system extension to link the Blackboard Learning System to the QuestionMark Perception assessment platform (Blackboard, 2004a). Grades from Perception assessments will be automatically entered into the Blackboard gradebook. This allows institutions to maintain student and instructor profiles within Blackboard while taking advantage of the powerful assessment features of QuestionMark Perception. Learners will be able to take portable data along with them as they move from one learning system to another. The learners' profiles will include data about their educational history and learning preferences (Syllabus, 2002).

WebCT is advocating the use of ePacks to promote partnerships with textbook publishers in developing course materials that can be readily integrated into the WebCT environment. Components of an ePack may include: (a) an electronic version of a textbook, (b) interactive media, (c) videos, (d) a question database with varied question types, (e) critical thinking activities that challenge students to apply knowledge or to expand their understanding on their own, such as case studies, essays, and simulations, and (f) instructor resources such as suggested answers to exercises and additional online resources. The availability of ePacks can be a big plus in course development.

select different color schemes or background image, edit the course menu items, and modify icons for hyperlinks (see Figure 9.13).

Online Quizzing

When evaluating the quiz functions of a course management system, questions we may need to ask include:

1. What types of questions are supported?
2. Is a question database (item bank) used to support reusability and portability of questions?
3. Can questions be batch imported and exported in standard format?
4. Is random selection of questions supported?
5. Is random ordering of quiz items supported?

FIGURE 9.13 **User Interface Customization in WebCT CE 4**

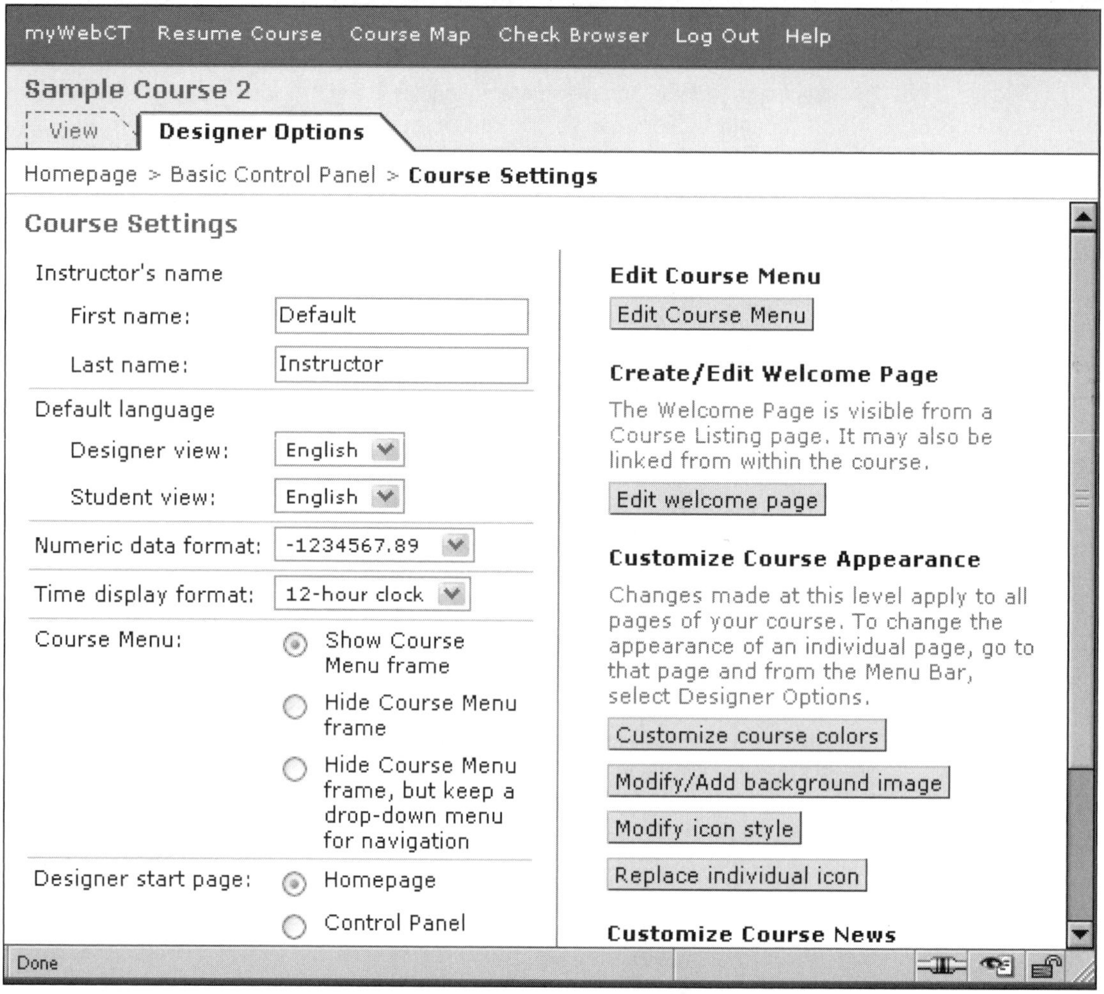

myWebCT Resume Course Course Map Check Browser Log Out Help

Sample Course 2

View | **Designer Options**

Homepage > Basic Control Panel > **Course Settings**

Course Settings

Instructor's name

First name: Default

Last name: Instructor

Default language

Designer view: English ▾

Student view: English ▾

Numeric data format: -1234567.89 ▾

Time display format: 12-hour clock ▾

Course Menu:
- ⦿ Show Course Menu frame
- ○ Hide Course Menu frame
- ○ Hide Course Menu frame, but keep a drop-down menu for navigation

Designer start page:
- ⦿ Homepage
- ○ Control Panel

Edit Course Menu

Edit Course Menu

Create/Edit Welcome Page

The Welcome Page is visible from a Course Listing page. It may also be linked from within the course.

Edit welcome page

Customize Course Appearance

Changes made at this level apply to all pages of your course. To change the appearance of an individual page, go to that page and from the Menu Bar, select Designer Options.

Customize course colors

Modify/Add background image

Modify icon style

Replace individual icon

Customize Course News

Done

6. Can a quiz be modified after it is created?

7. What kind of control do course designers have over the quiz settings, student grades, and the release of feedback?

8. What statistical reports are available?

Figure 9.14 illustrates factors to consider when choosing a quiz tool.

FIGURE 9.14   Things to Consider in Adopting a Quiz Tool

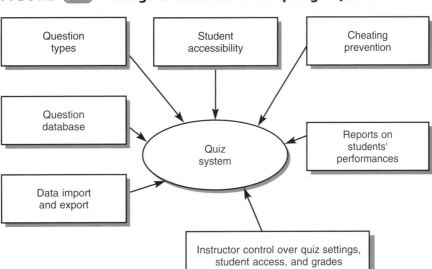

Types of Questions. Most quiz tools support multiple-choice and short-answer questions. One of the major advantages of computer-assisted quizzing is automated grading, which works best with multiple-choice questions. Multiple-choice questions have been a popular form of standardized objective test over the past few decades because such tests are easy to administer, broad in content coverage, generally high in validity and reliability, and can be scored by machine. These tests can be used to assess high levels of analytic and logical thinking skills.

Additional question types offered by course management systems include matching items, sequence ordering, filling in blanks, and calculated questions. Matching items is typically used to assess students' ability to identify related concepts. A simple example of matching items is given in Figure 9.15.

Filling in blanks is useful in testing students' language skills, particularly in areas of text coherence, text transition, and logical thinking. Calculated questions require the designer to enter a formula and a set of variable ranges. The quiz engine will generate a question with different variables for each student as they take the quiz (see Figure 9.16). The random generation of variables can help prevent cheating.

Question Database or Item Bank. Quiz questions can be very time consuming to develop. It saves time if questions can be reused in multiple quizzes or even in different courses. Some course management systems use

FIGURE 9.15   Matching Items in WebCT CE 4

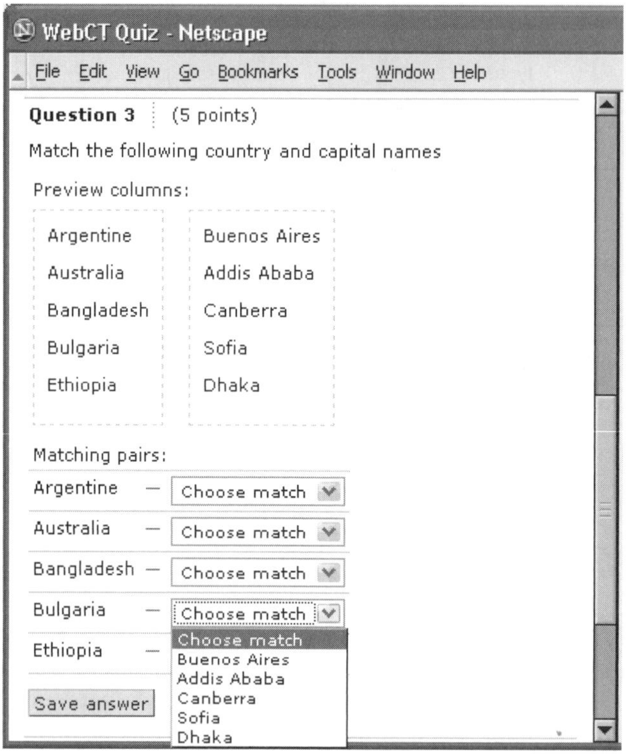

Note: © 2005 by WebCT, Inc. Reprinted with permission. All rights reserved.

a question database or item bank to store questions and let course designers pick questions from the bank when they create or edit a quiz. If there are enough items in the bank, the quiz engine can even support random selection of questions so that each student will see a different set of questions on the quiz. Random selection of questions can help prevent students from sharing questions and answers, which can be very easy in a network environment.

Batch Import and Export. Some course management systems support file upload for batch import of questions, but the data in the uploaded file must follow a specific format, which may require additional preparation. To reduce possible hassle in batch import, standard forms of data input usually need to be specified for instructors to use in preparing quiz questions. Data formats

FIGURE 9.16 Calculated Question in WebCT CE 4

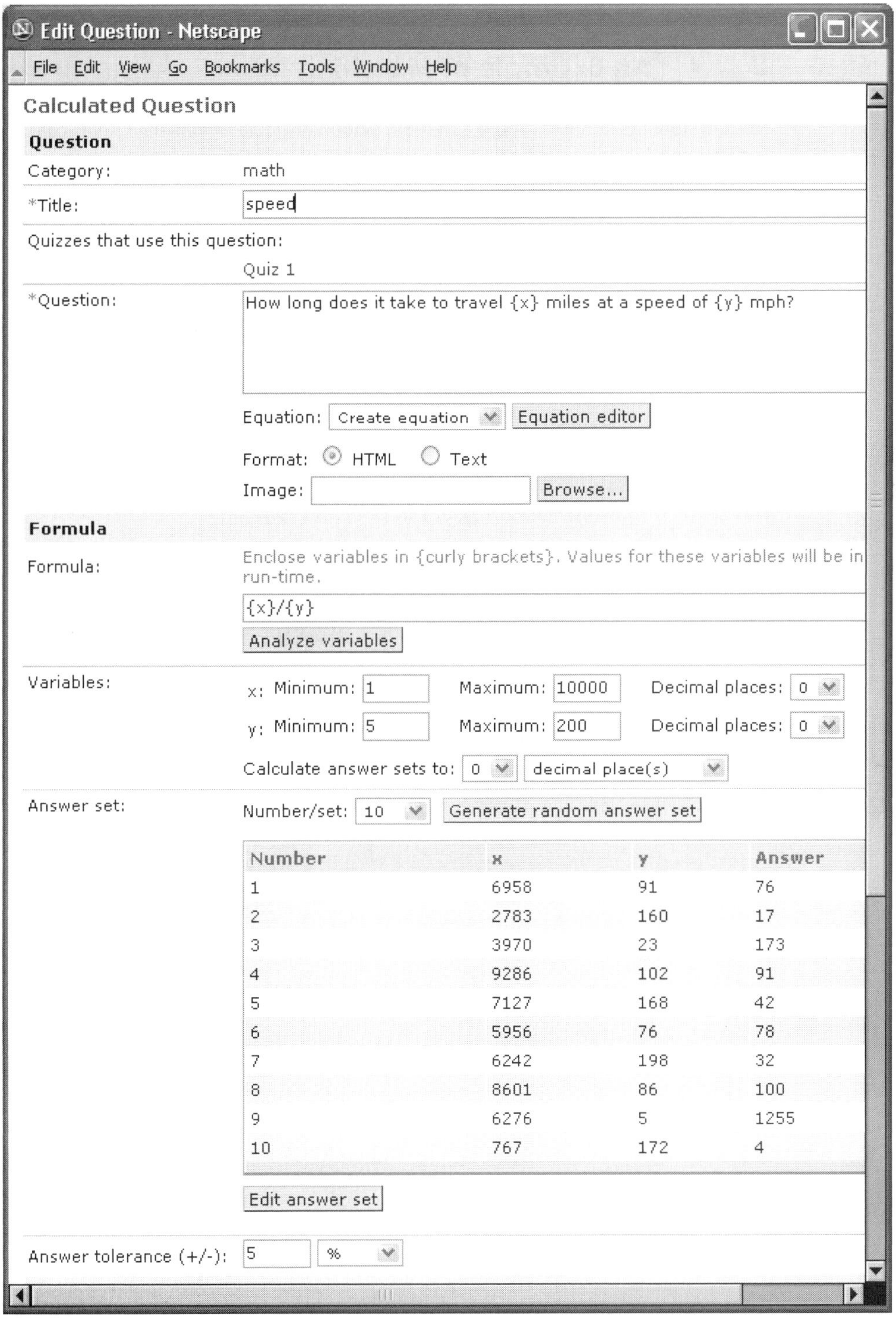
Edit Question - Netscape
File Edit View Go Bookmarks Tools Window Help
Calculated Question
Question
Category: math
*Title: speed
Quizzes that use this question:
Quiz 1
*Question: How long does it take to travel {x} miles at a speed of {y} mph?
Equation: Create equation
Equation editor
Format: HTML Text
Image:
Browse...
Formula
Formula: Enclose variables in {curly brackets}. Values for these variables will be in run-time.
{x}/{y}
Analyze variables
Variables:
x: Minimum: 1 Maximum: 10000 Decimal places: 0
y: Minimum: 5 Maximum: 200 Decimal places: 0
Calculate answer sets to: 0 decimal place(s)
Answer set: Number/set: 10
Generate random answer set
Number x y Answer
1 6958 91 76
2 2783 160 17
3 3970 23 173
4 9286 102 91
5 7127 168 42
6 5956 76 78
7 6242 198 32
8 8601 86 100
9 6276 5 1255
10 767 172 4
Edit answer set
Answer tolerance (+/-): 5 %

Note: © 2005 by WebCT, Inc. Reprinted with permission. All rights reserved.

C A S E S T U D Y　**An Example of Matching Items** ············

> ● For the students in the IS program at MSU, a good example of matching items can be a test on the open systems interconnection (OSI) model presented in chapter 5. The OSI model consists of seven layers: (1) physical, (2) data link, (3) network, (4) transport, (5) session, (6) presentation, and (7) application. Different layers are associated with different components of the TCP/IP protocol in network communication. We can list the components of TCP/IP in the left column and the seven layers in the right column, and ask students to match each component with the most closely related layer.

such as Microsoft Access, Microsoft Excel, and text files with comma separated values (CSV) are compatible with most standard data input and output through open database connectivity (ODBC), and are therefore generally recommended for preparing data for batch import and export.

Instructor Control Over Quizzes and Grades. Instructors need to be able to edit quizzes after they are created, such as modifying the title, changing the requirements, or resetting the dates. However, certain restrictions might be necessary. A future quiz should allow the most options for editing; a current quiz should allow only limited editing because some students may already have taken or are taking the quiz. Changing the title of a current quiz may confuse some students. Generally, the options for current quiz editing are limited to the reset of start/end dates and the release of feedback.

Some course management systems do not use a question database, so course designers have to enter all the questions when they build a quiz. Once the quiz is created, the course designer cannot add or remove any questions. More flexible course management systems allow course designers to add or remove questions after a quiz has been created, as long as the quiz has not been released to the students or no student has taken the quiz yet.

Reports on Student Performances. Most course management systems provide basic descriptive statistics on student performances, including individual student scores, class average, highest and lowest scores on each quiz, amount of time each student spent on a quiz, and number of attempts each student tried on a quiz if multiple attempts were allowed. More sophisticated course management systems may be capable of providing further instructionally informative data, such as a student error analysis and a graph of error distribution patterns.

Student Accessibility. For students taking online quizzes, the issue of accessibility often refers to the ability to resume a quiz session if the session is interrupted by various incidents, including network congestion, the server being down, Internet service provider (ISP) access difficulty, or the student's computer problem. If such incidents happen for distance students, we usually need to allow the student to resume the quiz. If the quiz consists of multiple parts and the student has been able to submit only the first part, we will let the student continue the quiz with the second part. Some quiz engines have the option of displaying one question at a time. This option can help control the sequence of question access. But most students seem to like having all the questions of each part of the quiz displayed at once, because it allows them to answer the questions in the order they prefer.

Another common accessibility need for students in general is to be able to view the correct answers and explanations after the quiz is over. Providing instant grading and immediate feedback can help students verify their answers and rectify their misunderstandings in a timely manner. The provision of automated grade check and feedback can also reduce the amount of time needed for the instructor to answer questions and explain the correct answers after a quiz. However, instant grading and immediate feedback may not always be desirable. For one thing, releasing correct answers will make these quiz items less reusable since the questions and answers may be disseminated by the quiz takers. More importantly, immediate release of grade and feedback may lead to spreading of the correct answers. For instance, if a quiz has 20 multiple-choice questions and a student gets 18 correct out of 20, the student's choices can serve as very reliable clues for others who have not taken the quiz yet. A course management system should allow course designers to withhold instant grading until every student has taken the quiz or the quiz expires.

Cheating Prevention. Because students in a distance class usually take the same quiz from different locations and far away from the instructor, it is possible for them to communicate with one another about the quiz questions and possible answers. One way to prevent such sharing of information is to randomize question generation. With enough questions in a question database, we can make the quiz engine randomly pick a given number of questions from the item bank for each student taking the quiz. However, this type of random selection requires the availability of a large number of questions, usually hundreds and thousands of them, depending on the number of questions to be picked each time. Random generation of questions can also make students' performances less comparable when students have different sets of questions for the same quiz. For multiple-choice questions, randomizing answer choice orders can make it more difficult for quiz takers to share answers.

Another common concern shared by many instructors in administering online quizzes is that students may be able to print out the questions, study the questions with the help of external resources, and then come back to answer the questions. We may prevent this type of problem by setting a time limit on each quiz and requiring the students to complete the quiz within the given timeframe. However, as we mentioned earlier, online quiz sessions can be interrupted by various incidents, and we usually have to allow students to resume the quiz if such interruptions occur.

Another popular way to prevent cheating in online quizzes is to have proctor supervision, which requires little technology support and is relatively easy to implement. The general practice of proctor supervision is to let the student nominate a person (usually a supervisor, teacher, parent, or colleague) as proctor, with the nomination approved by the instructor. Once approved, the proctor must be present to supervise each time the student takes a quiz. The proctor may need to sign in the student if the online quiz requires the proctor's password, or the proctor may need to send the instructor some form of verification through e-mail or a signature sheet. The most common problem with proctor supervision is when the proctor neglects his or her duties.

Support for Collaborative Learning

Most course management systems include basic online communication tools such as discussion boards and chat room. The primary advantage of these built-in tools is their integration with the system's user management and record keeping. Students' use of these tools can be connected to their course registration, assignment accomplishments, quiz performances, and other records of data. If you find the included communication tools inadequate to meet your instructional needs, you may consider using some external tools as a supplement, such as Internet conferencing tools to support real-time virtual space where students can hear and see one another, share files, work on a common set of data, and contribute to a team project. Since assessment of student performances in online communication activities is mostly subjective, using a discussion board system or chat tool outside the default course management system usually will not affect the normal functioning of the course management system.

Open-Source Endeavors

As we mentioned earlier in this chapter, there are some major constraints with the use of a proprietary course management system. Among other things, the ever-increasing cost of the annual license is a major concern for most institutions that have committed to a commercial proprietary CMS. In addition, the inability to customize or modify components of an adopted course management system is another major factor. As Ira Fuchs (2004) observes, if an institution finds the commercial CMS deficient or problematic in some way, it usually has to wait until the vendor decides if it is financially viable to provide an improvement or fix the problem. The ideal solution would be to have a self-developed in-house solution that the institution can customize to meet its needs without worrying about the annual license cost. However, because it is usually too costly for an individual institution to develop a course management system on its own, some institutions have started collaboration on open-source course management system development. Open source does not just mean open access to the source code. Open source also means free distribution and free modification of the source code. The openness encourages users and developers to contribute and improve the software. Successful stories of open source include the development of Apache, Linux, and MySQL. For higher education, open source can be more than sharing of software source code. It can mean a change in how the higher education community should join their efforts and resources in the development and utilization of technology (Brooks, 2004). Some notable examples of open-source CMS projects are Sakai, OpenCMS, Moodle, and Plone, briefly described here.

Sakai. A notable example is the Sakai project, undertaken by Indiana University, MIT, Stanford University, the University of Michigan, the uPortal Consortium, and the Open Knowledge Initiative (OKI), with the support of the Andrew W. Mellon Foundation. The goal of the Sakai project is to create a world-class production-ready system that is open, extensible, and scalable. Other colleges and universities can use the system and extend its functionality with modules developed by themselves or other schools. The Sakai Educational Partners Program (SEPP) has invited interested schools to participate in the project development, and approximately 50 schools have signed up as of this writing (Fuchs, 2004). Sakai 1.0 Final was released in October 2004, and Sakai 2.0 is available as of June 2005.

OpenCMS. OpenCMS has a WYSIWYG HTML editor with a user interface similar to that of well-known office applications. It helps the user create the contents, while a sophisticated template engine enforces a sitewide corporate layout. OpenCMS is built on Java and XML and runs in a full open-source environment that can be Linux, Apache, Tomcat, or MySQL as well as on commercial components such as Windows, IIS, and Oracle DB. OpenCMS is also completely free of licensing costs (OpenCMS, 2004).

Moodle. Like other open-source software, Moodle is free to download and use. Users can also freely customize and modify it. Moodle runs without modification on Unix, Linux, Windows, Mac OS X, Netware, and any other system that supports PHP, a server-side scripting language especially suited for Web development. Moodle is best supported by an open-source database such as MySQL and PostgreSQL, but it can also be used with Microsoft Access, SQL Server, and Oracle (Moodle 2004).

Plone. Plone has a click-and-run installer that makes it fairly easy to set up. Web pages created in Plone are compliant with U.S. Section 508 and the World Wide Web Consortium's AA rating for accessibility. Plone can interoperate with most relational database systems and can run on a range of platforms, including Linux, Windows, Mac OS X, Solaris, and BSD. The scripting language for Plone is Python (Plone, 2004).

So, should an institution choose an open-source course management system over a commercial package? Although open-source options are mostly free of an annual license cost, they generally require a considerable amount of technical expertise to set up, configure, customize, and troubleshoot. Much of the decision making will be based on what kind of computing infrastructure the institution has and how reliable the available support services will be. As indicated by the survey results at the Syllabus2004 Conference, a primary concern for most institutions in adopting an open-source CMS is the ability to secure dependable support (Blaisdell, 2005).

Apart from open-source endeavors such as the Sakai project, there are some other efforts by some institutions to develop course management systems that are more open than most proprietary course management systems and allow more customization by adopters. However, these systems are not open-source freeware and have to be acquired with a license fee. A notable example is ANGEL (A New Global Environment for Learning). ANGEL was initially developed in the CyberLab of Indiana University–Purdue University, Indianapolis. The CyberLab became a company called CyberLearning Labs, which later changed its name to ANGEL Learning. ANGEL is claimed to have been designed with an open architecture that is customizable to provide new functionality through a set of application programming interfaces (APIs). ANGEL is reported to be compliant with SCORM 1.2 (CyberLearning Labs, 2004).

Chapter Summary

This chapter starts by describing the key components of course management systems, including user management, file management, content structure and presentation, online quizzing, and communication tools. The chapter discusses some important issues to keep in mind when adopting a course management system. The issues include cost and portability, standardization and customization, online quizzing, support for collaborative learning, and possible open-source alternatives.

Review Questions

1. If your institution is going to adopt a new course management system such as Blackboard or WebCT, what components and functions do you think would be the most important?

2. If some of the instructors in your institution are quite experienced in using a stand-alone Web development tool such as DreamWeaver or FrontPage to author Web content, how would you assist the instructors in learning to use the new course management system?

3. What approaches other than those described in the chapter do you think could help prevent student dishonesty in taking online quizzes?

4. Do you think standardization is the most effective way to help ensure course content portability across different course management systems? What obstacles can you perceive in the modular approach of instructional content development?

Summary of Tips

1. When moving files in a course management system, make sure that related links from course pages are updated and do not become broken links.

2. Course designers need to be allowed to organize course content nodes in varied, flexible navigation schemes.

3. Use tracking functions to monitor learners' visits to course modules and their progress on course work in order to provide timely assistance and support where needed.

4. Use a question database (or item bank) to facilitate import and export of questions, promote item reusability, and support random generation of quiz questions.

5. Provide the option of withholding instant grading in online quizzes to prevent possible sharing of correct answers to questions.

6. Use random generation of quiz questions to help prevent cheating by spreading quiz questions and answers.

7. Give instructors the option to modify and reset student performance records so that a student can redo an exercise or retake a quiz.

8. Do not allow participants to change or delete their posted messages in online discussion, because such change or deletion may make follow-up responses appear off target or pointless.

9. Find out about content portability across systems when considering the adoption of a course management system.

10. Allow course designers and instructors to customize course page interface at least to some extent.

Exercises

1. Write a list of the key components and functions that you feel are essential in a course management system.

2. Explain why content portability across different course management systems is important.

3. Visit the related Web sites introduced in the chapter to learn about the most recent developments and major efforts made by various organizations and vendors to promote standardization in learning object development.

4. Interview some instructors and students who have taught or taken Web-based courses about their perceptions of online quizzing, particularly their views of cheating prevention in online quizzing.

5. Visit the Web sites introduced in this chapter and find out about the lastest developments in open source course management system endeavors.

6. WebCT Workbench is an online showcase that offers real courses created by real users to demonstrate how course content can be put in a course management system for Web-based instruction. Visit the site at http://www.webct.com/exemplary/, select one or two courses to browse through, and write a review of the managerial and instructional features of the course(s).

7. Discuss with colleagues or classmates the essential functions of a course management system. Explain why the functions are essential.

8. Conduct a general search to find out what kinds of ePacks are available for adoption in WebCT.

Resources on the Web

We have included some related Web resources at the end of each chapter. However, since Web resources are generally updated very frequently, we ask you to check out the Companion Website for updated and accurate resource links.

- Advanced Distributed Learning Initiative, the original source of SCORM (Shareable Content Object Reference Model) (http://www.adlnet.org).

- CMS Review collects information on over 350 proprietary CMS, open-source CMS, and CMS services hosted at application service providers. It also describes defining features of a CMS, parameters for comparing CMS, and steps to take to select a CMS (http://www.cmsreview.com).

- E-Learning Circuits has a collection of articles on e-learning and learning objects (http://www.learningcircuits.org).

- IEEE Learning Technology Standards Committee (LTSC) is a primary source of metadata (http://ltsc.ieee.org).

- IMS Global Learning Consortium is a primary source of learning object content packaging (http://www.imsproject.org).

- Learning Object and Standards Resources from Learnactivity (http://www.learnativity.com/standresources.html).

- MERLOT, open resources designed primarily for faculty and students of higher education. Links to online learning materials are collected along with annotations and peer reviews (http://www.merlot.org).

- Web Learning Resources Library, hosted by Robert Jackson (http://www.knowledgeability.biz/weblearning/).

- Getting Started in Using e-Pack (http://www.webct.com/quickstart/viewpage?name=quickstart_e-pack_quickstart).

- Sakai Project is a joint open-source course management project undertaken by Indiana University, MIT, Stanford University, and the University of Michigan (http://www.sakaiproject.org/).

- Moodle Project, an open source course management system that uses PHP as the system scripting language and is best integrated with MySQL as the supporting database (http://moodle.org).

- OpenCMS is an open source course management system that is built on Java (http://www.opencms.org).

- Plone is an open source course management system that uses Python as the default system scripting language (http://www.plone.org).

References

Advanced Distributed Learning Initiative (2004a). *About SCORM*. Retrieved December 1, 2004, from http://www.adlnet.org/index.cfm?fuseaction=scormabt.

Advanced Distributed Learning Initiative (2004b). *ADL overview*. Retrieved December 1, 2004, from http://www.adlnet.org/index.cfm?fuseaction=abtadl.

Blackboard (2004a). *Blackboard partners: QuestionMark*. Retrieved June 28, 2004, from http://www.blackboard.com/about/pc/partnerDetail.asp?tid=119.

Blackboard (2004b). *Frequently asked questions about Blackboard building blocks*. Retrieved June 28, 2004, from http://www.blackboard.com/addons/b2/faq.htm.

Blaisdell, M. (2005). It's the support, stupid! *Campus Technology, 18*(5), 36–39.

Brooks, L. (2004). Values of community source development. *Syllabus, 18*(1), 36–38.

Cisco Systems Inc. (2003) *Reusable learning object strategy*. Retrieved September 7, 2003, from http://www.cisco.com/en/US/netsol/ns460/networking_solutions_white_papers_list.html.

Cooper, L. (2000). Online courses: Tips for making them work. *The Journal, 27*(8), 87–92.

CyberLearning Labs (2004). About us. Retrieved December 1, 2004, from http://cyberlearninglabs.com/AboutUs/.

Fuchs, I. (2004). Learning management systems: Are we there yet? *Syllabus, 17*(12), 15–20.

Green, K. C. (2003). Tracking the digital puck into 2004. Retrieved December 1, 2004, from http://www.campus-technology.com/article.asp?id=8574.

IMS Global Learning Consortium (2004). *Specification*. Retrieved December 1, 2004, from http://www.imsglobal.org/specifications.cfm.

Longmire, W. (2000). *A primer on learning objects*. ASTD Learning Circuits. Retrieved August 18, 2002, from http://www.learningcircuits.org/2000/mar2000/Longmire.htm.

Merrill, M. D. (1983). Component display theory. In C. M. Reigeluth (Ed.), *Instructional-design theories and models: An overview of their current status* (pp. 279–334). Mahwah, NJ: Lawrence Erlbaum Associates.

Merrill, M. D. (1999). Instructional transaction theory (ITT): Instructional design based on knowledge objects. In C. M. Reigeluth (Ed.), *Instructional-design theories and models: A new paradigm of instructional theory (Vol. II)* (pp. 397–424). Mahwah, NJ: Lawrence Erlbaum Associates.

MERLOT (2004). Welcome to MERLOT. Retrieved November 28, 2004, from http://www.merlot.org.

Moodle (2004). Moodle. Retrieved November 30, 2004, from http://moodle.org.

OpenCMS (2004). Welcome to the OpenCMS Project. Retrieved November 30, 2004, from http://www.opencms.org/opencms/en/.

PITAC (2001). Report to the President on using information technology to transform the way we learn. President's Information Technology Advisory Committee. Retrieved December 19, 2004, from http://www.itrd.gov.

Plone (2004). What is Plone? Retrieved November 30, 2004, from http://www.plone.org.

Strauss, H. (2004). What's next: Course creation systems. *Syllabus, 17*(12), 62.

Syllabus (2002). The interactive campus: Administrative and course management system vendors take up the challenge. *Syllabus, 15*(11), 16–18, 42–43.

Young, J. R. (2004). Students have mixed views of technology's impact on teaching, survey finds. *The Chronicle of Higher Education,* August 4, 2004. Retrieved from http://chronicle.com/temp/email.php?id=s927fhbpjyz9r4rm0ivvwuzfs9c5ewqd.

Chapter 10

Utilizing Web Resources

CHAPTER INTRODUCTION

One of the biggest advantages of using the Web as a learning environment is having access to worldwide resources. However, Web resources are growing so fast that finding what you want is often a major challenge for less experienced Web users. Instructors can have a hard time selecting the best resources for a given instructional need. Learners have the same challenge: to find and evaluate quality resources that meet their learning needs. In this chapter, we will first introduce basic skills for finding resources on the Web, and then discuss strategies to filter and evaluate Web resources. The last section of the chapter will recommend a systematic approach toward management of Web resources.

This chapter will:

1. Highlight the growing importance of the World Wide Web as a source of information for learning.

2. Briefly describe the variety of resources and popular tools available for resource search on the Web.

3. Discuss some strategies for information filtering and resource evaluation.

4. Recommend a personal systematic approach to the management of Web resources.

LEARNING OBJECTIVES

After studying this chapter, the reader will be able to:

1. Explain the advantages of incorporating online resources into Web-based instruction.

2. Describe the major difficulties in managing an effective utilization of Web resources.

3. Categorize the primary types of resources available on the Web and their possible instructional values.

4. Describe the values of the offline and online resources available in the library, particularly journals, print books, and online databases.

5. Classify various types of search tools available on the Web and understand their search capabilities.

6. Distinguish between search engines, search agents, search directories, and specialized databases in terms of their functions, relative strengths, and limitations.

7. Know what types of online journals, reference resources, online books, and other primary data providers are available on the Web and how to find them.

8. Evaluate a Web resource using the criteria generally recommended by the Web community.

9. Plan a systematic approach to personal management of Web resource collection and evaluation.

10. Be able to categorize information skills needed for utilizing Web resources and know how each type of skill can be assessed.

⦿ A S E   S T U D Y ············

- Being involved in information technology, the instructors and students of the MSU IS program know that the World Wide Web is a great repository of resources to supplement their course materials. However, the vast amount of information and the uneven qualities of the resources present a major challenge for instructors and students with less Web experience in searching and evaluating online resources. Instructors and students in the IS program need guidance on the types of resources available on the Web and tips on utilizing Web resources. Specifically, they need training in effective use of search tools, filtering and evaluating resources, and developing a systematic approach to online information management that fits their personal and professional needs.

THE GROWTH OF THE WEB

Since its birth in the 1990s, the World Wide Web has been growing at an exponential rate. The amazing growth rate of the Web is a clear indication of its popularity with the general public. Why is the Web so popular?

1. The Web provides worldwide instant connection and electronic-speed communication, with both real-time interactivity and storage for later retrieval.

2. The Web allows truly worldwide sharing of resources. User access can be controlled by setting up different levels of permissions.

3. Digital data, text, graphics, audio, and video are much easier to distribute and edit than in traditional print and analog forms. Digital data are much easier to archive and store, too.

4. Searching through digital data is much more efficient, particularly so when there is database support.

5. The hypermedia structure allows flexible, nonlinear organization and presentation of content.

6. Multimedia can be easily incorporated into Web content.

Using the Web has become so paramount today that almost all businesses and institutions now find it crucial to have a Web presence. Today, many well-known magazines and newspapers have online versions, and some of them have free access, including the *New York Times, Los Angeles Times, Chicago Tribune, Newsweek,* and *Time* magazine. A prominent advantage of the online versions of these publications is their search capability, which allows you to find and retrieve documents from the archives within a few seconds.

Since most of the activities in Web-based instruction are conducted in the Internet environment, it is very convenient to incorporate Web resources in course materials. With its almost unlimited variety of resources, the Web can provide authentic materials for case studies and class discussions that relate to students' personal experiences. The rich information is also excellent for learning and practicing the three skills Mayer (1999) considers essential for constructive learning: (a) selecting material, (b) organizing material, and (c) integrating material.

Learn to Manage Web Resources

As the Web continues to grow, more and more resources will become available online. Although many of them may be valuable, there are also tons of subquality or junk materials out there. Whether we can make good use of the resources depends largely on the strategies we have for tapping them. Web resources can be difficult to utilize for several reasons:

1. The vast amount of data makes it difficult to find desired information.

2. There's little standard control over content quality, since every Web page author can produce Web content in his or her own ways.

3. Worldwide diversity in both content and form can cause compatibility problems for users with different computer systems.

4. Because digital data are so easy to edit and update, Web content can be extremely dynamic and changeable.

Mastering effective strategies to utilize Web resources is not only necessary for instructional designers and instructors, but also important for learners. More and more professions require people to keep acquiring new information and upgrading their existing knowledge. The ability to learn new knowledge is more important than the amount of knowledge one currently possesses. Therefore, in designing and teaching Web-based courses, we should help learners become acquainted with the scholarly and trade publications, leading professional associations and organizations, and popular Web resources in their disciplines.

Check Offline Resources First

Before going out to surf on the Web, you should check to see if you can get better or comparable resources offline. Browsing on the Web for an hour may not bring you what you can get within minutes from offline resources such as a reference book, a journal, or a CD-ROM.

Because of copyright concerns, many quality resources are not placed on the Web. When they are, a membership subscription or fee is often required to access them. This makes the Internet valuable more as a gateway to resources than as a collection of original professional content.

Generally, the quality of the primary content you can find on the Web is not as high as what you can find in libraries, where publications have been screened first by reviewers and editors, and then by professional librarians. Using the online catalog systems of state public libraries and university libraries, students can usually find a very broad range of materials and may be able to access materials through interlibrary loans or other means. If finding a desired book through the library system turns out to be difficult, you may want to try Amazon.com. Its book reviews by readers are valuable guides.

FINDING RESOURCES ON THE WEB

Given the vast amount and scope of information on the Web, search tools are needed to find relevant information in an efficient manner. Different types of search tools are available today, with varied capabilities for different user needs. Because search tools are constantly evolving, it is hard to recommend which search engines to use. Sometimes search tools merge with others or cease to exist because of market forces. For example, after being active for a few years, in 1998 the well-known Argus Clearinghouse ceased its content updating for lack of supporting funds and merged with the Internet Public Library (www.ipl.org).

To remain updated, you need to understand the evolving functions and growing capabilities of search tools. If you find it difficult to keep up with the trends, you can turn to some Web sites that analyze the current developments in search tools, such as Search Engine Watch (www.searchenginewatch.com) and Search Engine Showdown (www.searchengineshowdown.com). Based on the

FIGURE 10.1 Web Resources

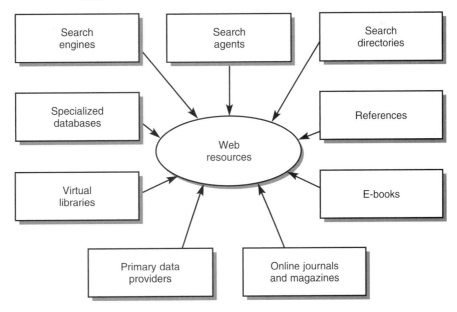

search methods used and ranges covered, search tools can be roughly grouped into five categories: (a) search engines, (b) search agents (meta–search engines), (c) search directories, (d) specialized databases, and (e) virtual libraries. We discuss them here, along with online journals and magazines, online references, e-books, and primary data providers. Figure 10.1 illustrates all these Web resources.

Search Engines

A search engine is in essence a computer program that crawls over the Internet, collects resources, and compiles the resources into searchable categories, indexes, or lists stored in databases. Search engines respond to user keyword queries by searching through the databases and displaying documents that match the search query based on the degree of relevance. Depending on the specificity of the keywords entered, the number of results returned by search engines can vary from dozens to millions. The success of a search often depends on appropriately formulating and specifying the keywords (Makinster, Beghetto, & Plucker, 2002). Learners may need to be trained in choosing the right keywords for a specific topic in order to get search results with better relevance. For example, if the search interest is Web page layout, the keywords "Web page layout" should be entered instead of a general term such as "Web page design." Specific keywords usually return better focused results with more relevance.

Furthermore, students may also need to be trained in using the initial returns from the starting search to refine further searches. Some research studies have found that inexperienced learners tend to use the Web for information gathering only. They simply collect and read the information returned from the initial search and do not use that information to refine the search for higher quality resources (Wallace, Kupperman, Krajcik, & Soloway, 2000; Vansickle, 2002).

Almost all search engines offer two levels of search: basic and advanced. The basic search simply provides a text box in which the user enters some keywords. There is no requirement for the use of Boolean operators such as *AND* and *OR* to join multiple keywords. When the user enters multiple words, the default Boolean operator *AND* (or +) is added between words. Most search engines also offer the option of advanced search, which lets the user specify search parameters to narrow down the search results. According to Nielson (2001) and others (Spink, Bateman, & Jansen, 1999; Spool, 2002), ordinary users usually do not read search tips or try the advanced option. If you want to encourage learners to use the advanced search option, you may need to convince them of the benefits offered by the advanced search functions and teach them how to use the functions.

Most search engines have special strengths that make them particularly useful for certain search tasks. For example, AltaVista searches the entire HTML file and gives the option of searching Usenet. Google caches documents (by storing documents in its server space) so that the user can still get a copy of the document found even if the original document is not available at the time.

It is difficult for search engines to screen for information quality, however, because search engines find relevant resources by matching keywords contained in the documents. When using search engines, it is up to the user to evaluate the quality of the resources returned.

IN PRACTICE   A Search Engine That Combines Text Search and Image Search Results

A separately branded and operated subsidiary of Amazon.com, A9.com is a search engine that combines text search and image search results enhanced by Google, Search Inside the Book results from Amazon.com, reference results from GuruNet, and movie results from IMDb. By asking you to sign in, A9.com can keep your own notes about your search preferences and results. With the A9 Toolbar installed as a plug-in on your browser, you can search through your whole history (and clear items you don't want kept). Using your search history, A9.com can recommend new sites, alert you to new search results, and let you know the last time you visited a page.

Source: http://www.a9.com

FIGURE  **Search Interface Screen of Copernic Agent Basic 6**

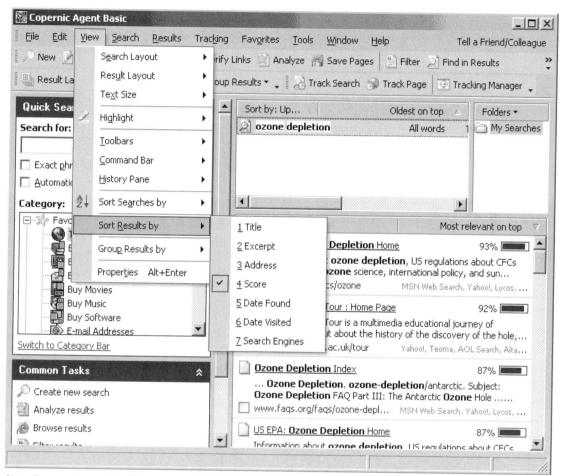

Note: Screen shot reprinted by permission from Copernic Technologies, Inc.

Search Agents

A search agent is a secondhand searcher that gets data from other search engines and is therefore called a meta–search engine. It searches multiple search engines through pipelines and displays results from these engines. As you would expect, search agents generally return more heterogeneous results than search engines.

Search agents generally have a browser-embedded interface, such as AskJeeve, Dogpile, Excite, MetaCrawler, and WebCrawler. However, some search agents are stand-alone applications, such as Copernic and WebFerret. Copernic lets the user sort search results by title, address, relevance score, and search engine (see Figure 10.2).

Most search agents are used for general searches, though there are search agents for special types of searches. For example, AskJeeves is a human-powered search service that aims to direct you to the exact page that answers your question. If it fails to find a match within its own database, it will provide matching Web pages from other search engines. Some search agents serve particular information needs, such as job search agents or the mega-dictionary www.onelook.com, which searches through multiple online dictionaries for definitions and explanations of target words.

Search Directories

The number of results returned by search engines and search agents can be overwhelming to less experienced users. For inexperienced users, a search directory is often a more manageable tool. A search directory collects and organizes resources into categories based on standard or self-developed subject headings. Yahoo! and Open Directory Project (http://dmoz.org/) are two such directories. Search directories take submissions from those who wish to be listed in the directories. Human editors also go out to the Internet to find Web sites they feel should be included in their directories. Annotations and comments are often added to the resources included in the directory listings. The human screening process helps ensure that resources selected are of acceptable quality. Because of the selective nature, the number of resources contained in search directories is generally smaller than what can be returned by search engines or agents, but the quality of the resources is usually higher.

In recent years, the distinction between search directory and search engine has become blurred. Many search engines have added optional directory listings to their starting pages (see Figure 10.3), and search directories such as Yahoo! have added search engine capabilities to their sites.

Because a directory organizes information in categories, it works particularly well for browsing general, categorized topics. If you are quite certain of the subject headings under which your topic is likely to be listed, a directory search often works better than using a search engine. Directory browsing is also usually more effective if you need to see a relatively complete list of well-established Web sites in a particular subject area. For example, to get a list of all public or private educational institutions in a particular state, you can go to Yahoo! and click through "education" > "colleges and universities" > "United States" > "public" or "private."

Because directories are compiled by human editors with more or less subjective views and preferences, categorization can differ among directories. For example, "education" may be listed in one directory as one of the top subject headings, but not be found in other directory listings.

Another important point to keep in mind is that each Web resource can be a source of related resources. A good Web resource on a specific topic in a particular field often contains links that lead to more quality resources in the field than a search engine or directory can provide.

FIGURE 10.3   Directory Listing

Arts	**Home**	**Regional**
Movies, Television, Music...	Family, Consumers, Cooking...	US, Canada, UK, Europe...
Business	**Kids and Teens**	**Science**
Jobs, Real Estate, Investing...	Arts, School Time, Teen Life...	Biology, Psychology, Physics...
Computers	**News**	**Shopping**
Internet, Software, Hardware...	Media, Newspapers, Weather...	Autos, Clothing, Gifts...
Games	**Recreation**	**Society**
Video Games, RPGs, Gambling...	Travel, Food, Outdoors, Humor...	People, Religion, Issues...
Health	**Reference**	**Sport**
Fitness, Medicine, Alternative...	Maps, Education, Libraries...	Baseball, Soccer, Basketball...

World
Deutsch, Español, Français, Italiano, Japanese, Nederlands, Polska, Svenska...

Specialized Databases

Specialized databases are collections of resources hosted by an institution or organization with a dedicated focus or interest. The resource collections may be in index form, or actually be stored in a database and dynamically retrieved in response to user queries. There are many specialized databases available. You can often find such databases through a search directory or search engine. Using a search directory, you can either browse by category or enter keywords. With a search engine, you can enter a content domain of your interest followed by the word "database." Try entering "instructional technology database" into the search box of one of your favorite search engines and see what you can find, and then try another search using the keywords "instructional technology" without the word "database."

Virtual Libraries

Some directories are highly selective in resource inclusion and are compiled with a particular audience in mind, such as Math Archives for math professionals and Social Science Information Gateway (SOSIG) for people in the field of social and behavioral sciences. Many of these directories can be considered virtual libraries. In the Resources on the Web section of this chapter, we have included some of these value-added directories and virtual libraries, with brief descriptions of their features and intended audiences. Some of the special directories and virtual libraries are free to the public. Most provide free search access to the public, but require a membership subscription or charge an access fee on a per-document basis. In terms of information quality, virtual libraries and specialized databases generally rank the highest, followed by search directories, and then search engines and search agents.

Online Journals and Periodicals

A major difficulty for most libraries today is to keep up with the ever-increasing cost of subscriptions to journals. Many libraries have had to cancel some of their journal subscriptions in order to maintain fiscal balance. Although the cost of journal subscriptions will probably continue to rise, there are some viable alternatives on the Web. Many libraries have institutional subscriptions to such online article providers as Infotrac and Lexis-Nexis Academic, but faculty and students usually have to access the subscribed services through computer terminals on campus. For distance learners, there are some more affordable alternatives. XanEdu (http://www.xanedu.com) offers thousands of full-text periodicals at $19.90 for three months or $49.90 a year. The eLibrary from High-Beam Research has full texts of articles from more than 600 periodicals; the membership fee is $19.95 a month or $99.95 a year.

Apart from fee-based portals to articles, free collections of articles are also available on the Web. HighWire Press (http://highwire.stanford.edu) from Stanford University is one such portal. Highwire hosts about 15,000,000 articles in over 4,500 Medline journals, and over 740,000 free full-text articles from 364 HighWire-hosted journals (HighWire, 2004). Another popular portal of free journal articles is FindArticles from LookSmart (www.findarticles.com), which allows users to search and read 2.8 million articles from more than 500 publications. The Social and Human Sciences Documentation Center at UNESCO (http://www.unesco.org/shs/shsdc/journals/shsjournals.html) has a collection of online periodicals with free access to specialized full-text articles from about 700 periodicals in the social and human sciences. Ellen Garvey's Resources for Research Periodicals (http://home.earthlink.net/%7Eellengarvey/rsapresource1.html) gathers a broad range of links to online journals and lets users go directly to sites with free access to full-text articles.

Online Reference Resources

Instead of going to a bookshelf, grabbing a thick volume, and flipping through the pages to find a specific piece of information, finding references online can be as simple as clicking a few links and entering a few keywords, provided that you know which online resources to try. Bartleby (http://www.bartleby.com) is a popular site that hosts some valuable resources, including the Columbia Encyclopedia (6th ed., 2001), which has over 50,000 articles, 40,000 bibliographic citations, and 80,000 cross-references; and the American Heritage Dictionary of the English Language (4th ed., 2000), which has over 90,000 entries featuring 10,000 new words and senses, 70,000 audio word pronunciations, 900 full-page color illustrations, language notes, and word-root appendixes. Other general-purpose online dictionaries include Merriam-Webster Online

CASE STUDY   Online Journals and Magazines for IS Students

• Remaining well informed about current developments in the IT industry is crucial for the students of the IS program. One of the ways to stay current is to subscribe to prominent journals and magazines in the IT field. Popular IT journals include:

▶ C|Net (http://www.cnet.com) carries reviews, news, and prices on computer technology products, and offers free downloads.

▶ ComputerWorld (http://www.computerworld.com) covers a broad range of topics including hardware, software, data management, networking, security, and mobile computing.

▶ Byte.com (http://www.byte.com) carries articles on wireless communication, computer security, software development, and embedded systems.

▶ eWeek (http://www.eweek.com) is targeted at core IT buyers with strategic news and reviews for making informed decisions in adopting technology solutions.

▶ Network Magazine (http://www.networkmagazine.com/) is one of the online publications from CMP Media.

▶ PC Magazine (http://www.pcmag.com) has over 5 million readers ranging from IT professionals to anyone interested in current computer technology. The magazine provides test reports and reviews on computer- and network-related products and services.

▶ TechWeb (http://www.techweb.com/) combines original content and one-stop access to the resources and technology publications from CMP Media.

▶ ZDnet (http://www.zdnet.com) features technology news, reviews, white papers, and purchasing advice for IT professionals.

(http://www.m-w.com/) and Cambridge Dictionaries Online (http://dictionary.cambridge.org/). See the Companion Website of this book for links to more online reference resources.

E-Books

Many people do not like reading extended text on a computer screen, but electronic texts do offer some advantages and conveniences. Among other things, it is easy to search through the contents of an electronic book to find specific material. Second, electronic books are easy to acquire. You can also download volumes and store them on CD, DVD, or another digital storage device that is smaller in size than a traditional book. Thousands of books are available in electronic form for free online. Most of these books are older titles published

ⒸⒶⓈⒺ   STUDY   **An Online Dictionary for IS Students**⋯⋯⋯⋯⋯

• One extremely helpful resource for the faculty and students of the IS program at Mid-State University is the Free On-Line Dictionary of Computing (FOLDOC). FOLDOC is a searchable online dictionary that contains common computing concepts and terms, including acronyms, jargon, programming languages, tools, architecture, operating systems, networking, theory, conventions, standards, telecommunications, electronics, institutions, companies, projects, products, and the history of computing. Edited by Denis Howe, the dictionary has been growing since 1985 and now contains over 13,000 definitions. Entries are cross-referenced to each other and to related resources elsewhere on the Web.

Source: http://foldoc.doc.ic.ac.uk/foldoc/

before 1923, since United States copyright law states that works published before 1923 are in the public domain, meaning that the works are not protected by the copyright law and are free for use by everyone. Two prominent virtual libraries with thousands of free electronic texts are the Electronic Text Center of the University of Virginia (http://etext.lib.virginia.edu/) and Project Gutenberg (http://gutenberg.net/). Project Gutenberg has over 10,000 electronic books available and adds more each month. The Electronic Text Center currently holds more than 70,000 humanities texts in thirteen languages, with more than 350,000 related images. Most of these texts and images are accessible to the public, although some of the electronic texts are not yet in the public domain; you cannot republish them without permission.

Primary Data Providers

Search tools can help us find Web resources, but they are generally less effective in getting primary data, particularly data that are frequently updated and accessible on a subscription or fee basis. To obtain primary data firsthand, we need to search through primary content providers. Primary content providers can be grouped into several categories, as listed in Table 10.1.

EVALUATING WEB RESOURCES

Given the uneven quality of Web resources and the difficulty in getting the desired quality of information online, inexperienced Web users generally need some guidelines before venturing into vast cyberspace. Quite a few Web resources provide guidelines on evaluation. Most guidelines call attention to site authorship, information accuracy, content objectivity, and content currency and stability (Alexander & Tate, 1999). Additional evaluation criteria are

TABLE 10.1 **Primary Content Providers**

Category	Sample resource domain names
News services	cnn.com; www.usatoday.com; abc.com
Special news services	www.wsj.com; www.ft.com
Library services	www.loc.gov; www.nlm.nih.gov; msdn.microsoft.com/library
Government agencies	www.ed.gov; www.dot.gov; edc.usgs.gov; www.eric.ed.gov
Organizations	www.unesco.org; www.w3.org; www.adlnet.org; www.imsglobal.org
Educational institutions	www.mcw.edu; www.siris.si.edu
Industry-specific content providers and trade publications	msdn.microsoft.com; www.mayoclinic.com; www.pcmag.com; www.nasa.gov; edc.usgs.gov
Subscription-required databases	infotrac.thomsonlearning.com; lexis-nexis.com; umi.com; netlibrary.com; consumerreports.com
Literary collections and archives	www.promo.net/pg/; digital.library.upenn.edu/books/; eserver.org

concerned about resource scope, nature of content, content uniqueness, accessibility, easy navigation, and information search (Alastair, 1997). Table 10.2 offers some criteria for judging a site.

Authorship

When a promising site pops up from your search results, the first thing you need to do is to discover the authorship. A responsible site should indicate authorship on its pages, whether the authorship is individual or institutional. The indication should include author contact information for further information or comments and suggestions. If applicable, the indication of authorship should include author affiliation and professional qualifications.

Sometimes, author affiliation may not be immediately visible on a Web page because the page is a "child" page subsumed under some higher-level

TABLE ⑩.2 Web Site Evaluation Criteria

Criteria	Things to check
Domain type	Academe, business, corporate, e-commerce, government, nonprofit organization, personal
Authorship	Author contact information, affiliation, qualifications, credentials
Intended audience and content nature	General introduction, professional forum, specialized knowledge
Content scope	Comprehensiveness, focus
Content currency and stability	Frequency of updating, archives of past materials
Content objectivity	Acknowledgement of limitations, reference to both pro and con arguments, other sites' reference to this resource
Information accuracy	Information verifiable
Accessibility and navigation	Speed of finding and retrieving documents and data
Privacy and security	Protection of sensitive personal information, security of confidential data

page or buried in a frame. In such a case, you can trace back to the higher-level URL to find the hosting institution or company domain. However, remember that such subsumed pages may not be official and may not represent the hosting domain. For example, personal home pages may be hosted under an institutional domain. Therefore, an .edu domain cannot guarantee academic quality. Web pages under an .edu domain can range from faculty research forums to student pages with just-for-fun content.

Site Goals

Evaluation of a site must be in line with the site goals and corresponding functions. Is the site maintained by an individual or an institution? Is the site for commercial promotion, political advocacy, individual vanity publishing, personal self-entertainment, or professional development? A site hosted by an advocacy group usually does not try to present an objective picture of an issue. A site for commercial promotion inevitably highlights its own positive points and downplays its competitors. However, many sites may have a mixture of professional information and commercial promotion. Sometimes it may be difficult to distinguish sponsor information from commercial promotion, and valuable information can be mixed with commercial promotion. Such mixing can be found in some business or even professional Web site content (Alexander & Tate, 1999). See whether there is a clear separation between the advertisement and the site information, and ask whether the information accuracy and truthfulness of the site content is affected by the sponsorship, advertising, or business orientation of the site itself.

Nature and Scope of Content

Content nature can be an important factor that draws an interested audience. If a Web resource provides unique information on a particular topic that cannot be found anywhere else, the resource would have some exclusive value. Related to content uniqueness is content scope, namely, breadth and depth of the content coverage. For general discussion, a site that has comprehensive coverage may be more helpful to a user with general interests than a site that has a narrow focus and deep exploration. However, for a user who wants to find in-depth discussions on a specialized topic, the latter type of site may be more valuable. If search tools are used, the content uniqueness of a site can be initially determined by comparing the description of the site with those of other sites in the search results, because sites with similar content are usually grouped together in results returned by search engines. To further determine content uniqueness, browse the site and scan the headings.

Accuracy and Credibility of Information

If you find a resource informative and are planning to cite the resource in your research, it is usually a good idea to verify the accuracy and truthfulness of the resource by comparing it with other resources. Resources from government agencies, professional organizations, academic publications, and renowned experts are usually more trustworthy. Generally, objectivity can be tested by looking for the inclusion of acknowledgement of limitations of the author's work, references to both pro and con sides of the issue, inclusion of counterarguments and opposing views, and verifiable research data and findings. If the target resource is a research paper, credibility can be enhanced if the author alludes to or displays professional knowledge of theories and related sources. Content credibility can also be checked by looking at other people's comments and reviews of the resource you are evaluating, and at links to the site you are examining (Henderson, 2002). Results returned by search engines often show related Web resources and tell you who has reviewed the site and who has linked to the site.

Currency and Stability of Content

Content currency and content stability may appear antithetical. The two ends can and should be consolidated. Content currency can mean two things. One is whether the content is periodically and recently updated, which usually can be checked by looking for a time stamp. The other is whether the actual content reflects the current status of the issue. The latter is more difficult to verify unless the reader is relatively well informed about developments in the field. If the reader is not well informed about the current status of the issue, it is a good idea to check by comparing the site with other resources.

Content stability means that when you visit the site again, you will be able to find what you saw last time. When the content is moved or archived, you will be able to find it through the site index or a search. Because more and more Web sites are using database management systems to dynamically generate data on the fly, bookmarks can quickly become invalid, and content stability is often hard to expect. Thus it is a good idea to record important Web information in archives on your local storage. We will discuss this later in the chapter.

Accessibility of Site and Ease of Navigation

The usefulness and practical value of a Web resource can be greatly affected by how easy it is for the user to find and get the wanted information. A site that has limited bandwidth or is frequently overloaded and hard to access is not a good resource even if it contains quality information. Similarly, a Web resource that has quality information but a poor navigation scheme may drive away interested visitors. Accessibility and usability are therefore two important factors to take into account in Web resource evaluation. In addition, characteristics such as graphic design, content legibility, text readability, syntax correctness, and accuracy in typing can all affect perception of site quality and credibility.

Privacy and Security

Some Web resources may require the visitor to register without charging any fee. Some may be fee-based and require users to subscribe. When registering with a Web site, check its protection of privacy and security of data transaction. If personal and confidential information is requested, is the site requesting more information than necessary? If confidential and sensitive information is transferred, is the transaction encrypted and protected through a secure data transfer protocol? When your browser is connected to a secure site, a padlock will appear in the bottom status line of your browser window. Clicking the padlock will make a window pop up displaying the secure certificate issued by a secure server certification authority. In addition, the protocol name that appears in the URL box will be HTTPS instead of HTTP.

Build Your Own Web Resource Repository

Despite the various search tools available to help people tap Web resources, few tools can satisfy all the information needs of a user. You need to develop a systematic approach and build up a resource repository that best meets your personal needs (Tomaiuolo, 2004). Such a systematic approach can help learners better utilize online resources in their lifelong learning.

In describing the systematic approach toward Web resources management, Hackathorn (1999) uses the term "Web farming" to suggest similarities between agricultural farming and information farming. As Hackathorn describes, Web farming is not haphazard surfing of the Web, wandering from one intriguing item to another, nor is it a one-time thorough search of the Web. Instead, Web farming is a continuous, systematic process of gathering and utilizing Internet-based resources that are relevant to the professional functions of an organization or individual.

Web farming is no easy task. A farmer has to apply great efforts and patience to cultivate crops with the help of natural and man-made resources, and the extent of success often depends on the cooperation of Mother Nature. Likewise, a Web farmer also has to work with diligence and persistence to make the virtual land productive. Such an undertaking must be carefully planned, systematic, and supported by appropriate and effective strategies and technologies. It requires considerable efforts to gather needed resources, sort through the data, extract useful information, integrate the information into the existing knowledge base, and make the resources ready for easy retrieval and use in the future. We cite Hackathorn's analogy here because we feel it helps to illustrate some features and requirements of systematic utilization of Web resources. However, we prefer to use the term *data warehousing* instead of Web farming in this text to emphasize the database management aspect of building up a personal repository of Web resources.

Recording and Archiving

Because digital data are easy to edit and transfer and because of the value placed on content currency, Web resources can be transient. What you find today may differ or disappear tomorrow. When you find a resource that you feel you'll need to cite in the future, it might be a good idea to make a note of the title and URL, and record the date when the resource was found. The date and URL information are needed when you cite the resources in your academic writing and publications. Sometimes, you may want to record part of the information that is too important to miss. If you do so, beware of copyright restrictions. Although browsers allow you to save a Web page, some authors may not allow their Web content to be downloaded and saved. Refer to chapter 8 for further discussion of copyright issues.

FIGURE 10.4   **Bookmark Tool Used to Organize Favorites in Internet Explorer 6**

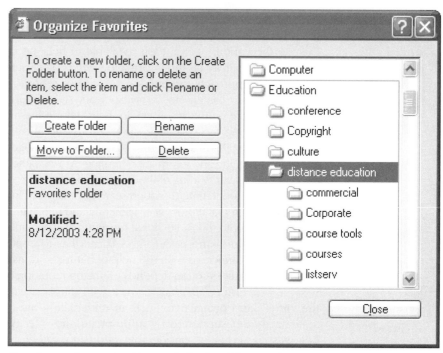

Note: Screen shot reprinted by permission from Microsoft Corporation.

Bookmarking

There are many strategies to deploy in personal data warehousing of Web resources. The simplest way to collect and organize Web resources is probably to use the bookmark tool of your browser. Categorization is the basic method of data organization in a bookmark system. Folders and subfolders can be created to organize links into categories (Figure 10.4).

If you use the bookmark tool extensively, make sure to back up your bookmarks regularly. In Mozilla Firefox 1.0, you can export the bookmarks (see Figure 10.5). Microsoft Internet Explorer 6 does not have an Export or Save As command for copying bookmarks, but you can make a copy of the Favorites folder that holds the bookmarks in Internet Explorer. In most cases, the Favorites folder should be stored under "C:\Documents and Settings\userName\."

Creating a Database

The primary advantage of the bookmark tool is that it makes it easy to record and retrieve links within the browser environment. But the bookmark tool is limited in its power to manage resources. As the list of your bookmarks grows, it can become unwieldy to organize and keep track of the records. If there are

FIGURE ⟨**10.5**⟩ **Bookmarks Manager Screen in Mozilla Firefox 1.0**

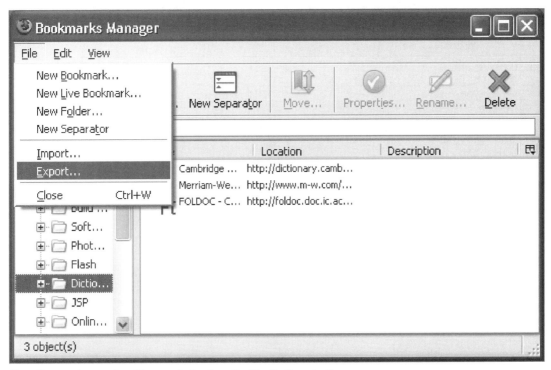

Note: Screen shot reprinted by permission from the Mozilla Organization.

more than three levels of subfolders, it is often difficult to find the embedded links in the subfolders. Furthermore, you cannot specify information attributes for the bookmarks, nor can you query in the bookmarks. For effective and efficient resource management, a database is a more helpful tool.

If you have never used a database before, database management might sound like a highly technical task for IT professionals only. This is not true. A personal database can be very easy to manage. For most people, a few tutorial sessions can help them start a simple database to store their personal resources such as music CD collections, student records, or Internet resources. Here we'll briefly describe some fundamental steps in using a database to store and manage Internet resources.

The first task in designing a simple database is to categorize data into relational entities and identify the data attributes of each entity. For example, "Internet resource" can be an entity, and the basic information attributes of this entity could include resource location (URL), resource title, media type (text, audio, video, graphic), file size, keywords, author name, and domain type (.com, .edu, .gov, .org, .net, etc.). To help track the utilization of the resources, we can add other logistic attributes such as the dates for first and last access. These attributes

FIGURE 10.6   Attributes (Field Names) and Data Types in Microsoft Access

⊞ Table1 : Table			
Field Name	**Data Type**	**Description**	
🔑 resource_URL	Text		
resource_title	Text		
media_type	Text	HTML, plain text, audio. video. graphic, etc	
file_size	Number	in kilo-bytes	
keywords	Text		
author_last_name	Text		
author_first_name	Text		
author_affiliation	Text		
domain_type	Text	.com .edu .gov .net .org	
domain_name	Text		
last_access_date	Date/Time		
description	Memo		
▶ comments	Memo ▾		

Field Properties

General	Lookup		
Format			
Caption			The data
Default Value			type
Validation Rule			determines
Validation Text			the kind of
Required	No		values that
Allow Zero Length	Yes		users can
Indexed	No		store in the
Unicode Compression	Yes		field. Press
IME Mode	No Control		F1 for help
IME Sentence Mode	None		on data
			types.

Note: Screen shot reprinted by permission from Microsoft Corporation.

are usually table column names. Additional columns may include a short description of the resource and your comments on the resource (see Figure 10.6).

Along with a field name, a data type must be selected for each field, as shown in Figure 10.6. The data type defines how much storage space needs to be reserved for the data and how the data should be processed by the database engine. Data types include text, number, and date. Each field can have format, validation rule, and other parameter settings.

The advantages of using Microsoft Access as a personal data management system include its user-friendly visual interface, integration with other Microsoft

IN PRACTICE   **Using Professional Experts to Build Collections of Resources**

As the amount of information resources keeps growing, it is becoming more and more of a challenge for an individual to find quality resources on the Web, even with the help of the search tools currently available. A search often turns out a very long list with resources that are rather uneven in quality. Steven Gilbert, president of the TLT Group, made a "modest proposal" suggesting that more academic professionals be encouraged to develop small "clusters," which are highly organized and focused sets of selected Web resources. These clusters do not need to be comprehensive or exhaustive, but should be developed with specific instructional needs in mind. These clusters could be shared among the faculty of a department, with faculty of other departments, or even with other institutions.

Source: Gilbert, S. W. (2002). Master clusters: Savvy Web searches? *Syllabus, 16*(5), 29, 36.

Please visit chapter 10 on the Companion Website (**http:// www.prenhall.com/ wang**) for a tutorial on using a Microsoft Access database for personal resource management, including creating tables and using queries to analyze data.

Office suite tools such as Word and Excel, and easy connectivity to other applications through Open Database Connectivity (ODBC). For example, you can easily export data from Access tables into Excel spreadsheets, XML documents, and plain text files, or vice versa.

Consulting Experts and Colleagues

The most direct, relevant, and valuable resource is probably advice and feedback from an expert on the topic or a colleague in the field. Through Web search, professional mailing lists, and discussion forums, you can find experts in various fields around the world. Most students may be hesitant to contact experts they have never seen or talked with. Actually, most experts are more willing to respond to students' questions than students would believe, especially if students' messages are composed in a very polite and professional manner, with clear, specific, carefully prepared questions (Gellis, 2000). Experts are not necessarily big names. Anyone who has made a focused study of a particular topic in a particular interest area can be considered a quasi-expert in that area.

Professional mailing lists and discussion forums are other places where you can get expert advice from those who have been working in your interest area for years. One of the well-known forums in the e-learning field is the Distance Education Online Symposium, or DEOS-L (http://lists.psu.edu/archives/deos-l.html).

ASSESSING STUDENTS' INFORMATION SKILLS

The biggest benefit of the Web is probably the easy access to worldwide information resources. As personal computers keep growing in power and portability, information access and resource sharing are becoming truly ubiquitous.

However, filtering through large numbers of possibly useful resources and picking out the most relevant and truly useful content is a major challenge for many inexperienced Web surfers, and yet this competence in information selection and evaluation is crucial for lifelong learning in the information age. Helping students become competent information searchers and researchers is an important component of Web-based instruction, and so is the assessment of students' development and mastery of the necessary skills.

Information Search and Evaluation Skills

How do we assess students' information skills? For a task that requires information gathering and evaluation, students first need to decide what information is needed and where to search for it. Once relevant resources are found, often in large quantity, students need to sort through the resources and evaluate their relevance and usefulness. The process requires the student to have a clear understanding of the learning task, its objectives, and needs for supporting information and resources. To assess students' information access and evaluation skills, we can have students document their search and research process, beginning with task analysis, followed by collecting relevant resources, filtering data, narrowing down choices, evaluating resource quality, and identifying interrelationships. The documentation of the process and a final report can be good indicators of student competence in information gathering, evaluation, and integration.

Information Presentation and Exchange Skills

Another aspect of information skills is information presentation, which can be assessed by asking students to report their findings. The Web supports a multitude of media for information presentation. Different media vary in their information attributes and strengths in conveying messages. Being able to select appropriate media and use the media effectively to convey a message to others is another important skill for our students. Students' Web presentations can be prepared by using tools such as HyperStudio, PowerPoint, Shockwave, or a combination of recorded audio narration, graphics, text description, and streaming video.

C A S E   S T U D Y   **Exercises on Resource Search and Research**

- For the IS students in our case study, learning tasks can be easily based on information gathering and evaluation over the Internet. For example, students can be asked to collect resources on open database connectivity (ODBC), pick the 10 most valuable resources, and write a report that synthesizes their research process and findings. Group work can also be organized to conduct a Web quest on topics that have information interest and research value for the course content.

Also important is competence in information exchange and online communication. For students in the Web-based learning environment, command of effective online communication skills is essential. There are two aspects of communicative competence in the online environment. One is the generic aspect applicable in the offline environment as well, such as the abilities to present a topic, raise a question, inform the audience, show respect for others, participate in a panel discussion, interact with guest speakers, negotiate for a solution, contribute to group maintenance, work toward the achievement of group goals, share team responsibilities, and solve problems with peer support. The other aspect is Internet-specific. Internet-specific communication competence includes appropriate use of netiquette, ability to select appropriate tools for particular communication tasks, and effective use of the tools to their advantage. Since most of the student communication and interaction is with peer learners, peer responses and reviews are often good indicators and valid measures of student communicative competence. Instructors can also sit in students' discussion, participate in online conferencing, and observe students' performance. See chapter 4 for further discussion of online communication and interaction.

Chapter Summary

This chapter began with an overview of the growth of the World Wide Web as a repository of information resources. We examined the forces that fostered the rapid growth and the benefits of the Web, and pointed out the difficulties in finding quality resources on the Web. We introduced several major types of Web search tools and highlighted their relative strengths and limitations. Resource search is followed by resource evaluation. We discussed some guidelines for filtering and evaluating Web resources in several key aspects. Given the vast scope of information on the Web, one should develop a systematic approach to Web resources management that best meets one's needs and circumstances. We suggested some primary strategies for building up a personal repository of Web resources. Finally, at the end of the chapter we recommend some Web resources that can help you do a better search job on the Web.

Review Questions

1. What search tools do you want to use to find Web resources on Andrew Lloyd Webber?

2. What search tools would be better choices for finding colleges and universities that offer online graduate programs in instructional technology?

3. What resources might be most helpful in finding research articles on information processing in the hypermedia environment?

4. When you find a Web resource that appears to provide information on a topic you're studying, what can you do to assure yourself of the information quality of the resource?

5. If you find conflicting information on the same topic from two or more related Web resources, what can you do to verify the accuracy of the information?

6. Do you think it is beneficial to develop a personal approach to managing and utilizing Web resources? What kind of approach do you feel fits you best?

Summary of Tips

1. Encourage students to use the advanced search option to limit search results to specific file types, such as Excel spreadsheets, audio recordings, or PDF files.

2. Use search engines to find specialized online databases.

3. Use search directories to look for information with categories and subcategories.

4. Use search directories for listing well-established Web sites in a particular subject area or field of study.

5. Look for related links in a good dedicated Web site to find more quality resources in the subject area.

6. Recommend to students a few good online references to facilitate Web-based learning.

7. Find and recommend some online journals related to the students' field of study. Select some articles for students' reading assignments.

8. Distinguish professional information from commercial promotion in evaluating information objectivity and truthfulness.

9. When citing information from a Web resource, verify the accuracy and objectivity of the information by comparing it with other resources.

10. Use reviews from related Web sites to check the credibility of a particular site. Use search engines to look for related Web resources.

11. Categorize and back up bookmarks you save with a browser.

12. Use a simple database to organize the Web resources you have collected so that data query and storage can be more effective and efficient.

13. Use primary data providers such as the U.S. Census Bureau for data that are frequently updated, such as Census data.

14. Encourage students to use professional mailing lists to get advice and feedback from experts and develop long-term relationships with colleagues in the field.

Exercises

The following series of activities should be assigned and carried out in sequence.

1. Conduct a survey in your class to find out the generally perceived difficulties in finding and utilizing Web resources. Report the findings to the class.

2. Design a general investigation of Web resource types to see if there are any other (new) primary types of resources available on the Web, other than those described in the chapter.

3. Compile a categorized list of the resources available from the local library. Compare the list with what's available on the Web and note the differences.

4. Select a topic of interest and search for resources on the topic through different types of search tools. Compare the results from the different search tools.

5. Conduct a comprehensive Web search to find online journals, reference resources, online books, and other primary data providers available in the field of your study. Compile a categorized list of your findings.

6. Evaluate the Web resource you found above using the criteria generally recommended by the Web community. Attach your evaluations to respective resources in your list.

7. Organize an online seminar, either synchronous through Internet conferencing or asynchronous through a discussion forum, to share your findings with classmates.

8. Make a plan for your personal systematic approach to the management of Web resources.

Resources on the Web

Please visit chapter 10 on the Companion Website (**http://www .prenhall.com/wang**) for updated and accurate resource links.

We have included some related Web resources at the end of each chapter. However, since Web resources are generally updated very frequently, we ask you to check out the Companion Website for updated and accurate resource links.

Tutorials on Searching the Web

- Bare Bones 101 is a Basic Tutorial on Searching the Web (http://www. sc.edu/beaufort/library/pages/bones/bones.shtml).
- Finding Information on the Internet is a Tutorial (http://www.lib.berkeley .edu/TeachingLib/Guides/Internet/FindInfo.html).

General Directories, Databases, and Virtual Libraries

- Open Directory Project is hosted and administered by Netscape Communication Corporation, is operated by a very small staff responsible for editorial policies and direction, community management and development, and systems engineering. Volunteer editors manage the directory's growth and development and ensure the directory is of superior quality. Netscape administers it as a noncommercial entity (http://dmoz.org).

- INFOMINE is a virtual library hosted by the University of California–Riverside, began in 1994 and is intended for faculty and students both within and outside the University of California. A unique feature is its use of an interactive crawler to integrate expert screening with automated Web resource searching and evaluation. This integration is an effective measure for managing the growing numbers of useful resources on the Web (Mitchell & Mooney, 1999) (http://infomine.ucr.edu).

- Internet Public Library (IPL) was started in 1995 as a class project in the School of Information and Library Studies at the University of Michigan. IPL contains several collections of resources, each created independently for a specific audience. Its chief strength lies in its human element; each resource collected has been identified, cataloged, and annotated by a real-life librarian or librarian-in-training. The information quality of the resources is therefore relatively high. Ironically, this is also its major weakness. Resource selection, subject to individual preferences, can be uneven in the selection of topics (Carter, 1999) (http://www.ipl.org).

- Librarians' Index is a searchable, annotated subject directory of more than 16,000 Internet resources (as of May 2005), selected and evaluated by librarians for their usefulness to users of public libraries. The site is meant to be used by both librarians and nonlibrarians as a reliable and efficient guide to described and evaluated Internet resources (http://lii.org).

- The Scout Report is hosted by the Department of Computer Sciences at the University of Wisconsin–Madison. Since 1994, a weekly Scout Report has been published containing annotated Internet resources recently found and screened by professional librarians, educators, and content experts. The report currently reaches 250,000 users every week (The Internet Scout Project, 2005) (http://scout.wisc.edu/).

- BUBL LINK is hosted by Strathclyde University, UK. Its mission is to provide value-added access to Internet resources for the UK higher education community. Although the number of resources currently held in BUBL LINK is not large, all the resources have been evaluated by professional staff members and are checked and fixed each month. The resources include tables of contents, abstracts, and the full text of hundreds of academic journals and magazines (Nicholson & Dawson, 1999) (http://bubl.ac.uk).

Special Directories, Databases, and Virtual Libraries

- Agricultural Network Information Center (AgNIC) is a voluntary alliance of the National Agricultural Library, land-grant universities, and other agricultural organizations (http://laurel.nal.usda.gov:8080/agnic/).

- CAREO (Campus Alberta Repository of Eduational Objects) is a project supported by Alberta Learning and CANARIE (Canadian Network for the Advancement of Research in Industry and Education) whose primary goal is the creation of a searchable, Web-based collection of multidisciplinary teaching materials for educators across the province and beyond. CAREO is undertaken by the Universities of Alberta and Calgary and Athabasca University in cooperation with BELLE (Broadband Enabled Lifelong Learning Environment) and CANARIE. The CAREO educational object repository is an ongoing research prototype; thus it may be offline periodically for updates and upgrades to the system as the project evolves and new theories about educational objects are tested and implemented (http://www.careo.org).

- Dissertation Abstracts (http://www.umi.com/dissertations/). Each institution that publishes with ProQuest Information and Learning receives free campuswide online access to the full text (in PDF format) of the dissertations and theses submitted to UMI.

- Edinburgh Engineering Virtual Library (EEVL) is an Internet guide to engineering, mathematics, and computing, resources for college faculty and students in engineering. EEVL is a free service created and run by a team of information specialists from a number of universities and institutions in the UK (http://www.eevl.ac.uk).

- FindLaw provides a comprehensive set of online resources for legal professionals, businesses, students, and individuals, including Web search utilities, cases and codes, legal news, an online career center, and community-oriented tools (http://www.findlaw.com).

- Math Archives is particularly strong in its collection of educational software in mathematics. It also contains extensive collections of links to Internet resources in mathematics (http://archives.math.utk.edu).

- Organizing Medical Networked Information (OMNI) hosted by Nottingham University, UK, offers free access to a searchable catalogue of selected and evaluated Internet resources in health and medicine (http://omni.ac.uk).

- Social Science Information Gateway (SOSIG) is a collection of selected Internet information for researchers and practitioners in the social sciences, business, and law. It is part of the UK Resource Discovery Network (http://sosig.ac.uk).

- The Educator's Reference Desk has links to over 3,000 resources on a variety of educational issues and a collection of over 2,000 unique lesson plans written and submitted by teachers from all over the United States (http://www.eduref.org).

Subscription-Required Databases

- InfoTrac College Edition contains over one million full-length articles from the last four years taken from scholarly and popular periodicals, including journals, magazines, encyclopedias, and newsletters. The articles cover a broad spectrum of disciplines and topics (infotrac.thomsonlearning.com).

- LEXIS-NEXIS is a leading provider of full-text resources in law, business, and current affairs (http://www.lexis-nexis.com).

- PsycINFO is an abstract (not full-text) database of psychological literature from 1887 to the present, hosted by the American Psychological Association (http://www.apa.org/psycinfo).

Collections of Online Journals and Periodicals

- BioMed Central provides free access to peer-reviewed research articles from more than 100 journals in the biomedical field (http://www. biomedcentral.com).

- PubMed is a service of the National Library of Medicine that includes over 14 million citations for biomedical articles back to the 1950s from MEDLINE and additional life science journals. PubMed includes links to many sites that provide full-text articles and other related resources (http://www. ncbi.nlm.nih.gov/).

- Electronic Journal Miner is part of a development effort by the nonprofit Colorado Alliance of Research Libraries (http://ejournal.coalliance.org).

- Internet Public Library Serials lists annotated links to online periodicals organized by subject area (http://www.ipl.org/div/serials).

- Magatopia provides a search collection of links to over 1,000 online magazines (http://www.magatopia.com).

- Yahoo! Directory of Online Journals organizes hundreds of links to online journals in categories including the arts, business, education, health, humanities, law, medicine, science, and technology (http://dir.yahoo.com/News_and_Media/Journals/).

Search Engines

- Search Engine Showdown (www.searchengineshowdown. com).

- Search Engine Watch (www.SearchEngineWatch.com).

Web Resource Evaluation

- Evaluating Web Resources, by Jan Alexander and Marsha Ann Tate, authors of the book *Web Wisdom: How to Evaluate and Create Information Quality on*

the Web (http://muse.widener.edu/Wolfgram-Memorial-Library/webevaluation/
webeval.htm).

- Evaluating Internet Research Sources, by Robert Harris (http://virtualsalt
  .com/evalu8it.htm).

- Information Quality WWW Virtual Library: The Internet Guide to Construction of Quality Online Resources, by Dr. T. Matthew Ciolek (http://www.
  ciolek.com/WWWVL-InfoQuality.html).

- Thinking Critically About World Wide Web Resources, by Esther Grassian,
  UCLA College Library (http://www.library.ucla.edu/libraries/college/help/
  critical/index.htm).

- Evaluating Information Found on the Internet from the Sheridan Libraries of
  the Johns Hopkins University (http://www.library.jhu.edu/researchhelp/
  general/evaluating/index.html).

References

Alastair, S. G. (1997). Testing the surf: Criteria for evaluating Internet information
 resources. *The Public-Access Computer System Review, 8*(3). Retrieved June 30,
 2004, from http://info.lib.uh.edu/pr/v8/n3/smit8n3.html.

Alexander, J. E., & Tate, M. A. (1999). *Web wisdom: How to evaluate and create
 information quality on the Web.* Mahwah, NJ: Lawrence Erlbaum Associates.

Carter, D. S. (1999). Internet Public Library (IPL). In A. T. Wells, S. Calcari, & T.
 Koplow (Eds.), *The amazing Internet challenge: How leading projects use library
 skills to organize the Web* (pp. 121–143). Chicago: American Library Association.

Gellis, M. (2000). Teaching research skills using the Internet. In R. A. Code (Ed.),
 Issues in Web-based pedagogy (pp. 349–363). Westport, CT: Greenwood Press.

Hackathorn, R. (1999). Web farming for the data warehouse. San Francisco: Morgan
 Kaufmann.

Henderson, J. R. (2002). ICYouSee: T is for thinking: A guide to critical thinking about
 what you see on the Web. Retrieved June 30, 2004, from
 http://www.ithaca.edu/library/Training/think.html.

HighWire (2004). Home page of HighWire Press. Retrieved July 5, 2004, from
 http://highwire.stanford.edu/.

Internet Scout Project. (2005). The Scout report. Retrieved May 15, 2005, from
 http://scout.wisc.edu.

Makinster, J. G., Beghetto, R. A., & Plucker, J. A. (2002). Why can't I find Newton's
 Third Law?: Case studies of students using the Web as a science resource. *Journal
 of Science Education and Technology, 11* (2), 155–172.

Mayer, R. E. (1999). Designing instruction for constructive learning. In C. M. Reigeluth
 (Ed.), *Instructional-design theories and models: A new paradigm of instructional
 theory* (Vol. II) (pp. 141–159). Mahwah, NJ: Lawrence Erlbaum.

Mitchell, S., & Mooney, M. (1999). INFOMINE. In A. T. Wells, S. Calcari, & T. Koplow
 (Eds.), *The amazing Internet challenge: How leading projects use library skills to
 organize the Web* (pp. 97–120). Chicago: American Library Association.

Nicholson, D., & Dawson, A. (1999). BUBL Information Service (BUBL). In A. T.
 Wells, S. Calcari, & T. Koplow (Eds.), *The amazing Internet challenge: How*

leading projects use library skills to organize the Web (pp. 53–75). Chicago: American Library Association.

Nielson, J. (2001). Search: Visible and simple. Alertbox—userit.com, May 13. Retrieved July 1, 2004, from http://www.useit.com/alertbox/20010513.html.

Spink, A., Bateman, J., & Jansen, B. J. (1999). Searching the Web: A survery of Excite users. *Internet Research: Electronic Networking Applications and Policy, 9*(2), 117–128.

Spool, J. (2002). *In search of the perfect search: Building the perfect on-site search.* CHI 2002 Tutorial.

Tomaiuolo, N. G. (2004). *The Web library: Building a world-class personal library with free Web resources.* Medford, NJ: Information Today.

Vansickle, S. (2002). Tenth graders' search knowledge and use of the Web. *Knowledge Quest, 30* (4), 33–37.

Wallace, R., Kupperman, J., Krajcik, J., & Soloway, E. (2000). Science on the Web: Students online in a sixth-grade classroom. *The Journal of the Learning Sciences, 9* (1), 57–104.

Chapter 11

Policy and Management for Web-Based Instruction

CHAPTER INTRODUCTION

As a course designer, distance instructor, or trainer you may wonder why you need to worry about the policies and management of Web-based instruction. E-learning is conducted by a systems approach. All the different aspects of distance learning affect each other. As an instructor or trainer you will find yourself on the front line giving support, be it technical or administrative. As a course designer, you need to understand how the entire distance learning system works so that you can create e-learning courses designed to address the many needs of distance students. Distance students need to feel they are part of the program and the institution, and much of that is accomplished through the course process. This chapter explains the types of distance learning institutions, how institutional policy must be adapted for distance delivery, and how a distance program is run.

LEARNING OBJECTIVES

After studying this chapter, the reader will be able to:

1. Outline the planning process for distance courses and programs.

2. Describe how to develop policies for courses and programs and how distance learning policies affect other units within the institution or organization.

3. Explain why a marketing plan is necessary for the courses or programs.

4. Describe how to provide services to distance students.

5. Explain the need for evaluating distance courses or programs.

ⒸASE STUDY

• You are part of a team that is planning the online delivery of the IS degree program at MSU. The administration has decided to venture from the current IVN delivery of the program. Now that the institution has made the decision to go forward with the project, the team is faced with the task of reviewing institutional policy to determine how online delivery will affect the institution.

▶ How does the team determine the significant issues that the institution will face in implementing an online program?

▶ What does the institution do to implement policy change?

▶ How do the policy changes affect individual faculty and courses in the online program?

Keep these questions in mind as you read through this chapter.

DISTANCE LEARNING INSTITUTIONS

Verduin and Clark (1991) discuss six different types of distance education organizations in their book, *Distance Education: The Foundations of Effective Practice*. Type I institutions are postsecondary educational institutions offering college degrees to students whom they have not taught. They award degrees for prior course work and work/life experience for which the students earn credit. Examples of such institutions are Excelsior College (formerly Regents College), Thomas Edison State College, and the Western Governors' University. Type II institutions are postsecondary educational institutions offering degrees to students whom they have taught, using the same alternative approaches as the Type I institutions. Examples of such institutions are Stephens College and Nova University.

Type III institutions are conventional universities that offer distance education through extension, independent study, and continuing education units. Most e-learning programs fall into this category. Type IV institutions involve consortia of education-related institutions. Type V institutions are those specifically designed to teach distance students, and Type VI involves educational media developed by recognized educational or informational organizations used without the assistance of an education organization by informal distance learners. In the decade since Verduin and Clark (1991) published their book, this area has grown steadily on the Web.

PLANNING YOUR E-LEARNING PROGRAM

The planning process is critical to the success of an e-learning program (Levy & Ramim, 2004). Any type of planning process can be used as long as it is followed through. Here is an example of a popular planning process developed by Boyle (1981).

The first step, establishing organizational and individual commitment, is what it takes to make it work. If you don't have top-down support within your institution or organization you will not succeed. It takes institutional support, with resources, to make an e-learning course or program function successfully. The second step is to analyze the situation. Design a needs assessment to identify your target audience and the academic programs it wants. Develop your niche market from those needs, keeping in mind that you must work within your institutional mission.

From your needs assessment you will work into step 3, identifying broad program objectives. These objectives must fall in line with your institutional and program missions and should include your academic goals along with your goals of service to your students.

Step 4, determining the needed resources and support, is where institutional support comes into play. When you determine your resource and support needs it is important that your institution be committed to providing that support. The initial development of a program is costly in monetary and human resources. Without institutional support your program will struggle. Ultimately a program can be self-sufficient, but institutional support until that point is reached is what will make it work.

The next two steps, designing the program and preparing an instructional plan, are the most time consuming. This is the heart of your program planning: developing the courses and the plan to implement them and to provide all the necessary services to your students. When you have completed that process, you are ready for step 7, in which you take action, implementing your program and managing the daily operations.

The final two steps are the assessment process. Determine the program's value and communicate the results. You need to plan up front how you will assess your courses or program so that you can make adjustments and improvements. However, the assessment process is not complete until the results are communicated to all the stakeholders in the program: the administration, the faculty and staff, and the students.

This was a quick overview of the process that goes on in program development. Faculty and course designers are part of the whole system of distance learning. It is important to understand how your part fits into the whole process.

To specifically address distance education program planning, let's look at the American Distance Education Consortium (ADEC) guiding principles for distance learning:

1. Design for active and effective learning. Early in distance course design, many faculty thought putting their lecture notes on the Web was a distance course. Courses need to be carefully designed to provide engaged learning, and should use learning strategies and provide learning outcomes. When working with an entire program at a distance, also keep in mind course sequences and having prerequisite courses offered in advance of upper level courses.

2. Support the needs of learners. Distance-delivered programs must offer the same services to distance students as to on-campus students, which include registration, financial services, bookstore and materials, advising, library, technical support, and placement, to name a few.

3. Develop and maintain the technological and human infrastructure. This goes hand in hand with services. Proper technical infrastructure is necessary to support student needs and course management systems. The human infrastructure is also vital. It is important for the distance student to be able to have human support—someone to talk to—when needed, to minimize the feelings of isolation many distance students encounter.

4. Sustain administrative and organizational commitment. Distance learning programs will not be successful unless they are a part of their institution's mission and have full administrative support.

Other distance planning processes are used as the basis of accrediting distance programs. An example is found on the Western Cooperative for Educational Telecommunications (WCET) site. This site is used by institutions as a guide for the self-study documents written to receive regional accreditation, particularly for the best practices document (WCET, 2004).

The categories used in self-study documents are:

1. Institutional context and commitment—the institution's role, support for, and commitment to delivering a distance program.

2. Curriculum and instruction—addresses the quality issues of course pedagogy and instructor qualification.

3. Faculty support—addresses issues such as faculty training and workload.

4. Student support—addresses all types of support provided to a geographically dispersed student population.

5. Evaluation and assessment—an often-overlooked area, where feedback from all stakeholders should be collected and used to improve distance programs.

 **ASE STUDY**

> • As the distance education program administrator, run an audit of the courses currently being delivered and those to be redesigned, ranking the cost benefits of redesigning the courses with the market potential.

Levy & Ramim (2004) have developed a cyclical plan for developing self-funding e-learning programs which includes the following eight elements: a strategic plan; administrative and institutional support; budget and funding; infrastructure; high-quality support and development team; policies and procedures; successful pilot program; and quality assurance.

There are many different planning models. Select the one that best suits the needs of your organization. What is crucial is that a planning process be used.

You may wonder why it is so important to plan an e-learning course or program. Any institution or organization is looking for a return on its investment in e-learning. Needs assessment was mentioned as an important part of the planning process. Robinson (2004) puts forth the transformative income generation (TIG) model as a resourceful way to determine the potential marketability of e-learning courses. For example, courses in the medical field can be used for nursing, pharmacology, and medical students. When looking at redesigning courses for distance delivery, rank courses not only for the educational benefits of the content but for the marketability potential.

DEVELOPING POLICY FOR YOUR E-LEARNING PROGRAM

The first step in developing high-quality courses and programs is to establish guidelines for official policies and procedures that are in line with the ones used for traditional courses (Levy & Ramim, 2004). This is also an area that often is not addressed until it is too late. It is much harder to develop policy on the fly than it is to think about it ahead of time, although there are times when a policy change may be needed as a situation occurs. Berge (1998) discusses some of the barriers that institutions hit when developing policy for distance programs. He provides the following group of policy issues: academic, fiscal, geographic, governance, labor-management, legal, and student support. Parisot (1997) provides a blueprint for policy that creates an environment for change, addressing the barriers and following the steps of acknowledgment, awareness, acculturation, and affirmation. First there is acknowledgment of the need for a change in policy; then awareness guides the process. Acculturation to the new ways of teaching and learning come from providing opportunities for professional development. Finally there is affirmation of the commitment to participate in distance learning. There are two main areas in which policy must be either created or changed for a distance program:

▶ Institutional support policies—staff and equipment, hiring faculty, policy for faculty compensation, training for faculty, including a faculty development lab, intellectual property, curriculum, and so on.

▶ Student services policies—admissions and registration, financial aid and fee payment, advising, library, technical support, student training for delivery method, receiving grades and transcripts, and so on.

It is important to understand that policy changes for your e-learning program will affect most units in the institution. You may or may not have a separate unit within the institution to handle distance services. If not, then your registrar needs to handle the admissions, registration, grades, and other such services. The financial aid office is affected, and the financial aid rules are different for distance programs. The colleges and departments must handle advising. It becomes a team effort within the institution. When there is a unit to handle the e-learning program, there is still interaction with all the institutional units because e-learning affects each of those units to some extent.

Table 11.1 provides a policy analysis framework for distance education, specifying the policy areas to be addressed and the key issues for each policy area. You will discover that developing policy for distance education in each of these areas will be a major task for your institution. As a course designer, distance instructor, or trainer, you will need to be familiar with the distance education policy to effectively support your distance students.

Table 11.2 provides an easy three-tier policy analysis framework to assist in the initial policy design.

Intellectual property policies are of particular importance to course designers, course instructors, and trainers. An institution's intellectual property policies include: intellectual property policies with respect to ownership of distance education courses; institutional and faculty rights and responsibilities after a course is created; faculty compensation, teaching load, and acceptance; student access and privacy; potential liabilities associated with distance education courses; and accreditation and approval beyond state and national borders.

According to an issue paper on distance education and intellectual property policy published by the American Association of University Professors (AAUP, 2005), the following questions should be considered in policy on ownership of intellectual property:

▶ What is "intellectual property"? It needs to be defined for your institution.

▶ Who owns the intellectual property? Is it the author, the institution, or both?

TABLE 11.1   **Policy Analysis Framework for Distance Education**

Policy area	Key issues
Academic	Calender, course integrity, transferability, transcripts, student/course evaluation, admission standards, curriculum/course approval, accreditation, class cancellations, course/program/degree availability, recruiting/marketing
Governance/administration/fiscal	Tuition rate, technology fee, full-time equivalent student counts (FTEs), administration cost, state fiscal regulations, tuition disbursement, space, single versus multiple board oversight, staffing
Faculty	Compensation and workload, development incentives, faculty training, congruence with existing union contracts, class monitoring, faculty support, faculty evaluation
Legal	Intellectual property; faculty, student, and institutional liability
Student support services	Advisement, counseling, library access, materials delivery, student training, test proctoring, videotaping, computer accounts, registration, financial aid, labs
Technical	Systems reliability, connectivity/access, hardware/software, setup concerns, infrastructure, technical support (staffing), scheduling, costs
Cultural	Adoption of innovations, acceptance of online/distance teaching, understanding of distance education (what works at a distance), organizational values

Source: Adapted from Gellman-Danley & Fetzner, 1998; Berge, 1998.

▶ Who may use the intellectual property? Is the work just for educational use?

▶ How are the funds to be distributed? Depending on how ownership is determined, how generated funds are distributed should be well defined.

▶ How are emerging issues and disputes resolved? Institutions should consider having an intellectual property committee to handle all related issues.

These issues should be reviewed at your institution before you begin Web-based course design (or during the process), and not after the fact, where problems could arise.

TABLE **11.2**   **Three-tiered Policy Analysis Framework
for Distance Education**

Policy area	Description
Faculty (including continuing education and cooperative extension)	Rewards (e.g., stipends, promotion and tenure, merit increases, etc.); support (e.g., student help, technical assistance, training, etc.); opportunities to learn about technology and new applications (e.g., release time, training, etc.); intellectual property (e.g., ownership of materials, copyright, etc.)
Students/ participants	Support (e.g., access to technology, library resources, registration, advising, financial aid, etc.); requirements and records (e.g., residency requirements, acceptance of courses from other places, transfer of credit, continuing education, etc.)
Management and organization	Tuition and fee structure; funding formula; collaboration (e.g., with other departments, units, institutions, consortia, intra- and interinstitutional, service areas, etc.); resources (e.g., financial resources to support distance education, equipment, new technologies, etc.); curricula/individual courses (e.g., delivery modes, course/program selection, plans to develop, individual sequences, course development, entire program delivery, interactivity requirements, test requirements, contact hour definitions, etc.)

Source: From J. W. King, et al., Policy frameworks for distance education: Implications for decision makers, http://www.westga.edu/~distance/king32.html

 ASE STUDY ········

> • As the distance education program administrator, review the campus policies and procedures that need to be established for e-learning courses and programs. Develop a plan, including specifying the principal stakeholders who need to be involved, to implement new policies and procedures.

MARKETING YOUR E-LEARNING PROGRAM

Two types of marketing need to be done, internal and external marketing. Let's briefly address internal marketing. Implementing an e-learning or distance program is a change to the institutional culture, and there is always resistance to change. Those involved need to internally market the distance program to the administration, faculty, staff, and students. Helping the university population understand what is involved in distance delivery and how it affects the institution is important for a successful program.

Once your internal community understands the distance program, it is time to market it to potential students. First review the needs assessments done in the planning stage of the program. You have begun your marketing plan by identifying the potential student population and the programs to develop. The potential e-learning environment is student focused and learner driven, including just-in-time learning (also known as anytime, anyplace learning—it is required by students right away), which is asynchronous and results oriented. It is different from traditional learning, which is campus based and must be marketed differently.

Jerry Feldberg, CEO of Embanet, advises, "you have to become a marketing guru" (Educational Pathways Newsletter, 2002). This can be a scary task as you wonder why you need to worry about marketing as a course designer or course instructor. In 2004, the American Marketing Association (AMA) updated its definition of marketing: "Marketing is an organizational function and a set of processes for creating, communicating, and delivering value to customers and for managing customer relationships in ways that benefit the organization and its stakeholders" (Sevier, 2005). By this definition, it is now the responsibility of everyone in an organization to help in marketing.

The following list of marketing tips has been collected from presentations, newsletters, and articles (Bourne, 2005; Donsky, 2004; Educational Pathways Newsletter, 2002; Embanet Newsletter, 2003; Ram, 1999; Sevier, 2005). It will be impossible to become a guru unless you want to. These tips can, however, inform you of the important aspects of marketing a distance course or program.

▶ Define potential customers/learners. Be able to understand and communicate to your customers/learners.

▶ Find and make connections to key market segments. Market to the right niche.

▶ Analyze and strategize; review your processes and planning strategies.

▶ Implement a communication plan to reach your market effectively, provide clear information, follow through.

▶ Give adequate advance notice of upcoming courses and/or programs.

▶ Focus on content, not technology—technology never sells a program.

▶ Don't forget to use the "soft touch" over a "hard touch"—don't be too pushy and be personal; don't overdo mass mailings

▶ Maximize your Web site; it's your best marketing tool.

▶ Keep it simple by sticking to one idea, one voice, one product at a time.

A good marketing plan for an e-learning program includes a combination of print-based and online advertising. It is important to understand that there will be extensive marketing for the program, and as an instructor or developer it is good to know where the marketing is directed. The course(s) and program(s) need to meet the needs of the potential students, and you should know who the marketing plan is targeting.

It is a good idea to develop a brand for your e-learning program. Many institutions find that developing a brand for their niche distance program assists in the recruitment and retention of students. The courses in the programs should be developed to include the brand and should have a consistent look, via a template, to portray the theme.

Word of mouth is the best marketing tool. Students who have a good learning experience will send more new students your way than will any other marketing campaign. Developing a quality course and providing excellent service to your students will bring them back, with their friends and co-workers.

Summing up marketing of distance education courses, there are five tips to remember: first, provide clear information on your courses and programs; second, maximize your Web site, including developing a brand for your program; third, find and make the right connections to help with marketing your courses and programs; fourth, analyze your strategies; and fifth, follow through with great customer service. Your goal should be to develop a brand for your courses or programs and establish a marketing plan that includes both internal and external marketing.

PROVIDING SERVICES TO DISTANCE STUDENTS

According to Moore and Kearsley (1996), administration of a distance education program includes all the activities that support the teaching/learning process:

▶ Potential students must be informed about proposed courses.

▶ Students must be registered and enrolled.

▶ Fees must be collected and accounts kept.

▶ Decisions must be made about what courses to produce.

▶ The process of designing, producing, and delivering course materials must be administered.

▶ Academic and administrative staff must be hired, supported, and supervised.

▶ Instructional and counseling services to students must be administered.

▶ Student grades, diplomas, degrees, and awards must be issued.

▶ Facilities, equipment, and materials must be obtained and maintained.

▶ The effectiveness, efficiency, and quality of the program must be constantly assessed.

Running through this list you will see the policy issues addressed earlier in the chapter. By providing these services the program is meeting most of the needs of distance students. As an instructor or course developer you need to know how your institution is providing these services. They should be included in your course information or syllabus. When students don't know whom to ask about a service or procedure, they will turn to the instructor for information and guidance first. The more informed you are about services and procedures for distance students, the less frustrated you will be with such inquiries.

EVALUATING YOUR E-LEARNING PROGRAM

The evaluation process completes the planning process and provides for quality control. The process should not be taken lightly, and, as stated earlier, needs to be part of the planning process. The instructor or course designer should carefully review feedback from students, but the questions asked of students need to be appropriate. It is important to assess how the technology works, how the content was delivered, and how feedback is given. When reviewing the student assessment, remember that students who are new to distance course delivery will be wary of how it works and it may not be their most comfortable learning style. Keep this in mind when reviewing evaluations and do not take comments personally. The feedback will be helpful, but is often very negative. Evaluations will range from very critical to extremely impressed. Students love it or hate it. However, sifting through the comments is helpful and will allow you to make important improvements for the next time.

Chapter Summary

This chapter was written to help you, as an instructor or trainer, course developer, or instructional designer, to better understand how an e-learning program is designed and administered. You will find yourself being the front line for student support, and understanding how the system works will help you. Keep informed about the policies developed by your institution for the distance program and for course delivery. Know whom to contact when students ask you support questions. Know how to direct students to the services they need on campus. This is one of the changing roles of the instructor in the e-learning environment. However, it is important to remember not to get so caught up in policy issues that you forget your most primary concern, teaching and learning.

Review Questions

1. Describe the planning process you would use to develop a distance course or program.

2. How would you review the current policies at your institution to adapt them for distance course and program delivery?

3. What steps would you take in developing a marketing plan for your distance course or program?

4. What type of program or course assessment does your organization conduct? How do you distribute the assessment information to the instructors and decision makers? If your organization does not conduct program or course assessment, how would you plan an assessment procedure?

Summary of Tips

1. Develop a plan to implement your online course or degree program, starting with a needs analysis.

2. Review institutional policy to adapt it for online course and program delivery, involving all stakeholders in the process.

3. Review or write intellectual property policy related to online course design and delivery.

4. Develop a marketing plan for your online courses and programs.

5. Develop a plan to provide all campus services to the online students.

6. Evaluate your online courses and programs and make necessary changes to the course and program delivery.

Exercises

1. After reviewing the types of distance learning institutions, determine what type of institution you work with.

2. Review the policies of your institution or online program and make note of the policies that would need to change to accommodate distance students.

3. Outline the planning process for distance courses and programs for your school or program.

4. Plan what services your institution should provide to distant students and what measures to take to ensure the effective provision of these services.

5. Prepare a report that explains the need for evaluating your distance courses or program and recommends actions to take to market the courses or program.

References

AAUP. (2005). Ownership of intellectual property. Retrieved March 15, 2005, from http://www.aaup.org/Issues/DistanceEd/Archives/speccmt/ipguiide.htm.

Berge, Z. L. (1998). Barriers to online teaching in post-secondary institutions: Can policy changes fix it? In *Online Journal of Distance Learning Administration, 1*(2), Summer 1998. Retrieved February 20, 2004, from http://www.westga.edu/~distance/Berge12.html.

Bourne, K. (2005). Marketing online programs: We are all marketers. Retrieved January 5, 2005, from http://www.sloan-c.org/publications/view/v4nl/marketing.htm.

Boyle, P. G. (1981). *Planning better programs.* New York: McGraw-Hill.

Donsky, A. (2004). Avoiding marketing mistakes. *Journal of Lifelong Learning, (4)*2, 1–3.

Educational Pathways Newsletter. (2002). Marketing distance education. Retrieved May 28, 2004, from http://www.edpath.com/marketing.htm.

Gellman-Danley, B., & Fetzner, M. J. (1998). Asking the really tough questions: Policy issues for distance learning. In *Online Journal of Distance Learning Administration, 1*(1), Spring 1998. Retrieved February 20, 2004, from http://www.westga.edu/~distance/danleyll.html.

Levy, Y., & Ramim, M. M. (2004). Financing expensive technologies in an era of decreased funding: Think big . . . start small . . . and build fast. In C. Howard, K. Schenk, & R. Discenza (Eds.), *Distance learning and university effectiveness: Changing educational paradigms for online learning.* Hershey, PA: Information Science Publishing.

Moore, M. G., & Kearsley, G. (1996). *Distance education: A systems view.* Belmont, CA: Wadsworth.

Parisot, A. H. (1997). Distance education as a catalyst for changing teaching in the community college: Implications for institutional policy. In C. L. Dillion & R. Cintron (Eds.), *Building a working policy for distance education.* New Directions for Community Colleges, 99, Fall 1997. San Francisco: Jossey-Bass.

Ram, S. (1999). How to develop an effective marketing plan. Presented at the DETC Marketing Workshop, October 24–26, 1999. Scottsdale, AZ.

Robinson, E. T. (2004). Return on investment for distance education offerings: Developing a cost effective model. In C. Howard, K. Schenk, & R. Discenza (Eds.), *Distance learning and university effectiveness: Changing educational paradigms for online learning.* Hershey, PA: Information Science Publishing.

Sevier, R. (2005). A new definition of marketing. Retrieved March 1, 2005, from http://www.universitybusiness.com/pageprint.cfm?p=751.

Verduin, J. R., Jr., & Clark, T. A. (1991). *Distance education: The foundations of effective practice.* San Francisco: Jossey-Bass.

WCET. (2004). Regional accrediting agency documents on electronically offered degree and certificate programs. Retrieved May 1, 2005, from http://www.wcet.info/resources/accreditation/index.asp.

GLOSSARY

Accessibility   Often specifically means making Web content accessible to people with disabilities, particularly those with vision and hearing impairments who rely on assistive technology to access and process digital information.

Adaptive hypermedia   A system designed to interact with an individual learner and to dynamically provide customized content and learning paths to meet the learning objectives, preferences, and knowledge needs of that individual.

Adaptive testing   Testing in which questions are selected from an item bank and presented to the test taker based on the test taker's responses to the preceding items. Primarily designed to improve the efficiency of test administration because fewer items and less time are needed to measure each examinee's proficiency. Results may be less comparable across test takers because each test taker may receive different sets of items.

Alternative assessment   General term covering a variety of assessment approaches that have grown largely out of dissatisfaction with the traditional objective test of student performance. Among the approaches are authentic assessment, performance assessment, and portfolio assessment.

Application sharing   Also called program sharing, it allows multiple participants to be connected to and work in the interface of the same application software. Each participant can both view and edit the data in the interface, and each person's contribution is reflected in real time in every other participant's view.

Associative learning   Learning fostered by association between ideas, which do not necessarily have a sequential or hierarchical relationship.

Asynchronous communication   Communication in which participants are usually separated by distance and a delay in response is expected.

Authentic assessment   Assessment that emphasizes authenticity of learning tasks, which may be part of what the student is currently doing in real life, or what the student is expected to do in real life in the near future. Learners find the assessment both a meaningful learning experience and a valuable life experience.

Bandwidth   In its original sense, the difference (width) between the highest and lowest frequencies of a transmission channel. However, also popularly used to mean data transfer rate or channel capacity—the amount of data that can be sent through a given data transfer channel in a certain amount of time, usually measured in bits per second.

Bit   Short for binary digit, generally considered the smallest unit of data storage in computing. A bit can be electronically on or off, signifying 1 or 0, true or false, yes or no. Eight bits make up one byte.

Blended learning   Distance learning that combines e-learning (using computer, Internet, telephone, television) and traditional media (face-to-face classroom setting, mail correspondence); often synonymous with hybrid distance learning.

Broadband   A telecommunication channel capable of supporting a wide range of frequencies and multiple signals by dividing the total capacity into multiple independent bandwidth channels; cable TV, DSL, fiber optic, and T1 are examples.

Browser   A software program for displaying Web pages and presenting hypermedia. With plug-ins, most browsers can display animation and play audio and video clips. Popular browsers include Microsoft Internet Explorer, Mozilla Firefox, Netscape Navigator, and Opera.

Byte   Smallest addressable unit of data storage in computing, larger than a bit but smaller than a word. A byte usually has eight bits and typically holds one character.

Client-side program   A program that runs on the user's computer only, typically in a browser environment, and does not need runtime support from any Web server.

CODEC   Short for compression/decompression or coder/decoder. In the former case, any technology for compressing and decompressing data. In the latter case, any technology that encodes and decodes signals, typically for converting data between analog and digital forms. CODEC can be implemented in software, hardware, or a combination of both.

Cognitive overload   The result of having too much information presented to be effectively processed, particularly memory overload.

Collaborative learning   A process in which each member of a group contributes personal experience, information, knowledge, perspective, skills, and views to achieve some shared learning goals. The objective is to maximize learning through collaboration to achieve learning outcomes that individuals will not be able to achieve on their own.

Constructive learning   Based on the belief that learners learn best when they gain knowledge and develop skills through exploration and relate new knowledge to prior experiences. Constructive learning is usually situated in realistic settings, and assessment is integrated with the learning task.

Correspondence study   Distance education conducted through traditional mail exchange without the help of telecommunication.

Course management system   A Web server software application package that provides an integrated online environment for administration of student enrollment, course setup, content creation and organization, online communication, online assessment, and student performance monitoring. Examples of commercial course management systems include Blackboard, Desire2Learn, and WebCT.

Criterion-referenced assessment   Assessment using a set of performance criteria to measure how well learner performances meet the criteria; often used in contrast with norm-referenced assessment.

Digital ink   Use of electronic signals to digitally represent handwriting and drawing. In a typical situation a digitizer laid under or over an LCD screen creates an electromagnetic field that captures the movement of a stylus and records the movement on the screen. The recorded handwriting is saved or converted to digital text using handwriting recognition technology.

Discussion board   An electronic message database, usually with a browser interface, where people can log in and post messages. Messages are generally topic-headed or threaded. Threaded messages are organized in outline format with responses indented directly under the message to which they reply.

Distance education   Educational practice in which the instructor is separated from the learners by physical distance; usually they are not on the same campus.

Distributed intelligence   Intelligence that is not just mental properties existing only in an individual's mind, but that is distributed in the artifacts created by humans.

Dynamic assessment   Conducted frequently during a learning process and designed to control the amount of help to be provided to a learner in performing a task. The purpose is to help the learner move from needing more help to less help and eventually be able to perform the task independently.

E-book   Short for electronic book; a book whose content is in electronic format and can be read on a computer or other digital device.

E-learning   Teaching and learning conducted via electronic media, including computers, the Internet, the World Wide Web, interactive television, and the telephone.

Formative assessment   Usually designed to provide a just-in-time basis for adjusting teaching and learning processes to accomplish the instructional objectives. Formative assessment is conducted frequently and closely integrated with teaching and learning activities.

GIF   Graphic Image File, a widely supported image format for graphic presentation on the World Wide Web. The color resolution of GIF is limited to 8 bits, or 256 colors. A series of GIF images can be successively displayed to create simple animation, known as animated GIF.

HTML   Hypertext markup language, a text document format that uses a set of tags to specify the format of a Web page. Each tag is enclosed in a pair of left angle < and right angle > brackets. To view the HTML source of a Web page, select Source from the View menu.

HTTP   Hypertext transfer protocol, which specifies how client and server should communicate in the Web environment. Each request from an HTTP client (browser) to a Web server and each response from a Web server to an HTTP client (browser) is an HTTP communication session.

Hybrid learning   Distance learning that uses both electronic media and face-to-face approaches to enable teaching and learning; often synonymous with blended learning.

Hyperlink   A reference (link) in hypertext that points to another document or node. A hyperlink is the traversable connection between two nodes.

Hypermedia   An extension of hypertext to include other media than text alone, such as sound, graphics, video, animation, and virtual reality.

Hypertext   Any text that contains hyperlinks to other documents or information nodes. These cross-reference links are provided so that readers can navigate (move from one node to another) in both linear and nonlinear ways.

Instant messaging   An Internet-based telecommunication service that enables you to have a real-time chat with another individual.

Internet conferencing   A tool that allows multiple participants to interact with one another in real time, usually in multimedia mode and in multiple channels, including text chat, audio conferencing, video conferencing, application sharing, and whiteboard.

Interactivity   Interaction between the learner and the instructional source.

Interactivity potential   Any intrinsic qualities of an instructional source that are expected to foster interactivity and/or interaction.

Java   An object-oriented programming language created by Sun Microsystems, originally designed for deployment on portable computing devices. Compiled Java programs can run on most computers because the Java runtime environment known as Java Virtual Machine is available for most operating systems.

JavaScript   A scripting language originally developed by Netscape and used primarily for deployment in a browser environment. JavaScript can be closely integrated with HTML, Document Object Model, and other scripting languages to create dynamic and interactive Web content.

Learning object   Any self-contained content module (often digital) that can be used, re-used, or referenced in a technology-supported learning environment.

Listserv   A specific mailing list server; like other such servers, it is an automated mail distribution service for a group of subscribers. To join and participate, a user sends a subscription message from an e-mail account.

Multimedia   The use of two or more media in an integrated way. The media can include text, graphics, audio, video, animation, and virtual reality.

Navigational disorientation   Losing one's sense of location and direction in a nonlinear hypermedia environment, which can be due to a poorly designed hypermedia system with insufficient context clues and navigation aids, or to lack of user experience in hypermedia navigation, or both.

Node   A basic organizational unit in hypermedia, which can consist of chunks of text, pictures, audio files, video clips, and hyperlinks that point to other nodes. Nodes are represented by and connected through hyperlinks.

Norm-referenced assessment   Assessment in which learner performance is measured in relation to other peer learners. Since it is based on the presumption of a normal distribution curve, the expectation is that only about half of the learners will perform above the average and half will fall below the average.

Objective test   A test with questions or items for which correct answers or responses can be prescribed in advance; performances can be assessed and scored by clerks or computers; and scores are not affected by the opinion or judgment of the scorer. Sometimes considered equivalent to a standardized test.

Open source   A software development approach and philosophy in which developers contribute to a common software project or technology and share responsibility to improve it. The source code of an open-source project is open to the public, and no individual or business can claim proprietary control over the source code.

Performance assessment   Assessment that involves direct observation of student performance on tasks that resemble those considered necessary in real life, though student performance may not be as authentic as in real life; and that values the process of problem solving more than the final result or product.

Pixel   Short for picture element, the smallest resolvable element in a digital graphic, either on a screen or stored in computer memory. A computer monitor screen can be divided into millions of pixels, arranged in rows and columns. The number of bits used to represent each pixel determines how many color variations can be displayed.

Plug-in   A software file to be downloaded and added to another software application to enhance or extend the functions of the parent application program. Most plug-in programs available on the Web today are for extending the multimedia functions of browsers.

Portfolio assessment   A combination of performance assessment and authentic assessment, based on a cumulative collection of a learner's work built over a period of time and usually involving multiple indicators and evidences to demonstrate a student's progress. A portfolio is a process as well as a product.

Scripting language   Programming language that can be distributed as script and compiled into binary code for execution in a runtime environment often called an "engine." Popular scripting languages include JavaScript, VBScript, Java Server Pages, and Perl.

Server-side program   A program that usually responds to a request from a remote user, executes functions on the server, and returns data to the user over the Internet. Given access permissions, a server-side program may also access resources such as databases and multimedia files on other servers.

Situated learning   A learning theory that holds that learning takes place in a real context through meaningful activities. The context and activities should be comparable to the expected future scenarios where the knowledge and skills learned will be applied.

Streaming media   Primarily designed for distributing large amount of multimedia data over the Internet. Instead of downloading the complete file before viewing, the recipient can start playing a streaming file as soon as a small amount of preloaded data is received and stored in the buffer on the recipient's computer. Once playing starts, the remaining data is continuously streamed to the recipient.

Summative assessment   Typically administered at some key points during the course of a program, often in the form of standardized tests to summarize learner performances against certain criteria.

Synchronous communication   Real-time communication in which participants continuously exchange messages, either face-to-face or through telecommunication. Feedback immediacy is expected.

URL   Short for uniform resource locator, the Internet standard for specifying the location of a Web page or other resources on the Internet. The URL is used in HTML documents to specify the target of a hyperlink and is used by a browser to locate and retrieve a Web page or node over the Internet.

Usenet   A distributed Internet discussion system. Usenet consists of a set of "newsgroups" with special interests and names, classified hierarchically by subject, therefore sometimes called newsgroups. A newsgroup requires users to subscribe in order to read and post messages, but Usenet does not send messages to subscribers.

Virtual reality   Computer simulations that use 3-D graphics to simulate real-world situations and allow the user to interact with the simulations by moving around, zooming in and out, and interacting with objects in ways similar to what happens in the real world.

VRML   Short for virtual reality modeling language, an evolving specification for describing virtual reality scenes and displaying three-dimensional objects in the Web environment. To view files created in VRML, you need a VRML browser or a VRML plug-in to a standard Web browser.

Web-based instruction   Instruction that uses the World Wide Web as the primary medium of course content delivery, class communication, and class management.

Whiteboard   An electronic "canvas" that allows multiple participants to share a common graphic work space in real time. Participants can draw, type, write, and copy and paste content on the shared canvas; the changes made by one participant are shown on every other participant's electronic canvas in real time.

INDEX

Access Board, 137
Accessibility
  and digital rights, 185
  of electronic forms, 138
  and image maps, 138
  to the Internet, 19, 203
  through video, 174
  of Web content, 136–140
Active Server Pages
      (software), 115
Adobe Acrobat, 184–185
Adobe Premiere, 176
Advanced Distributed Learning
      (ADL) Initiative, 226, 228
Advertising, 282. *See also*
      Marketing of courses
Agreements
  "click to accept," 198, 205
  licensing, 198
AltaVista, 248
Amazon.com, 246, 248
American Association of
      University Professors
      (AAUP), 278
American Distance Education
      Consortium (ADEC), 276
ANGEL (A New Global
      Environment for
      Learning), 237
Animation, water cycle, 180
Announcements, posting of, 73
Applications, sharing of, 22, 77, 89
Archives
  tools for, 214
  of Web information, 258
ARCS (attention, relevance,
      confidence and success)
      model, 99
Argus Clearinghouse, 246
Art of Poetry (Horace), 157
AskJeeves, 250
Assessments. *See also* Tests and
      testing
  alternative, 25–26, 45–53

authentic, 26, 48–49
of collaborative learning,
      52–53
criterion, 37–39
defined, 33
design of, 38, 64
dynamic, 36–37, 55
formative, 8, 35–37, 86
functions of, 32–33
importance of, 26
of information skills, 264
norm-referenced, 38–39
as part of instruction, 53
of performance, 26, 46–48, 55,
      100–101, 103
reliability of, 47, 49
self, 64, 112
summative, 8, 35–37, 52
supervision of, 25–26
and technology, 39–45
tools for, 208, 216–220
use of, 15
vs. objective tests, 47
Attention
  directing of, 99–100, 140–141,
      161–162
  split, 159
Audio
  digitizing, 203
  length of, 187
  production of digital, 170–172
  use of, 169–172, 185, 186–187
Ausubel, D. P., 127
Authors, finding rightful, 200–201,
      255–256

Backups, need for, 68, 214–215
Bandura, A., 23, 63
Bandwidth considerations, 71,
      178, 179
Beliefs and perceptions, 65–66
Berge, Z. L., 277
Bettex, M., 101
Blackboard, 17, 210, 228–229

Blodgett, H., 63
Bloom's taxonomy, 38, 39
Boettcher, Judith, 10
Bookmarks
  in Acrobat, 184
  attributes of, 261
  backing up, 260–263
  managing, 261
  options for, 149
  stability of, 148, 258
  tool for, 260
  use of, 150, 266
Book reviews, 246
Books, print, 183, 192
Borders, in window browsers,
      143, 144
Bork, A., 7
Braille, support for, 138
Branching, 105, 106, 118
Breadcrumb trails, 127, 134
Breadth and depth, balance
      between, 131
Broadband connections, 22
Brown, David, 83
Browsers
  and accessibility, 138
  compatibility of, 139–140,
      210, 245
  for 3-D graphics, 182
  plug-ins for, 112
  settings of, 146
Bruner, D., 67

Cache copies, 196
Camera Mouse, 138
Cameras, digital, 162
Cascading Style Sheet (CSS),
      135–136, 144, 152
Cell padding values, 143–144
Charts and diagrams
  tabular representation, 167
  text in, 166
  types of, 166
  use of, 167, 186

Chat rooms. *See also* Discussion
        boards
    in course management
        systems, 69, 88, 220
    on the Internet, 76–77
    problems with, 69–70, 76–77
    use of, 68
Cheating
    avoiding, 25–26
    prevention of, 33–37, 41, 218,
        235–236
    problems with, 34
Chicago public schools, 48
Chickering, A., 62
Clark, R., 160
Cloze tests, 108
Clusters, 263
CMS (course management
        systems). *See* Course
        management systems
CODEC (compression/
        decompression), 78, 170
Cognitive flexibility theory,
        21, 123
Cognitive overload, 102, 124, 129,
        131, 169
Communication
    alternative channels of, 71
    asynchronous, 8, 22–23,
        69–72, 80
    channels of, 37
    "common language" for, 66
    forums for, 8
    guidelines for online, 79
    importance of, 19, 22
    importance of online
        skills, 265
    instant messaging, 76
    interface of, 97
    options for, 80–81
    pedagogy of, 69–70
    psychology of, 71
    reliability of, 64
    between students, 68
    synchronous, 22, 23, 69–72,
        76, 84
    technology of, 71
    tools for, 73, 220–221
Communities, virtual, 81, 173–174

Conferences, audio, 68, 71,
        77–78
Conferencing
    Internet, 77–79, 221
    multimedia, 22, 77
    tools for, 236
    video, 78
Conflicts, dealing with, 85
Consistency, site-level, 135
Consortium of College and
        University Media
        Center, 203
Contact between students and
        instructors, 88
Content Aggregation Model
        (CAM), 228
Content mapping, 162
Content of courses
    accessibility of, 136–140
    adaptive, 106
    customization of, 228–229
    design of, 24
    flexibility of, 6
    hierarchical organization
        of, 147
    linkage across units of, 21
    modular approach to, 131–132,
        152, 217, 224, 225
    nature and scope of in Web
        sites, 257
    organization of, 7–8,
        215–216, 245
    portability of, 225, 239
    primary providers of, 255
    relevance of, 100, 117
    reusability of, 225
    shareable, 222
    supportive, 101
Context
    cues in, 151
    and graphic representation, 164
    in hypermedia, 132
    learning, 102, 124
    maintaining clarity of, 127
    and media, 160
    of projects, 103
    supportive, 101–102
Contributory infringement
        (copyright), 197

Copyright
    alternatives to, 200
    audits for infringement of, 199
    contributory infringement, 197
    defined, 192
    and e-books, 183–184
    establishing guidelines for, 199
    guidelines for, 205
    myths about, 194
    notices of, 197, 205
    and RAM (computer
        memory), 197
    and subscription services, 246
    violation notifications, 198
    and Web sites, 197, 259
Copyright Act, 193
Correspondence study, 3
Course management systems (CMS)
    changing, 20–21, 208
    compatibility, 226
    components of, 208–216
    considerations for, 17, 224
    cost of, 222, 224, 237
    and customization, 228–229
    evaluation of, 222, 223
    functions of, 209, 210
    and online quizzes, 229–230
    portability of, 222, 224
    reviews of, 222
    scalable, 212
    student perception of, 210
Courses online
    components of, 201
    controlling access to, 211–212
    coordination between,
        16–17, 28
    and copyrights, 196
    development of, 20–21,
        225, 275
    moving to new
        environment, 208
    ownership of materials, 201,
        202, 204, 278
    readiness of materials for,
        20–21
    sequences of, 276
    use of existing, 17
Cows, feeding of, 107
Crews, Kenneth, 195–197

CSF (content structure format), 228
Curriculum, planning, 276

Dahl, J., 196
Data
  archiving, 245
  distribution of, 245
  primary providers for, 254
  sharing of, 77
  storage of student's records, 113
  transfer, 78
Databases
  for managing bookmarks, 260–262, 266
  specialized, 251
  support for, 212
Data warehousing, 259
Deadlines, best time for, 72, 84, 87–88
Dede, Chris, 67, 70, 123, 160
Dee-Lucas, D., 124, 127
Design2Learn, 210
Dewey, John, 46, 48
Diagrams. *See* Charts and diagrams
Digital divide, 7
Digital Laboratory Manual, The (Gallik), 134, 135
Digital Millennium Copyright Act (DMCA), 194–197
Digital rights management (DRM), 196
Dillenbourg, P., 86
Directories
  browsing of, 250
  use of, 214, 215–216
Discussion boards
  accessibility of, 130
  and assessment, 236
  changing posts on, 221, 239
  distinguishing between messages on, 77
  instructor participation in, 79
  length of posts on, 85, 88
  management of, 84–85
  and newsgroups, 75
  public *vs.* private, 74

straying from topics, 79
students' views of, 71
threaded *vs.* unthreaded messages on, 74
tools for, 220, 221
use of, 23, 64, 72, 73–74, 79, 88, 263
Distance education
  access to, 196
  and copyright, 195–196
  guiding principles for, 276
  institutions offering, 274
  providers of, 4–5
Distance Education: The Foundations of Effective Practice (Verduin and Clark), 274
Distance Education Online Symposium (DEOS), 74, 263
DMCA, 195
DMCA (Digital Millennium Copyright Act), 194–197
DreamWeaver, 208
Drop-down list boxes, 108, 111
Dunlap, J., 132
Dwyer, F. M., 163–164

EagleEyes, 138
EArmyU, 4–5
E-books, 183–185, 253–254
Education
  distance, 3
  real-time, 69
Educational Testing Service (ETS), 40
Elaboration theory, 21, 127
E-learning
  assessments of program, 35, 275, 276, 284
  branding of, 282
  and copyrights, 193–198
  defined, 3
  effect on institution of, 278, 280–281
  funding for, 277, 279
  planning process for, 275
Electronic Privacy Information Center (EPIC), 196

Electronic Text Center, 254
ELibrary, 252
Elicitation, 111
E-mail
  copyright issues, 197, 203
  in course management systems, 220–221
  interface for, 220
  speed of, 71
  timeliness of, 72, 88
  use of, 64, 72–73, 79, 84, 88
Encoding, selective, 163–164
Encryption, 258–259
Engagement, cognitive, 100–101
"Entering the Mainstream" (Sloan Consortium), 4–5
EPIC (Electronic Privacy Information Center), 196
Error analysis, 42–44, 219–220, 234
Estrangement, types of, 45
Evaluations, 14–15, 32–33. *See also* Assessments
Expenses
  of attending college, 6
  of a course management system, 222, 224
Experts, contacting, 263
Expert systems, 99, 106, 107
Expressions
  colloquial, 170
  nonverbal, 169, 172

Faculty
  direction of, 65, 66
  entrepreneurial, 204
  expectations of, 65
  as independent contractors, 202
  issues for, 7–9
  readiness of, 17–18, 28
  role of, 16, 84–85
  support for, 276
  training for, 18, 244
Fair use, 192, 193–194. *See also* Copyright
FAQ pages, 88, 89
Feedback
  evaluative, 111
  immediacy of, 65, 68–69, 72, 84, 235

instructional, 107–112
need for, 22, 62
programmed instructional,
110–111
quality of, 86
remedial, 105, 111
from students on program, 283
and testing, 219–220
types of, 97
use of, 103
Feldberg, Jerry, 281
Field dependence *vs.* field
independence, 67
Files
audio, 170, 187
compression of, 170
management of,
212–215, 216
moving, 237
multimedia, 136–137
size of, 78
video, 177, 178, 180
zipped, 215, 216
Fischer, P. M., 133
Flash, 179–180
Flash movies, 113
Fonts
sizes, 146, 147
using, 145–146
Forms, accessibility of electronic,
138
Frame rate, 175
Frames and framesets, use of, 150
Freeware and shareware
and copyright issues, 198
open-source, 222, 237
FrontPage, 208
Fuchs, Ira, 236

Gallik, Stephen, 134, 135
Gamson, Z. F., 62
Gardner, H. E., 67–68
Gilbert, Steven, 263
Glaser, Robert, 45
Global account systems, 211–212
Google.com, 75, 248
Government agencies, information
from, 257
Grabinger, S., 132

Grading
automated, 230–231
and feedback, 219–220
instant, 219, 235, 239
Grading, automated, 218
Graphics. *See also* Visuals
and accessibility, 136–137
analogous representation, 164
color in, 137, 140–143, 161
contrast in, 140–141
3-D, 180, 181–182
gradient and shape, 161–162
interactive, 113
in interface design, 135
metaphorical and realistic
images, 165
realistic representation,
162–163
selective drawing, 164
in site navigation, 133–134
spatial representation,
166–168
text in, 145, 146
thumbnails for, 137
use of, 99, 186
Green, Casey, 5
Groups
composition of, 81–83
on discussion boards, 74
formation of, 64, 82, 221
instructor participation in,
52–53
members responsibilities in,
82–83
participation in, 22–23, 52–53
size of, 83
Group work, 46–47, 64, 66, 74
Guest speakers, 86, 87, 89
Guidelines, posting of, 84–85

Hackathorn, R., 259
Harper, William Rainey, 3
Headings, use of, 117, 132
Help functions, 106
Hiltz, S. R., 80
Home pages, 129–130, 132–133,
256
Horace, 157
Horn, R. E., 164

Horton, S., 150
HTML
and e-books, 184
editing in, 211, 212
style sheets in, 136
tables in, 143
tags, 136, 137, 145, 147–148
use of, 140
Hyperlinks
defined, 122
organization of, 125
updating of, 216
visibility of in text, 141–142
Hypermedia
adaptive, 104
and content modules, 225
defined, 122–123
design of, 21
frames in, 148
organization of, 150
strengths of, 123
student readiness for, 19
use of, 7–8, 15, 124–125, 151
Hypertext, 127, 141

Icons, 162, 163–164
Ideas, exchange of, 63–64
Image maps, 138
IMS Global Learning Consortium,
222, 225–226
IMS specifications, 225–227
Information
accessing, 263–264
accuracy of in Web sites,
257–258
background, 170
"bias" in, 159
evaluation of, 264, 266
finding, 245
flexibility of, 8
presentation of, 122–123,
264–265
quality of, 252
Instant messaging, 76
Institution
commitment of, 276
readiness of, 16–17
services provided by, 282–283
support of, 275, 278

Instruction
  adaptive, 103–107, 106,
    113, 118
  and assessment, 33, 35
  development of, 14–15
  follow-up help, 68–69
  quality of adaptive, 103
Instructional design, 7–9, 14–15
Intellectual property policy. *See
    also* Copyright
  changing, 202
  terms of, 201–202, 278–279
Intelligence
  artificial, 99, 111
  distributed, 98–99
Interaction
  cognitive effects of, 62
  and copyright issues, 201–202
  design and management of, 80
  effectiveness of, 81–82
  factors affecting, 65
  importance of, 61–63
  and learning, 65–69, 118
  principles of, 62
  quality of, 86, 110
  student, 97
Interactive videoconferencing
    networks (IVN), 158
Interactivity
  defined, 97–98
  factors affecting, 98–99
  levels of, 99–103
  media, 158
  need for, 24–25
  potential for, 98
  server-supported, 112–116
Interfaces
  browser-based, 208, 210–211
  customization of, 230, 239
  look of, 135
Internet2, 78
Internet Public Library, 246
ISPs and copyright, 197
Item banks, 229–230, 231–232,
    235, 239

Jamison, D., 157
JAWS, 138
Jonassen, D., 71, 133

Jones, Dennis, 10
Journals, online, 252, 253

Kearsley, G., 282–283
Keegan, D., 7
Keeves, J. P., 32–33
Keller, John, 99
Keyboards, on-screen, 139
Keyword matching, 109
Keyword searches, 183, 247,
    252–253
KIS principle, 202
Knowledge
  ability to learn, 246
  hierarchical structure of, 128
  interconnections of, 123
  prior, 106, 157
  procedural, 125–126
  retention of, 63
Knowledge Web (Moe and
    Blodgett), 63
Kommers, P., 132

Laboratory manual, digital, 134
Larkin, J. H., 124
Learner authenticity, 25–26, 33–34,
    35, 53
Learning
  active, 276
  active vs. passive, 6, 102, 118
  associative, 126
  associative *vs.* sequential, 7–8
  asynchronous, 28
  behavioral, 157
  blended and hybrid, 4
  cognitive approach, 157
  collaborative, 6, 8, 23, 52–53,
    62, 63–64, 123, 236
  constructive, 21–22, 26, 36, 70
  designing for, 21–22
  developing skills for, 245
  effects of media on, 67–68
  interaction with media, 157
  just-in-time, 281
  levels of, 99
  lifelong, 5–6, 264
  meaningful, 46
  peer, 70, 265
  rote, 33

  social, 36
  student-centered, 8
  styles of, 65, 67, 123–124
  synchronous, 28
Learning Management System
    (LMS), 228
Learning objectives, 118
Learning objects, 225, 226
Learning outcomes, 6, 7–8, 14–15
Learning paths, 105–107, 108, 118,
    124
Learning tasks, 84
Lectures, and retention of
    knowledge, 63
Levy, Y., 277
Lexis-Nexis Academic, 252
Libraries
  database-supported, 24, 99
  online access to, 17
  use of catalogs of, 246
  virtual, 251–252, 254
Licenses
  fees, 236
  nonexclusive, 202
  software, 224
  for use of copyrighted
    works, 195
Links
  and copyright issues, 198, 199
  in frames, 148
  levels of, 127, 129–130
  organization of, 131
  updating, 239
Listening tasks, length of, 169
Lists, drop down, 108, 111
Listserv, 80
L-Soft Listserv List, 74–75
Lynch, P. J., 150

Macromedia Director, 180
Mailing lists, 74–75, 79, 88, 263, 266
Mandl, H., 133
Marketing of courses, 280–282, 284
Masters, G. N., 32–33
Matching items, 232, 234
Materials, digitizing
  audio, 203
  and copyrights, 196
  video, 175, 203

Math Archives, 251
Mayer, R. E., 159, 245
Mckenzie, J., 198
McLuhan, Marshall, 157
Measurement, 32–33. *See also*
        Assessments
Media
    choices in, 67–68
    combining, 159
    and context, 160
    effects on learning of, 159, 185
    importance of, 67, 157
    instructional effectiveness
        of, 160
    role of in learning, 160
Memory, human system, 123
Mentoring, 77, 86
Menus, use of, 133–135
MERLOT project, 226
Merrill, D., 26
Metadata, and PDF documents,
        184–185
Meta-search engines, 249–250. *See
        also* Search engines
Methods, flexibility of, 15
Microsoft Access, 262–263
Microsoft Visio, 168
Mini DV, 175–176
Moe, M., 63
Moodle, 237
Moore, D. M., 97, 124
Moore, M. G., 282–283
Moreno, R., 159
Motivation
    effects of interaction on, 63
    and engagement, 86
    promoting, 71
    of students, 65, 66, 81–82
Mouse and stylus, use of, 110
Multimedia
    copyright issues in, 202–203
    tools for, 44–45
    use of, 22, 76–77
    vs. single medium, 159

Nav bars, 133
Navigation
    branching, 105–107
    cues for, 133–135

guidance for, 132–135
    and page layout, 147
    schemes for, 108, 125–132,
        135, 151
    within Web sites, 124, 258
Navigational disorientation, 124, 129
Navigation bars, 133
Needs analysis, 14–21, 281, 284
Netiquette, 75, 84–85, 265
Network traffic, managing, 112
Newsgroups, advantages of, 76
Nielsen, J., 150
Nodes
    defined, 122
    in grid structures, 128
    organization of, 125, 239
    in tree structures, 214
Nuremberg (movie), 173

Objectives
    aligning tests with, 45
    of e-learning programs, 275
    macro and micro, 36
Objects, learning, 225–226, 228
Office hours, virtual, 77, 84, 85
Olson, D., 67
OnMouseOver, 138
OpenCMS, 237
Open Database Connectivity
        (ODBC), 113, 115,
        262–263, 264
Open database connectivity
        (ODBC), 232, 234
Open Directory Project, 250
"Openness" continuum, 40–41
Open standards, 222. *See also*
        Freeware and shareware
Open systems interconnection
        (OSI) model, 109
Output, student, 109
Outside resources
    e-books, 183

Palumbo, D., 67
Participation, assessment of,
        84–85, 86
Passwords, use of, 199, 203
Paths, cascading, 127, 151
Patton, M. Q., 32–33

Peers
    grading by, 83
    interaction of, 84
    interaction with, 63, 65–66
    reviews by, 51, 55, 265
Permission letter, 200
Permissions. *See also* Copyright
    asking for, 200, 203, 205
    need for, 197, 198, 204
    policies on, 193, 204
    restrictions in, 196
Pew Learning and Technology
        Program report
        (Twigg), 201
Picciano, A. G., 199
Plone, 237
Plug-ins, 112
Policies and procedures
    analysis framework for,
        279, 280
    guidelines for, 277–278
    informing students of, 283
    review of, 284
Portal for Online Objects in
        Learning (POOL), 226
Portfolios
    assessment of, 26, 27, 49–52, 55
    developing, 47, 50, 51
    Web-based, 125
President's Information
        Technology Advisory
        Committee (PITAC), 224
Privacy, 258–259
Problem solving, 26
Programming, technical limitations
        of, 104
Programs
    client-side, 112–113, 118
    legacy, 116
    protection of source code, 113
    text entry in, 109
Project Gutenberg, 254
Public Broadcasting Service, 3
Public domain, 192, 253–254. *See
        also* Copyright

Questions
    calculated, 218, 231, 233
    database for, 231–232, 234

effective, 66
in expert systems, 106
for good hypermedia, 133
import and export of, 232, 234
multiple-choice, 40, 230–231
prior to topics, 118
quality and quantity of, 85
random selection of,
231–232, 239
reusability of, 218, 219
student, 85, 88
types of, 216, 218, 230–231
QuickTime VR, 181–182

Radio, instruction delivered by, 3
Radio buttons, 108
Ramim, M. M., 277
RAM (random access memory),
and copyright, 197
Realism, and information
processing, 163–165
RealMedia, 177, 179
RealServer, 179
Records, restoration of, 214–215
Reigeluth, C. M., 15, 97, 127
Relationships, interpersonal, 72,
80–81
Research papers, on the Web,
257–258
Resources
copyright crash course, 198
evaluation of, 254–255
offline, 246
online, 25, 252–253
quality of, 8, 245, 248,
254–255
repository of Web, 259
sharing of, 244
use of external, 28, 43, 84–86,
124, 235, 244
on the Web, 245–246, 263
Return messages, 110–111
Revision of work, 51
Robinson, E. T., 277
Romiszowski, A. J., 116
Rubrics, 37–39, 47–48, 50, 53
Run-Time Environment
(RTE), 228
Russell, Tom, 158

Sakai Educational Partners
Program (SEPP), 237
Salomon, G., 67, 98, 160
Scaffolding, 36–37, 63, 103
Schimmel, B. J., 110
Scores, overriding of, 219
SCORM (shareable content object
reference model), 222,
228, 237
Screen action, capturing, 174–175
Screen readers, 138
Screen size, computer, 143
Scrolling, avoidance of, 150
Search agents, 249–250
Search directories, 250–251
Search engines, 247–248, 249–250,
251, 266
Search Engine Showdown, 246
Search Engine Watch, 246
Searches, 245
in e-text, 253–254
levels of online, 248
refining, 248, 250, 266
results from, 249, 250
tools for online, 246–247
Search interface screen, 249
Section 508, 137–138
Section 107 (Copyright Act of
1976), 193
Security, 258–259
SEPP (Sakai Educational Partners
Program), 237
Sequencing and Navigation
(SN), 228
Servers, Web, 112–116, 196
Shockwave, 112–113, 174,
179–180
Social Science Information
Gateway (SOSIG), 251
Software
and accessibility, 138
Active Server Pages, 115
adaptive hypermedia tools, 104
Blackboard, 17
for chart and diagram
creation, 168
chat, 76
client-side programs, 112–113
communication tools, 64

course management systems,
17, 41, 124, 133,
208–216, 210
digital audio, 171
digital rights management
(DRM), 185
digital video, 175–180
e-mail interfaces, 73
graphics, 112–113
HTML, 110, 114
interactive, 110
Java Applet Service (JAS), 110
JavaScript, 111–112
mailing list, 74–75
for menus, 134–135
Microsoft Word, 140
open source, 114–115, 236–238
PDF, 184
Perception Secure Browser, 34
Perl, 114–115
PHP, 115
Portfolio Builder, 51–52
to prevent cheating, 34
proprietary features of, 222
Scientific Notebook, 9
screen action capture,
174–175
scripting languages, 114
search agents, 249
server-side programs, 113–116
SLO (Student Learning
Objectives), 27
streaming media, 179
style sheets, 135–136
UNIX, 114–115
use of, 8–9
video conferencing, 78
virtual reality, 182
for virtual reality, 181–182
WebCT, 17, 124, 133
Web presentation, 264
WIDS (Worldwide Instructional
Design System), 20
Space, flexibility of, 81
Speech *vs.* reading, 170
Speed, to access Web sites,
136–137
Standardization, 224–226, 229,
232, 234

Standards, organizations for
    development of, 224–225
Streaming media, 78, 179
Structures, site
    deciding on navigational, 131
    flexibility in, 126
    grid, 128–129
    hierarchical, 126–128
    linear, 125–126
    mesh, 128–131
    vertical, 126
Students
    adult, 3, 101
    anticipating needs of,
        103, 106
    attitudes of, 65–66
    backgrounds of, 66–67
    challenges for, 9
    concerns of, 72–73, 169
    control of content, 102
    engagement of, 86. *See also*
        Motivation
    groups, 212
    guidance for, 111
    helping, 36–37, 47
    marketing to, 281
    monitoring, 212
    nontraditional, 22, 35, 49
    eadiness of, 18–19
    recruitment and retention
        of, 282
    response opportunities for,
        107–112
    support for, 276, 278, 284
    technical capabilities of,
        19, 28, 71
    tracking of, 213
    work as intellectual property,
        198, 201–202, 203
Studies
    course management
        systems, 210
    of media, 160
    media comparison, 157–158
    navigation, 132
    online search actions, 248
    open-source CMS, 237
Subscriptions, 246, 251–252,
        258–259

Suppes, P., 157
Syllabuses, use of, 35–36, 211, 283

Tables
    borders of, 143–144
    and page layout, 150
TabletPC, 44
TARGET attribute, 147–148
Tasks. *See also* Deadlines, best
        time for nature of, 65, 67
    timeframe for, 84, 87–88
TEACH Act, 196
TEACH (Technology, Education,
        and Copyright
        · Harmonization), 195–197
Teamwork
    and groups, 82
    value of, 64
Teamwork, training for, 23, 52
Technical support
    need for, 67–68, 275, 276
    and open-source software, 237
    use of, 8–9
Technology
    assistive, 137–139
    availability of, 4, 7
    digital ink and tablet, 44
    and e-books, 183
    infrastructure of, 16–17
    reliability of, 68
    student access to, 68
Television, instruction delivered
        by (ITV), 3, 61, 97
Tests and testing. *See also*
        Assessments
    adaptive, 43–44
    advantages of computerized,
        39–40
    calculated questions, 218
    computer-assisted, 216, 218
    editing quizzes, 234
    interruption of quizzes, 234–235
    item banks, 41–42, 43, 55
    minitests, 37
    multiple-choice, 40
    objective, 40–41, 47
    online, 41–43
    online quizzes, 229–230
    open-book exams, 54

options for, 34
proctors for, 34, 41, 236
question database, 219, 235
question reusability, 218, 219
quiz management, 42, 55
quiz tools, 231
releasing answers to, 42, 217
restarting quizzes, 239
scoring of, 41, 218–219
self-tests, 112
standardized, 26, 35, 39, 40,
        45–46
of student readiness, 19
time limits for, 235–236
Web resources inside, 43
Text
    in charts, 166
    copies of recordings, 170
    delimiting area of, 143–144
    digital copies of, and
        copyright, 196, 205
    digital *vs.* print, 183
    electronic, 253–254
    graphic, 146
    legibility of, 142, 152
    length of, 132
    line length, 142–143
    space between lines in, 144
    tags for, 137
Text-to-speech conversion, 185
Thinking, active, 110
Time
    flexibility of, 69, 80
    management of, 19, 28, 87–88
    in test taking, 41
    video compression of, 174
Time flexibility, 5, 6, 9, 19, 22
Time management, 9
Title IV, 195
Topics, for adult learners, 101
Tree structures, 212, 214
Troubleshooting, 77
Turn-taking, 83
Tutoring sessions, 66
Twigg, Carol, 201

URLs (Uniform Resource Locators)
    bookmarking of, 148
    defined, 122

U.S. Army, web instruction of, 4–5
Usenet (newsgroups), 75–76
Users
    management of, 211–212, 213
    needs of, 104
    orientation of, 132–133

Verduin and Clark, 274
Video
    advantages of, 172–173
    digital, 175–176, 186
    digitizing, 175, 203
    editing of, 176
    investment in, 177–178
    length of segments, 178
    presentations, 44–45
    screen action capturing, 175
    slow motion, 174
    use of, 158, 172–175, 187
    when to use, 177–178
Virtual reality, 99, 181–182
Vision, persistence of, 175
Visual memory, 162
Visuals, functions of, 160–161,
        185. *See also* Graphics
Voice recognition
        technology, 110
VRML, 181
Vygotsky, L. S., 23, 61, 63, 103

Web Accessibility Initiative, 137
Web-based instruction (WBI)
    advantages of, 5, 79
    attributes of, 15
    best subject matters for, 8
    chemistry, 178
    costs and returns of, 9
    defined, 3

and degree programs, 16–17
design of, 7–9
institutional readiness for, 17
principles for building, 11
technical needs of, 10
time needed to prepare
        materials for, 20
Webcams, use of, 26. *See also*
        Video
Web Content Accessibility
        Guidelines (WCAG), 138
WebCT
    backups in, 215
    content organization in,
        215–216, 217
    and customization, 228–229
    discussions in, 221
    interface of, 211
    monitoring students in, 212
    quiz, 232
    release condition settings
        in, 217
    use of, 17, 208, 210
    zipped files in, 215
Web farming, 259
Web forms, 108, 109
Web sites
    bias in, 257
    contrast, foreground and
        background, 140–141.
        See also Graphics
    and copyright, 197, 199
    creating a database of,
        260–263
    downloading from, 198
    evaluation of, 256
    fonts on, 99, 135, 145, 146
    goals of, 256–257

importance of, 245, 281
judging objectivity of, 257–258
legibility of, 140–142, 183
length of pages, 150
lines in, 144, 152
print outs of, 143, 149–150
privacy and security on,
        258–259
recording of, 259
repository of resources, 259
stability of, 258
text layout of, 142–147
Web Style Guide (Lynch and
        Horton), 150
Wellman, B., 80
Wells, S., 157
Western Cooperative for
        Educational
        Telecommunications
        (WCET), 276
Whiteboard, 77, 221
Wie, Chu Ryang, 110
Wiggins, Grant, 48
Windows Narrator, 138–139
Work-for-hire doctrine, 202
World Wide Web
    popularity of, 244–245
    presence on, 245, 281
World Wide Web Consortium
        (W3C), 135, 137, 138
Writing, guidelines for, 132

Yahoo!, 250–251
Yang, C. S., 124

Zone of proximal development
        (ZPD), 36, 61, 63, 103
Zooming, 173